THE
JUNIOR
LEAGUE
CELEBRATION
COOKBOOK

D0459040

THE
JUNIOR
LEAGUE
CELEBRATION
COOKBOOK

THE ASSOCIATION OF

JUNIOR LEAGUES INTERNATIONAL INC.

AN ELLEN ROLFES BOOK

G. P. PUTNAM'S SONS

NEW YORK

ACKNOWLEDGMENTS

AJLI wishes to thank all the Junior Leagues that generously submitted recipes from their League cookbooks. Our appreciation goes to the Ad Hoc Cookbook Committee members for their support and for sharing their invaluable cookbook marketing experiences: Susan Rehfeld, JL of Huntsville, AL; Susan Carley, JL of Atlanta, GA; Ella Herlihy, JL of Atlanta, GA; Holly Kay Walters, JL of Memphis, TN; Cynthia Stanford, JL of Cincinnati, OH; Pam Murray, JL of Charleston, SC; Jamie Young, JL of El Paso, TX; Ann Perrino, JL of Portland, ME; Marsha Powell, JL of Monroe, LA; Gwen E. Barron, JL of Monroe, LA; and Cristina de Perez-Verdeda, JL of Mexico City, Mexico.

The Junior League Celebration Cookbook would not have been possible without the leadership of AJLI Executive Director Jane Silverman and the hard work of AJLI Director of Communications and Development Anne Lieberman and Communications Associate Jannell Khu.

In addition, special thanks to Sara, Wally, and Buntz Watkins.

To the spirit of voluntarism, and to all those individuals
who do indeed change the world through their acts of caring

THE ASSOCIATION OF JUNIOR LEAGUES INTERNATIONAL INC.

The Association of Junior Leagues International Inc. is an organization of women committed to promoting voluntarism, developing the potential of women, and improving the community through the effective action and leadership of trained volunteers. Its purpose is exclusively educational and charitable.

The Association of Junior Leagues International Inc. reaches out to women of all races, religions, and national origins who demonstrate an interest in and commitment to voluntarism.

"Junior League" is a registered trademark of The Association of Junior Leagues International Inc. It is in use in four countries: the United States, Canada, Mexico, and Great Britain. Reg. U.S. Pat. & Tm. Off.

G. P. Putnam's Sons
Publishers Since 1838
A member of Penguin Putnam Inc.
375 Hudson Street, New York, NY 10014

Library of Congress Cataloging-in-Publication Data

The Junior League celebration cookbook / by the Association of Junior Leagues International, Inc.
　　　p.　cm.
　　"An Ellen Rolfes book."
　　ISBN 0-399-14658-X
　　1. Cookery, American.　I. Title: Celebration cookbook.　II. Association of Junior Leagues International.

TX715.J9716　　2000　　　　　00-041745
641.5—dc21

Printed in the United States of America

10 9 8 7 6 5 4 3 2 1
This book is printed on acid-free paper ∞

Book design by Barbara C. Aronica-Buck

CONTENTS

INTRODUCTION

Great-grandmother's tattered dime-store notebook, where she wrote down the family recipes, doesn't just list ingredients and provide instructions for creating dishes—the deeper message behind this precious family heirloom is one of love that nourishes the body and the soul. Her cookbook is a legacy that she left behind for her family; the recipes are a tradition she instilled in future generations to preserve.

The Junior Leagues have published cookbooks for over fifty years and know a thing or two about leaving behind legacies. The cookbooks capture and preserve the food traditions of the community, offering portraits of the myriad ways that the women of the Junior League cook for celebrations, for special events and for everyday. But these cookbooks are also a testament to the countless Junior League volunteers who dedicate themselves to meeting the needs of their communities through successful programs that have improved and transformed the lives of thousands of people.

Junior Leagues publish cookbooks to raise money to help fulfill the organization's mission: "to promote voluntarism, develop the potential of women and improve communities." Over the years, cookbook revenues have helped communities to build parks, playgrounds, museums,

educational programs, and shelters for women and children. In other words, Junior Leagues have used their cookbooks as a means to an end—the improvement of their local community based on a careful assessment of what is needed.

Sprinkled throughout this book are some "Recipes for a Better Community," which illustrate the extraordinary achievements of women who came together with a shared vision and took action to make a difference in their communities. These "Recipes" describe a sampling of the many projects that Junior Leagues have funded *and* founded through money raised by their cookbooks. In many cases, the cookbooks and their revenue have empowered Junior Leagues to take their place at the table . . . the table of community decision-making where neighborhoods are strengthened, programs are green-lighted, and needs are strategically met. These cookbooks have helped give voice to generations of women's community leaders who would otherwise have been working silently in the background.

While Leagues have raised funds since their inception in 1901, this "can do" entrepreneurial spirit really took off with the first published cookbook in the 1940s. Through the cookbooks, those postwar Junior League members took command of something that was personal and very close to their hearts. They took what they knew—home and hearth—and turned it into gold. Junior League cookbooks have sold more than eighteen million copies and have generated tens of millions of dollars—money that has been fed back into the community.

Over the course of producing high-quality, award-winning cookbooks, League members have mastered business development, marketing, packaging, and sales techniques. They have become experts at managing and running national wholesale and retail mail-order businesses. Their cookbooks sell on television shopping channels, in national bookstores, and on the Internet. After hugely successful first cookbooks, many Leagues have published their second and third books. And recently, the Junior League of Boca Raton, Florida, produced a CD-ROM version of its cookbook.

Just as handwritten cookbooks safeguard and transmit families' traditions and customs, Junior League cookbooks preserve and document regional food celebrations, culture, and history. Both the James Beard Foundation and the Radcliffe Institute's Schlesinger Library hold large collections of Junior League cookbooks. In fact, Junior League cookbooks are widely regarded as having set the standard for, and raised the bar on, community cookbooks. What makes a Junior League cookbook so special is that it holds so many treasured home-tested family recipes that have been handed down from one generation to the next. Heirloom recipes whose flavors describe another time and place nestle against contemporary dishes that accommodate today's hurried cook and take advantage of widely available, sophisticated ingredients.

But Junior League cookbooks don't just list ingredients and provide instructions for creating dishes. The deeper story of these cookbooks and the time-honored recipes that they hold is one of love. The books make manifest the dedication of thousands of women volunteers who transform their communities and, in the process, transform themselves. This book celebrates the work and love that two hundred and ninety-six Junior Leagues demonstrate to their communities through their collaborations, their commitment, and their cooking.

—Jane Silverman, AJLI Executive Director

APPETIZERS

NORTHEAST AND MID-ATLANTIC

Extending down half of the Eastern Seaboard, the Northeast and Mid-Atlantic region speaks with a range of accent that reflects the diversity of our inhabitants. Our little states of Rhode Island, Maryland, Connecticut, and New Jersey nestle against Massachusetts, New York, and Pennsylvania, and everyone gets along. Only when someone asks, "Which is better, Manhattan or New England clam chowder?" or "Who grows the best corn and tomatoes?" is there bound to be trouble.

Opinions on these and other culinary matters run deep and strong, testimony to the kind of pride this region takes in its food. The Mid-Atlantic states share the nation's longest history, with nine states being among the original thirteen colonies. In the early 1600s from Jamestown, Virginia, to Plymouth Rock, Massachusetts, European settlers began developing America's first cooking traditions. Not that they were alone.

Our food history goes back further still. For eons before the Europeans arrived, American Indians cultivated the land, fished the waterways, and hunted in a primeval paradise of verdant fields and deep forests. Their agriculture and hunting skills sustained the struggling settlers during their first years in America. Some of the dishes taught to our forefathers still survive, such as the Algonquin combination of corn and lima beans known as succotash. America's treasured national holiday of Thanksgiving—a rich celebration of the harvest's bounty and our own good fortune—began here.

The region's cooking spans centuries, cultures, and lifestyles. From the rural farm fare of the Pennsylvania Dutch to the sophisticated dishes in the harbor cities of Boston and New York, Northeasterners embrace it all. We will just as happily roll up our sleeves, spread out some newspaper, and grab a nutcracker to enjoy the spice and savor of a Maryland crab boil as we will don our finest clothes to pay homage to lobster Newburg.

Despite customs that embrace the extremes of Yankee thrift in Maine to Southern hospitality in Virginia, there is more that we hold in common than what sets us apart. Generations of Northeastern cooks have perfected the recipes their families have enjoyed in a glorious processional of fall and winter hearty soups and stews, as well as steamed puddings and yeasted breads; spring and summer bring fruit pies and cobblers, cooling salads, fish fries, and clambakes.

America revels in the foods from the Northeast. In today's world, Maine lobster, Maryland crab cakes, Virginia ham, and Vermont Cheddar are just an e-mail away. And while we may battle within our borders over the best chowder, we agree they are all satisfying, thick, and delicious when made with the shellfish dug from our shores. We debate the merits of Jersey tomatoes versus Pennsylvania's, Maryland corn versus New York's, and those arguments will go on forever. But there is clear consensus that, whether transformed into feather-light cornbread and heavenly corn pudding, soothing tomato soup and spicy tomato sauce, or simply picked from our fields and sprinkled with salt, our corn and tomatoes are unbeatable.

On these points we will not yield. We give thanks for an abundance of wondrous ingredients, cooking styles based on bounty, and an abiding respect for local, seasonal food. These precepts have worked throughout our history and cannot be improved upon now.

—Patricia Mack, *The Record,* Northern New Jersey

MAINE LOBSTER BAKE

Lobster bakes are part of what makes Maine famous, from the corn on the cob to the fresh steamed lobsters. The real down-home-style lobster bakes are made out of doors over an open fire, layering water, seaweed, lobsters, clams, corn on the cob (still in the husks), and hard-cooked eggs. Occasionally the clams are placed in mesh-style bags in individual servings along with new potatoes, corn, and an egg. These are covered with seaweed and steamed together. Add melted butter . . . and begin the seaside feast!

Submitted by *RSVP*, Portland, ME

CAPE SHORE LOBSTER BAKE 230

CORNBREAD 283

SOUR CREAM POTATO SALAD 64

DEB'S BLUEBERRY BUCKLE 325

YARMOUTH SPICED TEA 48

MARYLAND CRABFEST

The crabfest is the highlight of summer entertaining in Maryland. Picking crabs is a slow task, so the crabfest has evolved into a leisurely outdoor event spiced with good food and conversation. A crabfest is perfect entertainment for a crowd. It is an art—a feast of fresh food and a celebration of old and new friendship. Who can be standoffish having once been elbow to elbow at a picnic table surrounded by crab shells?

Submitted by *Of Tide & Thyme,* Annapolis, MD

PIERSIDE MARYLAND
STEAMED CRABS   235

ANNAPOLIS HARBOR BOIL   239

OYSTERS SALISBURY   20

STRAWBERRY AND SPINACH SALAD   68

CREAMY PEACH-BLACKBERRY COBBLER   367

BUBBLY PEACH PUNCH   52

RECIPE FOR A BETTER COMMUNITY

JUNIOR LEAGUE OF CINCINNATI, OHIO COMMUNITY PROJECT:

Withrow College and Career Center

Before the Junior League of Cincinnati became involved with Withrow, this large urban public high school had a disappointing graduation rate of only 34 percent. Since the Junior League of Cincinnati's Withrow College and Career Center opened in December 1997, the graduation rate has jumped by 20 percent. The center's objectives are to raise students' academic expectations, increase college acceptances, and provide job training programs. The League continues to be active in the Center by providing volunteer support, acting as a support mechanism for the Center Coordinator, and organizing special events. In addition, the League is involved in the grant writing process to secure additional funding for the Center.

The cookbook that helped to make it happen: *I'll Cook When Pigs Fly* funded half of the Withrow College and Career Center.

Did you know? *I'll Cook When Pigs Fly* garnered great publicity as a result of the cover art drawn by nationally syndicated editorial cartoonist Jim Borgman.

HOT CHEESE PUFFS

MAKES 10 TO 12 SERVINGS

4 ounces cream cheese
¾ teaspoon grated onion
½ cup homemade mayonnaise
1 tablespoon chopped chives
⅛ teaspoon ground red pepper
   (cayenne)
2 tablespoons grated Parmesan cheese
½ small loaf white bread

Preheat the oven to 350F. Combine the cream cheese, onion, mayonnaise, chives, cayenne pepper, and cheese in a medium bowl. Mix well. Cut the bread into circles (1½-inch rounds) and spread each with cheese mixture. Arrange on a baking sheet and bake 15 minutes, or longer for a crispier puff.

NOTE: The bread may be cut and spread with cheese mixture, then frozen. Bake when ready to use.

Plantation Cookbook, New Orleans, LA

BACON BISCUIT PUFFS

MAKES 30

1 (8-ounce) can refrigerated biscuits
2 cups (8 ounces) grated Cheddar or
   Swiss cheese
½ cup mayonnaise (or more if needed
   for desired consistency)
1 small onion, chopped
1 (3-ounce) jar bacon bits
2 tablespoons sugar
¼–½ teaspoon garlic salt
5 drops hot pepper sauce

Preheat the oven to 350F. Separate each biscuit into 3 pieces. Place on a baking sheet. Combine the cheese, mayonnaise, onion, bacon bits, sugar, garlic salt, and hot pepper sauce in a medium bowl; mix well. Place a spoonful of the mixture, spreading evenly, on each biscuit round. Bake 10 minutes or until golden.

I'll Cook When Pigs Fly, Cincinnati, OH

SCALLOP PUFFS

MAKES 12 DOZEN

3 tablespoons unsalted butter or
    margarine
1 pound bay scallops, quartered
2 teaspoons lemon zest, finely minced
3 small cloves garlic, minced
3 tablespoons chopped fresh dill
3½ loaves small, thin white sandwich
    bread (such as Pepperidge Farm)
2 cups shredded Gruyère cheese
2¼ cups mayonnaise
Dash of Tabasco
Salt and freshly ground pepper to
    taste
Sweet Hungarian paprika
Lemon slices and dill sprigs (optional)

Melt the butter in a medium skillet over medium-high heat. Add the scallops, lemon zest, and garlic. Cook 2 to 3 minutes, stirring constantly, until scallops are just done, being careful not to overcook. Add the dill and cook 30 more seconds. Remove from heat and cool to room temperature. (The scallop mixture will keep covered and refrigerated up to 4 days.)

Preheat the broiler. Cut the bread into 1-inch rounds, place on baking sheet(s), and toast lightly on both sides. Combine the cheese, mayonnaise, Tabasco, salt, pepper, and scallops in a medium bowl; mix well. Place the toast rounds ½ inch apart on baking sheets. Top each round with a heaping teaspoon of scallop mixture, and sprinkle lightly with paprika. Broil 5 inches from the heat for 2 to 3 minutes or until puffed and golden. Serve hot. Garnish with lemon slices and dill sprigs, if desired.

Thymes Remembered, Tallahassee, FL

GOAT CHEESE TORTA

MAKES 12 TO 16 SERVINGS

2 (8-ounce) packages cream cheese,
    softened
7 to 8 ounces mild goat cheese
2 cloves garlic, minced
4 teaspoons snipped fresh oregano or
    1 teaspoon dried oregano, crushed
⅛ teaspoon freshly ground pepper
¼ cup prepared pesto
½ cup sun-dried tomatoes packed in
    oil
1 to 2 tablespoons slivered almonds,
    toasted
Fresh oregano or parsley sprigs
Stone-ground-wheat crackers or thinly
    sliced baguette

Line a 1-quart loaf pan or soufflé dish with clear plastic wrap. In a food processor bowl or large mixer bowl, combine the cream cheese, goat cheese, garlic, oregano, and pepper. Process or beat with an electric mixer until smooth. Spread one-third of the cheese mixture in the bottom of the pan. Top with the pesto, spreading evenly. Layer with another one-third of the cheese mixture. Drain the sun-dried tomatoes, reserving one tomato for garnish. Chop the remaining tomatoes and spread them evenly over the cheese mixture. Top with the remaining cheese mixture. Cover with plastic wrap and press gently to pack the cheese. Chill several hours.

Uncover the cheese; invert onto a serving plate and remove the plastic wrap. Cut the reserved sun-dried tomato into thin slices. Garnish the torta with thin slices of sun-dried tomato, the toasted almonds, and fresh oregano or parsley. Serve with stone-ground-wheat crackers or sliced baguette.

Heart & Soul, Memphis, TN

ITALIAN TORTA

MAKES 10 SERVINGS

1 package (16 to 20) sun-dried
    tomatoes
12 slices provolone cheese
½ cup pesto
2 (8-ounce) packages cream cheese,
    softened
1-2 cloves garlic, minced

Place the tomatoes in a medium-size bowl and pour in enough boiling water to cover. Let stand for 8 to 10 minutes or until softened. Drain well. Chop fine. Cut a piece of cheesecloth large enough to cover the bottom and sides as well as extend over the top of a loaf pan. Dampen with water and arrange in the pan. Line the pan with 4 slices of the provolone cheese, covering the entire bottom and sides of the pan by overlapping the slices. Spread half the pesto over the provolone.

Combine the cream cheese and garlic in a bowl. Layer half the cream cheese mixture, half the tomatoes, and half the provolone in the prepared pan. Spread with the remaining ¼ cup pesto. Layer the remaining cream cheese mixture, tomatoes, and provolone over the top. Pull the cheesecloth tightly across the top; press down to remove excess oil and to mold the torte to the pan. Chill in the refrigerator for at least 4 hours. Bring to room temperature before serving. Turn out on a serving platter and remove the cheesecloth. Serve with crackers or sliced bread.

NOTE: May be stored in the refrigerator for up to 3 days. You may use sun-dried tomatoes packed in oil, drained, and rinsed well, instead of the packaged sun-dried tomatoes.

Dining by Design, Pasadena, CA

BLUE RIBBON DIP

MAKES 1 ½ CUPS

8 ounces blue cheese, crumbled
2 cloves garlic, crushed
½ cup olive oil
2 tablespoons red wine vinegar
1 tablespoon lemon juice
½ cup chopped red onion
½ cup minced fresh parsley
¼ teaspoon freshly ground black pepper

Combine all the ingredients in a medium bowl and spread into a shallow serving dish. Refrigerate for at least 1 hour or up to 2 days. Serve with baguette slices, crackers, or fresh vegetables.

Gold 'n Delicious, Spokane, WA

SAVORY BLUE CHEESE CAKE

MAKES 12 TO 16 SERVINGS

¼ cup fine dry bread crumbs
⅓ cup finely grated Parmesan cheese
8 ounces bacon
1 Vidalia or white onion, minced
3 (8-ounce) packages cream cheese,
    softened
4 large eggs
½ cup heavy cream
12 ounces Gorgonzola, Stilton, or
    Roquefort cheese, crumbled
Salt and white pepper to taste
Dash of Tabasco

Preheat the oven to 300F. Coat a greased 10-inch springform pan with bread crumbs mixed with Parmesan cheese.

Cook the bacon in a skillet until crisp-fried and crumbly. Drain the bacon, reserving 1 tablespoon of drippings. Crumble the bacon and set aside. Sauté the onion in the reserved drippings until transparent.

Process the cream cheese, eggs, and cream in a blender or food processor until well combined. Add the crumbled bacon, onion, and Gorgonzola cheese and process well. Add the salt, white pepper, and Tabasco sauce. Process until nearly smooth.

Pour into the prepared pan. Bake 1½ hours or until the middle springs back when lightly touched. Turn off the oven. Let stand in the oven for 1 hour.

Bay Tables, Mobile, AL

HARRIS MANSION CHEESE PÂTÉ

MAKES 8 TO 10 SERVINGS

2 (8-ounce) packages cream cheese
1½ teaspoons dried Italian herb
    seasoning
Salt and freshly ground black pepper,
    to taste
½ cup shredded Gruyère cheese
¼ cup finely chopped pecans
3 ounces Roquefort cheese, crumbled
½ cup snipped fresh parsley
½ cup crumbled crisply cooked bacon
Fresh parsley sprigs
Assorted crackers

Lightly oil a 6 x 4-inch loaf pan. Line with plastic wrap, leaving a 2-inch overhang on each side. Beat the cream cheese in a medium bowl to soften. Beat in the herb seasoning, salt, and pepper.

Spread one-third of the cream cheese mixture evenly in the prepared pan. Top with the Gruyère cheese and pecans. Spread this layer with half of the remaining cream cheese mixture, then with the Roquefort cheese, parsley, and bacon. Top with the remaining cream cheese mixture. Press down firmly. Cover with overhanging plastic wrap and refrigerate overnight.

Invert onto a serving plate and remove the plastic. Bring to room temperature, garnish with parsley sprigs, and serve with crackers.

A Capital Affair, Harrisburg, PA

POLENTA STARS

MAKES 12 SERVINGS

1 package instant polenta
Olive oil
4 ounces goat cheese
1 tablespoon chopped fresh dillweed
1 tablespoon dry white wine
8 oil-packed sun-dried tomatoes,
    drained and chopped
Sprigs of dillweed

Prepare the polenta according to the package directions. Spread evenly in a 13 x 9-inch pan. Let stand until cool, then turn out onto a work surface. Cut into shapes with a star cookie cutter.

Heat ¼ inch of olive oil in a large heavy skillet. Fry the polenta stars until light brown on both sides; drain on paper towels.

Mash the goat cheese with a fork in a bowl. Stir in the chopped dillweed, 1 tablespoon of olive oil, the wine, and half the tomatoes. Spread the cheese mixture on the stars. Top with the remaining tomatoes. Arrange on a serving platter and top with sprigs of dillweed.

Celebrate Chicago: A Taste of Our Town, Chicago, IL

TUSCANY TOAST

MAKES 2 DOZEN

2 large firm, ripe tomatoes, chopped
1 cup loosely packed, chopped fresh
    basil
¼ cup chopped Belgian endive
¼ cup virgin olive oil
Salt and freshly ground pepper
1 loaf Italian bread

Preheat the broiler.

Mix the chopped tomatoes, basil, endive, and olive oil in a medium bowl; let stand at room temperature. Add the salt and pepper to taste. Slice the bread, arrange the slices on a baking sheet, and toast under the broiler until golden brown on both sides. Watch carefully so it does not burn. Top the hot toasts with the tomato mixture and serve.

A Matter of Taste, Morristown, NJ

WALNUT-AND-PECAN CARAMELIZED BRIE

MAKES 8 TO 10 SERVINGS

⅔ cup lightly packed brown sugar
⅓ cup water
½ cup heavy cream
⅛ teaspoon grated nutmeg
⅛ teaspoon ground cinnamon
5 tablespoons butter
¼ cup pecan halves
¼ cup walnut halves
1 (8-inch) round of Brie cheese, with
   top rind removed
4 ounces red seedless grapes
1 Granny Smith apple, sliced
Assorted crackers

Bring the brown sugar and the water to a boil in a heavy saucepan; boil 4 minutes. Remove from heat, and let cool slightly. Stir in the cream, nutmeg, and cinnamon. Bring the mixture to a boil; boil 3 to 4 minutes or until slightly thickened. Remove from the heat; stir in the butter and nuts.

Center the Brie on a 12-inch round serving plate; place the grapes, apple slices, and crackers around the edges. Pour the caramel evenly over the top of the cheese, allowing it to run over the sides. Evenly distribute the nuts over the top using a spoon.

Victorian Thymes & Pleasures, Williamsport, PA

PESTO BRIE

MAKES 8 SERVINGS

1 pound Brie cheese
1 ripe plum tomato, seeded and
   chopped
2 green onions, thinly sliced
¼ cup pesto
1 loaf French bread, sliced and toasted

Preheat the oven to 350F. Trim the rind from the cheese and cut the cheese into chunks. Layer the cheese, tomato, and green onions in a baking dish. Dot with the pesto. Bake until the cheese melts and the pesto begins to run. Serve warm with bread slices.

Generations, Rockford, IL

ERIC'S CHAMPAGNE CHEESE BALL

MAKES 12 TO 16 SERVINGS

2 pounds sharp Cheddar cheese,
  grated
2 tablespoons butter
6 ounces cream cheese, softened
½ cup Champagne or ⅓ cup dry
  white wine
¼ cup finely chopped onion
1 clove garlic, minced
1 teaspoon Worcestershire sauce
¼ teaspoon salt, or as needed

TOPPING:
1¼ cups chopped walnuts
1 tablespoon chopped parsley
1 teaspoon paprika
1 teaspoon chili powder
1 teaspoon curry powder
1 teaspoon dillweed

Combine the Cheddar cheese, butter, and cream cheese in a large bowl; mix thoroughly. Add the Champagne slowly, stirring constantly. Add the onion, garlic, Worcestershire sauce, and salt to taste. Cover the mixture and chill for 1 hour.

Form the cheese mixture into a ball. Combine the walnuts, parsley, paprika, chili powder, curry powder, and dill in a small bowl. Spread the walnut mixture on waxed paper and roll the cheese bowl over it until thoroughly coated. Wrap the ball in a clean sheet of waxed paper and chill for 1 hour longer. Serve with crackers.

Junior League of Philadelphia's Bicentennial Cookbook, Philadelphia, PA

GRAND MARNIER BALL

MAKES 15 TO 18 SERVINGS

4 (8-ounce) packages cream cheese,
  softened
2 tablespoons vanilla extract
1 pound powdered sugar
½ cup Grand Marnier
¼ cup packed light brown sugar
Fresh strawberries

In an electric mixer or food processor, beat the cream cheese, vanilla, powdered sugar, and Grand Marnier until fluffy. Mound the mixture into a ball on a serving platter or pack the mixture into a decorative mold that has been lined with plastic wrap.

Refrigerate for several hours and gently remove the plastic wrap. The cheese ball will remain semisoft. To serve, sprinkle the brown sugar over the top and surround with strawberries. Serve with gingersnaps or chocolate wafer cookies.

And Roses for the Table, Tyler, TX

CHEESE RING

MAKES 8 TO 10 SERVINGS

1 pound sharp Cheddar cheese, grated
1 cup chopped pecans
¾ cup mayonnaise
1 small onion, grated
1 clove garlic, pressed
½ teaspoon Tabasco
1 cup strawberry preserves

Combine the cheese, pecans, mayonnaise, onion, garlic, and Tabasco in a medium bowl; mix well. Spoon into a ring mold that has been lined with plastic wrap. Chill in the refrigerator.

When ready to serve, unmold onto a platter and top with the strawberry preserves. Serve with crackers.

Charlotte Cooks Again, Charlotte, NC

PARMESAN PITA CRISPS

MAKES 4 DOZEN

4 (6-inch) pita rounds
6 tablespoons olive oil
1 teaspoon dried whole oregano leaves
1 teaspoon garlic powder
½ cup grated Parmesan cheese
1½ tablespoons sesame seeds

Preheat the oven to 425F.

Separate each pita round into two circles. Cut each circle into 6 wedges. Place the wedges, rough side up, on an ungreased baking sheet. Combine the oil, oregano, and garlic powder in a small bowl; mix well. Brush lightly onto the wedges. Combine the Parmesan cheese and sesame seeds in a small bowl. Sprinkle on top.

Bake 10 minutes or until lightly browned. Cool. Store in an airtight container.

Dining by Fireflies, Charlotte, NC

Mexican Cheesecake with Salsa Roja and Guacamole

Makes 14 servings

Salsa Roja:

3 large tomatoes, peeled, seeded, and
    diced
1 red onion, minced
1 clove garlic, minced
2 serrano chile peppers, seeded and
    minced
1 bunch fresh cilantro, minced
¼ cup fresh lime juice
Salt and freshly ground pepper to
    taste

Cheesecake:

1½ cups crushed tortilla chips
4 tablespoons (½ stick) unsalted
    butter, melted
2 (8-ounce) packages cream cheese,
    softened
8 ounces Monterey Jack cheese or
    jalapeño Jack cheese, shredded
    (2 cups)
3 large eggs
1 cup sour cream
1 (4-ounce) can diced green chiles
1 cup picante sauce

Guacamole:

2 avocados, pitted and peeled
2 tablespoons minced onion
1 teaspoon chopped fresh cilantro
Juice of ½ lime
Dash of Tabasco
1 teaspoon minced fresh jalapeño
    pepper
Salt to taste

Salsa roja: Combine the tomatoes, onion, garlic, serranos, cilantro, and lime juice in a serving bowl. Season with salt and pepper. Cover and chill.

Cheesecake: Preheat the oven to 350F. Combine the chips and melted butter. Press the mixture into the bottom of a greased 9-inch springform pan. Bake for 10 minutes. Combine the cream cheese and Monterey Jack in a food processor. Add the eggs and ½ cup of the sour cream and pulse to combine. Add the green chiles and picante sauce. Pulse again to thoroughly combine. Pour the cheese mixture over the chilled crust and spread evenly. Place the pan on a baking sheet and bake for 40 minutes. Spread the remaining ½ cup of sour cream on the hot cheesecake. Cool to room temperature and chill.

Guacamole: Mash the avocados with a fork in a medium bowl. Add the onion, cilantro, lime juice, Tabasco, and jalapeño pepper, mixing well. Season with salt.

To serve, unmold the cheesecake onto a serving platter. Top with dollops of salsa roja and guacamole. Serve with tortilla chips.

Stop and Smell the Rosemary, Houston, TX

CRAWFISH CHEESECAKE

MAKES 8 SERVINGS

1 cup grated Parmesan cheese
1 cup fresh bread crumbs
½ cup butter, melted
1 tablespoon olive oil
1 cup chopped onion
½ cup chopped green bell pepper
½ cup chopped red bell pepper
1 pound crawfish tails, chopped
2 teaspoons minced garlic
2-3 tablespoons Creole seasoning
2 dashes Worcestershire sauce
2 dashes Tabasco
2 tablespoons lemon juice
28 ounces cream cheese, softened
4 large eggs
½ cup heavy cream
1 cup shredded smoked Gouda cheese
2½ cups Green Mayonnaise (see
    below)

Preheat the oven to 350F.

Combine the Parmesan cheese, bread crumbs, and melted butter in a bowl. Press the mixture into the bottom of a 9-inch springform pan. Heat the olive oil in a large skillet over high heat. Add the onion and bell peppers and sauté for 2 minutes. Add the crawfish, garlic, Creole seasoning, Worcestershire, Tabasco, and lemon juice. Sauté for 1½ minutes. Remove from the heat.

Beat the cream cheese and eggs with an electric mixer in a large bowl for 5 minutes or until thick and frothy. Stir in the heavy cream, Gouda cheese, and crawfish mixture. Beat for 2 minutes or until well mixed and creamy. Pour the filling into the crust and bake for 1 hour or until firm. Cool to room temperature.

Spoon green mayonnaise onto 8 plates. Top with a slice of crawfish cheesecake.

GREEN MAYONNAISE:

MAKES 2½ TO 3 CUPS

¾ cup chopped green onions
½ cup chopped fresh parsley
1 tablespoon chopped shallots
1 tablespoon chopped garlic
2 large eggs (see Note)
1 teaspoon salt
Freshly ground pepper
1½ cups vegetable oil

Purée the green onions, parsley, shallots, and garlic in a blender or food processor. Add the eggs, salt, and pepper and process until mixed. Add the oil in a slow, steady stream with the machine running. Process until thickened.

NOTE: Raw eggs are used in this sauce. If the possibility of salmonella is a concern, substitute 1 cup of commercial mayonnaise mixed with ½ cup of sour cream or plain yogurt for the eggs and oil. Adjust seasoning to taste.

Crescent City Collection: A Taste of New Orleans, New Orleans, LA

Chile con Queso Mexicano

MAKES 4 TO 6 SERVINGS

6 fresh green chiles, roasted, peeled,
   seeded, and cut in lengthwise slices
1 onion, chopped
2 tablespoons bacon drippings
1 clove garlic, minced
2 large fresh tomatoes, peeled and
   finely chopped
2½ cups shredded Monterey Jack or
   Longhorn cheese
Salt to taste

In a skillet, sauté the chiles and onion in the bacon drippings over medium heat for 5 minutes or until softened. Add the garlic and cook for 60 seconds. Stir in the tomatoes, cheese, and salt. Heat until the cheese melts. Serve hot as a dip with corn chips.

Seasoned with Sun, El Paso, TX

Hot Onion–Cream Cheese Dip

MAKES 12 TO 16 SERVINGS

3-4 cups chopped onion (4 medium
   onions), or 12-16 ounces frozen
3 (8-ounce) packages cream cheese,
   softened
2 cups grated Parmesan cheese
½ cup mayonnaise
Corn chips or assorted crackers

If you are using frozen onions, thaw them and roll them in paper towels, squeezing to remove excess moisture. Preheat the oven to 425F.

Stir together the onions, cream cheese, Parmesan cheese, and mayonnaise until well combined. Transfer to a shallow 2-quart soufflé dish. Bake about 15 minutes or until the top is golden brown. Serve with corn chips or assorted crackers.

Heart & Soul, Memphis, TN

CRAB MUFFINS

MAKES 12 SERVINGS

1 jar Old English cheese spread
4 tablespoons (½ stick) butter, at room
  temperature
½ teaspoon seasoning salt
¼ teaspoon garlic powder
1 tablespoon mayonnaise
1 (6-ounce) can crabmeat, drained
1 package (6) English muffins

Preheat the oven to 450F.

Combine the cheese spread and butter in a medium bowl. Add the salt, garlic powder, mayonnaise, and crabmeat; mix well. Spread the mixture on the English muffin halves and place on a baking sheet (may be frozen before baking). Bake for 10 minutes or until they begin to bubble and brown.

Udderly Delicious, Racine, WI

CRAB AND CAPER DIP

MAKES 16 TO 20 SERVINGS

2 cups chopped onions
2 tablespoons butter
2 cups mayonnaise
2 cups shredded Swiss cheese
1 (3½-ounce) jar capers, drained
1 (6-ounce) can fancy lump crabmeat,
  drained
1 round loaf of bread

Preheat the oven to 350F.

Sauté the onions in the butter in a small skillet for 5 minutes or until soft. Combine the onions with the mayonnaise, cheese, capers, and crabmeat in a medium bowl; mix well.

Cut the top off the bread and hollow out the loaf; save the bread pieces for dipping. Spoon the crabmeat mixture inside the loaf. Wrap in foil and bake for 1 hour.

NOTE: Do not double or halve this recipe.

Gracious Gator Cooks, Gainesville, FL

CRAB MOUSSE

MAKES 12 SERVINGS

1 tablespoon unflavored gelatin
3 tablespoons cold water
¼ cup mayonnaise
1 tablespoon prepared mustard
2 tablespoons fresh lemon juice
1 tablespoon chopped fresh parsley
1 tablespoon chopped fresh chives
Salt and pepper to taste
1 pound fresh crabmeat, picked over to
    remove bits of cartilage
⅔ cup heavy cream, whipped

Stir the gelatin and water together in a small saucepan and let stand for 5 minutes, then place over medium heat for 1 to 2 minutes or until dissolved. Remove from the heat and cool slightly. Fold in the mayonnaise and mustard. Add the lemon juice and seasonings. Stir in the crabmeat and gently fold in the whipped cream.

Pour into an oiled 5-cup mold. Chill at least 4 hours. Unmold onto a chilled plate. Serve with assorted crackers.

Very Virginia, Hampton Roads, VA

CRAB-STUFFED MUSHROOM CAPS

MAKES 16

1 tablespoon butter
¼ cup finely diced onion
¼ cup finely diced celery
2 tablespoons white wine
1 teaspoon salt
¼ teaspoon white pepper
½ teaspoon thyme
1 teaspoon lemon juice
4 ounces king, snow, or lump
    crabmeat, picked over
2 tablespoons heavy cream or half-
    and-half
¼ cup shredded Swiss cheese
½ cup dry bread crumbs
16 large mushrooms, stems removed
16 small thin slices Swiss cheese

Preheat the oven to 375F.

Melt the butter in a medium skillet and sauté the onion and celery until tender. Add the wine, seasonings, lemon juice, and crabmeat; simmer 3 minutes. Add the cream and shredded cheese; cook until cheese melts. Add bread crumbs.

Spoon the crab mixture into the mushroom caps. Top with slices of the Swiss cheese. Arrange on a baking sheet and bake 12 to 15 minutes or until the cheese is lightly browned.

Great Beginnings, Grand Finales, South Bend, IN

HERB CHEESE–STUFFED MUSHROOMS

MAKES 8 TO 10 SERVINGS

2 (8-ounce) packages cream cheese,
    softened
1 (1-ounce) package ranch dressing
    party mix
¼ cup mayonnaise
2 tablespoons minced onion
1 tablespoon chopped fresh parsley
¼ cup grated Parmesan cheese
1½ pounds mushrooms, washed and
    stems removed
1 cup crushed herbed stuffing mix
8 tablespoons (1 stick) butter, melted

Preheat the oven to 350F. Grease a quiche dish or a glass pie plate.

Mix the cream cheese, party mix, mayonnaise, onion, parsley, and Parmesan cheese in a food processor or blender. Stuff the mushrooms with the cheese mixture. Dip the top of the filled mushrooms into the crushed stuffing.

Place the mushrooms in the prepared baking dish. Pour the melted butter over the top. Bake 30 minutes.

NOTE: These come out of the oven very hot, so give them a moment to cool.

Sound Seasonings, Westchester on the Sound, NY

OYSTERS SALISBURY

MAKES 4 DOZEN

4 dozen oysters in their shell
Coarse or kosher salt
2 tablespoons butter
2 tablespoons all-purpose flour
2 cups milk
½ cup shredded Swiss cheese
¾ teaspoon Worcestershire sauce
¼ teaspoon grated nutmeg
Salt to taste
⅛ teaspoon pepper
½ (10-ounce) package frozen chopped
    spinach
Parmesan cheese for topping

Open the oysters, letting them remain in the deep half of the shell (fish and seafood shops will do this for you). Pour a thick layer of coarse salt on each of two large baking sheets and arrange the oysters on the salt, pushing them down to steady them.

Melt the butter in a 1-quart saucepan. Blend in the flour and slowly stir in the milk. Simmer for 5 minutes on low heat, stirring occasionally. Add the Swiss cheese and stir until melted. Stir in the Worcestershire sauce, nutmeg, salt, and pepper.

Cook the spinach as directed on the package and squeeze out all additional moisture. Blend the spinach into the cheese sauce and let the mixture cool. Top each oyster with 1 tablespoon of the spinach mixture. Sprinkle with the grated Parmesan cheese (can be covered and refrigerated to this point). Bake in a preheated 400F oven for 10 to 15 minutes. Serve immediately.

Of Tide & Thyme, Annapolis, MD

SEVICHE

MAKES 8 SERVINGS

1 pound thin white fish fillets
   (flounder, sole, or other flatfish) (see
   Note)
1 cup lemon or lime juice
5 large tomatoes, chopped
1 large onion, chopped
15 stuffed green olives, chopped
1 tablespoon vegetable oil
1 tablespoon chopped parsley
¼ teaspoon marjoram
¼ teaspoon thyme
½ teaspoon sage
2 (4-ounce) cans chopped green chiles

Cut the fillets into bite-size pieces, place in a bowl, and add the lemon or lime juice. Cover the bowl and leave in the refrigerator at least 4 hours or overnight. Stir occasionally.

Combine the tomatoes, onion, and olives with the fish. Add all the other ingredients. Let stand at least 4 to 6 hours. Serve well-chilled as an appetizer with saltines or tostadas or as a seafood cocktail.

NOTE: Since the fish is "cooked" only in the lemon juice, it is essentially served raw, so you will want to use perfectly fresh fillets.

Seasoned with Sun, El Paso, TX

TORTILLA PINWHEELS

MAKES 3 DOZEN

1 (4-ounce) can diced green chiles,
   drained
1 (2¼-ounce) can chopped ripe olives,
   drained
1 (2-ounce) jar sliced pimiento,
   drained
1 (8-ounce) package cream cheese,
   softened
7-10 flour tortillas
Salsa (optional)

Combine the chiles, olives, pimiento, and cream cheese in a small bowl, mixing well. Spread the mixture on each tortilla and roll up jellyroll fashion. Cover with a damp paper towel and plastic wrap to prevent drying out; chill for several hours. To serve, slice tortillas into 1-inch segments. Dip in salsa, if desired.

Nuggets, Colorado Springs, CO

LONE STAR FONDUE

MAKES 12 TO 15 SERVINGS

1 (1½-pound) round firm loaf of
    bread
2 tablespoons vegetable oil
1 tablespoon butter, melted
1½ cups sour cream
8 ounces sharp Cheddar cheese, grated
1 (8-ounce) package cream cheese,
    softened
1 cup diced cooked ham (3 ounces)
½ cup chopped green onions
1 (4-ounce) can green chiles, drained
    and chopped
1 teaspoon Worcestershire sauce

Preheat the oven to 350F.

Slice off the top of the bread and set it aside. Hollow out the insides with a small paring knife, leaving a half-inch shell. Cut the removed bread into 1-inch cubes (about 4 cups).

Combine the oil and butter in a large skillet. Add the bread cubes and stir until thoroughly coated. Place on a cookie sheet. Bake for 10 to 15 minutes, turning occasionally, until golden brown. Remove the cubes from the oven and set aside.

Combine the sour cream, Cheddar cheese, and cream cheese in a large bowl. Stir in the ham, green onions, chiles, and Worcestershire sauce. Spoon the cheese mixture into the hollowed bread shell. Replace the top of the bread. Wrap the filled loaf in several layers of heavy foil. Set the loaf on a cookie sheet. Bake for 1 hour and 10 minutes or until the cheese filling is melted and heated through. When the fondue is ready, remove the wrap and transfer the loaf to a serving dish with the bread cubes placed around it for dipping.

The Wild, Wild West, Odessa, TX

JALAPEÑO BITES

MAKES 6 TO 8 SERVINGS

1 (8-ounce) package cream cheese,
    softened
8 ounces grated Parmesan cheese
3 tablespoons chopped jalapeño
    peppers
2 large egg yolks
2 cups dry bread crumbs

Preheat the oven to 350F. Combine the cream cheese, Parmesan cheese, jalapeño peppers, and egg yolks in a bowl and mix to form a paste. Shape ½ tablespoonful at a time into ¼-inch rounds. Roll in the bread crumbs. Place on an ungreased baking sheet. Bake for 10 to 15 minutes or until golden brown. Serve warm.

Meet Us in the Kitchen, St. Louis, MO

JALAPEÑO PIE

MAKES 8 SERVINGS

1 (11-ounce) can pickled, seeded
    jalapeño peppers, sliced lengthwise
10 ounces sharp Cheddar cheese,
    grated
4 eggs, beaten

Preheat the oven to 275F. Oil a glass pie pan and line it with the jalapeño peppers. Sprinkle cheese over the top. Pour in the eggs. Bake for 45 minutes. Slice and serve hot or at room temperature.

NOTE: Green chiles may be substituted for the jalapeño peppers for a milder flavor.

Fiesta, Corpus Christi, TX

HOT APPETIZER PIE

MAKES 12 SERVINGS

1 (8-ounce) package cream cheese,
    softened
2 tablespoons milk
1 (2½-ounce) jar dried beef, rinsed in
    boiling water, drained and sliced
    into strips
2 tablespoons finely chopped green
    pepper
2 tablespoons finely chopped onion
½ teaspoon freshly ground pepper
½ cup sour cream
1½ teaspoons curry powder, optional
¼ cup or more chopped walnuts

Preheat the oven to 350F. Beat the cream cheese with the milk in a medium bowl. Add remaining ingredients, except nuts, and mix well. Pat into an 8-inch pie pan. Spread the nuts over top. Bake for 15 minutes. Serve hot with crackers or Melba toast.

Bound to Please, Boise, ID

ASPARAGUS FOLDOVERS

MAKES 75

3 loaves fresh soft sandwich bread
Butter, softened
Grated Parmesan cheese
3 cans green asparagus spears
Melted butter

Remove the crusts from the bread and roll each slice flat between two sheets of waxed paper. (These may be done ahead and frozen.) Spread each slice with softened butter, and sprinkle well with the Parmesan cheese. Drain the asparagus; then place on paper towels to absorb all excess moisture. Place one spear on a corner of each bread slice and roll up. Secure with toothpicks. These may be done the day before serving and refrigerated.

Preheat the oven to 400F. Before baking, brush each roll with melted butter and sprinkle with more cheese. Bake for 10 to 12 minutes. Serve hot.

The Silver Collection, Memphis, TN

HOT ARTICHOKE SPREAD

MAKES 6 SERVINGS

1 (14-ounce) can artichoke hearts,
*   drained and chopped*
1 cup mayonnaise
1 cup grated Parmesan cheese
Garlic powder to taste

Preheat the oven to 350F. Mix all ingredients in a medium bowl. Spoon into a ramekin. Bake for 20 minutes or until the mixture bubbles. Serve with crackers for spreading or chips for dipping.

Southern Accent, Pine Bluff, *AR*

ARTICHOKE CHEESE DIP

MAKES 12 SERVINGS

1 cup mayonnaise
1 cup grated Parmesan cheese
2 cups shredded mozzarella cheese
2 (8-ounce) cans artichoke hearts,
    drained and chopped in quarters
½ – 1 teaspoon garlic powder
Paprika

Preheat the oven to 350F. Combine the mayonnaise, cheeses, artichoke hearts, and garlic powder in a 1½-quart baking dish. Sprinkle with the paprika. Bake for 25 minutes. Serve hot with crackers for dipping.

Brunch Basket, Rockford, IL

ARTICHOKE SQUARES

MAKES 10 TO 12 SERVINGS

3 (6-ounce) jars marinated artichoke
    hearts in oil
1 clove garlic, crushed
½ cup chopped onion
4 large eggs
¼ cup seasoned bread crumbs
½ pound sharp Cheddar cheese, grated
2 tablespoons minced fresh parsley
¼ teaspoon salt
⅛ teaspoon dried oregano
⅛ teaspoon freshly ground pepper
⅛ teaspoon Tabasco
Watercress or parsley sprigs

Preheat the oven to 325F. Drain the oil from 1 jar of the artichoke hearts into a 2-inch skillet and, using moderate heat, gently heat the oil. Sauté the garlic and onion in the oil for 5 minutes and set aside. Drain and discard the oil from the remaining 2 jars of artichoke hearts. Chop the hearts finely and set aside.

In a medium-sized bowl, beat the eggs until foamy and blend in the bread crumbs, cheese, parsley, salt, oregano, pepper, and Tabasco. Add the finely chopped artichoke hearts to the egg mixture and stir gently to blend. Add the onion and garlic; mix well. Spoon into a greased 9 x 9-inch pan. Bake 30 minutes. Cool well before cutting into 2-inch squares. Before serving, bake 10 to 12 minutes, then place on a warm serving plate garnished with watercress or parsley sprigs.

The California Heritage Cookbook, Pasadena, CA

WHITE GUACAMOLE

MAKES 12 SERVINGS

¾ *cup mayonnaise*
¾ *cup sour cream*
3 tablespoons canned chopped green
   chiles, drained
1 tomato, finely chopped and drained
2 tablespoons lemon juice
2 avocados, mashed
Garlic salt to taste
Salt and freshly ground pepper to
   taste
Tortilla chips

Blend all the ingredients in a bowl, except tortilla chips; mix well. Cover and refrigerate at least 1 hour. Serve with chips.

NOTE: This must be prepared ahead in order for the flavors to blend.

Plain and Fancy, Richardson, TX

CARROT DIP

MAKES 15 SERVINGS

1 (8-ounce) package cream cheese,
   softened
1 cup (packed) grated carrots
1 tablespoon grated onion
1 tablespoon mayonnaise
Salt and ground red pepper (cayenne)
   to taste
2 dashes lemon juice
Parsley sprigs (optional)

Combine all the ingredients, except the parsley, in a medium bowl; mix well. Shape the mixture into a carrot shape or roll into a ball; decorate the top with parsley, if desired. Serve with crackers. This keeps in the refrigerator for 3 weeks.

Charlotte Cooks Again, Charlotte, NC

JOANNE'S SPICY SHRIMP SALSA

MAKES 2 CUPS

2 large ripe tomatoes or 1 (14-ounce)
    can whole tomatoes, drained
½ cup diced red onion
⅛ cup (about 4) seeded and diced
    jalapeño peppers
8 ounces small bay shrimp, cooked
    and shelled, or medium shrimp,
    coarsely chopped
1 tablespoon chopped fresh cilantro
½ teaspoon cumin
2 cloves garlic, minced
4 teaspoons lime juice
½ teaspoon salt
¼ teaspoon freshly ground black
    pepper

Drop the fresh tomatoes into a small pan of boiling water for about 2 minutes or until the skins blister. Remove from the water, cool, and peel.

Coarsely chop the fresh or canned tomatoes and place in a large bowl. Stir in the remaining ingredients. Cover and refrigerate at least 4 hours. Serve with baked tortilla chips or as a side dish.

NOTE: For a thicker salsa, combine all the ingredients except shrimp in a food processor; pulse 3 times or until desired consistency. Stir in shrimp.

Gold 'n Delicious, Spokane, WA

JALAPEÑO CHILE SALSA

MAKES 1 CUP

4 small fresh jalapeño chiles, seeded
    and chopped (see Note)
2 large tomatoes, peeled and chopped
1 onion, minced
½ teaspoon garlic powder
Dash of salt

Thoroughly mix all ingredients. Serve with crackers or as a chile sauce for tacos or any Mexican dish.

NOTE: For a spicier salsa, leave in some or all of the seeds.

Seasoned with Sun, El Paso, TX

Black Bean Salsa

MAKES 12 SERVINGS

2 (15-ounce) cans black beans,
 drained and rinsed
1 (16-ounce) can white shoepeg corn,
 drained
6 tablespoons fresh lime juice
6 tablespoons olive oil
1½ teaspoons ground cumin
½ cup finely chopped red onion
¼ cup chopped fresh cilantro
½ teaspoon salt
1 cup peeled and chopped tomato
Chopped jalapeño pepper (optional)

Combine the beans, corn, lime juice, olive oil, cumin, onion, cilantro, and salt in a large bowl; mix well. Cover and refrigerate overnight. Add the chopped tomato just before serving. You may also want to add a little more lime juice and a chopped jalapeño pepper. Serve with tortilla chips.

St. Louis Days . . . St. Louis Nights, St. Louis, MO

Easy Shrimp Dip

MAKES 6 TO 8 SERVINGS

1 (4-ounce) can small shrimp
4 tablespoons mayonnaise
3 tablespoons cream-style horseradish

Drain and chop the shrimp (a pastry blender is helpful for this); add the mayonnaise and horseradish and mix well. Add more or less mayonnaise and horseradish according to how runny and "hot" you want it to be. Serve with crackers.

The Charlotte Cookbook, Charlotte, NC

SHRIMP BUTTER

MAKES 2½ CUPS

8 tablespoons (1 stick) butter, softened
1 (8-ounce) package cream cheese,
    softened
4 tablespoons mayonnaise
8-12 ounces shrimp, cleaned, cooked,
    and minced
½-1 teaspoon garlic salt
Salt and freshly ground pepper to
    taste
2-3 tablespoons finely minced onion
Dash of lemon juice

Combine the butter, cream cheese, and mayonnaise in a medium bowl. Blend the shrimp with the butter mixture. Add the seasonings to taste. Serve with crackers or as a canapé spread on toast rounds.

Out of Our League, Too, Greensboro, NC

SHRIMP QUESO

MAKES 8 SERVINGS

½ cup evaporated milk
8 ounces sharp Cheddar cheese, grated
8 ounces Monterey Jack cheese, grated
1 cup picante sauce
2 cups cooked and chopped shrimp

Heat the milk in the top of a double boiler; add the cheeses and stir until melted. Add the picante sauce and the shrimp; mix well. Serve warm with tortilla chips.

¡Viva! Tradiciones, Corpus Christi, TX

GARLIC PRAWNS

MAKES 8 SERVINGS

¼ cup red wine vinegar
¼ cup tarragon vinegar
½ cup olive oil
¼ cup finely chopped fresh parsley
¼ cup finely chopped shallots
4 teaspoons Dijon mustard
8 small cloves garlic, minced
1-2 teaspoons crushed red pepper
    flakes
1-2 pounds frozen cooked prawns or
    large shrimp, thawed

Whisk the wine vinegar, tarragon vinegar, oil, parsley, shallots, mustard, garlic, and pepper flakes in a small bowl. Place the prawns in a shallow baking dish. Pour in the vinegar mixture. Marinate, covered, in the refrigerator for 6 to 10 hours. May be served with sliced baguette toasts.

Dining by Design, Pasadena, CA

CURRIED LOBSTER AND SHRIMP CROUTONS

MAKES 24 SERVINGS

1 loaf party-size French bread,
    unsliced
6 to 8 tablespoons olive oil
1 cup mayonnaise
¼ cup mango chutney, chopped
1 teaspoon curry powder
12 large shrimp, cooked, peeled,
    deveined, and cut in half
6 ounces fresh Florida lobster meat,
    cooked and chopped
Ground red pepper (cayenne)
Kumquat branches, watercress, or
    parsley (garnish)

Preheat the oven to 350F. Cut the bread into 24 slices ¼ to ½ inch thick. (Save extra bread for another use.) Brush both sides of the bread slices with olive oil; place on a baking sheet. Bake on the center shelf of the oven until crisp, about 10 minutes, turning after 5 minutes. Remove from the oven; cool; cover until ready to use.

Combine the mayonnaise, chutney, and curry powder in a small bowl, mixing well. Spread a generous ½ tablespoon of the mayonnaise mixture on each crouton; top with shrimp or lobster meat. Sprinkle lightly with cayenne. Arrange on a serving tray; garnish as desired. Serve immediately.

Tampa Treasures, Tampa, FL

CONFETTI SHRIMP

1 medium red bell pepper
¼ cup olive oil
1½ pounds (about 24) large shrimp,
   peeled and deveined
1-1½ tablespoons minced fresh ginger
2 cloves garlic, minced
1½ tablespoons fresh lemon juice
1 tablespoon fresh lime juice
¼ teaspoon salt
½ teaspoon Chinese hot (red chile) oil
¼ cup minced fresh chives

Roast the pepper under the broiler, turning until charred all over, about 5 minutes. Place the pepper in a paper or plastic bag and let steam 10 minutes. Remove the skin, stem, and seeds. Mince the pepper and set aside in a small bowl.

In a large, heavy skillet, heat 2 tablespoons of the olive oil over high heat. Add the shrimp, stirring constantly for 2 to 3 minutes or until pink. Transfer to a medium bowl and let cool. Reduce the heat to moderately low and add the ginger and garlic to the skillet. Stir constantly for 3 minutes or until the garlic turns golden (do not let it burn). Spoon the garlic mixture into a small bowl, and whisk in the lemon juice, lime juice, and salt. Whisk in the remaining 2 tablespoons of olive oil and the chile oil. Pour the mixture over the cooled shrimp, stirring to coat. Marinate several hours. Before serving, bring to room temperature. Stir in the chives and minced red pepper and transfer to a serving bowl.

Very Virginia, Hampton Roads, VA

THAI SHRIMP AND SPINACH CURRY

1 (14-ounce) can unsweetened coconut
   milk, chilled
2 teaspoons Thai red curry paste
1 pound large shrimp, shelled and
   deveined
2 tablespoons nam pla (fish sauce)
2 carrots, thinly sliced
1 red bell pepper, seeded and thinly
   sliced
¾ pound fresh spinach, cleaned and
   spun dry
3 tablespoons chopped cilantro

Spoon ⅓ cup of the thick coconut cream from the top of the chilled coconut milk into a skillet. Cook over medium heat 2 to 3 minutes, whisking constantly. Add the curry paste, whisking for 1 minute. Add the shrimp. Sauté over medium–high heat for 2 minutes or until the shrimp turn light pink. Add the remaining coconut milk and the fish sauce. Simmer, uncovered, 1 minute, stirring occasionally, or until the shrimp are thoroughly cooked.

Transfer the shrimp to a serving bowl, using a slotted spoon. Cover with aluminum foil to keep warm. Add the carrots and red pepper to the skillet. Simmer 5 minutes. Add the spinach in batches, stirring until each batch is wilted. Return the shrimp to the skillet; simmer 1 minute. Sprinkle with cilantro. Serve over rice.

Capital Celebrations, Washington, D.C.

Icy Prawns with
A Trio of Celestial Dipping Sauces

MAKES 8 SERVINGS

*1 pound jumbo shrimp, peeled
   (leaving tail intact) and deveined*

Put the shrimp in a large pot of boiling salted water. Reduce the heat at once and simmer 2 to 4 minutes or until pink. Remove from the heat. Drain and run under cool water to prevent further cooking. Serve on ice surrounded by dipping sauces.

Fiery Tomato-Onion Dipping Sauce:

MAKES ABOUT 1 CUP

*3 large tomatoes, peeled, seeded, and
   finely chopped*
*2 fresh green chiles, minced, or 1
   (7-ounce) can diced green chiles,
   drained*
1 small onion, minced
1 tablespoon minced fresh cilantro
1 tablespoon olive oil
1 tablespoon fresh lime juice
1 teaspoon salt or to taste
*¼ teaspoon freshly ground pepper or
   to taste*
Pinch of sugar

Combine all the ingredients in a food processor and blend just until finely chopped, approximately 2–3 pulses. (Do not over-process or the ingredients will turn to liquid.) Cover and refrigerate.

PESTO DIPPING SAUCE:

MAKES 1 CUP

1 cup loosely packed parsley leaves
¼-½ cup fresh basil leaves or 1
    tablespoon dried basil
¼ cup grated Parmesan cheese
2 large cloves garlic, minced
1 cup mayonnaise
Pine nuts for garnish

Process all the ingredients, except pine nuts, in a food processor or blender and purée until smooth. Place in an airtight container. (Cover and refrigerate up to 3 days.) At time of serving, garnish with pine nuts.

PEANUT-CURRY DIPPING SAUCE:

MAKES ABOUT 1½ CUPS

8 ounces cream cheese, softened
½ cup sour cream
1 tablespoon curry powder, or more to
    taste
1 small clove garlic, minced
½ teaspoon salt
½ cup peanuts, finely chopped
2 slices bacon, cooked and crumbled
2 green onions, finely chopped

Combine the cream cheese, sour cream, curry powder, garlic, and salt in a medium bowl; mix until smooth. Stir in the peanuts and bacon. (Refrigerate, covered, up to 3 days.) Let come to room temperature before serving. Garnish with green onions.

Dining by Fireflies, Charlotte, NC

CREAMED SHRIMP AND ARTICHOKE BOTTOMS

MAKES 12 TO 16 SERVINGS

4½ tablespoons butter
4½ tablespoons all-purpose flour
½ cup milk
¾ cup heavy cream
Salt and freshly ground pepper to
    taste
¼ cup dry vermouth
1 tablespoon Worcestershire sauce
1½ pounds shrimp, cooked, shelled,
    deveined, and coarsely chopped
2 (16-ounce) cans artichoke bottoms,
    drained and coarsely chopped
¼ cup freshly grated Parmesan cheese

Melt the butter in a large skillet and stir in the flour. When blended, gradually add the milk and cream, stirring constantly with a wire whisk. When the mixture is thickened and smooth, season with salt and pepper. Add the vermouth and Worcestershire sauce to the cream sauce. Combine with the shrimp and artichokes. Heat through, then pour into a chafing dish. Sprinkle with the Parmesan cheese. Serve with buttered toast rounds.

The Silver Collection, Memphis, TN

CRUNCHY SPINACH DIP

MAKES 6 TO 8 SERVINGS

1 (10-ounce) package frozen chopped
    spinach, thawed, with juice
    squeezed out thoroughly
1 package Knorr vegetable soup mix
¼ cup chopped green onions
1 cup water chestnuts, chopped
1 cup mayonnaise
1 cup sour cream
Lemon juice to taste
Tabasco to taste

In a large bowl, combine all the ingredients. Mix thoroughly. Chill well in the refrigerator before serving. Serve in a round loaf of hollowed-out bread with chunks of bread or crackers on the side.

Rare Collections, Galveston County, TX

SPINACH BALLS

MAKES ABOUT 100

2 (10-ounce) packages frozen chopped
    spinach
6 large eggs, slightly beaten
8 tablespoons (1 stick) butter, softened
2 cups herb-seasoned stuffing
1 teaspoon garlic salt
½ cup freshly grated Parmesan cheese
1 small onion, grated
1-2 tablespoons olive oil
8 ounces feta cheese, crumbled

Preheat the oven to 350F. Thaw the spinach and drain, pressing to remove all excess liquid. Combine the spinach and remaining ingredients in a large mixing bowl, Roll the mixture by tablespoonfuls into 1-inch balls. Place the balls on a lightly greased baking pan. Bake for 20 minutes or until golden.

NOTE: Unbaked spinach balls may be stored in the freezer. If spinach balls are frozen, do not thaw before baking.

Very Virginia, Hampton Roads, VA

CAVIAR AND EGG HORS D'OEUVRES

MAKES 8 TO 10 SERVINGS

6 hard-cooked eggs, peeled and
    chopped fine
8 tablespoons (1 stick) butter, softened
¼ cup mayonnaise
⅓ cup finely chopped onion
½ teaspoon lemon juice
Salt, if desired
⅛ teaspoon freshly ground black
    pepper
1 (8-ounce) container sour cream
1 (3½-ounce) jar whitefish caviar

In a small bowl, combine the eggs, butter, mayonnaise, and onion. Add the lemon juice, salt, and pepper; mix thoroughly. Line a medium-size bowl with aluminum foil. Firmly pack the egg mixture into the foil-lined bowl. Chill in the refrigerator overnight.

When ready to serve, invert onto a serving plate. Remove the foil. Frost with the sour cream. Spoon the caviar around this mixture. Serve crackers on the side.

Rare Collections, Galveston County, TX

Texas Caviar

Makes 40 servings

¾ cup cider vinegar
1 tablespoon water
½ cup vegetable oil
1 cup sugar
1 teaspoon salt
½ teaspoon freshly ground pepper
1 (15-ounce) can pinto beans, drained
1 (15-ounce) can garbanzo beans,
    drained
1 (15-ounce) can black beans, drained
1 (15-ounce) can black-eyed peas,
    drained
2 (11-ounce) cans white shoepeg corn,
    drained
2 (4-ounce) cans chopped green chiles,
    drained
1 (2-ounce) jar finely chopped
    pimiento, drained
1 cup finely chopped green bell pepper
1 cup finely chopped celery
1 small onion, finely chopped

Combine the vinegar, water, oil, sugar, salt, and pepper in a saucepan. Bring to a boil, stirring occasionally. Cool the marinade to room temperature. Combine the beans, peas, corn, green chiles, and pimiento in a large bowl. Add the green pepper, celery, and onion. Add the marinade; mix well. Chill, covered, for 24 hours. Serve with tortilla chips.

The Best of Wheeling, Wheeling, WV

Eggplant Caviar

Makes 6 to 8 servings

1 large eggplant
3 tablespoons finely chopped onion
⅓ cup chopped tomato
2 tablespoons chopped fresh parsley
1 tablespoon chopped fresh basil
¼ teaspoon minced garlic
2 tablespoons olive oil
2 tablespoons lemon juice
¼ teaspoon salt
¼ teaspoon freshly ground pepper

Preheat the oven to 450F. Pierce the eggplant several times with a fork and place on a baking sheet. Bake for 20 minutes or until the skin darkens and the eggplant is tender. Let stand until cool.

Peel the eggplant and coarsely chop the pulp. Combine the eggplant, onion, tomato, parsley, basil, garlic, olive oil, lemon juice, salt, and pepper in a medium bowl; mix well. Serve with toasted French bread slices.

Beyond Cotton Country, Decatur, AL

APPLE AND CHEESE QUESADILLAS
WITH CINNAMON-YOGURT DIPPING SAUCE

MAKES 32

2 tablespoons butter, softened
16 (7-inch) flour tortillas
⅓ cup orange marmalade
1 cup shredded Monterey Jack cheese
1 cup shredded Cheddar cheese
1 large apple, peeled and finely
  chopped
⅓ cup golden raisins
Cinnamon-Yogurt Dipping Sauce (see
  below)

Preheat the oven to 350F

Spread the butter on one side of each tortilla. Place the tortillas, butter side down, on waxed paper. Spread the marmalade on the non-buttered side of each tortilla. Combine the cheeses in a small bowl. Sprinkle evenly over the tortillas. Top each with the apple and raisins.

Fold the tortillas in half. Place on an ungreased baking sheet and bake for 12 minutes or until the cheese is melted and the tortillas are golden brown. Cut the quesadillas in half and serve with the dipping sauce.

CINNAMON-YOGURT DIPPING SAUCE:

1 cup vanilla or lemon yogurt
¼ teaspoon ground cinnamon

Combine the yogurt and cinnamon in a small bowl. Mix well and refrigerate until ready to serve.

Dining by Fireflies, Charlotte, NC

THAI PEANUT DIP FOR CRUDITÉS

MAKES 2 CUPS

1 tablespoon minced shallots
¾ teaspoon Asian sesame oil
¾ cup creamy peanut butter
¼ cup lemon juice
¼ cup soy sauce
½ cup water
1 teaspoon crushed red pepper flakes
2 cloves garlic, crushed
2 tablespoons shredded coconut
2½ tablespoons brown sugar

Sauté the shallots in the sesame oil in a saucepan until transparent. Add the peanut butter, lemon juice, soy sauce, water, red pepper flakes, garlic, and shredded coconut. Cook, stirring constantly, over medium-low heat for 4 minutes. Add the brown sugar. Simmer, covered, 10 minutes, stirring frequently. If sauce thickens, add more water. Serve warm with crudités.

Capital Celebrations, Washington, D.C.

MEXICAN CORN DIP

MAKES 10 SERVINGS

2 (11-ounce) cans Mexican-style
 corn, drained
1 (4-ounce) can chopped green chiles,
 drained
2 jalapeño peppers, seeded and
 chopped
5 green onions, chopped
1 tablespoon sugar
1 cup mayonnaise
1 cup sour cream
2 cups grated sharp Cheddar cheese

Combine all the ingredients in a bowl, mixing well. Refrigerate overnight. Serve with tortilla chips. Keeps in the refrigerator for up to 5 days.

Capital Celebrations, Washington, D.C.

CURRIED CHUTNEY DIP

MAKES 30 TO 40 SERVINGS

3 (8-ounce) packages cream cheese,
  softened
1 (10-ounce) jar Bengal hot chutney,
  chopped
1 (10-ounce) jar mango chutney,
  chopped
1 (5-ounce) can crushed pineapple,
  drained
½ (4-ounce) box crystallized ginger,
  finely chopped (may be softened in
  pineapple juice)
3 tablespoons curry powder
1 tablespoon garlic powder
1 (11-ounce) can cashew nuts,
  chopped
1 (8-ounce) carton sour cream
King-size Fritos or crackers

Beat the cream cheese in a medium bowl until smooth. Add the chutneys, pineapple, ginger, curry powder, and garlic powder; mix well. Just before serving, stir in the cashews and sour cream. Serve with Fritos or crackers.

Second Round: Tea-Time at the Masters, Augusta, GA

CRANBERRY CHUTNEY

MAKES 2 QUARTS

3½ cups sugar
1 cup cider vinegar
1 (10-ounce) package frozen chopped
  onions
1 cup currants or raisins or ½ cup of
  each
1 teaspoon ground allspice
3 tablespoons grated fresh gingerroot
2 (12-ounce) packages cranberries
1 cup walnuts, pecans, or almonds

Combine the sugar, vinegar, onions, currants, allspice, and ginger in a nonaluminum medium saucepan. Cook, uncovered, on medium-high heat until the sugar dissolves. Add the cranberries and cook on medium heat for 10 minutes or until all of them have popped. Stir in the nuts and remove from the heat.

Pour into 1-cup jars and seal with paraffin, or freeze in freezer-safe containers. To serve, spoon over a block of cream cheese and accompany with crackers.

Bound to Please, Boise, ID

TEXAS TRASH

MAKES 8 POUNDS

1 (16-ounce) box Alphabets cereal

1 (16-ounce) box Cheerios cereal

1 (16-ounce) box wheat, rice, or corn
   Chex cereal

1 (16-ounce) box Captain Crunch
   cereal

1 (16-ounce) box pretzel sticks

2 pounds pecan halves

1 (12-ounce) bottle Worcestershire
   sauce

4 tablespoons savory salt

4 tablespoons celery salt

4 tablespoons chili powder

2 teaspoons Tabasco

4 tablespoons (½ stick) margarine

2 cups bacon drippings

2 tablespoons liquid smoke

Preheat the oven to 200F.

Combine the cereals, pretzels, and pecans in a large roasting pan. Combine the remaining ingredients in a large saucepan. Bring to a boil. Pour over the dry mixture, spreading evenly and mixing well. Bake for 1½ hours or until all the liquid is absorbed, stirring every 10 minutes. Let cool; store in 2-pound coffee cans.

Some Like It Hot, McAllen, TX

BEVERAGES

APPALACHIAN AND PIEDMONT

Community cookbooks are to regional food traditions what historic preservationists are to a city's architectural richness. The recipes collected and handed down so carefully tell us not just what the inhabitants of a particular place eat, but how they live and what they value as well.

The foods eaten by residents of the mountains and valleys of eastern Tennessee and Kentucky and the Piedmont of North Carolina reflect a rich Southern tradition. They also show the influence of the crops and wildlife indigenous to this specific area, and even in today's world of assimilation, our cuisine remains unique.

The geography of our region is as magnificent as it is diverse. From craggy mountains to fertile valleys, from thunderous streams to tamed rivers, the land and its waters have nourished its people for centuries. The early settlers of the high and low terrain grew many of the same crops that are raised on today's farms. Corn and sorghum fields still spread across the flatlands, and apple orchards dot the rural mountainsides.

This area is blessed with distinct seasons: hot summers, cool falls, icy winters, and warm springs, each blending gently into the next. Meals also follow this pattern, with cooks taking advantage of harvest time to prepare (as well as freeze and can) just-picked delicacies.

In the summer, we gather for Sunday dinner in grandmother's dining room, where the table presents a plate of peeled and sliced tomatoes sprinkled with cucumber slices. Bowls of stewed corn and bacon-flavored green beans vie for space with casseroles of crooknecked squash rich with cheese and platters of the ubiquitous fried chicken and country ham. Buttery biscuits are served with a pitcher of molasses. For dessert, we devour blackberry cobbler made with the berries picked late Saturday afternoon from our secret patch in the woods.

Autumn calls for a tailgate picnic in the field beside the football stadium. We have cooked for days and packed everything into warmers and coolers that we transport along with an amazing array of collapsible furniture, tablecloths, and dinnerware. Clutching mugs of hot spiced cider to warm our hands, we feast on pumpkin bread spread with cream cheese, vegetable chowder, buns stuffed with smoked brisket, and marinated slaw. Sweet with the first crop of Winesaps, apple cake is a fitting finish to the pregame meal.

To escape the chill of January, friends crowd around a roaring fire in a mountain-top home and enjoy cocktails before a wild game supper. Venison and dove, the fruits of a late-November hunt, have been carefully frozen for this special party and are now roasted as the main course. They are served with scalloped winter vegetables, wild rice pilaf, and corn muffins. Syllabub, a festive wine punch spiked with Kentucky bourbon and topped with meringue and nutmeg, is offered in wineglasses as a finale.

The first shoots of asparagus in the spring are a harbinger for an informal Saturday brunch at a lake cottage. For this noonday repast, the hosts choose rainbow trout, caught from a nearby mountain brook and grilled with herbs, to complement side dishes of asparagus with Hollandaise, parsley-flecked new potatoes, and tomato aspic on baby lettuce. Yeasty rolls, served with last summer's blackberry jelly, and a lemon mousse round out the menu.

While our current tastes have been embellished with cosmopolitan touches and various ethnic flavors, we will always claim our Appalachian and Piedmont heritage for its distinct qualities that enrich our palates and our lives.

—Karin Glendenning, *The Chattanooga Times*
Chattanooga, TN

DINING ON THE PATIO

Dining outside on a moonlit night, amid the glow of candles and fireflies, is truly a summertime delight. Friends and families gather on patios, on porches, or in backyards to relax and dine in the lazy warm weather, while children spend time playing and chasing fireflies. Grilled fare and ice cream are always a hit. And there is always plenty of bug spray on hand if needed!

Submitted by *Dining by Fireflies,* Charlotte, NC

SUN-KISSED CITRUS BOURBON SLUSHES 53

ICY PRAWNS WITH A TRIO OF CELESTIAL DIPPING SAUCES 32

GRILLED MAPLE-GLAZED BABY BACK RIBS 201

HOT CORNBREAD STICKS 285

COLD DILLED NEW POTATOES WITH CARROTS AND SCALLIONS 63

SWEET-AND-SOUR BROCCOLI, CORN, AND RED PEPPERS
IN TOMATO CUPS 93

MOONLIT BLUEBERRY PIE WITH ALMOND CRÈME CHANTILLY 336

CELEBRATE SPRING

Springtime explodes with freshness and color—a true delight for the senses. The air feels new, as the eye beholds vibrant azaleas in bloom. The dogwoods, which blend into the natural foliage three seasons a year, now refuse to go unnoticed. Overhead, birds whistle and call one to another, and the earthy smell of a newly turned garden announces the promise of flowers, fruits, and vegetables. Suddenly it is spring, and no one can stay inside. Families and friends gather outdoors for brunches and supper parties. Weddings and receptions are planned for porches, patios, and gardens. The season is a time of celebration.

Submitted by *Very Virginia,* Hampton Roads, VA

CRAB MOUSSE 19

GRILLED BUTTERFLIED LEG OF LAMB 205

ROASTED NEW POTATOES 161

MARINATED ARTICHOKE SALAD 88

WALNUT CRUST CHEESECAKE 329

RECIPE FOR A BETTER COMMUNITY

JUNIOR LEAGUE OF JOHNSON CITY, TENNESSEE COMMUNITY PROJECT:

Watauga Mental Health Center

The Junior League of Johnson City initiated and funded a family mental health center in 1960, and today it is the largest in the region. The League continues to be involved by sitting on the board.

The cookbooks that made it happen: *Smoky Mountain Magic* and *Treasures of the Smokies* have brought in $400,000.

Did you know? *Smoky Mountain Magic* includes authentic regional recipes that date back to one hundred years.

MINT TEA

MAKES 3½ QUARTS

6 cups hot water
5 regular-size tea bags
6 (3- to 4-inch) mint sprigs
2 cups sugar
¾ cup lemon juice
2½ cups pineapple juice
1 liter ginger ale, chilled

Boil the water, tea bags, and mint in a large saucepan for 5 minutes. Remove the mint and squeeze the tea bags before removing from the water. Add the sugar, lemon juice, and pineapple juice to the tea. Stir well until the sugar is dissolved. Pour into a large pitcher and chill in the refrigerator. Before serving, add the ginger ale and serve over ice.

Celebrations on the Bayou, Monroe, LA

AMBER TEA

MAKES 8 (1-CUP) SERVINGS

2 cups boiling water
5 tea bags
½ cup sugar
½ cup lemon juice
2 cups orange juice
3½ cups apricot nectar
1½ cups ginger ale
Lemon slices

Pour the boiling water over the tea bags in a heatproof pitcher; let stand for 5 minutes. Discard the tea bags. Stir in the sugar, lemon juice, orange juice, and apricot nectar. Chill, covered, in the refrigerator until cold. Stir in the ginger ale just before serving. Serve with the lemon slices.

Dining by Design, Pasadena, CA

ICED TEA PUNCH

MAKES 3½ QUARTS

1 cup sugar
4 cups strong hot tea
4 cups lemonade
4 cups orange juice
1 cup pineapple juice
Fresh mint, for garnish

Dissolve the sugar in the tea. Pour into a large pitcher. Add the lemonade, orange juice, and pineapple juice, mixing well. Serve over ice in tall glasses; garnish each serving with a sprig of mint.

Heart of the Palms, West Palm Beach, FL

YARMOUTH SPICED TEA

MAKES 50 SERVINGS

5 cups sugar
8 quarts water
2 cinnamon sticks
1 (12-ounce) can frozen orange juice
   concentrate
1 (6-ounce) can frozen orange juice
   concentrate
1 (6-ounce) can frozen lemonade
   concentrate
1 cup tea leaves
4 cups boiling water

Boil the sugar, 2 quarts of the water, and cinnamon sticks in a large saucepan for 5 minutes. Add the orange juice and lemonade concentrates. Stir in the remaining 6 quarts of water and chill.

Steep the tea leaves in the 4 cups of boiling water for 5 minutes; strain and allow to cool. Pour into the first mixture just before serving over ice.

RSVP, Portland, ME

PARTY TIME FRUIT PUNCH

MAKES 12 TO 15 SERVINGS

2 fresh limes (or lemons)
2 (6-ounce) cans frozen orange juice
  concentrate
2 (6-ounce) cans frozen lemonade
  concentrate
1 (20-ounce) can crushed pineapple
  with juice
2 (10-ounce) packages frozen
  strawberries or raspberries
2 quarts ginger ale
36 ice cubes

Cut the limes in half, then in slices. Shortly before serving, combine all ingredients in a large (6- to 7-quart) punch bowl. Stir well.

Udderly Delicious, Racine, WI

T. REX PUNCH

MAKES 20 SERVINGS

1 (6-ounce) can frozen lemonade
  concentrate, thawed
1 (6-ounce) can frozen limeade
  concentrate, thawed
6 (6-ounce) cans water
½ (46-ounce) can grapefruit juice
½ (46-ounce) can pineapple juice
½ to 1 cup sugar to taste
Green food coloring
1 (32-ounce) bottle ginger ale

Combine the lemonade and limeade concentrates, water, grapefruit and pineapple juices, sugar, and green food coloring in a large bowl. Pour into round plastic containers and freeze. To serve, partially thaw punch, break into chunks and place in a punch bowl. Add ginger ale just before serving.

Children's Party Book, Hampton Roads, VA

CALIFORNIA SUNSET

MAKES 4 SERVINGS

3 cups cranberry juice
¼ cup lemon-lime soda
¾ cup orange juice

Mix all ingredients well. Serve chilled.

California Sizzles, Pasadena, CA

CITRUS FRAPPÉ

MAKES 2 SERVINGS

½ cup orange juice
¼ cup lemon juice
½ teaspoon grated lemon rind
1 cup lemon sherbet
10 crushed ice cubes
2 tablespoons dry sherry (optional)

Combine the first 3 ingredients in a blender. Process for 5 seconds. Add sherbet and ice cubes; process for 1 minute or until frothy. Process again while adding sherry. Serve in parfait or wine glasses immediately.

Junior League of Philadelphia's Bicentennial Cookbook, Philadelphia, PA

PI PHI MOCHA PUNCH

MAKES 2 QUARTS SYRUP

1 cup unsweetened cocoa powder
1½ cups cold water
2½ cups boiling water
2¾ cups sugar
Pinch of salt
1 teaspoon vanilla extract
Coffee, double strength
Milk
Vanilla ice cream

Mix the cocoa and cold water into a paste in a large saucepan. Add the boiling water, sugar, and salt to the paste mixture. Simmer slowly for 1 hour, stirring often. Cool the syrup mixture and add vanilla. Refrigerate. Make double-strength coffee and set aside.

To make 3 or 4 servings of punch, mix 8 ounces of cold coffee, 8 ounces of cold milk, and 2 tablespoons of the chocolate syrup mixture. Serve over 1 pint of ice cream in a punch bowl. The syrup will keep in the refrigerator for up to 2 months.

Superlatives, Oklahoma City, OK

SALLY'S WINE COOLER

MAKES 60 SERVINGS

4 (10-ounce) boxes frozen sliced
    strawberries, thawed
4 (6-ounce) cans frozen lemonade
    concentrate, thawed
1 gallon rosé wine
2 quarts club soda

Combine all the ingredients in a large container; mix thoroughly. Serve chilled.

Rare Collections, Galveston County, TX

BUBBLY PEACH PUNCH

MAKES 20 SERVINGS

2 (10-ounce) cans frozen peach
    daiquiri mix
1 (12-ounce) can frozen orange juice
    concentrate
1 (12-ounce) can frozen limeade
    concentrate
4 cups water
2 liters ginger ale
1 bottle Champagne or seltzer
Fresh peach slices

Mix the frozen fruit concentrates with the water. Pour over ice. Add the ginger ale and champagne. Garnish the glasses with fresh peach slices.

Of Tide & Thyme, Annapolis, MD

CRANBERRY CRUSH

MAKES 2 SERVINGS

½ cup whiskey or rum
½ cup whiskey sour mix
½ cup cranberry juice

Combine all the ingredients and pour into a freezer container; freeze. Remove from the freezer and stir until slushy before serving in parfait or wine glasses.

Junior League of Philadelphia's Bicentennial Cookbook, Philadelphia, PA

SUSTAINER'S SLUSH

MAKES 12 TO 16 SERVINGS

1 (12-ounce) can frozen lemonade
  concentrate
4½ cups water
3 cups bourbon
3 tablespoons frozen orange juice
  concentrate

Combine the lemonade concentrate, water, bourbon, and orange juice concentrate in a freezer container and mix well. Freeze until firm. Spoon into goblets.

Sunny Side Up, Greater Fort Lauderdale, FL

SUN-KISSED CITRUS BOURBON SLUSHES

MAKES 16 TO 18 SERVINGS

2 tea bags
7½ cups water
12 ounces frozen orange juice
  concentrate
12 ounces frozen lemonade concentrate
6 ounces frozen limeade concentrate
2 cups bourbon

Steep the tea bags for 5 minutes in 1 cup of the water that has been brought to a boil. Discard the tea bags. Combine the tea and the remaining ingredients in a large bowl; mix well. Pour into a freezer container and freeze until slushy, about 2 to 4 hours. Remove from the freezer and pour into a glass pitcher for "pour your own" drinks.

Dining by Fireflies, Charlotte, NC

BRANDY SLUSH

2 cups sugar
7 cups water
4 tea bags
2 cups boiling water
1 (12-ounce) can frozen lemonade
  concentrate, thawed
1 (12-ounce) can frozen orange juice
  concentrate, thawed
2 cups brandy
Lemon-lime soda

Add the sugar to the 7 cups of water in a saucepan. Bring to a boil and set aside. Steep the tea bags in the 2 cups of boiling water for 5 minutes. Discard the tea bags and combine the tea with the lemonade, orange juice, and brandy. Place in a freezer container and freeze. When ready to serve, spoon the slushy frozen mixture into a glass so it is three-fourths full. Add enough lemon-lime soda to fill the glass.

Udderly Delicious, Racine, WI

COSMOPOLITAN COCKTAIL

MAKES 2 SERVINGS

3 scoops ice cubes
¼ cup vodka
3 teaspoons cranberry juice
Juice of ½ lime
2 thin strips lime peel

Place the ice, vodka, cranberry juice, and lime juice in a cocktail shaker. Shake to mix well. Serve in martini glasses, garnished with the lime peel.

Dining by Design, Pasadena, CA

VODKA SLUSH

MAKES 12 SERVINGS

1 (6-ounce) can frozen orange juice
  concentrate
2 (6-ounce) cans frozen lemonade
  concentrate
2 (6-ounce) cans frozen limeade
  concentrate
3½ cups water
2 cups vodka
1 cup sugar
Sprite

Thaw the frozen juices and mix together in a large bowl. Add the water, vodka, and sugar. Place in the freezer for 48 hours, stirring occasionally. To serve, put ⅔ cup of the slush in an 8-ounce glass and fill with Sprite.

Some Like It South!, Pensacola, FL

BLOODY MARYS BY THE GALLON

MAKES 16 SERVINGS

5 tablespoons celery salt
3 tablespoons freshly ground pepper
2 tablespoons prepared horseradish
¼ cup Worcestershire sauce
½ cup lime juice
3 quarts tomato juice
1 fifth vodka
Celery ribs

Mix the celery salt and pepper in a small bowl. Mix the horseradish, Worcestershire sauce, and lime juice in a small bowl. In a gallon container, combine both mixtures with the tomato juice and vodka, stirring well. Serve over ice and garnish with celery.

NOTE: May be prepared ahead, omitting vodka, and refrigerated.

Texas Sampler, Richardson, TX

SANGRITA

MAKES 10 CUPS

1 (46-ounce) can tomato juice
2 cups orange juice
6 tablespoons lime juice
6 tablespoons Worcestershire sauce
Tabasco
2 teaspoons onion juice
Salt and freshly ground pepper
1 cup tequila

Combine all the ingredients in a large bowl; mix well. Pour over a block of ice in a punch bowl. Serve with brunch or before lunch.

Fiesta, Corpus Christi, TX

NEW WAVE MARGARITAS

MAKES 4 SERVINGS

1 (6-ounce) can frozen limeade
   concentrate
6 ounces tequila
2 ounces Triple Sec
Crushed ice
1 lime, cut in half
Salt

Pour the limeade, tequila, and Triple Sec into a blender. Fill with ice and blend until smooth. Serve in stemmed glasses that have been prepared by rubbing the cut lime around the top rims and dipping the rims into a saucer of salt to coat.

Delicioso, Corpus Christi, TX

HOT BUTTERED RUM

MAKES 64 SERVINGS

2 sticks (½ pound) butter, softened
½ pound packed light brown sugar
½ pound powdered sugar
1 teaspoon ground cinnamon
1 teaspoon grated nutmeg
1 pint vanilla ice cream, softened
Light rum
Boiling water

Cream the butter with the brown sugar, powdered sugar, cinnamon, and nutmeg in a large bowl. Blend in the ice cream. Store, covered, in the freezer. When ready to use, put 1 tablespoon of the mixture and 1½ ounces of light rum into a mug and fill with boiling water. Serve warm.

Out of Our League, Too, Greensboro, NC

BUFFALO FREEZE

MAKES 18 SERVINGS

9 cups water
2 cups dark rum
1 (12-ounce) can frozen lemonade
   concentrate
1 (12-ounce) can frozen orange juice
   concentrate
3 tablespoons grenadine
1 tablespoon maraschino cherry juice

Combine the water, rum, lemonade and orange juice concentrate, grenadine, and cherry juice in a freezer container and mix well. Freeze to the desired consistency.

Great Lake Effects, Buffalo, NY

SALADS AND SALAD DRESSINGS

SOUTHEAST

It's not unusual for Atlanta tourists to find themselves in a dinnertime daze. Since the Olympic games brought worldwide attention to the heart of the Sun Belt, new restaurants of every style, price range, and ethnicity have been popping up at a breakneck pace. And the trend shows no signs of abating.

But where can one experience the true flavor of the city—or the region it represents? Longtime natives may suggest a favorite barbecue joint, or perhaps some near-forgotten meat-and-three-sides that still turns out an honest platter of fried chicken, cornbread, and marshmallow-covered sweet potatoes. Better yet would be an invitation to a traditional home-cooked meal. There in the kitchen, you'll likely spot a spiral-bound cookbook, spattered and dogeared, filled with culinary clues that distinguish the community it represents from all others.

The cuisine of the Southeast is as varied as its geography—from the north Georgia mountains, to the marshlands of South Carolina Low Country, to the shores of the Florida Keys. Situated in the foothills between the Appalachians and the coastal plains, Atlanta has a cooking style that has always been a blending of its surrounding influences.

Atlantans have a special fondness for dishes that feature not only prominent Georgia crops, such as peaches, peanuts, pecans, and the highly prized sweet Vidalia onion, but also its drink of choice, Coca-Cola. Invented by an Atlanta pharmacist in 1886, it remains deeply ingrained in the city's identity and is used as an ingredient in some of the city's most enduring dishes, including cakes, gelatin molds, and baked ham. *The Cotton Blossom,* the Junior League of Atlanta's 1947 cookbook, features a suggestion for a cream cheese dip to serve "for your next morning Coca-Cola party."

Heading eastward, through moss-draped Savannah and into South Carolina's verdant Low Country, the cuisine changes as dramatically as the topography. From its waters comes an abundance of wonderful seafood: shrimp, crabs, oysters, sturgeon, and shad. The locals celebrate it enthusiastically, with shrimp-and-grits breakfasts, fish fries, oyster roasts, and perhaps the most popular, Frogmore stew—a seafood boil made of shrimp, crabs, corn, and sausages. And even though most of the rice crops that built Charleston's aristocracy have long since dried up, rice remains a dietary staple, in side dishes such as pilau and hoppin' John, as well as breads, stuffing, savory pies, and sweet rice pudding.

No Low Country cocktail party would be complete without benne crackers, a dainty sesame-seed wafer served with drinks. Benne (sesame) seeds were brought by West African slaves, along with peanuts, okra, and other plants, from their homeland. Their dialect, Gullah, is still spoken in some parts of the coast. When the Junior League of Charleston released its first edition of *Charleston Receipts* in 1950, they peppered it with Gullah phrases in an attempt to preserve the dialect.

Farther down the coastline into Florida, a similar form of fusion cooking had begun hundreds of years earlier. After Ponce de Leon landed in St. Augustine in 1513, Spaniards brought cattle, hogs, peaches, and citrus. Inland African Americans and Anglos from Southern colonies created a style of farm cooking with Spanish touches known as Cracker cooking. Tories from the Bahamas contributed hot bird peppers, conch salad, and Key lime pie. By the late 1800s, railroad wives in South Dade County were experimenting with local seafood and exotic fruits such as carambola and mangoes.

Then in 1959 came the largest migration, when refugees poured into Miami from Cuba. Soon Cuban sandwiches and black beans were as standard as hamburgers and French fries.

A far cry from Southern food? Flip through the Junior League of Atlanta's *True Grits: Tall Tales and Recipes from the New South*. Like its humbler predecessors, this slick collection published in 1995 contains the perfunctory fried chicken and cheese grits. But the very first recipe is for black bean cakes flavored with mojo criollo, a Spanish marinating sauce.

—Susan Puckett, *Atlanta Constitution*
Atlanta, GA

DINNER BY THE BAY

Living by the bay is delightful. Bountiful seafood from nearby waters and fresh fruits and vegetables grown in the vicinity present the fare for a bayside menu to enjoy with friends.

Submitted by *Tampa Treasures,* Tampa, FL

YBOR CITY DEVILED CRAB 233

GAZPACHO 115

YBOR CITY VEGETABLE PAELLA 152

RED SNAPPER EN PAPILLOTE 224

FLAN DE LECHE NUEVO 355

BRUNCH ON THE FAIRWAYS

Imagine yourself among prestigious pines, brilliant azaleas, and resplendent dogwoods. As you spread your checkered tablecloth on the velvety grass, the bobwhites and the rushing creek beckon, leaving an indelible mark on your memory. Watch a round of golf and enjoy a fairways brunch.

Submitted by *Second Round: Tea-Time at the Masters,* Augusta, GA

CURRIED CHUTNEY DIP 39

BUTTERNUT ROLLS 292

SENSATIONAL SALAD 73

DIRTY SHRIMP 240

ROBIN K'S CHOCOLATE MOUSSE WITH RASPBERRY SAUCE 363

RECIPE FOR A BETTER COMMUNITY

JUNIOR LEAGUE OF CHARLESTON, SOUTH CAROLINA COMMUNITY PROJECT:

The Charleston Speech and Hearing Center

In 1947, Charleston League members concentrated their efforts on establishing the first school in South Carolina for children with speech defects. In 1955, the school was incorporated and a community board was formed. In 1991, the Junior League of Charleston received the Distinguished Service Award of the American Speech-Language-Hearing Association for founding the center and for its continuous support since 1947. The award drew congratulations from First Lady Barbara Bush and visits from South Carolina's Governor and U.S. Senators to the school.

The cookbook that made it happen: *Charleston Receipts* has provided funds in excess of $700,000.

Did you know? To promote *Charleston Receipts,* Mrs. Huguenin, one of the cookbook editors, invited the food editor of the *New York Herald Tribune* to Charleston. While in Charleston, the food editor was so impressed by the League's cookbook and the city's hospitality that she ranked Charleston along with San Francisco, New Orleans, Chicago, and New York.

COLD DILLED NEW POTATOES WITH CARROTS AND SCALLIONS

MAKES 8 SERVINGS

14 small new potatoes, scrubbed clean
6 hard-cooked eggs, peeled and
    quartered
1 medium carrot, peeled and grated
2 medium scallions, thinly sliced
3 tablespoons chopped fresh dill, or 1
    tablespoon dried
2 tablespoons chopped fresh parsley
1 tablespoon caraway seeds
½ teaspoon salt
½ teaspoon freshly ground black
    pepper
¾ cup sour cream
¾ cup mayonnaise

Bring water to a boil in a medium saucepan. Add the potatoes and cook until just tender, 20 to 25 minutes. Drain, cool, and cut in half. Combine the potatoes, eggs, carrot, and scallions in a large bowl. Add the dill, parsley, caraway seeds, salt, and pepper and gently toss to combine. Fold in the sour cream and mayonnaise. Refrigerate the salad, tightly covered, for several hours before serving. (Can be prepared 1 day ahead.)

Dining by Fireflies, Charlotte, NC

SOUR CREAM POTATO SALAD

⅓ cup chopped chives
1 teaspoon salt
*¼ teaspoon freshly ground black
    pepper*
*1 tablespoon chopped onion, or to
    taste*
¼ cup salad oil
¼ cup cider vinegar
*7 cups warm boiled, peeled, and sliced
    potatoes (2 to 2½ pounds)*
½ cup chopped celery
*½ cup peeled, seeded, and diced
    cucumber*
¾ cup sour cream
¾ cup mayonnaise

Combine the chives, salt, pepper, onion, oil, and vinegar in a medium bowl, and gently mix with the warm potatoes. Chill.

Combine the celery, cucumber, sour cream, and mayonnaise in a small bowl; chill. Fold the potato mixture and the sour cream mixture together before serving.

Magic, Birmingham, AL

AUNT SADIE'S POTATO SALAD

1 head red or green cabbage, shredded
*10 potatoes, boiled in jackets, peeled,
    and sliced*
*Salt and freshly ground pepper to
    taste*
Celery seed to taste
3 onions, sliced in rings
2 green bell peppers, sliced in rings
3 hard-cooked eggs, peeled and sliced
1 quart mayonnaise or salad dressing
Paprika (for garnish)

Place one layer of cabbage in a large bowl. Add a layer of sliced potatoes. Add salt and pepper; then sprinkle with celery seed. Add a layer of onion rings and a layer of pepper rings. Add a layer of sliced eggs and then spread mayonnaise over all. Continue layering until all ingredients are used. End with mayonnaise and eggs. Garnish with paprika. Refrigerate at least 24 hours before serving.

Cotton Country Collection, 25th Anniversary Edition, Rockford, IL

PEANUT POTATO SALAD

MAKES 6 TO 8 SERVINGS

3 pounds red potatoes
12 slices bacon, crisp-fried, crumbled
1 cup salted Spanish peanuts
1 medium red bell pepper, chopped
2 ribs celery, chopped
4 green onions, chopped
¼ cup chopped cilantro
¼ cup chopped parsley
Peanut Butter Dressing (see below)
Salt and pepper to taste

Boil the potatoes in water to cover in a saucepan until tender. Drain and let cool. Cut into 1-inch cubes. Combine the potatoes, bacon, peanuts, bell pepper, celery, green onions, cilantro, and parsley in a large bowl and mix well. Pour the dressing over the salad. Season with salt and pepper.

PEANUT BUTTER DRESSING:

¾ cup mayonnaise
½ cup chunky peanut butter
3 tablespoons cider vinegar

Whisk the mayonnaise, peanut butter, and vinegar together in a small bowl.

Beyond Burlap: Idaho's Famous Potato Recipes, Boise, ID

SOUTHWESTERN PASTA SALAD

MAKES 4 TO 6 SERVINGS

8 ounces elbow macaroni

1 (6-ounce) package deli thin-sliced
  ham, chopped

½ cup diced yellow bell pepper

½ cup diced red bell pepper

1 cup peeled, seeded, and chopped
  tomato

¼ cup diced red onion

1 tablespoon plus 1½ teaspoons
  minced cilantro

1 clove garlic, minced

1 small jalapeño pepper, seeded and
  minced

1 tablespoon olive oil

1 tablespoon red wine vinegar

¼ cup crumbled feta cheese

2 tablespoons pine nuts, toasted

Cook the macaroni according to package directions. Drain and set aside. Combine the ham and next 9 ingredients in a large bowl. Stir in the macaroni. Cover and chill at least 2 hours. Top with the cheese and pine nuts just before serving.

Texas Sampler, Richardson, TX

COUSCOUS SALAD

MAKES 6 TO 8 SERVINGS

1 package couscous

¼ cup mayonnaise

¼ cup rice wine vinegar

1 tablespoon curry powder

1 teaspoon dry mustard

1 teaspoon garlic powder

Salt and pepper to taste

1 (15-ounce) can marinated artichoke
  hearts, drained and chopped

1 red bell pepper, chopped

½ cup chopped pimiento-stuffed olives

4 hearts of palm, sliced

6 green onions, sliced

2 tablespoons capers

Cook the couscous following the package directions. Whisk together the mayonnaise, vinegar, curry, mustard, garlic powder, salt, and pepper in a medium bowl. Combine with the couscous. Fold in the artichokes, bell pepper, olives, palm, green onions, and capers. Chill, covered, up to 12 hours.

NOTE: To serve as a main course, add 1 pound cooked, peeled, deveined shrimp.

Southern on Occasion, Cobb-Marietta, GA

MARINATED SLAW

MAKES 12 TO 15 SERVINGS

1 large head cabbage, chopped or
   shredded
1 small green bell pepper, finely
   chopped
1 small onion, finely chopped
1 cup vegetable oil
1 cup vinegar
¾ cup sugar
1 tablespoon dillweed
1 tablespoon celery seed
½ teaspoon salt

Combine the cabbage, green pepper, and onion in a large bowl.
Combine the oil, vinegar, sugar, dillweed, celery seed, and salt in a
saucepan and mix well. Bring to a boil, then pour evenly over the
slaw. Let stand without stirring for 1½ to 2 hours. Stir to mix.
Chill, covered, for several hours.

NOTE: This slaw keeps well in the refrigerator.

Beyond Cotton Country, Decatur, AL

ORIENTAL COLESLAW

MAKES 4 TO 6 SERVINGS

2 packages beef-flavor ramen noodles,
   uncooked
1 (16-ounce) bag coleslaw mix
1 cup sunflower seeds
1 small bunch green onions, chopped
   (use only white and pale green
   parts)
Oriental Dressing (see below)
⅓ cup sliced almonds, toasted

Crush the dry noodles and combine with the coleslaw mix, sunflower seeds, and onions in a large bowl. Toss with the dressing.
Sprinkle with the toasted almonds. Refrigerate overnight to blend
flavors.

ORIENTAL DRESSING:

1 cup olive oil
⅓ cup red wine vinegar
½ cup sugar
2 packets beef seasonings from ramen
   noodles

Combine all the ingredients in a jar and shake well.

Gracious Gator Cooks, Gainesville, FL

ORANGE-SPINACH SALAD WITH HONEY-MUSTARD DRESSING

MAKES 6 SERVINGS

¾ cup safflower oil
¼ cup red wine vinegar
¼ cup honey
¼ cup Dijon mustard
¼ cup sesame seeds, toasted
2 cloves garlic, minced
½ teaspoon salt
½ teaspoon freshly ground pepper
10 ounces fresh spinach, washed, spun
   dry, and stemmed
2 large oranges, peeled and sectioned
1 small red onion, thinly sliced
8 ounces bacon, cooked until crisp,
   crumbled

Combine the safflower oil with the vinegar, honey, mustard, sesame seeds, garlic, salt, and pepper in a small bowl; mix well. Chill. Tear the spinach into bite-size pieces and place in a large salad bowl. Add the orange sections and onion slices. To serve, toss the salad with enough of the dressing to coat. Sprinkle with the bacon.

Nuggets, Colorado Springs, CO

STRAWBERRY AND SPINACH SALAD

MAKES 8 SERVINGS

1 pound fresh spinach, washed, spun
   dry, stemmed, and broken into
   pieces
1 pint strawberries, washed, hulled,
   and sliced
Sweet French Dressing (see below)

Prepare the spinach and strawberries and return to the refrigerator to chill. Make the dressing and chill. Just prior to serving, toss the spinach and strawberries with enough dressing just to coat the spinach leaves

SWEET FRENCH DRESSING:

⅓ cup sugar
½ cup vegetable oil
¼ cup white vinegar
¼ teaspoon salt
¼ cup ketchup
½ tablespoon Worcestershire sauce

Combine all the ingredients and stir or whisk until the sugar is dissolved.

Of Tide & Thyme, Annapolis, MD

BASKETS OF SPINACH-STRAWBERRY SALAD

MAKES 8 SERVINGS

1 quart fresh strawberries, hulled

1 large bag fresh spinach, washed and
    spun dry, stems removed

½ cup sugar

1½ teaspoons minced onion

¼ teaspoon Worcestershire sauce

¼ teaspoon paprika

¼ cup cider vinegar

½ cup vegetable oil

2 tablespoons sesame seed

1 tablespoon poppy seed

Peanut oil for frying

8 egg roll wrappers

Chill the strawberries and the spinach. Combine the sugar, onion, Worcestershire sauce, paprika, and vinegar in a blender. With the blender running, slowly add the vegetable oil. Stir in the sesame seed and the poppy seed. Chill the dressing.

Heat a 3-inch depth of peanut oil to 375F in a deep fryer. Plunge one egg roll wrapper into the hot oil and immediately press down on its center with a soup ladle. Keep the ladle in place until the "basket" is browned. Remove and drain upside down on paper towels. Repeat the process with the remaining wrappers. To serve, toss the spinach and the strawberries with the dressing. Divide the salad among the "baskets."

Brunch Basket, Rockford, IL

SIDBURY HOUSE SALAD

MAKES 12 SERVINGS

1 (10-ounce) package fresh spinach

1 head iceberg lettuce

8 ounces fresh mushrooms, sliced

½ pound bacon, fried until crisp,
    crumbled

Cottage Cheese Dressing (see below)

Wash and dry the spinach and lettuce and tear into bite-size pieces, discarding the spinach stems. Refrigerate. Just before serving, toss the greens with the mushrooms, bacon, and dressing.

COTTAGE CHEESE DRESSING:

¼ cup sugar

1 teaspoon salt

1 teaspoon dry mustard

2 tablespoons minced onion or
    scallions

⅓ cup cider vinegar

1 cup vegetable oil

½ pint large-curd cottage cheese

Combine all the ingredients in a glass jar. Shake to blend.

Delicioso, Corpus Christi, TX

CAESAR SALAD I

1 clove garlic
1 large egg or 1 tablespoon egg
   substitute
¼ teaspoon dry mustard
¼ teaspoon coarse ground pepper
½ teaspoon salt
½ cup Parmesan cheese, grated
6 tablespoons olive oil
4 tablespoons lemon juice
2-3 heads romaine lettuce
Croutons

Grate the garlic clove into a wooden salad bowl. Beat in the egg. Add the mustard, pepper, salt, Parmesan, olive oil, and lemon juice and mix with a wire whisk. Clean and dry the romaine leaves; tear into bite-size pieces if you wish. Toss with just enough dressing to lightly coat the greens. Add croutons and serve.

Rare Collections, Galveston County, TX

CAESAR SALAD II

MAKES 8 SERVINGS

1 clove garlic, halved
½ cup olive oil
1 teaspoon salt
½ teaspoon dry mustard
Freshly ground pepper
1½ teaspoons Worcestershire sauce
2 heads romaine, washed, spun dry,
   and chilled
Coddled egg
1 lemon
Garlic croutons
½ cup grated Parmesan cheese
2 ounces anchovy fillets, drained
   (optional)

Just before serving, rub a large salad bowl with a clove of garlic. Add the oil, salt, mustard, pepper, and Worcestershire sauce; mix thoroughly. Tear the romaine into bite-size pieces; add to the oil mixture, tossing until the leaves glisten. Break the egg onto the romaine. Squeeze on juice from the lemon; toss until the leaves are well coated. Sprinkle the croutons, cheese, and anchovies, if desired, over the salad and toss.

Udderly Delicious, Racine, WI

FIELD GREENS WITH CRUMBLED BLUE CHEESE AND SPICY PECANS

MAKES 8 SERVINGS

VINAIGRETTE:

⅔ cup sugar

1 teaspoon dry mustard

1 teaspoon salt

⅔ cup distilled white vinegar

3 tablespoons apple cider vinegar

4½ teaspoons onion juice

2 tablespoons Worcestershire sauce

1 cup vegetable oil

SALAD:

8-10 cups mixed field greens

2 green onions, chopped

4 ounces blue cheese, crumbled (1 cup)

1 Granny Smith apple, cored, seeded,
    and chopped

¼ cup coarsely chopped Spicy Pecans
    (see below)

Make the vinaigrette: Combine the sugar, dry mustard, salt, and vinegars in a small bowl. Stir until the sugar is dissolved. Whisk in the onion juice and Worcestershire sauce. Add the oil slowly, whisking continuously until blended.

To make the salad, combine the greens, green onions, blue cheese, apple, and pecans in a salad bowl. Add just enough vinaigrette to coat the greens. Toss until well combined.

SPICY PECANS:

2 large egg whites

1½ teaspoons salt

¼ cup sugar

2 teaspoons Worcestershire sauce

2 tablespoons Hungarian paprika

1½ teaspoons ground red (cayenne)
    pepper

4½ cups pecan halves

6 tablespoons unsalted butter, melted
    and cooled

Preheat the oven to 325F.

Beat the egg whites with the salt until foamy. Add the sugar, Worcestershire sauce, paprika, and cayenne. Fold in the pecans and melted butter. Spread the pecans evenly on a baking sheet. Bake 30 to 40 minutes, stirring every 10 minutes. Remove from the oven and cool. Store the pecans in an airtight container.

Stop and Smell the Rosemary, Houston, TX

CRUNCHY ROMAINE SALAD

MAKES 10 TO 12 SERVINGS

SWEET-AND-SOUR DRESSING:
1 cup sugar
¾ cup canola oil
½ cup red wine vinegar
1 tablespoon soy sauce, or to taste
Salt and pepper to taste

SALAD:
1 (3-ounce) package ramen noodles
1 cup chopped pecans
¼ cup (½ stick) unsalted butter
1 bunch broccoli, coarsely chopped
1 head romaine, washed, spun dry,
  and torn into bite-size pieces
4 green onions, chopped

For the dressing, combine the sugar, oil, vinegar, soy sauce, salt and pepper in a jar with a tight-fitting lid. Shake until blended.

For the salad, break the ramen noodles into small pieces, discarding the flavor packet. Brown the noodles and pecans in the butter in a skillet. Drain on paper towels. Let stand until cool. Combine the noodles, pecans, broccoli, romaine, and green onions in a salad bowl and mix gently. Add 1 cup or more of the dressing, tossing to coat.

Down by the Water, Columbia, SC

MIXED GREENS AND PEAR SALAD WITH WALNUT VINAIGRETTE

MAKES 4 SERVINGS

1 medium shallot
½ cup extra virgin olive oil
3 tablespoons walnut oil
2 tablespoons red wine vinegar
1 tablespoon Dijon mustard
½ teaspoon sugar
¼ teaspoon salt
Freshly ground pepper
½ cup walnut pieces
1 large firm Bartlett pear, unpeeled,
  halved lengthwise, and cored
10 cups torn mixed greens

Mince the shallot in a food processor or blender. Add the olive oil, 2 tablespoons of the walnut oil, the vinegar, mustard, sugar, salt, and pepper; process until well blended. Set the dressing aside.

Heat the remaining tablespoon of walnut oil in a small skillet over medium heat. Add the walnuts. Cook about 4 minutes or until light brown and fragrant, stirring frequently. Transfer to a bowl; cool.

Cut each pear half into ¼-inch slices. Place in a small bowl; pour dressing on top. Place the mixed greens in a salad bowl. Using a slotted spoon, remove pear slices. Add dressing to the greens and toss gently. Divide greens among 4 plates. Arrange 3 to 4 pear slices on each, overlapping slightly. Sprinkle with walnuts.

A Cleveland Collection, Cleveland, OH

SENSATIONAL SALAD

MAKES 10 TO 12 SERVINGS

*2 large heads romaine, washed, spun
    dry, and torn into bite-size pieces*
1 bunch parsley, chopped
1 cup grated Romano cheese
*1 (4-ounce) package blue cheese,
    crumbled*
Freshly ground pepper to taste

Combine the lettuce and parsley in a large bowl. Just before serving, pour enough vinaigrette to moisten the greens over the lettuce mixture. Toss well. Sprinkle with the Romano and blue cheeses; toss again. Season with the pepper.

GARLIC VINAIGRETTE:

½ cup vegetable oil
½ cup olive oil
2½ tablespoons fresh lemon juice
1½ tablespoons vinegar
2 cloves garlic, minced
1 teaspoon salt
Freshly ground black pepper to taste

Combine all the ingredients in a small bowl; blend well.

Second Round: Tea-Time at the Masters, Augusta, GA

CHEF SALAD–STUFFED PITA

MAKES 20 SERVINGS

½ –¾ head of lettuce, shredded
¼ pound ham, cut into thin strips
¼ pound chicken or turkey, cut into
    thin strips
¼ pound Monterey Jack cheese, cut
    into thin strips
1 (4½-ounce) can black olives, sliced
2 tomatoes, chopped
2 stalks celery, chopped
2 green onions, thinly sliced
½ green bell pepper, chopped
8 slices bacon, fried crisp and crumbled
2 avocados, peeled, pitted, and
    chopped
1 cup mayonnaise
Salt and freshly ground black pepper
Lemon-pepper seasoning
10 whole-wheat pita pockets, cut in half
Alfalfa sprouts (optional)

Combine the lettuce and the next 10 ingredients in a large salad bowl. Toss with the mayonnaise. Season with salt, black pepper, and lemon pepper; toss lightly. Serve in the pita pockets and garnish with sprouts, if desired.

Celebrations on the Bayou, Monroe, LA

MEXICAN CHEF SALAD

MAKES 6 TO 8 SERVINGS

4 tomatoes, chopped
1 large head lettuce, chopped
1 bunch green onions, chopped
6 ounces grated Cheddar cheese
2 avocados, chopped
Italian salad dressing
1 (6-ounce) bag tortilla chips
1 pound lean ground beef
1 (15-ounce) can ranch-style beans
Salt and freshly ground pepper to taste
Tomato and avocado wedges (optional)

Combine the chopped tomatoes, lettuce, green onions, cheese, and avocado in a large bowl; moisten with Italian dressing. Crush the chips and mix into the salad.

Brown the ground beef in a medium skillet, stirring to break up chunks. Stir in the undrained beans. Simmer for 10 minutes. Add salt and pepper to taste. Cool to room temperature. To serve, combine the meat mixture and the salad mixture. Garnish with tomato and avocado wedges, if desired.

Fiesta, Corpus Christi, TX

COLD STEAK SALAD I

MAKES 6 SERVINGS

2 pounds lean boneless sirloin, cut
    into ½-inch-thick strips
8 tablespoons (1 stick) butter, divided
12 ounces mushrooms, sliced
1 (10-ounce) package frozen artichoke
    hearts, cooked, drained, cooled
1 cup chopped celery
2 cups small cherry tomatoes
2 tablespoons chopped fresh chives
2 tablespoons chopped fresh parsley
2 cups Dijon Dressing (see below)
Lettuce leaves

Sauté the beef in batches in 4 tablespoons of the butter in a large skillet over high heat until medium-rare. Do not overcrowd the pan. As the meat is cooked, transfer to a colander to drain. Let stand until cool. Sauté the mushrooms in the remaining butter in the same skillet; drain. Let stand until cool.

Combine the beef, mushrooms, artichokes, celery, cherry tomatoes, chives, and parsley in a bowl and mix gently. Add the Dijon dressing, tossing to coat. Marinate, covered, in the refrigerator for 8 to 10 hours, stirring occasionally. Spoon onto lettuce-lined salad plates.

DIJON DRESSING:

2¼ cups vegetable oil
¾ cup wine vinegar
⅓ cup chopped fresh parsley
6 shallots, finely chopped
2 teaspoons Dijon mustard
1½ teaspoons dried dillweed, or ⅓ cup
    chopped fresh dillweed
⅛ teaspoon Tabasco
Salt and freshly ground pepper to
    taste

Combine the oil, vinegar, parsley, shallots, mustard, dillweed, Tabasco, salt, and pepper in a jar with a tight-fitting lid. Cover the jar and shake to mix. Store in the refrigerator.

Sunny Side Up, Greater Fort Lauderdale, FL

COLD STEAK SALAD II

MAKES 8 SERVINGS

DRESSING:

¼ cup olive oil

⅓ cup white wine vinegar

2 tablespoons Dijon mustard

2 cloves garlic, minced

1 teaspoon soy sauce

½ teaspoon Worcestershire sauce

1 teaspoon onion salt

Freshly ground black pepper

SALAD:

2 pounds grilled or broiled steak,
    chilled

2 (8-ounce) cans artichoke hearts,
    drained and quartered

1 cup roasted red peppers, sliced

1 pound mushrooms, sliced

¾ cup diced celery

2 tablespoons chopped fresh chives

3 tablespoons chopped fresh parsley

Combine all dressing ingredients in a container with a tight-fitting lid and shake well. Thinly slice the steak and cut into bite-size pieces. Combine the steak with the remaining salad ingredients. Toss the salad with the dressing, cover, and chill for 6 or more hours. Stir and serve.

A Matter of Taste, Morristown, NJ

GAZPACHO SALAD

MAKES 6 TO 8 SERVINGS

2 envelopes unflavored gelatin
1 (10-ounce) can tomato juice, divided
⅓ cup red wine vinegar
1 teaspoon salt
Dash of hot pepper sauce
2 small tomatoes, peeled and diced
1 medium cucumber, pared and diced
1 medium bell pepper, seeded and diced
½ cup chopped onion
1 tablespoon chopped chives
Avocado Dressing (see below)

In a medium saucepan, sprinkle the gelatin over ¾ cup of the tomato juice and let stand for 5 minutes to soften. Place over low heat and stir constantly until the gelatin is dissolved. Remove from the heat. Stir in the remaining tomato juice, the vinegar, salt, and hot pepper sauce. Set the saucepan in a bowl of ice, stirring occasionally, for about 15 minutes, until the mixture is the consistency of unbeaten egg whites.

Fold in the tomato, cucumber, bell pepper, onion, and chives. Pour the mixture into a 1½-quart mold that has been rinsed in cold water. Refrigerate until firm, at least 6 hours. Unmold onto a chilled platter and serve with avocado dressing.

AVOCADO DRESSING:

1 large ripe avocado, peeled, pitted,
    and cut into chunks
½ cup sour cream
½ cup light cream
1 tablespoon grated onion
Dash of ground red pepper (cayenne)
1½ teaspoons salt
⅛ teaspoon sugar
1 clove garlic, crushed
1 tablespoon lemon juice

Combine all the ingredients in a blender and blend until smooth. Place plastic wrap directly on the surface of the dressing. Refrigerate, covered, for several hours to blend the flavors.

Seasoned with Sun, El Paso, TX

CARDINAL CHICKEN SALAD

MAKES 8 SERVINGS

2 cups diced peeled apples
1 tablespoon lemon juice
4 cups finely chopped cooked chicken
1½ cups finely diced celery
1 cup green seedless grapes, sliced
1 cup mayonnaise-type salad dressing,
    divided
½ teaspoon salt
¼ teaspoon freshly ground pepper
1 (8-ounce) package cream cheese,
    softened
Grapes, lemon slices, mint leaves, or
    parsley for garnish

Sprinkle the apples with the lemon juice. Add the chicken, celery, grapes, ¾ cup salad dressing, salt, and pepper. Mix lightly. Press the mixture into a 1½-quart bowl. Cover with plastic wrap placed directly on the surface and chill for several hours. Unmold onto a serving platter.

Combine the remaining ¼ cup salad dressing and the cream cheese. Blend well. Frost the salad mold with this mixture and garnish with grapes, lemon, mint, or parsley.

Dinner on the Diner, Chattanooga, TN

CHICKEN RICE SALAD WITH ARTICHOKES

MAKES 6 SERVINGS

½ cup sliced cooked artichoke hearts
1 cup chopped celery
½ cup chopped green bell pepper
½ cup zesty Italian salad dressing
1 (6-ounce) package long grain and
    wild rice mix
2 whole chicken breasts, cooked and
    chopped
½ cup mayonnaise
8 ounces mushrooms, sliced
Lettuce leaves

Combine the artichoke hearts, celery, green pepper, and salad dressing in a bowl; mix well. Marinate in the refrigerator overnight.

Cook the rice according to the package directions, reducing the amount of water by ½ cup. Cool. Combine the rice with the chicken and mayonnaise in a bowl; add the mushrooms and marinated vegetables, mixing well. Chill until serving time. Serve the salad on lettuce-lined plates.

Generations, Rockford, IL

Fiesta Chicken Salad with Lime-Cilantro Vinaigrette

½ cup chopped shallots

¼ cup fresh lime juice

¼ cup chopped fresh cilantro

1 tablespoon minced garlic

Salt and freshly ground pepper to taste

½ cup vegetable oil

3 cups thinly sliced red leaf lettuce

3 cups thinly sliced Napa cabbage

1 cup diced cooked chicken breast

2 Roma tomatoes, seeded and chopped

½ red bell pepper, thinly sliced

½ yellow bell pepper, thinly sliced

½ avocado, peeled and diced

⅓ cup crumbled tortilla chips

¼ cup cooked fresh corn kernels

¼ cup pumpkin seeds, toasted

¼ cup thinly sliced onion

½ cup feta cheese (about 2 ounces), crumbled

Whisk together the shallots, lime juice, cilantro, garlic, salt, and pepper. Gradually add the vegetable oil, whisking until well blended. Set the vinaigrette aside.

Combine the red leaf lettuce and the remaining salad ingredients, except the cheese, in a large bowl. Toss with enough of the vinaigrette to coat. Top with cheese.

And Roses for the Table, Tyler, TX

CHICKEN PASTA SALAD

MAKES 8 TO 10 SERVINGS

2 whole chicken breasts, cooked and
    chopped
4 tablespoons balsamic or red wine
    vinegar
Salt to taste
8 ounces pasta
1 tablespoon olive oil
1 cup mayonnaise
1½ teaspoons salt
½ teaspoon dillweed
⅛ teaspoon freshly ground pepper
1 cup chopped celery
½ cup chopped bell pepper
3 tablespoons chopped green onion
2 tablespoons chopped pimiento
½ teaspoon celery seed
½ cup chopped parsley
¼ teaspoon Creole seasoning
2 teaspoons lemon juice

Sprinkle the chicken with the vinegar and some salt to taste. Refrigerate for up to 24 hours.

Cook the pasta following package directions; drain, toss with the olive oil, and set aside to cool. Combine the mayonnaise with the remaining ingredients in a bowl; mix well. Add the chicken and the pasta; toss until combined. Refrigerate for several hours. Adjust the seasonings as needed. Serve on lettuce leaves.

Selections, Huntsville, AL

CHICKEN SALAD INDIENNE

MAKES 4 TO 6 SERVINGS

2 to 3 cups diced cooked chicken
1 (13-ounce) can pineapple tidbits,
    drained (1 cup)
3 ribs celery, diagonally sliced
4-5 scallions, sliced, including some
    green portion
¼ cup salted peanuts
⅔ cup mayonnaise
2 tablespoons chopped chutney
½ teaspoon grated lime zest
2 tablespoons lime juice
½ teaspoon curry powder
¼ teaspoon salt

Toss the chicken, pineapple, celery, scallions, and peanuts in a large bowl. Combine the remaining ingredients in a small bowl, stirring to blend. Pour the mayonnaise mixture onto the chicken mixture and stir together well. Chill until ready to serve, preferably 3 hours to overnight for flavors to blend. Serve on salad greens.

Sound Seasonings, Westchester on the Sound, NY

GREEK CHICKEN SALAD

MAKES 6 SERVINGS

3 cups cubed cooked chicken
2 medium-size cucumbers, peeled,
    seeded, and chopped
10 ounces feta cheese, crumbled
⅔ cup sliced pitted black olives
¼ cup snipped parsley
1 cup mayonnaise
2 cloves garlic, crushed
½ cup plain yogurt
1 tablespoon ground or crushed dried
    oregano
Lettuce or pita bread pockets
    (optional)

Mix the chicken, cucumbers, feta cheese, olives, and parsley in a large bowl; set aside. Mix the mayonnaise, garlic, yogurt, and oregano in a small bowl. Add the mayonnaise mixture to the chicken mixture. Toss lightly. Cover and chill.

Serve on a bed of Boston lettuce or in pita bread pockets with romaine.

Savor the Brandywine Valley, Wilmington, DE

CHICKEN SALAD GALORE

2½ cups mayonnaise
½ cup sour cream
1 tablespoon curry powder
3 cups cold cooked rice
5 cups chopped cooked chicken breasts
1½ cups chopped green bell pepper
3 cups chopped celery
¼ cup seedless raisins
1¼ cups slivered almonds
3 (11-ounce) cans mandarin oranges,
    drained
2 (8-ounce) cans sliced water
    chestnuts, drained
Salt and freshly ground pepper to taste

Combine the mayonnaise, sour cream, and curry powder in a large bowl; mix well. Add the rice, chicken, green pepper, celery, raisins, almonds, mandarin oranges, water chestnuts, salt, and pepper; toss to mix well. Spoon into a serving bowl.

Dining in the Smoky Mountain Mist, Knoxville, TN

CURRIED TURKEY SALAD

MAKES 6 SERVINGS

2 cups cooked turkey, cubed
1 large stalk celery, thinly sliced
½ cup slivered almonds
¼ cup golden raisins
1 green onion, thinly sliced
2 tablespoons mango chutney
4 tablespoons Curry Mayonnaise (see
　　below), divided
Red leaf lettuce
Garnishes: hard-cooked eggs, halved;
　　boiled new potatoes, sliced thin;
　　cucumber slices; fresh pineapple or
　　melon chunks; tart apple slices;
　　blanched vegetables
Mayonnaise

Combine the turkey, celery, almonds, raisins, green onion, and chutney in a medium bowl. Add 2 tablespoons of the curry mayonnaise to the mixture and toss to blend.

Spoon the turkey mixture over the lettuce leaves. Arrange any or all garnishes in pairs around the salad. Thin the remaining 2 tablespoons curry mayonnaise with additional mayonnaise and pass as a sauce for the garnishes.

CURRY MAYONNAISE:

3 tablespoons mayonnaise
1 tablespoon curry powder
1 tablespoon Dijon mustard
1 teaspoon fresh lemon juice
1 large clove garlic, minced

Combine all the ingredients in a small bowl; mix well.

Thymes Remembered, Tallahassee, FL

COLD SHRIMP CURRY

MAKES 8 SERVINGS

*4 tablespoons (½ stick) butter or
    margarine*
1 cup peeled and chopped apple
2 cups chopped green onions
1 teaspoon crushed coriander seed
1 teaspoon ground ginger
1 tablespoon curry powder
1 teaspoon all-purpose flour
1 large orange, peeled and chopped
½ cup coconut liquid or coconut milk
1½ teaspoons sugar
2 cups mayonnaise
*Salt and freshly ground black pepper
    to taste*
Dash of ground red pepper (cayenne)
2 tablespoons lemon juice
3 pounds cooked and peeled shrimp

Melt the butter in a large skillet. Add the apple and onions and sauté for 8 to 10 minutes or until softened. Add the coriander seed, ginger, curry powder, and flour; mix well. Add the orange. Combine the coconut liquid and sugar in a small bowl and stir until dissolved. Add coconut liquid to the mixture in the skillet, 1 teaspoon at a time, using just enough to form a smooth paste.

Cool the paste and mix with the mayonnaise. Add the salt, black pepper, cayenne, and lemon juice. Stir in the shrimp and chill.

NOTE: If desired, serve in scooped-out pineapple halves. Garnish with cubed pineapple and toasted, grated coconut.

Jambalaya, New Orleans, LA

DILLY RICE SALAD

MAKES 6 SERVINGS

2 cups chicken broth
1 cup regular rice, uncooked
⅓ cup chopped green onions
⅓ cup chopped green bell pepper
*⅓ cup sliced pimiento-stuffed green
    olives*
*1 (7-ounce) jar marinated artichoke
    hearts, drained and chopped*
⅓ cup chopped celery
½ cup mayonnaise
¼ cup chopped fresh dill, or to taste
*Salt and freshly ground pepper to
    taste*
Lettuce leaves
Green olives for garnish

Bring the chicken broth to a boil in a medium saucepan. Add the rice, cover, and cook over very low heat for 17 minutes or until all the liquid is absorbed. Cool.

Combine the rice and the onions, green pepper, olives, artichoke, celery, mayonnaise, and seasonings in a medium bowl; chill well. Serve on lettuce leaves and garnish with sliced olives.

Georgia on My Menu, Cobb-Marietta, GA

SHRIMP SALAD VERMICELLI

MAKES 8 SERVINGS

*2 pounds shrimp, boiled, peeled, and
   cut in half lengthwise*
*12 ounces vermicelli, broken into
   2-inch lengths, cooked, drained,
   and cooled*
1 cup chopped celery
⅓ cup chopped red bell pepper
½ cup chopped green onions
¼ cup capers, drained
2 hard-cooked eggs, chopped
Creamy Garlic Dressing (see below)
Tomato slices for garnish

Combine the shrimp, vermicelli, celery, bell pepper, onions, capers, and eggs in a large bowl; toss gently. Add the dressing, tossing well to cover all the ingredients. Top with the tomato slices.

CREAMY GARLIC DRESSING:

¾ cup mayonnaise
2 tablespoons lime juice
1 clove garlic, minced
⅓ cup vegetable oil
2 teaspoons seasoned salt
*1 teaspoon freshly ground black
   pepper*

Combine all the ingredients in a glass jar; shake well, and refrigerate until ready to use.

¡Viva! Tradiciones, Corpus Christi, TX

SHRIMP RÉMOULADE

MAKES 8 SERVINGS

RÉMOULADE SAUCE:
¼ cup tarragon vinegar
2 tablespoons horseradish-flavored
    mustard
½ teaspoon salt
¼ teaspoon ground red pepper
1½ teaspoons paprika
1 tablespoon ketchup
1 clove garlic, minced
½ cup vegetable oil
¼ cup finely chopped green onion
¼ cup finely chopped celery
2 pounds shrimp, cooked, peeled, and
    deveined

To make the rémoulade sauce, combine all the ingredients except the shrimp in a small bowl; blend well.

Pour the mixture over the shrimp and marinate for several hours or overnight.

Some Like It South!, Pensacola, FL

VERMICELLI SALAD

MAKES 8 TO 10 SERVINGS

2 (16-ounce) packages vermicelli
3 tablespoons vegetable oil
3 tablespoons fresh lime or lemon juice
1 cup chopped celery
1 green bell pepper, chopped
1 bunch green onions, chopped
1 (7-ounce) jar sliced pimientos,
    drained and chopped
1 (8-ounce) can black olives, drained
    and chopped
2 cups mayonnaise
1 (10-ounce) package frozen green
    peas, unthawed
Coarsely ground black pepper
Beau Monde spice to taste
Garlic salt or powder to taste
¼ cup Catalina salad dressing
    (optional)

Boil the vermicelli in a large saucepan in salted water until just tender (do not overcook). Drain and rinse in cold water. Combine the vegetable oil and lime juice in a large bowl. Add the vermicelli, stirring well. Marinate in the refrigerator overnight.

Remove the vermicelli from the refrigerator about 1 hour before serving. Stir in the celery, bell pepper, green onions, pimiento, black olives, mayonnaise, and green peas. Season to taste. Add the Catalina dressing, if desired. Return to the refrigerater until ready to serve.

Some Like It Hot, McAllen, TX

Southwest Black Bean and Wild Rice Salad

MAKES 10 SERVINGS

1½ cups cooked and drained black beans
1 head each romaine and red leaf
    lettuce, washed, spun dry, and torn
    into bite-size pieces
1 bunch green onions, chopped
1 cucumber, peeled, seeded, and sliced
2 tomatoes, chopped
2 avocados, peeled, pitted, and chopped
2 cups blue-corn chips, broken
1 cup shredded Cheddar cheese
2 cup shredded pepper Jack cheese
1 teaspoon chili powder
1 teaspoon ground cumin
1 teaspoon ground red pepper
    (cayenne)
1 teaspoon garlic powder
¾ cup cooked wild rice
French dressing

Mix the beans, lettuces, onions, cucumber, tomato, avocado, chips, and cheeses in a large bowl. Combine the chili powder, cumin, cayenne, garlic powder, and wild rice in a separate bowl; mix well. Add to the black bean mixture and mix well. Moisten with French dressing; toss until combined. Serve immediately.

Reflections Under the Sun, Phoenix, AZ

MARINATED ARTICHOKE SALAD

MAKES 10 TO 12 SERVINGS

3 (10-ounce) packages frozen
  artichoke hearts
2-3 yellow bell peppers, seeded and
  cut into thin strips
3 tablespoons Dijon mustard
¾ cup red wine vinegar
1 tablespoon sugar
1½ teaspoons salt
1½ teaspoons freshly ground black
  pepper
1½ cups olive oil or ¾ cup olive oil
  and ¾ cup vegetable oil
1 pound fresh snow peas, trimmed

Cook the artichokes according to the package directions and drain. Combine the artichokes and peppers in a large bowl; set aside.

Whisk together the mustard, vinegar, sugar, salt, and pepper in a small bowl. Slowly add the oil, whisking constantly until the mixture thickens. Pour the dressing over the artichokes and peppers. Cover and refrigerate overnight. Blanch the snow peas in a small amount of boiling water for 30 seconds. Plunge into ice water to stop the cooking process; drain well. Refrigerate overnight.

Remove the artichoke mixture from the refrigerator. Stir in the snow peas. Let stand at room temperature 1 hour before serving.

Very Virginia, Hampton Roads, VA

SALADE AUX HARICOTS VERTS

MAKES 4 SERVINGS

1½ pounds fresh green beans
1 clove garlic, finely minced
1 tablespoon Dijon mustard
2 tablespoons red wine vinegar
6 tablespoons vegetable oil
Salt and freshly ground pepper to
  taste
¼ cup chopped fresh parsley
2 thin slices red onion, separated into
  rings

Trim or snap off ends of beans and remove strings, if necessary. Drop the beans into a medium saucepan of boiling salted water and cook 5 to 10 minutes, or until tender. Do not overcook. Pour the beans into a colander and rinse with cold water; drain.

Combine the garlic, mustard, and vinegar in a large bowl; mix well. Add the oil a little at a time, whisking continuously until all the oil is added and the dressing thickens. Season with salt and pepper and half the parsley. Add the green beans to the dressing and toss gently. Garnish with the remaining parsley and thinly sliced red onion rings.

Thymes Remembered, Tallahassee, FL

CITRUS BEAN SALAD

MAKES 8 SERVINGS

½ cup olive oil
¼ cup red wine vinegar
1 teaspoon sugar
2 (11-ounce) cans mandarin orange
    sections, drained
1 (19-ounce) can garbanzo beans,
    drained
1 (19-ounce) can red kidney beans,
    drained
½ cup very thinly sliced red onion
¼ cup chopped parsley

Whisk the olive oil, vinegar, and sugar together in a bowl. Add the mandarin oranges, garbanzo beans, kidney beans, onion, and parsley; toss to mix well. Chill until serving time.

Wild Thymes and Other Temptations, Tucson, AZ

AVOCADO AND MOZZARELLA SALAD

MAKES 4 SERVINGS

4 plum tomatoes, chopped
¼ cup pitted kalamata olives
3 tablespoons julienned fresh basil
    leaves
¼ cup olive oil
3-4 tablespoons rosemary vinegar or
    tarragon vinegar
1 tablespoon balsamic vinegar
1 avocado, peeled, pitted, and chopped
1 cup coarsely chopped drained water-
    pack mozzarella cheese
Salt and freshly ground pepper to
    taste

Combine the tomatoes, olives, basil, olive oil, herb vinegar, and balsamic vinegar in a bowl and mix well. Chill, covered, 2 to 24 hours. Add the avocado and mozzarella cheese and mix gently. Season with salt and freshly ground pepper.

Wild Thymes and Other Temptations, Tucson, AZ

CORNUCOPIA CHICKEN SALAD

MAKES 6 SERVINGS

3 tablespoons sugar
½ cup sliced almonds
½ head green leaf lettuce, washed,
    spun dry, and torn into bite-size
    pieces
½ head romaine lettuce, washed, spun
    dry, and torn into bite-size pieces
1 cup chopped celery
4 green onions, chopped
1 (11-ounce) can mandarin orange
    sections
1 avocado, peeled, pitted, and cut into
    chunks
1 apple, peeled (if desired) and diced
¼ cup dried currants
½ cup crumbled blue cheese
3 boneless, skinless chicken breast
    halves, cooked and shredded
Vinaigrette Dressing (see below)

Melt the 3 tablespoons of sugar in a large dry frying pan with the sliced almonds, stirring continuously until the almonds are coated. Don't let the sugar burn. Remove the almonds and spread out on foil to cool.

Mix both the lettuces, the celery, onions, oranges, avocado, apple, currants, blue cheese, and chicken in a large bowl; stir in the almonds. Toss with the dressing and serve.

VINAIGRETTE DRESSING:

½ teaspoon salt
½ teaspoon freshly ground pepper
¼ cup vegetable oil
1 tablespoon chopped parsley
2 tablespoons sugar
2 tablespoons white wine vinegar

Combine all the ingredients and mix well with a wire whisk.

California Sizzles, Pasadena, CA

ZORBA'S GREEK OLIVES

MAKES 2 POUNDS OLIVES

½ cup vegetable oil
½ cup olive oil
3 tablespoons fresh lemon juice
2 tablespoons red wine vinegar
2 teaspoons dried oregano, crumbled
Salt and freshly ground black pepper
    to taste
1 pound pitted black olives
1 pound pitted green olives

Combine the vegetable and olive oil, with the lemon juice, vinegar, oregano, salt, and pepper in a medium bowl; mix well. Add the olives. Cover and refrigerate at least 1 day before serving. Serve on a platter with sliced fresh tomatoes, green onions, and feta cheese.

NOTE: Either kalamata or ripe black olives absorb this marinade well.

Celebrations on the Bayou, Monroe, LA

SQUASH PICKLES

MAKES 8-10 PINTS

10 small summer squash, thinly sliced
2 medium onions, thinly sliced
4 green bell peppers, thinly sliced
¼ cup salt
3 cups sugar
2 cups vinegar
2 teaspoons mustard seed
2 teaspoons celery seed

Layer the squash, onions, and bell peppers in a large nonaluminum stockpot. Sprinkle with the salt. Cover with ice and water and let stand for 1 hour. Pour off the water. Combine the sugar, vinegar, mustard seed, and celery seed in a saucepan; bring to a boil. Pour over the squash and bring back to a boil for 1 minute. Pack in sterilized jars, and seal while hot.

Celebrations on the Bayou, Monroe, LA

HUCKLEBERRY DRIZZLE SALAD

MAKES 8 SERVINGS

HERBED VINAIGRETTE:
¼ cup vegetable oil
1 tablespoon lemon juice
1 tablespoon white vinegar
1 clove garlic, minced
¼ teaspoon salt
¼ teaspoon sugar
⅛ teaspoon dry mustard
⅛ teaspoon onion salt
⅛ teaspoon paprika
⅛ teaspoon dried oregano
Pinch of thyme

SALAD:
8 cups red and/or green leaf lettuce,
    rinsed, spun dry, and torn into
    bite-size pieces
½ cup blanched slivered almonds,
    toasted
¼ cup crumbled feta cheese
½ cup huckleberry syrup

Combine the vinaigrette ingredients in an electric blender and blend well. Toss the lettuce with the desired amount of dressing and mound on individual salad plates. Sprinkle each salad with toasted almonds and feta cheese. Drizzle with huckleberry syrup.

Gold 'n Delicious, Spokane, WA

SUMMER TOMATO AND BASIL SALAD

MAKES 8 SERVINGS

5 medium tomatoes, sliced and salted
⅓ cup sliced, pitted black olives
½ cup crumbled feta cheese
½ cup olive oil
⅓ cup red wine vinegar
¼ cup lightly packed fresh basil leaves,
    chopped
1 garlic clove, minced
⅛ teaspoon coarsely ground black
    pepper

Arrange the sliced tomatoes in a 13 x 9-inch dish. Top with the olives and cheese. Combine the remaining ingredients in a jar and shake vigorously. Pour over the tomatoes, cover, and chill for at least 2 hours.

A Southern Collection—Then & Now, Columbus, GA

SWEET-AND-SOUR BROCCOLI, CORN, AND RED PEPPERS IN TOMATO CUPS

MAKES 8 SERVINGS

1 cup olive oil
2 pounds broccoli, trimmed and cut
    into ¾-inch pieces
2 cups fresh corn kernels or frozen
    corn, thawed
2 large red bell peppers, seeded and
    chopped
4 tablespoons white wine vinegar
4 tablespoons sugar
6 tablespoons lemon juice
½ teaspoon ground cinnamon
½ teaspoon freshly ground black
    pepper
½ cup raisins
½ cup pine nuts, toasted
4 medium tomatoes

Heat the oil in a large skillet and add the broccoli. Cook over moderate heat until tender, approximately 12-15 minutes. Stir in the corn, bell peppers, vinegar, sugar, lemon juice, cinnamon, and pepper; simmer the mixture for 5 minutes. Add the raisins and pine nuts; simmer for 2 to 3 minutes longer, until the mixture thickens slightly. Remove from the heat. Cover and refrigerate until chilled, approximately 2 hours. (Can be prepared 1 day ahead up to this point.)

Cut the tomatoes in half and scoop out the seeds, discarding pulp. Turn over and drain on paper towels. Cover and refrigerate. Just before serving, stuff the tomatoes with the sweet-and-sour broccoli mixture.

Dining by Fireflies, Charlotte, NC

FINLEY AVENUE SUMMER SALAD

MAKES 4 SERVINGS

2 ears fresh corn
2 cups fresh baby okra
½ cup chopped sweet onion
½-1 cup chopped red bell pepper
¼ cup chopped fresh basil
White wine vinegar or herb vinegar
Salt and freshly ground black pepper
    to taste

Steam the corn in a saucepan 1 minute. Cut the kernels from the cobs. Steam the okra 1 minute; slice. Combine the corn kernels, sliced okra, onion, bell pepper, and basil in a medium bowl. Toss with vinegar to taste. Season with salt and pepper to taste. Chill.

Food for Thought, Birmingham, AL

SAUTÉED APPLE SALAD

¼ cup red wine vinegar
1 tablespoon chopped fresh thyme
½ cup plus 2 tablespoons olive oil
Salt and freshly ground pepper to
*   taste*
5 medium-size Granny Smith apples,
*   peeled and sliced*
1 tablespoon sugar
6 cups torn young lettuce leaves
1 cup crumbled blue cheese
½ cup chopped toasted walnuts

Combine the vinegar and thyme in a small bowl. Add ½ cup of the olive oil gradually, whisking constantly until blended. Season with salt and pepper. Set the dressing aside.

Sauté the apples and sugar in the remaining 2 tablespoons oil in a large skillet over medium-high heat until the apples are slightly tender. Cool. Arrange the lettuce in a large salad bowl; layer the apple mixture over the top. Sprinkle with the blue cheese and walnuts. Add the oil and vinegar dressing, tossing gently to coat.

Sweet Home Alabama, Huntsville, AL

NORTHWEST AUTUMN SALAD

MAKES 6 SERVINGS

1 head red leaf lettuce
1 head Bibb lettuce
1 cup watercress leaves
2 Red Delicious apples (see Note)
¾ cup toasted walnuts, chopped
¾ cup crumbled blue cheese
½ cup walnut or vegetable oil
¼ cup cider vinegar
2 tablespoons minced shallots
2 tablespoons freshly squeezed lemon
*   juice*
1 tablespoon maple syrup
¼ teaspoon salt
¼ teaspoon freshly ground pepper

Tear the lettuces into bite-size pieces and place in a large salad bowl. Add the watercress leaves. Cut the apples into very thin wedges and place on top of the greens. Sprinkle the toasted walnuts and blue cheese evenly over the salad. Combine the oil, vinegar, shallots, lemon juice, maple syrup, salt, and pepper in a small jar with a tight-fitting lid. Shake until evenly combined. Drizzle the dressing over the salad. Toss gently and serve immediately.

NOTE: Apples should be sliced just before serving so they do not discolor. The rest of the salad can be prepared in advance and refrigerated until ready to be tossed with the dressing and served.

Simply Classic Cookbook, Seattle, WA

APPLE AND BLUE CHEESE TOSSED SALAD

MAKES 4 SERVINGS

2 Golden Delicious apples, chopped
2 tablespoons (or less) lemon juice
3-4 cups torn red leaf lettuce
3-4 cups torn spinach
½ cup coarsely chopped cashews
½ cup crumbled blue cheese
6 slices bacon, crisp-fried, crumbled
½ cup sliced raw mushrooms
Red Wine Vinaigrette (see below)

Toss the apples with the lemon juice to slow the browning process. Combine the apples with the lettuce, spinach, cashews, blue cheese, bacon, and mushrooms in a large salad bowl. Pour in the red wine vinaigrette and toss to coat. Serve.

NOTE: Omit the lemon juice if the apples are chopped immediately before serving.

RED WINE VINAIGRETTE:

¼ cup red wine vinegar
⅓ cup salad oil
1 teaspoon Worcestershire sauce
1 clove garlic, crushed
½ teaspoon salt
¼ teaspoon oregano
2 tablespoons sugar
Dash of freshly ground pepper

Whisk the vinegar, oil, Worcestershire sauce, garlic, salt, oregano, sugar, and pepper in a small bowl.

Dining by Design, Pasadena, CA

STEGOSAURUS SALAD

MAKES 6 SERVINGS

6 lettuce leaves
12 maraschino cherries, chopped
1 (3-ounce) package cream cheese,
    softened
6 canned peach halves, drained
12 grapes
Slivered almonds

Wash the lettuce leaves, blot dry, and place 1 leaf on each salad plate. Using a fork, blend the cherries with the cream cheese until well mixed. Place a rounded teaspoon of the cheese mixture in the center of each lettuce leaf and cover with a peach half, cut side down. Cut 6 grapes into quarters. Place 4 pieces around each peach half as "feet" and 1 whole grape as the "head." Insert the slivered almonds in a row across the peach for "spikes."

Children's Party Book, Hampton Roads, VA

PICKLED PEACH SALAD

MAKES 10 SERVINGS

1 jar pickled peaches
1½ (3-ounce) packages lemon gelatin
½ cup water
½ cup orange juice
Juice of 1 lemon
Pinch of salt
1 jar light-skinned sweet cherries,
    drained and chopped
1 cup chopped pecans

Drain the peaches, saving 1 cup of juice; cut up the fruit and set aside. Place the gelatin in a medium bowl. Bring the juice to a boil in a small saucepan. Pour over the gelatin and stir until dissolved. Add the water, orange juice, lemon juice, and salt. Refrigerate for 1 to 1½ hours, until the gelatin is slightly thickened. Fold in the peaches, cherries, and nuts.

Rinse an 8-cup ring mold, shake out excess water, and pour in the gelatin mixture. Cover and refrigerate for about 3 hours or until set. Unmold onto a serving dish.

NOTE: You can soak the fruit in sherry for several hours before making the salad.

Huntsville Heritage Cookbook, Huntsville, AL

HEAVENLY ORANGE FLUFF

2 (3-ounce) packages orange gelatin
2 cups boiling water
1 (6-ounce) can frozen orange juice
    concentrate
2 (10-ounce) cans mandarin orange
    sections, drained
1 (15-ounce) can crushed pineapple,
    not drained
Lemon Topping (see below)
6 maraschino cherries, halved

LEMON TOPPING:

1 (3-ounce) package instant lemon
    pudding
1 cup milk
½ pint whipping cream or frozen
    whipped topping, thawed

Place the gelatin in a medium bowl. Pour in the boiling water and stir until dissolved. Add the orange juice, stirring until melted. Cool. Add the oranges and pineapple. Let the mixture congeal in a 13 x 9-inch pan or individual molds. Before serving, spread the lemon topping over the gelatin and top with the cherry halves.

Beat the pudding and milk together in a small bowl until slightly firm, about 4 minutes. Whip the cream. Fold into the pudding mixture.

The Charlotte Cookbook, Charlotte, NC

PTERODACTYL EGGS

6 hard-cooked eggs, shells removed
1½ teaspoons prepared mustard
¼–⅓ cup mayonnaise
1½–2 tablespoons sweet pickle relish
Paprika for garnish

Cut the eggs lengthwise into halves. Carefully remove the yolks and set the white portion aside. Using a fork, mash the yolks until smooth. Add the mustard, mayonnaise, and relish, adjusting the amount of mayonnaise to taste. Fill the egg white halves with the yolk mixture, using a spoon or pastry bag with a wide tip. Garnish with the paprika.

Children's Party Book, Hampton Roads, VA

SOUPS

AND

STEWS

DEEP SOUTH

From christenings and graduations to weddings and anniversaries, Southerners seize any chance to celebrate with great fanfare and great food. Food is taken seriously and heated arguments come to a boil over the merits of white or yellow cornmeal in the cornbread, Memphis-style barbecue, drop dumplings or rolled. You can pinpoint a person's birthplace by the type of dressing she prefers with her Thanksgiving turkey. But from the catfish fries of inland regions to the oyster roasts of the coasts, the unifying elements are abundance and the gracious plenty that so often describes the celebratory tables of the Deep South.

Some of the South's most famous foods are rooted in a community sensibility, and are seldom prepared at home just for the family. Brunswick stews of Tennessee are assembled in giant iron pots and then rhythmically stirred by strong volunteers equipped with boat paddles. Gumbos and jambalayas at Cajun *fais do-dos* are enjoyed communally and traditionally in rural dance halls. These centerpiece foods star, by and large, in an outdoor, male domain. It takes space, muscle, stamina, and camaraderie to barbecue and baste a 200-pound pig for 15 hours or more.

Women's roles at these gatherings are to showcase their creative prowess, providing the appetizers, side dishes, salads, breads, and desserts they prepare with so much care and love. At potluck occasions, such as dinners-on-the-grounds, you'll see good cooks hovering proudly near their contributions, ever ready to accept their accolades.

The triumphs of the modern family table trace their origins to recipes compiled in community cookbooks. Future food historians will see how cooks of the era updated traditional recipes. Grandma's buttermilk biscuits may get a bit of cheese worked into the dough. Traditional fried chicken, the dish most universally associated with the South, is still enjoyed at tailgate parties, family reunions, and charity events. But now it might be fried in canola oil rather than rendered bacon fat, and served with a vegetable in lieu of rich gravy.

Southern cuisine is primarily the product of the early settlers, who combined the blander European foods with the lively spicy flavors of Africa to come up with dishes that transcend their origins. In Louisiana, this fusion cooking became even more complex and exciting. European chefs of wealthy plantation owners and French Acadians from Nova Scotia prepared local ingredients with the cooking styles of the Spanish, American Indians, and African-American residents, and the outcome was Creole and Cajun cooking. Classic French techniques melded with local produce to give us sophisticated Creole cuisine. Cajun cooking is earthier, typified by pungent and peppery single-pot meals.

While Southern cooks take ownership of their ancestral recipes, they are once again enthusiastically embracing new ethnic flavors brought by the wave of immigrants from the former Soviet Union, Southeast Asia, and Latin countries. In the hands of clever Southern cooks, those culinary wizards of adaptation and experimentation, the outcome will surely be nothing short of masterful.

—Chris Gang, *The Commercial Appeal*
Memphis, TN

FOURTH OF JULY FISH FRY

As the sun sets over the lakes of the Deep South and the heat settles as much as it is going to, swimsuit-clad frolickers come off the boats and out of the water to join family and friends for the ritual that has become tradition. The cooker is brought out to fry the fish, and the ice cream freezer is cranked up to make the dessert. The side dishes have been ready and waiting in the refrigerator since yesterday. The only hot things on the table are the fish and hush puppies. It's no accident that everyone sits down to eat just as the fireworks begin to explode and reflect on the river.

Submitted by *Beyond Cotton Country*, Decatur, AL

EGGPLANT CAVIAR WITH TOASTED FRENCH BREAD 36

TENNESSEE RIVER CATFISH WITH JALAPEÑO TARTAR SAUCE 220

SOUTHERN HUSH PUPPIES 166

MARINATED SLAW 67

CONFETTI CORN TOSS 148

PREVIEW PARTY BROWNIES 346

CARAMEL PEANUT BARS 371

DREAMY VANILLA ICE CREAM 370

COTTON PICKIN' PICNIC

Cotton is still king in Louisiana, and a midday feast for today's gentleman planter offers a contemporary twist on a classic theme. It's not the usual wicker-basket fare but, instead, provides chicken and beef and even chef salad in pita bread pockets. So go with the whim! Polish the silver, if you so desire, and head for the field—or the tailgate party—wherever the picnic spirit finds you.

Submitted by *Celebrations on the Bayou*, Monroe, LA

CREAMY POTATO LEEK SOUP 105

PITA POCKETS:

FAJITA CHICKEN FILLER 265

MARINATED BEEF SALAD 190

CHEF SALAD STUFFING 74

ZORBA'S GREEK OLIVES 91

SQUASH PICKLES 91

HARVEST LOAF 287

RECIPE FOR A BETTER COMMUNITY

JUNIOR LEAGUE OF COBB-MARIETTA, GEORGIA COMMUNITY PROJECT:

Cobb Parenting Initiative

Cobb Parenting Initiative is a program that provides parenting training and resources. The program was launched in 1998, and the League continues to facilitate the community-wide initiative.

The cookbooks that helped to make it happen: *Southern on Occasion* and *Georgia on My Menu* have funded $73,000 to the Cobb Parenting Initiative over a five-year period.

Did you know? The Junior League of Cobb-Marietta entered its cookbooks in many local and national contests and it paid off. *Southern on Occasion* won the coveted Tabasco Community Cookbook Award and an award at the Atlanta Gourmet Show, thereby receiving great publicity, which resulted in more book sales!

CREAMY POTATO LEEK SOUP

8 cups rich chicken broth

4 medium potatoes, peeled and diced

6 stalks celery, cut into pieces

3 leeks, thoroughly washed, cut into
    1-inch pieces, or 9 chopped green
    onions

Salt and freshly ground pepper to
    taste

2 tablespoons butter (optional)

1 cup sour cream

Chopped chives

Combine the broth, potatoes, celery, and leeks in a large saucepan; add salt and pepper to taste. Place over medium heat and gradually bring to a boil. Reduce the heat and cook until the vegetables are tender. Purée the vegetables in batches in a food processor or blender with some of the liquid.

Return the purée to the saucepan, blending well. Taste and adjust seasoning. Bring to a simmer over medium heat. Add the butter, if desired, for a richer soup. Stir until the butter melts. Ladle the soup into bowls and serve with a dollop of sour cream and a sprinkle of chives.

Celebrations on the Bayou, Monroe, LA

BUTTERNUT SQUASH SOUP

MAKES 6 SERVINGS

3 tablespoons butter, divided
1 (2-pound) butternut squash, seeded,
    cut into 8 pieces
1 pound parsnips, peeled and cut into
    2-inch slices
¼ cup water
1 onion, thinly sliced
2 teaspoons chopped fresh thyme, or ¾
    teaspoon dried
4 cups chicken broth
1 cup half-and-half
Salt and freshly ground pepper to
    taste

Preheat the oven to 375F. Butter a large roasting pan with 1 tablespoon of the butter. Arrange the squash skin-side down and the parsnips in the pan; add the water. Cover with foil. Bake 50 minutes or until the vegetables are very tender. Let cool.

Melt the remaining 2 tablespoons of butter in a small skillet over medium-low heat. Add the onion and thyme. Sauté 8 to 10 minutes or until the onion is tender and golden. Remove from the heat.

Remove the squash peel when it is cool enough to handle. Combine the squash, parsnips, and onion in a food processor bowl. Process until puréed. Add the chicken broth; process until blended. Pour the mixture into a large heavy saucepan. Whisk in the half-and-half. Bring to a simmer. Season with the salt and pepper.

NOTE: May be made ahead and stored, covered, in the refrigerator for 1 day.

Dining by Design, Pasadena, CA

CURRIED BUTTERNUT SQUASH SOUP

1 (2½-pound) butternut squash,
   halved
1 tablespoon unsalted butter or
   margarine
Salt to taste
1 cup chopped onion
2 tablespoons vegetable oil
4 cloves garlic, finely chopped
2 teaspoons curry powder, or to taste
1 teaspoon ground cumin
Ground red pepper (cayenne) to taste
3 cups chicken broth
3 cups water
1 pound tart apples, peeled and
   chopped
Freshly ground black pepper to taste

Remove the seeds from the squash and spread them on a double thickness of microwave-safe paper towels. Microwave on high for 3 to 5 minutes or until dry. Cool to room temperature. Sauté the seeds in the butter in a skillet over medium high heat for 2 minutes or until golden brown, stirring constantly. Drain on paper towels. Season with salt.

Peel the squash and cut it into thin slices. Set aside.

Sauté the onion in the oil in a large heavy saucepan over medium heat for 10 to 12 minutes or until golden brown. Add the garlic, curry powder, cumin, and cayenne pepper. Cook for 30 seconds, stirring constantly. Add the squash, chicken broth, 3 cups of water, and apples. Simmer, covered, for 25 minutes or until the squash is tender.

Purée the mixture in several batches in a blender or food processor. Return to the saucepan and season with salt and black pepper. Cook until heated through. Sprinkle the servings with the toasted squash seeds.

Generations, Rockford, IL

AUTUMN PUMPKIN SOUP

MAKES 8 SERVINGS

1 cup diced onion
2 tablespoons diced leek, white part
    only
1 tablespoon butter
3 cups chicken broth
1 (16-ounce) can solid pumpkin
½ teaspoon salt
Freshly ground white pepper to taste
½ teaspoon sugar
¼ teaspoon grated nutmeg
1 tablespoon fresh lemon juice
1 tablespoon grated orange zest
½ cup half-and-half
⅓ cup roasted sunflower kernels

Sauté the onion and leek in butter in a large saucepan until tender, about 5 to 8 minutes. Stir in the chicken broth and pumpkin and heat thoroughly. Add salt and white pepper. Purée in a food processor until smooth. Add the sugar, nutmeg, lemon juice, and orange zest. Return to the pan and slowly whisk in the half-and-half. Heat to serving temperature. Sprinkle with sunflower kernels.

Women of Great Taste, Wichita, KS

ROASTED EGGPLANT SOUP

MAKES 6 SERVINGS

2 medium eggplants
2 tablespoons vegetable oil, divided
4 medium cloves garlic, minced
2 cups chopped onion
8 cups chicken stock
1 (6-ounce) can tomato paste
1 cup lightly packed fresh basil leaves
    or ¼ cup dried basil
½ teaspoon salt
¼ teaspoon freshly ground pepper

Preheat the broiler. Cut each eggplant in half lengthwise and place on oiled baking sheets, skin side up. Rub the skin with 1 tablespoon of the oil and place under the broiler. Broil 10 to 15 minutes or until the skins are charred and blistered; cool.

Peel the eggplant and cut the pulp into chunks. Heat the remaining tablespoon of oil in a large skillet. Add the eggplant, garlic, and onion. Sauté about 15 minutes or until the vegetables are softened. Put the chicken stock in a large, heavy pot over medium heat. Add the sautéed vegetables, tomato paste, basil, salt, and pepper. Simmer about 15 minutes. Puree the soup in batches in a food processor or blender. Return the soup to the pot and simmer gently until heated through. Serve immediately.

Simply Classic Cookbook, Seattle, WA

CREAM OF WATERCRESS SOUP

2 bunches watercress
¼ cup minced onion
2 tablespoons butter
¼ teaspoon salt
2 tablespoons all-purpose flour
4 cups boiling chicken stock
2 large egg yolks
1 cup heavy cream
Freshly ground pepper to taste

Trim and rinse the watercress; drain. Reserve several perfect leaves for garnish.

Sauté the onion in the butter over medium heat in a large saucepan for 8 to 10 minutes or until tender. Add the watercress; sprinkle with ¼ teaspoon salt. Cook, covered, over medium-low heat 5 to 10 minutes or until the watercress is wilted. Stir in the flour. Cook 5 minutes, stirring occasionally. Gradually stir in the boiling stock; mix well. Cook 5 minutes. Process the mixture in a food processor until puréed.

Bring the puréed mixture to a simmer in a clean saucepan just before serving. Beat the egg yolks and cream in a bowl until blended. Add some of the puréed mixture gradually to the egg mixture, whisking constantly until blended. Return the mixture to the saucepan. Heat, but do not allow to simmer, stirring constantly. Season with salt and pepper to taste. Ladle into soup bowls. Top with the reserved watercress.

NOTE: May be prepared 1 day in advance and served chilled.

Sweet Home Alabama, Huntsville, AL

CILANTRO SOUP

6 cups chicken broth
1 pound zucchini, coarsely chopped
½ onion, coarsely chopped
1½ cups fresh cilantro leaves
1 tablespoon butter
2 teaspoons flour
½ cup heavy cream (optional)
Salt and freshly ground pepper to
   taste
½ cup vegetable oil
6 corn tortillas, cut into thin strips
½ cup cubed farmer cheese

Heat the chicken broth in a saucepan, then add the zucchini and onion, and simmer until tender. Cool slightly. In a blender, purée the zucchini mixture with the cilantro leaves until smooth. In another large saucepan, melt the butter and stir in the flour until it bubbles. Slowly add the cilantro mixture, whisking constantly. Gradually stir in the cream, if you desire, and season the soup with salt and pepper.

Meanwhile, heat the oil in a skillet until very hot but not smoking and fry the tortilla strips until golden. Remove and drain the tortilla strips on paper towels. Serve the soup decorated with tortilla strips and cheese cubes.

Behind the Walls, Mexico City, Mexico

TORTILLA SOUP

MAKES 6 SERVINGS

1 small onion, chopped
1 (4-ounce) can chopped green chiles,
    drained
2 cloves garlic, crushed
2 tablespoons vegetable oil
1 cup peeled and chopped tomatoes
1 (10-ounce) can condensed beef
    bouillon
1 (10-ounce) can condensed chicken
    broth
1½ cups water
1½ cups tomato juice
1 teaspoon ground cumin
1 teaspoon chili powder
1 teaspoon salt
⅛ teaspoon freshly ground pepper
2 teaspoons Worcestershire sauce
1 tablespoon bottled steak sauce
3 corn tortillas, cut into ½-inch strips
¼ cup shredded Cheddar cheese

Sauté the onion, chiles, and garlic in the oil in a large heavy saucepan until soft. Add the tomatoes, bouillon, chicken broth, water, tomato juice, cumin, chili powder, salt, pepper, Worcestershire sauce, and steak sauce. Bring the soup to a boil; lower the heat, and simmer, covered, 1 hour. Add the tortillas and cheese and simmer 10 minutes longer. Serve hot.

Seasoned with Sun, El Paso, TX

SPICY TORTILLA SOUP

MAKES 8 TO 10 SERVINGS

½ onion, chopped
2 cloves garlic, minced
1 tablespoon vegetable oil
1 (16-ounce) can stewed tomatoes
2 (8-ounce) cans tomato sauce
1 cup water
4 cups chicken broth
1 teaspoon ground cumin
½ teaspoon freshly ground black pepper
Tortilla chips
Monterey Jack cheese, grated

Sauté the onion and garlic in the oil in a small skillet until tender. Purée the stewed tomatoes and their juice in a food processor and transfer to a large soup pot. Add the tomato sauce, water, chicken broth, cumin, and pepper and simmer for 15 minutes.

To serve, place some chips and grated cheese in serving bowls. Spoon the hot soup over the chips and cheese. Serve immediately.

And Roses for the Table, Tyler, TX

SOPA DE TORTILLA

MAKES 8 SERVINGS

6 stale corn tortillas
½ cup vegetable oil
1 onion, finely chopped
½ cup tomato purée
2 quarts chicken or beef stock
1 tablespoon chopped fresh cilantro
Grated Parmesan cheese
2 ripe avocados, peeled, pitted, and
   sliced

Cut the stale tortillas into ¼-inch strips. Heat the oil in a large skillet until very hot but not smoking. Fry the strips in batches until golden. Remove with a slotted spoon to drain on paper towels; keep warm.

Sauté the onion in the same oil for 5 minutes, until soft. Add the tomato purée and simmer for 5 minutes. Add the stock and the tortilla strips and simmer 25 minutes. Top with cilantro and grated Parmesan cheese right before serving. Garnish with avocado slices.

Delicioso, Corpus Christi, TX

FATHER DEMSKE'S MUSHROOM SOUP

MAKES 8 SERVINGS

2 tablespoons chicken bouillon
   granules
3 cups hot water
1 large onion, chopped
4 tablespoons (½ stick) butter
1 pound mushrooms, trimmed and
   sliced
⅓ cup minced fresh parsley
3 tablespoons tomato paste
1 clove garlic, crushed
¼ teaspoon freshly ground pepper
½ cup dry white wine
½ cup shredded Jarlsberg cheese
½ cup shredded Asiago cheese
½ cup shredded sharp Cheddar cheese

Dissolve the bouillon granules in the hot water and mix well. Sauté the onion in the butter in a stockpot over medium heat just until tender, about 5 minutes. Stir in the mushrooms. Sauté briefly. Add the bouillon mixture, parsley, tomato paste, garlic, and pepper; mix well. (The soup may be prepared in advance up to this point and stored in the refrigerator.)

Shortly before serving, stir in the white wine. Return the soup to a boil and simmer, covered, for 5 minutes, stirring occasionally. Ladle into soup bowls. Sprinkle with the Jarlsberg cheese, Asiago cheese, and Cheddar cheese. Serve immediately.

Great Lake Effects, Buffalo, NY

ELEGANT MUSHROOM SOUP

MAKES **4** SERVINGS

1 pound mushrooms, trimmed and
    coarsely chopped
4 green onions with tops, coarsely
    chopped
8 tablespoons (1 stick) butter
⅓ cup all-purpose flour
¼ teaspoon dry mustard
2 teaspoons salt
Ground red pepper (cayenne) to taste
¼ teaspoon freshly ground black
    pepper
2 cups chicken broth
2 cups heavy cream or half-and-half
⅓ cup sherry (optional)

Sauté the mushrooms and green onions in the butter in a large
saucepan for 5 minutes. Stir in the flour, dry mustard, salt, cayenne,
and black pepper. Gradually stir in the chicken broth and cream.
Simmer until thickened and smooth, stirring constantly. Add the
sherry, if desired. Serve hot.

Generations, Rockford, IL

WILD MUSHROOM SOUP

MAKES **6** TO **8** SERVINGS

5 tablespoons butter
1 small onion, minced
2 large shallots, minced
¾ pound fresh wild mushrooms,
    cleaned, trimmed, and finely
    chopped
3 tablespoons all-purpose flour
1 (10-ounce) can beef consommé
1 (13-ounce) can beef broth
3 bay leaves
Salt and freshly ground pepper to
    taste
½ cup heavy cream
Parsley for garnish

Melt the butter in a large heavy saucepan. Add the onion and
shallots, and sauté lightly. Stir in the mushrooms and cook until quite
soft. Sprinkle in the flour, stirring constantly. Gradually stir in the
consommé and broth. Add the bay leaves and season to taste with
salt and pepper. Cover and simmer for 5 minutes. Remove the bay
leaves and stir in the cream just before serving. Garnish with
parsley.

Settings . . . From Our Past to Your Presentation, Philadelphia, PA

MOUNTAIN APPLE AND VIDALIA SOUP

MAKES 8 SERVINGS

1 quart beef stock
1½ cups apple cider
1 bay leaf
½ teaspoon thyme
1 teaspoon coarsely ground black
    pepper
½ teaspoon salt
2 tablespoons butter
1 pound Vidalia onions, thinly sliced
⅛ teaspoon sugar
⅓ cup dry sherry
Garlic croutons
Parmesan cheese, freshly grated
Gruyère cheese, thinly sliced
⅔ cup finely diced red apple, chilled,
    for garnish

Combine the beef stock and apple cider in a large stockpot. Bring to a light boil. Add the bay leaf, thyme, black pepper, and salt. Simmer, partially covered, for 1 hour.

Melt the butter in a medium skillet and sauté the onions until soft. Add the sugar and continue cooking until the onions are browned. Deglaze the skillet with sherry and add the mixture to the beef stock. Simmer for 1 more hour. Remove the bay leaf.

When ready to serve, preheat the broiler. Place 8 ovenproof soup bowls on a baking sheet. Ladle the soup into the bowls and top each bowl with the croutons. Cover with grated Parmesan cheese and put a slice of Gruyére cheese on top. Slide under the broiler for 1 to 2 minutes or until the cheese melts and browns. Garnish with diced apple before serving.

Dining by Fireflies, Charlotte, NC

COLD ZUCCHINI SOUP

MAKES 8 SERVINGS

5-6 medium zucchini
1 large onion, thinly sliced
1½ teaspoons curry powder
3 (10-ounce) cans chicken broth
1½ cups half-and-half
Salt to taste
White pepper to taste

Rinse the zucchini and pat dry. Trim off the ends. Cut the zucchini into 1-inch lengths, then cut each length into quarters. Place the zucchini in a saucepan. Add the onion slices and sprinkle with curry, stirring to coat the vegetable pieces. Add the broth; bring to a boil, reduce the heat, and simmer, covered, 30 minutes. Transfer to a blender and purée. Add the half-and-half. Season with salt and white pepper to taste. Chill and serve.

Selections, Huntsville, AL

ANNABANANA SOUP

MAKES 4 TO 6 SERVINGS

2 cups chicken broth
1 onion, thinly sliced
1 potato, peeled and thinly sliced
1 tart green apple, peeled and chopped
1 banana, sliced
2-3 teaspoons mild curry powder
2 cups half-and-half
Sour cream
Fresh chives, minced

In a saucepan over medium heat, slowly heat the chicken broth. Add the onion, potato, apple, and banana and simmer until the vegetables are tender. Remove from the heat and add the curry powder. Purée the mixture in a blender or food processor.

Pour into a large bowl. Stir in half-and-half and chill at least 1 hour. To serve, pour into individual bowls and garnish with a dollop of sour cream and fresh chives.

From Portland's Palate, Portland, OR

LOBSTER GAZPACHO

MAKES 4 TO 6 SERVINGS

4 or 5 ripe tomatoes
2 cucumbers, peeled and seeded
1 yellow onion
3 ribs celery
1 yellow bell pepper
½ cup red wine vinegar
¼ cup olive oil
1 clove garlic, crushed
Tabasco to taste
Salt and freshly ground black pepper
   to taste
2 (12-ounce) cans vegetable juice
   cocktail
⅓ cup chopped fresh cilantro
2 Florida lobster tails, steamed

Blanch the tomatoes in a saucepan of boiling water for 15 seconds. Transfer to a bowl of ice water to cool. Peel, seed, and chop the tomatoes. Coarsely chop the cucumbers, onion, celery, and bell pepper.

Combine the tomatoes with the chopped vegetables in a bowl and mix well. Purée one-fourth of the vegetable mixture in a blender or food processor until smooth. Stir the puréed mixture into the chopped vegetables.

Whisk the vinegar and olive oil in a bowl. Stir in the garlic, Tabasco, salt, and black pepper. Add to the vegetable mixture and mix well. Stir in the vegetable juice cocktail and cilantro. Chill, covered, in the refrigerator.

Remove the meat from the lobster tails and chop. Ladle the vegetable mixture into soup bowls. Add a portion of the lobster meat to each bowl just before serving.

Made in the Shade, Greater Fort Lauderdale, FL

GAZPACHO

1 large (46-ounce) can tomato juice

1 medium onion, finely chopped

2 large ripe tomatoes, peeled and
    chopped

1 green bell pepper, cored, seeded, and
    finely chopped

1 cucumber, peeled, seeded, and diced

2 whole green onions, minced

1 clove garlic, minced

¼ cup chopped fresh parsley

2 tablespoons olive oil

2 tablespoons lime juice

2 tablespoons red wine vinegar

1½ tablespoons lemon juice

1 tablespoon fresh tarragon leaves or 1
    teaspoon dried

1 tablespoon minced fresh basil or 1
    teaspoon dried

1 teaspoon honey

½ teaspoon salt

¼ teaspoon freshly ground black
    pepper

¼ teaspoon ground cumin

Dash of Tabasco

1 whole green onion, sliced, for garnish

In a large bowl, combine all ingredients except the sliced green onion; stir to mix well. Taste and adjust seasoning. Chill at least 2 hours. Serve in soup bowls or mugs; garnish with sliced green onion.

Tampa Treasures, Tampa, FL

L. S. Ayres Chicken Velvet Soup

MAKES 6 TO 8 SERVINGS

12 tablespoons (1½ sticks) butter,
    softened
¼ cup all-purpose flour
1 cup warm milk
6 cups hot chicken stock or broth,
    divided
1 cup warm light cream or half-and-half
1½ cups chopped cooked chicken
¾ teaspoon salt
Freshly ground pepper

Melt the butter in a Dutch oven over low heat. Stir in the flour; cook until smooth and bubbly. Combine the milk, 2 cups of the chicken stock, and the cream; gradually whisk in to the flour mixture. Cook and stir until well blended. Add the remaining 4 cups of stock, the chicken, salt, and pepper. Heat through and serve.

Winners, Indianapolis, IN

Rogue River Salmon Soup

MAKES 8 TO 10 SERVINGS

FISH STOCK:
3 cups clam juice
½ cup white wine
1 medium onion, chopped
1 bay leaf
2 sprigs parsley
4 peppercorns

SOUP:
1 pound cooked fresh salmon fillet or
    1 (14-ounce) can pink salmon
3 tablespoons butter
1 medium onion, chopped
½ cup finely chopped celery
3 cups fish stock
3 tablespoons all-purpose flour
1 cup whole milk
Salt to taste
¼ teaspoon lemon-pepper seasoning
3 tablespoons cream
Chopped parsley for garnish

Place all the fish stock ingredients in a medium saucepan and mix well. Cook over medium heat for 5 to 10 minutes. Remove from the stove, strain, and set aside.

Mash the cooked salmon with a fork. If using canned salmon, drain and mash in a bowl. Melt the butter in a large heavy saucepan. Add the onion and celery; sauté for 5 minutes or until soft but not brown. Add the strained fish stock and simmer, covered, 5 minutes.

In a small jar with a lid, shake the flour and a little milk together to make a smooth paste. Add the remaining milk and shake until smooth. Stir the milk mixture into the soup to thicken it. Add the salmon; season with the salt and lemon-pepper. Stir in the cream; heat but do not boil. Serve in soup bowls garnished with chopped parsley.

Rogue River Rendezvous, Jackson County, OR

CHICKEN VEGETABLE SOUP

MAKES 8 SERVINGS

1 (3- to 4-pound) chicken, cut up
5 cups water
1 teaspoon salt
½ teaspoon freshly ground pepper
1 medium onion, chopped
2 cups chopped celery
2 cups diced carrots
2-3 cups cooked rice
4 chicken bouillon cubes
1 pound processed cheese (such as
    Velveeta), cubed

Place the chicken pieces in a large stockpot and add the water, salt, pepper, onion, and celery. Bring to a boil, lower the heat, cover, and cook for 1 hour or until the chicken falls off the bone.

Remove the chicken; skin, debone, and chop it and place the meat back in the broth. Add the carrots, rice, and bouillon cubes; cook over low heat for 1½ hours. Add the cheese; heat until the cheese melts. Serve immediately.

The Junior League of San Angelo Cookbook, San Angelo, TX

CORN CHOWDER

MAKES 4 TO 6 SERVINGS

4 slices bacon
1 cup chopped onion
2 cups pared and diced potatoes
2½ cups water, divided
1 teaspoon salt
¼ teaspoon freshly ground pepper
2 (16-ounce) cans whole-kernel corn
    or 2 cups cooked fresh corn
1½ cups milk
¼ cup all-purpose flour
Paprika

Cook the bacon in a skillet until crisp; remove from the pan and set aside. Sauté the onion in bacon drippings for 5 to 8 minutes or until soft. Add the potatoes, 2 cups of the water, the salt, and pepper. Simmer, covered, 15 minutes or until the potatoes are tender. Stir in the corn with its liquid and the milk.

Blend the flour with the remaining ½ cup water until smooth, then stir into the chowder. Cook, stirring constantly, over medium heat until it thickens and heats thoroughly. Serve sprinkled with crumbled bacon and paprika.

Treasures of the Smokies, Johnson City, TN

ITALIAN WEDDING SOUP

MAKES 16 SERVINGS

2 whole chicken breasts with skin and
  bone
4 quarts water
3 cups chopped celery
1 medium onion, chopped, plus ¼ cup
  minced onion
⅔ cup chopped fresh parsley, divided
Freshly ground pepper to taste
4 chicken bouillon cubes
1 small head escarole
1 pound lean ground beef
2 large eggs
⅔ cup grated Romano cheese, divided
¾ teaspoon salt
¾ cup bread crumbs
½ cup pastina or other small pasta

Rinse the chicken. Place in a stockpot with the water, celery, the chopped onion, ⅓ cup of the parsley, pepper, and bouillon cubes. Bring to a boil, lower the heat, and simmer until the chicken is barely cooked through, about 10 minutes. Remove the chicken to a platter. Chop the chicken, discarding skin and bones. Return the meat to the stockpot.

Bring the escarole and enough water to cover to a boil in a large saucepan. Boil for 7 minutes; drain. Chop the escarole. Stir into the chicken mixture.

Make meatballs: Combine the ground beef, remaining ⅓ cup of parsley, 1 beaten egg, ⅓ cup of the Romano cheese, the ¼ cup of minced onion, salt, and bread crumbs in a bowl; mix well. Shape into ½-inch balls.

Bring the chicken mixture to a boil; add the meatballs. Stir in the pastina. Simmer for 20 minutes or until the meatballs are cooked through, stirring occasionally.

Bring the soup to a boil just before serving. Stir in 1 beaten egg and the remaining ⅓ cup of Romano cheese. Ladle into soup bowls. Serve immediately.

The Best of Wheeling, Wheeling, WV

CHEESY CHOWDER

MAKES 4 TO 8 SERVINGS

1 cup chopped onion
½ cup chopped carrot
½ cup chopped celery
2 tablespoons butter
1½ teaspoons paprika
3 cups chicken broth
6 ounces Cheddar cheese, grated
   (1½ cups)
3 ounces Swiss cheese, shredded
   (¾ cup)
½ cup light cream
⅓ cup all-purpose flour
1 cup milk
½ teaspoon Worcestershire sauce
⅛ teaspoon freshly ground pepper
Grated Parmesan cheese

In a heavy saucepan, sauté the onion, carrot, and celery in the butter for 5 minutes. Blend in the paprika. Add the chicken broth. Heat to boiling, reduce heat, and simmer, covered, for 10 minutes. Add the cheeses, stirring until melted. Add the cream. Blend the flour with the milk in a small bowl, and add to the chowder. Cook and stir until slightly thickened. Add the Worcestershire sauce and pepper. Ladle into soup bowls. Sprinkle with the Parmesan cheese.

Bound to Please, Boise, ID

IDAHO-IOWA CORN AND POTATO CHOWDER

MAKES 6 TO 8 SERVINGS

3 slices bacon, diced
1 pound skinless, boneless chicken
   breasts
¾ cup chopped onion
¾ cup chopped celery
4 cups whole-kernel corn, divided
4 cups chicken broth, divided
2 cups pared and cubed potatoes
Salt to taste
1 cup heavy cream
2 tablespoons chopped parsley
Freshly ground pepper to taste

Brown the bacon until crisp in a heavy saucepan. Remove the bacon to a paper towel and pour off all but 2 tablespoons of drippings. Cut the chicken into cubes. Add the chicken, onion, and celery to the drippings in the saucepan. Cook for 10 to 15 minutes or until the chicken and vegetables are tender, stirring constantly.

Combine 2 cups of the corn and 1 cup of the chicken broth in a blender container; process until smooth. Add the puréed corn, the remaining broth, the remaining corn, the potatoes, and salt to the chicken mixture. Bring to a boil and reduce the heat. Simmer 30 minutes or until the potatoes are tender. Stir in the cream and the parsley. Simmer 5 minutes. Add the bacon, salt, and pepper. Ladle into soup bowls.

Beyond Burlap: Idaho's Famous Potato Recipes, Boise, ID

HEARTY CLAM CHOWDER

MAKES 4 SERVINGS

6 slices bacon
2-3 carrots, sliced
2 stalks celery, chopped fine
1 small onion, chopped fine
½ small green bell pepper, chopped
1 clove garlic, minced
1¼ pounds red-skin potatoes
2 (8-ounce) bottles clam juice
6 (4-ounce) cans clams, chopped with
* juice*
1 pint heavy cream
1 pint half-and-half
½ teaspoon Worcestershire sauce
½ teaspoon Tabasco
1 bay leaf
½ teaspoon thyme
Salt to taste
¼ teaspoon freshly ground pepper

Chop the bacon and cook in a skillet until crisp. Remove the bacon to drain on paper towels and pour off all but 2 tablespoons of drippings. Sauté the carrots, celery, onion, green pepper, and garlic in the drippings until the onion is transparent.

Slice the potatoes, leaving on the skins. In a large saucepan, simmer the sliced potatoes in clam juice for about 15 minutes. Add the sautéed vegetables, the chopped clams, cream, half-and-half, and the seasonings. Heat until simmering. Ladle into soup bowls and serve.

Udderly Delicious, Racine, WI

CHICKEN VEGETABLE GUMBO, SOUTH TEXAS STYLE

MAKES 12 SERVINGS

2 whole chickens, about 3 pounds
    each, cut into serving pieces
½ head cabbage, shredded
3 large onions, chopped
1 (16-ounce) can peeled tomatoes or 1
    pound fresh
1 stalk celery, chopped
1 pound carrots, peeled and sliced
1 bunch cilantro, chopped
1 (16-ounce) package frozen corn
1 (16-ounce) package frozen cut green
    beans
4 tablespoons ground black pepper
4 tablespoons garlic powder or 2 cloves
    garlic, chopped
Texjoy seasoning to taste (optional)
2 tablespoons oregano
1 cup raw rice

Place the chicken pieces in 1 gallon of water in a large stockpot. Bring to a boil, lower the heat, and simmer about 1 hour or until tender. Skim off foam as it accumulates. Remove the chicken, debone, and set aside.

Add the cabbage and the remaining ingredients, except rice, to the broth; cook for 30 to 60 minutes. Chop the chicken and add to the stockpot. Stir in the rice. Bring to a boil. Simmer until rice is cooked.

Some Like It Hot, McAllen, TX

TURKEY GUMBO

MAKES 4 SERVINGS

1 turkey carcass
¼ cup all-purpose flour
¼ cup bacon drippings
1 cup chopped green onions
1 cup chopped celery
¼ cup chopped parsley
2-3 bay leaves
½ teaspoon thyme
1 cup chopped spicy smoked sausage
3 cups turkey meat from carcass
Salt and freshly ground pepper to
   taste
1 pint shucked oysters and their liquid
1 tablespoon gumbo filé
2 cups cooked rice

Break up the turkey carcass and place in a soup kettle. Cover with at least 8 cups of water and boil gently for about 1 hour, or until the meat is easily removed from the bone. Remove the carcass and pick the meat off the bones. Strain the broth; if necessary, boil to reduce to 6 cups. Set aside.

To make a roux, brown the flour in bacon drippings until the mixture is a rich dark brown. (Be careful not to let it burn.) Add the onions, celery, and parsley; sauté 5 minutes. Slowly add the reserved broth to the roux; add the bay leaves, thyme, sausage, and turkey meat. Season with salt and pepper to taste. Cook over low heat for 1½ to 2 hours, adding oysters during the last 5 minutes of cooking. Add the filé just before serving, being careful not to let the mixture boil once it has been added. Remove the bay leaves and serve the gumbo over hot rice. If planning to freeze, do not add oysters and filé until reheating to serve.

Plantation Cookbook, New Orleans, LA

PEGGY'S CHILI

MAKES 4 SERVINGS

1 pound lean ground beef
¼ cup bacon drippings
½ teaspoon salt
½ teaspoon freshly ground black
   pepper
2 tablespoons chili powder
1 tablespoon all-purpose flour
1 teaspoon unsweetened cocoa powder
1 teaspoon sugar
1 medium green bell pepper, chopped
1 medium onion, chopped
2 cloves garlic, chopped
1 (6-ounce) can tomato paste
Water

Brown the meat in the bacon drippings in a large skillet, stirring to break up lumps. Add the salt, pepper, chili powder, flour, cocoa, and sugar; mix well over low heat. Add the bell pepper, onion, and garlic. Cook until the onion is transparent. Add the tomato paste; mix thoroughly. Add enough water to cover the mixture in the pan. Simmer 45 minutes.

Fiesta, Corpus Christi, TX

DOVE GUMBO

30 doves (squab), cleaned
3 onions, quartered, divided
4 stalks celery, quartered, divided
2 teaspoons peppercorns
1 bay leaf
⅔ cup all-purpose flour
½ cup vegetable oil
2 cloves garlic, minced
2 quarts chicken or beef broth,
    approximately
1 (14-ounce) can diced tomatoes
4 green onions, chopped
½ teaspoon ground red pepper
    (cayenne)
2 tablespoons chopped parsley
1 (12-ounce) can beer
Salt to taste
2 cups okra, fresh or frozen
Hot cooked rice
Filé powder (optional)

In a large stockpot, cover the doves with water seasoned with 1 quartered onion, 2 stalks celery with leaves, the peppercorns, and the bay leaf. Bring to a boil, reduce the heat, and simmer, skimming frequently, until the doves are tender, about 1 hour. Remove the doves and debone. Strain the broth, reserving the liquid.

Make a roux by sautéing the flour in the oil until coffee colored, stirring constantly. (Do not let it burn.) Add the remaining 2 quartered onions and the remaining celery to the roux and cook until the onion is transparent.

Add enough chicken broth to the reserved liquid to make 1 gallon. Gradually add the roux to the broth in small batches, stirring constantly to avoid lumps. Add the dove meat, tomatoes, green onions, cayenne, parsley, beer, and salt. Simmer 3 hours. Add the okra during the last hour. Serve over the hot rice. Sprinkle with filé powder.

¡Viva! Tradiciones, Corpus Christi, TX

SEAFOOD GUMBO

MAKES 8 SERVINGS

ROUX:
1 cup peanut oil
2 cups all-purpose flour

GUMBO:
3-4 medium onions, chopped fine
7 stalks celery, chopped fine
Garlic to taste (fresh or minced)
3-4 tablespoons butter
*4 (10-ounce) cans chicken stock or 5
    cups fresh*
*1 pound fresh okra, chopped, or 1 (10-
    ounce) package frozen chopped okra*
2 (28-ounce) cans tomatoes, undrained
*Salt, Tabasco, and Worcestershire sauce
    to taste*
2 pounds peeled raw shrimp
*2 pounds crabmeat, picked over to
    remove bits of cartilage*
Crab claws or bodies, if available
2 tablespoons filé
Hot steamed rice

Make the roux: Pour the oil into a hot skillet. When oil is hot, pour the flour into it, stirring so it won't be lumpy. Reduce the heat to medium-low to medium and brown the flour very slowly. Stir constantly; do not burn or let stick. If black specks appear, the roux is burned and you must start over. A dark roux will take a pretty good while, approximately 1 hour, so be patient. You can tell when it's done by the odor and by the dark brown color.

For the gumbo: Sauté the onions, celery, and garlic in the butter in a large skillet until soft, about 8 minutes. Add to the roux and let simmer on the back of the stove while heating the stock. Heat the stock in a large soup pot. Slowly add the roux and stir until smooth. Add the okra, tomatoes, salt, Tabasco, and Worcestershire sauce; simmer about 3 hours. Add the shrimp, crabmeat, and crab bodies. Cook about 30 minutes. Remove from the heat, stir in the filé, and serve in large bowls over rice.

Winning Seasons, Tuscaloosa, AL

SEATTLE SEAFOOD STEW

MAKES 6 SERVINGS

½ cup olive oil

3 medium cloves garlic, minced

1 cup each *finely chopped onion,
    celery, and fennel bulb*

4 cups chicken stock

2 cups dry white wine

1 cup clam juice

2 (15-ounce) cans diced tomatoes,
    undrained

1 tablespoon tomato paste

1 teaspoon freshly ground pepper

1 teaspoon each *saffron threads and
    fennel seed, crushed*

½ teaspoon dried thyme

¼ teaspoon dried red pepper flakes,
    crushed

1 pound clams

1 pound mussels

1 pound large shrimp

1 pound firm fish (cod, snapper, sea
    bass)

1 tablespoon Pernod (optional)

½ cup minced parsley

In a heavy 8-quart pot, combine the oil, garlic, onion, celery, and fennel. Sauté 7 minutes or until softened. Add the chicken stock, wine, clam juice, tomatoes, tomato paste, pepper, saffron, fennel seed, thyme, and red pepper flakes. Simmer 45 minutes.

Scrub the clams and, if necessary, debeard the mussels. Discard any open shells that do not close when tapped. Shell and devein the shrimp. Cut the fish into 1-inch pieces.

In a heavy saucepan, place the clams in 2 inches of water. Cover and cook over high heat 5 minutes. Add the mussels to the pan; cook, covered, 3 minutes more. Discard any unopened shells. Add the clams and mussels to the large pot. Strain the cooking liquid and add to the pot along with the shrimp, fish, Pernod, and parsley. Simmer 5 minutes longer or until the shrimp turn pink and the fish is opaque. Serve immediately.

Simply Classic Cookbook, Seattle, WA

SHRIMP AND SAUSAGE JAMBALAYA

MAKES 10 SERVINGS

1 pound smoked sausage, thinly sliced
3 tablespoons olive oil
⅔ cup chopped green bell pepper
2 cloves garlic, minced
¾ cup chopped fresh parsley
1 cup chopped celery
2 (14-ounce) cans tomatoes, chopped,
    undrained
2 cups chicken broth
1 cup chopped green onions
1½ teaspoons dried thyme
2 bay leaves
2 teaspoons dried oregano
1 tablespoon Creole seasoning
½ teaspoon salt
¼ teaspoon ground red pepper
    (cayenne)
¼ teaspoon freshly ground black
    pepper
2 cups uncooked long-grain converted
    rice
3 pounds raw shrimp, peeled

Sauté the sausage in 1 tablespoon of the oil in a 4-quart saucepan. Remove with a slotted spoon and reserve. Add the remaining oil, the bell pepper, garlic, parsley, and celery and sauté 5 minutes. Add the tomatoes with their juices, chicken broth, green onions, thyme, bay leaves, oregano, Creole seasoning, salt, cayenne pepper, and black pepper, keeping the pot over low heat.

Wash and rinse the rice 3 times and add to the saucepan mixture. Stir in the sausage and cover. Cook over low heat, stirring occasionally, for 30 minutes or until most of the liquid is absorbed. Add the shrimp and cook until pink.

Preheat the oven to 350F. Transfer the mixture to an oblong baking dish. Bake uncovered for about 25 minutes.

Jambalaya, New Orleans, LA

TRADITIONAL CINCINNATI CHILI

MAKES 6 TO 8 SERVINGS

2 pounds ground beef
4 medium-size onions, minced
1 clove garlic, minced, or 1 teaspoon
 garlic powder
1 (8-ounce) can tomato sauce
4 cups water
2 dashes Worcestershire sauce
1½ tablespoons vinegar
Salt and freshly ground black pepper
 to taste
¼ cup chili powder
1 teaspoon ground red pepper (cayenne)
1 teaspoon ground cinnamon
5 bay leaves
35 whole allspice
1 (16-ounce) can kidney beans

In a Dutch oven, brown the beef with the onion and garlic, stirring to crumble. Drain off excess fat. Stir in the tomato sauce, water, Worcestershire sauce, vinegar, salt, black pepper, chili powder, red pepper, and cinnamon. Enclose the bay leaves and allspice in a cheesecloth bag; secure tightly, and add to the mixture. Bring to a boil, stirring frequently. Add the beans, reduce the heat, and simmer, covered, 3 hours. Remove the cheesecloth bag and ladle the chili into individual bowls. Serve hot.

I'll Cook When Pigs Fly, Cincinnati, OH

BLACK BEAN CHICKEN CHILI

MAKES 8 SERVINGS

2 small skinless, boneless chicken breast
 halves cut into 1-inch pieces
1 cup chopped onion
1 cup chopped green bell pepper
2 cloves garlic, minced
2 tablespoons skimmed broth or bouillon
2 (28-ounce) cans stewed tomatoes
2 (15-ounce) cans black beans, rinsed
 and drained
1 teaspoon salt
½ teaspoon hot sauce
2 cups medium salsa
2 tablespoons chili powder
1 teaspoon ground cumin
Shredded Cheddar or Jack cheese
 (optional)

Simmer the chicken, onion, green pepper, and garlic in the 2 tablespoons of broth in a stockpot until the chicken is cooked through. Add the tomatoes, black beans, salt, hot sauce, salsa, chili powder, and cumin; mix well. Simmer 30 to 45 minutes. Serve with shredded cheese, if desired.

Seaboard to Sideboard, Wilmington, NC

SONORAN CHICKEN CHILI

1 tablespoon olive oil
½ cup chopped shallots
3 cloves garlic, minced
2 (14-ounce) cans chopped tomatoes
    with garlic, oregano, and basil
1 (14-ounce) can whole tomatoes,
    chopped
1 (14-ounce) can no-salt-added
    chicken broth
1 (4-ounce) can chopped green chiles
½ teaspoon oregano
½ teaspoon ground coriander
¼ teaspoon ground cumin
4 cups chopped cooked chicken
1-2 (16-ounce) cans white kidney or
    navy beans, drained
3 tablespoons freshly squeezed lime
    juice
¼ teaspoon freshly ground pepper
Shredded Cheddar cheese for garnish

Heat the olive oil in a large saucepan over medium-high heat. Add the shallots and garlic. Sauté about 5 minutes or until the shallots are soft. Add the seasoned tomatoes, chopped tomatoes, broth, chiles, oregano, coriander, and cumin. Bring to a boil. Reduce the heat; simmer for 20 minutes.

Add the chicken and beans; mix well. Cook until heated through. Stir in the lime juice and pepper. Ladle into bowls and garnish with cheese.

Reflections Under the Sun, Phoenix, AZ

WHITE CHICKEN CHILI

MAKES 6 SERVINGS

1 pound dried white navy beans
4 skinless, boneless chicken breast
   halves
1 (14-ounce) can chicken broth
1 teaspoon salt
½ medium onion, chopped
2 cloves garlic, minced
1 tablespoon vegetable oil
1 (4-ounce) can chopped green chiles
2 teaspoons each ground cumin, dried
   oregano, and ground coriander
Pinch each of ground cloves and
   ground red pepper (cayenne)
½ cup shredded Monterey Jack cheese
   (2 ounces)
4 green onions, thinly sliced

Rinse and sort the beans. Combine the beans with enough water to cover by 1 to 2 inches in a large stockpot. Let soak for 8 to 10 hours; drain.

Place the chicken in a saucepan with enough cold water to cover. Bring to a boil; reduce the heat. Simmer, covered, for 10 to 15 minutes or until chicken is tender; drain, reserving broth. Cool the chicken slightly; cut into bite-size pieces. Chill in the refrigerator.

Add enough canned chicken broth to the reserved broth to measure 6 cups. Combine the 6 cups of broth, the beans, salt, and half the onion and garlic in a large stockpot. Simmer, covered, for 1½ to 2 hours or until the beans are tender, stirring occasionally and adding additional broth if needed.

Sauté the remaining onion and garlic in the oil in a small skillet until tender, about 5 minutes. Add the green chiles, cumin, oregano, coriander, cloves, and cayenne; mix well. Cook for 20 minutes over low heat, stirring frequently. Add to the bean mixture. Stir in the chopped chicken. Heat until piping hot. Spoon into bowls. Top with the cheese and green onions.

Dining in the Smoky Mountain Mist, Knoxville, TN

SNOWY DAY WHITE CHILI

MAKES 8 SERVINGS

1 pound dried Great Northern beans
2 pounds skinless, boneless chicken breasts
2 medium onions, chopped
1 tablespoon olive oil
4 cloves garlic, minced
2 (4-ounce) cans chopped green chiles
2 teaspoons ground cumin
1½ teaspoons dried oregano
¼ teaspoon ground cloves
¼ teaspoon ground red pepper (cayenne)
6 cups chicken broth
2 cups shredded Monterey Jack cheese
   (8 ounces)
Salt and freshly ground black pepper
   to taste
Sour cream, salsa, chopped fresh
   cilantro (for garnish)

Pick through the beans and rinse them. Soak the beans according to the package directions; drain well.

Place the chicken in a large Dutch oven and cover with boiling water; simmer 15 minutes or until tender. Drain and let cool. Cut the chicken into cubes.

Sauté the onion in hot oil in the Dutch oven over medium heat for 10 minutes; add the garlic, chiles, cumin, oregano, cloves, and cayenne, and cook for 2 minutes. Add the beans and broth; bring to a boil. Reduce the heat, and simmer, stirring occasionally, 2 hours or until the beans are tender. Add the chicken and cheese; cook, stirring constantly, until the chili is thoroughly heated and cheese is melted. Season with the salt and black pepper. Serve immediately with desired toppings.

Victorian Thymes & Pleasures, Williamsport, PA

Vegetables and Side Dishes

MIDWEST

Chances are, when people hear the line "O beautiful for spacious skies, for amber waves of grain" from *America the Beautiful,* they picture the windswept grain fields of the Midwest. Blessed with rich fertile soil, the Midwest grows an abundance of wheat, barley, oats, rye, soy, and corn and can rightfully claim the title America's Breadbasket.

Covering a wide swath of land from Illinois to Missouri, the Corn Belt produces more than 80 percent of the nation's corn. Corn is also the main food source for the area's livestock, another staple of the Midwesterner's diet. It is not surprising that corn is featured in many of the region's recipes, including freshly home-baked cornbread and muffins, delicate corn soufflés like those served in Des Moines' finest restaurants, or corn on the cob simply grilled and slathered with sweet dairy butter as eaten at county fairs. Midwesterners know that on the farm you wait until the water has reached the boil before running out to the field to pick the corn. That way, the sugar in the plump kernels has only moments to begin to turn starchy.

But the Midwest produces more than just grain and corn. In fact, "the land of milk and honey" best describes the rich abundance of the Midwest region. Hog and chicken farms flourish in rural Illinois. Tens of thousands of dairy cows graze on Wisconsin's green pasture lands, earning that state the title of America's dairyland and its football fans the sobriquet "cheese heads." It is easy to see why meat and dairy foods feature prominently in the Midwesterners' diet. But not to be overlooked are the region's fruits: Michigan's juicy plums, sweet cherries, and blueberries and Wisconsin's crisp apples and luscious raspberries and strawberries.

The Midwest's early settlers combined their culinary traditions from the old country with the bounty of their new homeland. The Germans who settled in Wisconsin celebrated Oktoberfest and introduced hearty sausages, the wursts, to be washed down with cold dark beer, another grain product. The Polish who settled in Chicago introduced pierogi, plump dumplings stuffed with meat and cheese, and *placki kartolane,* a light potato pancake. The Norwegians who settled in Minnesota brought with them their beloved rice porridge pancakes eaten with sweet preserved fruit jams. In the copper mines of Michigan's Upper Peninsula, pasties are a favorite—a tradition of meat pies that dates back 800 years to Cornwall, England, where miners enjoyed them for lunch. And the American Indians, who called the area home long before the settlers arrived, have shared their recipes for authentic roasted corn soup and wholesome honey acorn bread.

It is through community cookbooks that treasured heirloom recipes and food traditions are passed down from generation to generation, preserving the fiber of American regional cooking. The Midwest recognizes the importance of community cookbooks in America, with the largest cookbook collection housed at the Lilly Library in Indianapolis. The collection includes more than 400 books on cookery including some dating back to the 1700s. A relaxed browse reveals that traditions hold strong over the centuries.

—Lucio Guerrero, *The Chicago Sun-Times*
Chicago, IL

REGATTA DINNER

On a summer day, on the shores of Lake Michigan, residents and visitors alike watch boats compete in a sailing regatta. Warm breezes off the lake gently rustle your hair and your napkin as you dine on some of your favorite foods, especially those from the water.

Submitted by *Udderly Delicious,* Racine, WI

CRAB MUFFINS 18

HEARTY CLAM CHOWDER 120

CAESAR SALAD 70

SEAFOOD TETRAZZINI 232

SANDCAKE WITH RASPBERRY SAUCE 319

PARTY TIME FRUIT PUNCH 49

COMPANY DINNER PARTY

Nothing says more about you than the meals you prepare and serve at home. With today's busy lifestyles, entertaining at home becomes more and more difficult. For those who still like to invite family and friends for dinner, creative recipes help make that plan a reality. And your friends will adore you for inviting them.

ICY PRAWNS WITH TRIO OF CELESTIAL DIPPING SAUCES   32

ITALIAN TORTA   9

BEEF WELLINGTON   182

GREEN BEANS IN YELLOW PEPPER BUTTER   150

HOT CURRIED FRUIT   172

ROBIN K'S CHOCOLATE MOUSSE WITH RASPBERRY SAUCE   363

SALLY'S WINE COOLER   51

RECIPE FOR A BETTER COMMUNITY

JUNIOR LEAGUE OF SPRINGFIELD, MISSOURI COMMUNITY PROJECT:

ABC's & 123's

More than 600 women and children are housed at the Family Violence Center, a "safe haven" for women and children victims of domestic violence. The Junior League supports ABC's & 123's, providing an elementary classroom, salary for a teacher, and supplies. League members serve as volunteer tutors to assist children with homework. The program was launched in 1997, and the League still provides partial funding.

The cookbooks that made it happen: $200,000 from the sales of *Sassafras!, The Ozarks' Cookbook,* and *Women Who Can Dish It Out* was allotted to fund this project.

Did you know? The Junior League of Springfield features their cookbooks in an annual holiday cooking extravaganza called "Celebrate the Season." This past year, they netted more than $10,000 from this one evening.

FRESH TOMATO TART

Pastry for a 1-crust pie, unbaked
3 large ripe tomatoes
Seasoned salt and freshly ground
  pepper to taste
1 tablespoon chopped fresh basil or 1
  teaspoon dried
½ cup mayonnaise
½ cup freshly grated Parmesan cheese
⅛ teaspoon garlic powder
¼ cup cracker crumbs

To prepare the crust, preheat the oven to 400F. Line a 10-inch tart pan with the pastry. Prick the sides and bottom thoroughly with a fork and bake until golden brown, about 20 minutes. Remove to a rack; maintain the oven heat.

Slice the tomatoes and place in layers in the tart shell. Sprinkle with the seasoned salt, pepper, and basil. Combine the mayonnaise, Parmesan cheese, and garlic powder in a small bowl. Spread the mixture over the tomatoes (it will not completely cover them). Sprinkle with the cracker crumbs. Bake the tart for 15 minutes. Serve warm or cold.

Thymes Remembered, Tallahassee, Fl

TOMATOES BERGERETTE

MAKES 8 SERVINGS

8 firm ripe tomatoes
½ teaspoon salt
1 teaspoon Dijon mustard
3 green onions, minced
2 tablespoons finely chopped green bell
    pepper
2 tablespoons minced parsley
2 tablespoons finely chopped pimiento
    (optional)
4 anchovy fillets, minced
1½ cups firm cooked rice
⅓ cup heavy cream, whipped
Vinaigrette (see below)
Parsley sprigs
Ripe olives

Slice the tops off the tomatoes. Remove the pulp and reserve, discarding seeds and juice. Sprinkle shells with salt; invert to drain.

Mix the tomato pulp with the mustard, onions, green pepper, parsley, pimiento, anchovies, and rice. Fold in the whipped cream.

To serve, spoon 1 teaspoon of the vinaigrette into each shell and fill with rice mixture. Garnish with parsley and ripe olives.

VINAIGRETTE:

½ cup olive oil
3 tablespoons vinegar
½ teaspoon salt
⅛ teaspoon freshly ground black
    pepper
2 cloves garlic, minced

Combine all the ingredients in a small bowl; mix well.

Plain and Fancy, Richardson, TX

EGGPLANT PASTA SAUCE

MAKES 2 QUARTS

2-3 cloves garlic, minced
⅓ cup olive oil
1 medium (1-pound) eggplant,
    unpeeled and chopped
2 green bell peppers, seeded and diced
3 cups fresh or canned peeled and
    chopped tomatoes
¾ cup sliced black olives
4 tablespoons capers
1 teaspoon crushed oregano
½ teaspoon crushed basil
12 ounces tomato paste
2 cups dry white wine
Salt and freshly ground pepper to
    taste

Sauté the garlic in the oil in a large skillet for 1 to 2 minutes, until golden. Add the eggplant, bell pepper, tomatoes, olives, and capers; stir well. Stir in the oregano, basil, tomato paste, wine, salt, and pepper. Cover and simmer for 1 hour, stirring occasionally. Add more white wine if necessary.

The refrigerated sauce will keep three weeks. May be served cold as a vegetable or hot over pasta.

Some Like It Hot, McAllen, TX

EGGPLANT-TOMATO BAKE

MAKES 6 TO 8 SERVINGS

1 large eggplant (1¼ pounds)
4 teaspoons salt, divided
2 large eggs, beaten
2 tablespoons butter, melted
¼ teaspoon freshly ground pepper
½ teaspoon dried oregano
½ teaspoon dried basil
1 clove garlic, minced, or ¼ teaspoon
    garlic powder
½ cup fine dry bread crumbs
1 small onion, chopped
4 ounces Cheddar cheese, grated and
    divided
2 large ripe tomatoes, sliced
¼ cup grated Parmesan cheese
Paprika

Preheat the oven to 350F.

Peel and slice the eggplant. Place in a saucepan; add water to cover and 2 teaspoons of the salt. Cook, covered, for 10 minutes. Drain and mash in a medium bowl. Stir in the eggs, butter, remaining 2 teaspoons of salt, the pepper, oregano, basil, garlic, bread crumbs, onion, and half the Cheddar cheese.

Grease a 2-quart casserole and arrange half the tomato slices on the bottom. Add the eggplant mixture and top with the remaining tomato slices. Sprinkle evenly with the remaining Cheddar cheese and the Parmesan cheese. Sprinkle with the paprika. Bake for 1 hour.

Settings . . . From Our Past to Your Presentation, Philadelphia, PA

Mushroom Soufflé

MAKES 4 SERVINGS

1 pound mushrooms, cleaned and
    chopped fine
1 tablespoon minced onion
6 tablespoons butter, divided
6 tablespoons all-purpose flour
2 cups scalded milk
½ cup grated sharp cheese
Dash of Tabasco
¼ teaspoon thyme
½ teaspoon marjoram
Salt and freshly ground pepper
6 large eggs, separated
½ cup chopped almonds, toasted

Combine the mushrooms, onion, and 3 tablespoons of the butter in a medium saucepan. Cook over low heat until soft. Cover and let steam for 5 minutes. Push the mushroom-onion mixture to one side of the pan. To the liquid in the pan add the remaining 3 tablespoons of butter; blend in the flour. Add the hot milk gradually, stirring until thick and well blended. Add the grated cheese, Tabasco, and herbs. Season lightly with salt and pepper. Cool but do not chill.

One hour before serving, preheat the oven to 325F. Beat the egg yolks until thick in a small bowl. Stir into the mushroom mixture. Using clean beaters and a clean bowl, beat the egg whites with an electric mixer until stiff. Fold into the mushroom mixture carefully. Pour the mixture into a 1½-quart buttered casserole dish; sprinkle with almonds. Bake 50 to 60 minutes. Serve at once.

Smoky Mountain Magic, Johnson City, TN

Basil Mushrooms

MAKES 12 SERVINGS

1 small onion, minced
2 cloves garlic, minced
8 tablespoons (1 stick) butter
1 pound fresh mushrooms, cleaned
    and trimmed
¼ cup chopped fresh basil, or 1
    teaspoon dried
1 teaspoon oregano
½ teaspoon thyme
½ teaspoon Tabasco
2 tablespoons fresh lime juice
¼ cup dry sherry
½ teaspoon salt

Sauté the onion and garlic in the butter in a large skillet over low heat for 6 to 8 minutes or until tender. Add the mushrooms; stir to coat them well. Add the basil, oregano, thyme, Tabasco, lime juice, sherry, and salt; mix well. Simmer, covered, until most of the liquid has evaporated. Serve as an appetizer or an accompaniment to beef or veal.

Sweet Home Alabama, Huntsville, AL

CAULIFLOWER AND BROCCOLI SPECIAL

MAKES 8 SERVINGS

1 large head cauliflower, cut into
   florets
Florets from 1 large head broccoli
3 tablespoons grated Parmesan cheese
2 tablespoons butter
¼ cup sour cream
Salt and freshly ground pepper to
   taste
⅓ cup fine dry bread crumbs

Preheat the oven to 350F.

Boil the cauliflower in a large pot of salted water for 5 minutes. Remove with a slotted spoon to a colander. Boil the broccoli in the same water for 5 minutes; drain.

Place the cauliflower in a 2-quart baking dish. Sprinkle with the Parmesan cheese.

Purée the broccoli in a blender with the butter and sour cream. Season the broccoli mixture with salt and pepper and spoon over the cauliflower. Top with the bread crumbs. Bake 20 minutes.

¡Viva! Tradiciones, Corpus Christi, TX

BROCCOLI WITH A TWIST

MAKES 6 SERVINGS

1½ cups mayonnaise or salad dressing
¾ cup sugar
2 tablespoons cider vinegar
1 tablespoon lemon juice
5 cups broccoli florets
½ cup raisins
½ cup chopped pecans, toasted
½ cup chopped red onion
12 slices bacon, cooked crisp and
   crumbled

In a small bowl, combine the mayonnaise, sugar, vinegar, and lemon juice. Mix well. Cover and chill at least 2 hours.

Place the broccoli florets in a large bowl. Add the raisins, pecans, onion, and bacon. Stir gently to mix. Add the mayonnaise mixture; toss lightly to coat. Serve immediately or cover and chill until serving time.

Heart & Soul, Memphis, TN

PUMPKIN SHELL CASSEROLE

MAKES 4 TO 6 SERVINGS

1 small pumpkin, 7 inches in
diameter
2 cups peeled chopped apples
1 cup raisins
1 cup chopped pecans
⅓ cup sugar
1 teaspoon lemon juice
¼ teaspoon grated nutmeg
¼ teaspoon ground cinnamon
Sour cream (optional)

Preheat the oven to 350F. Wash the pumpkin; cut a lid, and scrape out the seeds. Combine the remaining ingredients except the sour cream in a mixing bowl; toss gently. Spoon the mixture into the pumpkin shell. Replace the lid and place the pumpkin on a lightly greased cookie sheet. Bake 1 hour and 15 minutes. Remove from the oven. To serve, spoon portions of pumpkin and filling from the shell and top with sour cream, if desired. This may be served hot or cold.

Nutbread & Nostalgia, South Bend, IN

ONION CASSEROLE

MAKES 6 SERVINGS

3 large onions, thinly sliced
3 tablespoons butter, melted and
divided
1 roll of round buttery crackers, such
as Ritz
3 tablespoons milk, plus additional as
needed
1 cup shredded sharp Cheddar cheese

Preheat the oven to 350F.

Sauté the onion in 2 tablespoons of the butter in a large skillet until soft but not brown, 6 to 8 minutes. Crush the crackers in a bowl with the 3 tablespoons of milk and remaining tablespoon of melted butter. Layer half the cracker mixture on the bottom of a 2-quart casserole. Layer the onions and then the cheese in the casserole. Top with the rest of the cracker mixture. Sprinkle a few drops of milk over the top. Bake for 20 to 30 minutes or until hot in the center.

First Impressions: Dining with Distinction, Waterloo–Cedar Falls, IA

ORANGE-GLAZED ASPARAGUS

MAKES 6 SERVINGS

2 pounds fresh asparagus
½ cup orange juice
2 teaspoon grated orange zest or ½
    teaspoon crushed dried orange peel
1 tablespoon sugar
1 tablespoon minced fresh ginger
2 teaspoons soy sauce

Trim the asparagus, snapping off the tough bottoms, and place in a covered container. Combine the remaining ingredients and pour over the asparagus. Refrigerate for 2 to 24 hours, turning occasionally.

Preheat the broiler. Drain the asparagus and reserve the marinade. Place the asparagus on a baking sheet. Broil for 5 minutes or until tender, turning several times to prevent burning.

Meanwhile, put the marinade in a small saucepan and bring to a boil. Continue to simmer, uncovered, until the marinade is reduced by half. Transfer the cooked asparagus to a serving dish and top with the marinade.

Gold 'n Delicious, Spokane, WA

LUNCHEON ASPARAGUS

MAKES 4 SERVINGS

3 tablespoons butter
3 tablespoons all-purpose flour
1 cup warm milk
1 cup grated cheese
Salt and freshly ground pepper
1 onion, thinly sliced
1 (3-ounce) can button mushrooms,
    drained
¼ cup sherry, optional
1 (14-ounce) can asparagus spears,
    drained
4 split and toasted English muffins
8 pieces crisp bacon, crumbled

Melt the butter in the top of a double boiler. Add the flour, blend, and cook for several minutes. Add the milk gradually, stirring until thickened. Add the cheese and allow to melt. Season with salt and pepper to taste. Stir in the onion and mushrooms, and add the sherry if desired.

Place the asparagus spears on the toasted muffin halves. Pour the sauce over them and sprinkle with bacon pieces.

Gasparilla Cookbook, Tampa, FL

GLAZED CARROTS

MAKES 4 SERVINGS

1 medium bunch carrots, peeled and
   sliced
8 tablespoons (1 stick) butter
⅓ cup packed light brown sugar
1 teaspoon grated nutmeg
3 tablespoons orange juice
¼ cup honey

Steam the carrots in a saucepan for 5 to 6 minutes, until slightly tender. Sauté them briefly in the butter in a medium skillet; add the sugar, nutmeg, orange juice, and honey. Cook, stirring constantly, until the sugar melts and the carrots are well glazed.

A Southern Collection—Then & Now, Columbus, GA

HEAVENLY CARROTS

MAKES 16 SERVINGS

2 pounds carrots, peeled and sliced
   into circles or cut on the diagonal
1 small green bell pepper, sliced
1 medium onion, sliced
1 (10-ounce) can tomato soup
½ cup salad oil
1 cup sugar
¾ cup vinegar
1 teaspoon prepared mustard
I teaspoon Worcestershire sauce
Salt to taste

Boil carrots in salted water in a medium saucepan until crisp-tender. Drain. Place the cooked carrots, green pepper, and onion in layers in a shallow serving dish. Combine the tomato soup, oil, sugar, vinegar, mustard, Worcestershire sauce, and salt in a medium bowl; mix well. Pour over the carrots. Refrigerate at least overnight.

Cotton Country Collection, 25th Anniversary Edition, Rockford, IL

ORANGE-RAISIN CARROTS

MAKES 4 SERVINGS

1 pound carrots, peeled and sliced
¾ cup water
½ teaspoon salt
2 tablespoons cornstarch
1 cup orange juice
½ cup raisins
1 tablespoon sugar

Combine the carrots, water, and salt in a medium saucepan. Bring to a boil, then reduce the heat. Simmer uncovered until the carrots are crisp-tender. Mix the cornstarch slowly with the orange juice and add to the carrots. Add the raisins and sugar. Cook over medium heat until the sauce has thickened.

Selections, Huntsville, AL

CARROT PURÉE WITH COGNAC

MAKES 4 SERVINGS

1½ pounds carrots (about 10 to 12),
    peeled and chopped
4 tablespoons (½ stick) butter, melted
Dash of salt
¼ teaspoon freshly ground pepper
2 tablespoons heavy cream
2 teaspoons cognac, or to taste

Cook the carrots in boiling water to cover until tender; drain. In a food processor fitted with the metal blade, process a third of the carrots until finely chopped. Repeat two times, adding the remaining carrots. If necessary, stop the processor and scrape down the sides of the workbowl.

Add the butter, salt, and pepper. Process 30 seconds. Add the cream and cognac and process until combined. Taste and adjust seasoning.

Sound Seasonings, Westchester on the Sound, NY

SHRIMP SUCCOTASH

MAKES 4 SERVINGS

½ cup dried baby lima beans

5 cups (or more) water

1 (1-inch-thick) onion slice, plus 1
    small onion, chopped

1 stalk celery with leaves

2 garlic cloves, pressed

1 bay leaf

8 ounces uncooked large shrimp

1 slice bacon

2 cups fresh or thawed frozen corn
    kernels

Salt and freshly ground pepper to
    taste

2 tablespoons chopped chives or green
    onions

Place the beans in a bowl and cover with cold water by 3 inches. Let stand overnight. Drain.

Combine 5 cups of water, the onion slice, celery stalk, garlic, and bay leaf in a medium saucepan. Bring to a boil and boil for 5 minutes. Add the shrimp and simmer for 3 minutes or until the shrimp are pink. Remove the shrimp with tongs to a bowl. Reserve the cooking liquid. Peel, devein, and cut the shrimp into ½-inch pieces. Set aside.

Add the drained beans to the cooking liquid. Cover and simmer for 40 minutes or until the beans are tender and the liquid is reduced to ½ cup. Add more water during cooking if necessary. Remove the bay leaf, onion slice, and celery stalk and discard.

Cook the bacon in a large skillet over medium heat for 5 minutes or until crisp. Remove to paper towels to drain. Crumble the bacon and set aside. Pour off all but 1 teaspoon of the bacon drippings. Add the chopped onion to the skillet and sauté over medium-low heat for 10 minutes or until golden brown. Stir in the corn and the beans with their cooking liquid. Cook for 8 minutes or until the corn is tender. Stir in the shrimp and bacon and cook for 3 minutes or until heated through. Season with salt and pepper and sprinkle with the chives.

NOTE: The shrimp and beans can be made 1 day ahead. Cover separately and chill.

Crescent City Collection: A Taste of New Orleans, New Orleans, LA

SPANAKOPITA (SPINACH PIE)

MAKES 18 SERVINGS

2 sticks (½ pound) plus 4 tablespoons
    (½ stick) butter
½ cup finely chopped onion
3 (10-ounce) packages frozen chopped
    spinach, thawed
3 large eggs
½ pound feta cheese, crumbled
2 tablespoons chopped parsley
1 teaspoon salt
⅛ teaspoon freshly ground pepper
1 pound frozen phyllo pastry, thawed
    according to package directions

Preheat the oven to 350F.

Melt the 4 tablespoons of butter in a medium saucepan. Sauté the onion in the butter until golden, about 5 minutes. Add the spinach; stir well. Remove from the heat. In a large bowl beat the eggs, cheese, parsley, salt, and pepper; stir in the spinach-onion mixture. Mix well.

Melt the 2 sticks of butter. Remove the phyllo leaves from the package and place on a work surface. Keep the stack of leaves covered with a sheet of waxed paper over which you have placed a damp kitchen towel. Trim the dough into 13 x 9-inch sheets; save the scraps for another use. Brush a 13 x 9-inch baking pan lightly with some of the melted butter. Place 1 phyllo leaf in the pan and brush it with melted butter. Continue with 7 more leaves, brushing each with melted butter. Spread the top leaf evenly with the spinach mixture. Cover with 8 more leaves, brushing each with butter. With a sharp knife, cut through the top pastry layer to form 18 rectangles about 3 x 2 inches. Bake 30 to 35 minutes or until the top crust is puffy and golden. Remove from the oven and slice the rectangles through to the bottom of the pan. Serve hot.

Sugar Beach, The Emerald Beaches, FL

CORN FRITTERS

MAKES 4 SERVINGS

1 cup fresh or canned corn kernels
1 large egg, separated
3 tablespoons all-purpose flour
½ teaspoon salt
¼ teaspoon freshly ground pepper
½ cup vegetable oil, or as needed

Combine the corn, egg yolk, flour, salt, and pepper in a medium bowl. Beat the egg white in a separate bowl until stiff peaks form. Gently fold the egg white into the corn mixture. Heat the oil in a heavy skillet until it is hot but not smoking. Drop 1 tablespoon of batter per fritter into the hot oil. Cook on one side, then turn over. Add more oil to the pan as needed. Drain on paper towels.

Almost Heaven, Huntington, WV

CONFETTI CORN TOSS

MAKES 8 CUPS

2 (15-ounce) cans whole-kernel sweet
   corn, drained
1 (15-ounce) can black beans, rinsed
   and drained
1 (14-ounce) can hearts of palm,
   drained, rinsed, and sliced
2 large ripe tomatoes, seeded and
   chopped
½ cup chopped red onion
⅓ cup minced fresh cilantro
¼ cup vegetable oil
3 tablespoons lime juice
1½ teaspoons chili powder
½ teaspoon ground cumin
Fresh cilantro sprigs (for garnish)
Tortilla chips (for garnish)

Combine the corn, beans, hearts of palm, tomatoes, onion, and cilantro in a large bowl; mix well. Combine the oil, lime juice, chili powder, and cumin in a small bowl; mix well. Drizzle the oil mixture over the vegetable mixture and toss gently. Chill, covered, for 3 hours. Garnish with the cilantro sprigs and tortilla chips.

Beyond Cotton Country, Decatur, AL

HOT HOMINY

MAKES 6 TO 8 SERVINGS

1 large onion, chopped
4 slices bacon, fried until crisp,
   crumbled (reserve drippings)
1 (16-ounce) can tomatoes, chopped,
   with their juice
2 jalapeño peppers, seeded and diced
3 (15-ounce) cans hominy, drained
½ pound sharp Cheddar cheese, grated

Preheat the oven to 350F.

Cook the onion in the bacon drippings for 5 minutes or until limp. Add the tomatoes and jalapeños; mix well. Add the hominy, stirring to combine all the ingredients.

Transfer the mixture to a baking dish and top with the cheese and bacon. Bake about 40 minutes, or until bubbly.

Georgia on My Menu, Cobb-Marietta, GA

LUMBERJACK BEANS

MAKES 10 TO 12 SERVINGS

¾ cup packed dark brown sugar
¼ cup cider vinegar
1 teaspoon dry mustard
1 teaspoon ground ginger
1 teaspoon salt
1 small onion, chopped
6-8 slices bacon, browned and
  crumbled
1 (16-ounce) can butterbeans, drained
1 (16-ounce) can lima beans, drained
1 (16-ounce) can kidney beans,
  drained
1 (16-ounce) can pork and beans

Combine the brown sugar, vinegar, dry mustard, ginger, salt, and chopped onion in a saucepan. Simmer 30 minutes. Preheat the oven to 350F. Mix the bacon, vinegar mixture, and beans together. Place in a baking dish. Bake 1 hour.

NOTE: This can be cooked in a Crock-Pot on low heat for 4 hours.

Almost Heaven, Huntington, WV

GREEN BEANS EXCELSIOR HOUSE

MAKES 8 TO 10 SERVINGS

½ pound bacon strips, cut in half
  crosswise
2 (16-ounce) cans vertical-packed
  green beans
1 cup bean juice
¼ cup packed dark brown sugar
Dash of salt
Dash of freshly ground pepper
½ teaspoon ground allspice

Preheat the oven to 375F. Wrap the half-slices of bacon around 10 to 12 beans; fasten with toothpicks. Place the bundles in a baking dish.

Mix the bean juice and the brown sugar together in a small bowl and pour over the beans. Sprinkle the salt, pepper, and allspice over the bean bundles. Bake 25 minutes (don't overcook). Turn once during cooking and baste.

Cooking Through Rose-Colored Glasses, Tyler, TX

GREEN BEANS WITH BALSAMIC VINEGAR

MAKES 4 TO 6 SERVINGS

1 pound fresh green beans, trimmed
1 tablespoon minced shallot
1½ tablespoons Dijon mustard
1½ tablespoons balsamic vinegar
¼ cup olive oil
½ teaspoon lemon juice
Salt and freshly ground pepper to
    taste
2 tablespoons chopped fresh dill

Cook the green beans in a saucepan of boiling salted water until crisp-tender. Drain and keep warm. Combine the shallot, mustard, vinegar, olive oil, and lemon juice in a small saucepan or microwavable dish. Add salt and pepper to taste. Whisk together. Heat the mixture, then pour over the green beans; toss to coat. Sprinkle with the dill. Serve immediately.

Food for Thought, Birmingham, AL

GREEN BEANS IN YELLOW PEPPER BUTTER

MAKES 8 SERVINGS

6 tablespoons plus 1 tablespoon butter,
    softened
1 medium yellow bell pepper, coarsely
    shredded, plus 1 large yellow bell
    pepper, cut into julienne strips (1
    cup)
¼ cup pine nuts
1 tablespoon lemon juice
Salt
⅛ teaspoon freshly ground pepper
1½ pounds fresh green beans, trimmed

Melt the 1 tablespoon of butter in a small saucepan. Add the shredded bell pepper. Cook over medium-high heat for 5 minutes or until crisp-tender.

Combine the 6 tablespoons softened butter and the pine nuts in a food processor bowl or blender jar. Process until almost smooth. Add the shredded bell pepper, lemon juice, ¼ teaspoon salt, and pepper. Process until almost smooth. Set aside and keep warm.

Pour a small amount of salted water into a medium saucepan. Bring to a boil. Add the beans. Cook, covered, for 12 minutes; remove to a colander with tongs. Add the bell pepper strips to the liquid in the saucepan and cook for 3 minutes; drain.

Put the beans in a serving bowl. Add half the butter mixture; toss to coat. Arrange the pepper strips around the edge. Serve the remaining butter on the side or reserve for another use.

Dining by Design, Pasadena, CA

GREEN BEANS À LA GRECQUE

MAKES 6 SERVINGS

1 pound green beans, washed and
  trimmed, cut into 1-inch lengths
2 tablespoons olive oil
1 medium onion, thinly sliced and
  separated into rings
2 large cloves garlic, minced
¼ cup red wine vinegar
1 tablespoon dried oregano, crumbled
2 large tomatoes, peeled, seeded, and
  coarsely chopped
6 tablespoons crumbled feta cheese
Salt and pepper to taste

Bring a large saucepan of water to a boil. Add the beans and simmer until crisp-tender, 3 to 5 minutes. Drain, refresh in ice water, and drain again. Set the beans aside or, if prepared early in the day, wrap in paper towels and store in a plastic bag in the refrigerator.

Heat the oil in a large skillet over medium heat. Add the onion and garlic. Sauté until soft but not browned, about 5 minutes.

Add the vinegar, oregano, and tomatoes to the onion mixture. Simmer 5 minutes, stirring frequently. Add the green beans and simmer, stirring frequently, until heated through. Remove from the heat.

Sprinkle with the feta cheese and toss gently. Taste first and then season with salt and pepper.

Transfer the beans to a bowl or platter. Serve immediately or cool to room temperature before serving.

NOTE: The beans are best if combined with the dressing within an hour of serving time.

California Sizzles, Pasadena, CA

YBOR CITY VEGETABLE PAELLA

MAKES 8 SERVINGS

⅓ cup olive or vegetable oil

1 medium onion, diced

2 small zucchini (about 6 ounces each), cut into bite-size pieces

½ pound medium mushrooms, cut in half or quartered

1 eggplant (about 1 pound), cut in half lengthwise, each half cut crosswise into ½-inch-thick slices

2 medium-size fresh tomatoes, cut into ¼-inch slices

3 (14-ounce) cans chicken broth

1 (16-ounce) package converted rice

1 (10-ounce) package frozen artichoke hearts, thawed

¼ teaspoon salt

½ teaspoon saffron threads, crushed (optional)

¼ teaspoon freshly ground pepper

1 (16-ounce) can garbanzo beans, drained

1 (3-ounce) jar pimiento-stuffed olives, drained

1 (10-ounce) package frozen peas

Preheat the oven to 350F.

Heat the oil in a 4-quart ovenproof saucepan over medium-high heat; add the onion and cook until tender. Add the zucchini and mushrooms; cook, stirring occasionally, until the vegetables are golden brown. Add the eggplant and 1 tablespoon oil, if needed; cook, stirring frequently, until the eggplant is softened. Stir in the tomatoes, broth, rice, artichoke hearts, salt, saffron, and pepper; heat to boiling over high heat.

Place the saucepan in the oven; bake, uncovered, about 50 minutes or until the rice is tender and the liquid is absorbed. Remove from the oven; stir in the garbanzos, olives, and frozen peas. Return to the oven and heat through, about 15 minutes.

Tampa Treasures, Tampa, FL

MARINATED VEGETABLE MEDLEY

CHOOSE ANY 5 OF THE FOLLOWING ITEMS:

1 can green beans, drained

1 can asparagus, drained

1 can carrots, drained

1 can artichoke hearts, drained

2 cups (½ pound) fresh mushrooms, cleaned

2 cups cherry tomatoes

2 cups sliced raw summer squash

2 cups sliced cucumber

2 cups (1 small head) cauliflower florets

2 cups (1 bunch) broccoli florets

2 medium green peppers, sliced

1 small red onion, sliced and separated into rings

MARINADE:

1 cup vegetable oil

½ cup white wine vinegar

½ cup sugar

1 tablespoon dried Italian herb seasoning

2 teaspoons dry mustard

1 teaspoon salt

Combine your choice of vegetables in a large mixing bowl or storage container. Combine the marinade ingredients and pour over the vegetables; toss well. Chill, covered, overnight. Drain and arrange on a platter for serving.

Out of Our League, Too, Greensboro, NC

JARLSBERG VEGETABLE BAKE

MAKES 6 TO 8 SERVINGS

3 medium zucchini, sliced
1 cup sliced fresh mushrooms
½ cup green bell pepper strips
½ cup sliced green onions
1 clove garlic, minced
¼ cup olive oil
1 cup cherry tomato halves
½ teaspoon salt
⅛ teaspoon freshly ground pepper
2 cups shredded Jarlsberg cheese

Preheat the oven to 350F.

Sauté the zucchini, mushrooms, green pepper, green onions, and garlic in the olive oil in a skillet for 5 to 6 minutes or until the vegetables begin to soften. Stir in the tomatoes, salt, and pepper. Layer the vegetable mixture alternately with the cheese in a greased 1½-quart baking dish until all the ingredients are used, ending with cheese. Bake uncovered for 30 minutes.

Generations, Rockford, IL

VEGETABLE PIZZAZZ

MAKES 6 DOZEN

2 packages refrigerator crescent dinner roll dough
2 (8-ounce) packages cream cheese, softened
1 cup mayonnaise
1 package Italian salad dressing mix
1 large carrot, peeled and diced
⅓ cup chopped red bell pepper
⅓ cup chopped raw green beans
⅓ cup sliced fresh mushrooms
1 pint cherry tomatoes, cut in half
1 cup small broccoli florets
⅓ cup grated Monterey Jack cheese
⅓ cup grated Cheddar cheese

Preheat the oven to 350F. Spread the roll dough on a cookie sheet, pressing together and making a slightly raised edge. Bake 10 minutes; cool.

Mix the cream cheese, mayonnaise, and Italian dressing mix and spread on the baked crust. Decorate the top with an assortment of the raw vegetables. Gently press the vegetables into the cream cheese mixture. Sprinkle the grated cheeses on top. Cut into 1½-inch squares and arrange on a serving platter.

A Matter of Taste, Morristown, NJ

GRILLED MIXED VEGETABLES

MAKES 4 SERVINGS

1 yellow squash, washed and stemmed
1 zucchini, washed and stemmed
1 green bell pepper, cored and seeded
1 small onion, peeled
6 large mushrooms, wiped
Nonfat Italian dressing

Prepare a hot fire in a charcoal or gas–fired grill.

While the grill is heating, cut the yellow squash and zucchini into 1-inch chunks. Cut up the green pepper into large pieces, quarter the onion, and halve or quarter the mushrooms, depending on their size.

Mix the vegetables together and spread them on a large piece of aluminum foil. Sprinkle Italian dressing over all.

Close the foil tightly, making a flat package, and place on the grill rack. Grill for about 15 minutes or until the vegetables are tender.

Serve at once or cool and serve at room temperature.

Treasures of the Smokies, Johnson City, TN

DIVINE WISDOM FETTUCCINE

MAKES 4 TO 6 SERVINGS

1 (8-ounce) package cream cheese
8 tablespoons (1 stick) butter
1 (12-ounce) can evaporated milk
½ cup freshly grated Parmesan cheese,
    divided
¼ cup minced parsley
1 (16-ounce) package fresh fettuccine,
    cooked and drained
Cracked pepper

In the top of a large double boiler over simmering water, melt the cream cheese and butter. Stir in the evaporated milk and whisk until creamy. Add ¼ cup of the Parmesan cheese and the minced parsley. Toss the warm fettuccine into the sauce. Serve immediately with cracked pepper and the remaining Parmesan cheese.

¡Viva! Tradiciones, Corpus Christi, TX

PESTO PRESTO OVER LINGUINE

MAKES 8 SERVINGS

2 cloves garlic, peeled
2 cups lightly packed fresh basil leaves
½ cup olive oil
1 teaspoon salt
2 tablespoons pine nuts
½ cup freshly grated Parmesan cheese
3 tablespoons butter, softened
1 tablespoon or more hot water
2 pounds dried linguine

Put the garlic cloves in a food processor and mince at high speed. Add the basil and process until basil is finely chopped. With the processor running, add the olive oil through the feeder tube in a steady stream. Process until well blended. Add the salt and pine nuts and process until combined. Transfer to a bowl and sprinkle the Parmesan cheese over the pesto. Blend well. Add the softened butter and stir until thoroughly combined.

Cook the linguine according to package instructions. Drain, reserving a tablespoon or more of the water in which the pasta has been boiled. Thin the pesto with the hot water, spoon the sauce over the pasta, and toss until well combined. Serve immediately.

A Matter of Taste, Morristown, NJ

MEDITERRANEAN ORZO

MAKES 8 SERVINGS

1 cup orzo (rice-shaped pasta)
½ ounce sun-dried tomatoes
1 cup crumbled feta cheese
¼ cup finely chopped red onion
¼ cup chopped yellow bell pepper
¼ cup chopped red bell pepper
¼ cup chopped green bell pepper
2 tablespoons chopped fresh parsley
2 tablespoons sliced black olives
¼ teaspoon freshly ground black
    pepper
2 tablespoons red wine vinegar
1½ teaspoons olive oil, or more to
    taste

Cook the orzo according to the package directions; if desired, omit the salt and butter. Drain; reserve 1 cup of the cooking liquid and bring to a boil in a small saucepan. Stir in the tomatoes. Cook, covered, for 2 minutes or until tender; drain. Chop the tomatoes.

Combine the orzo, tomatoes, feta cheese, onion, bell peppers, parsley, olives, black pepper, vinegar, and oil in a large bowl; toss to combine. Garnish with parsley or additional sliced olives.

Dining by Design, Pasadena, CA

ORZO WITH MYZITHRA AND BASIL

MAKES 6 SERVINGS

3 tablespoons butter or margarine
1½ cups orzo (rice-shaped pasta)
2 cloves garlic, minced
3 cups chicken broth
⅔ cup Myzithra or Parmesan cheese,
    grated (see Note)
6 tablespoons chopped fresh basil or
    1½ teaspoons dried basil
Salt and freshly ground pepper to
    taste
Fresh basil sprigs for garnish

Melt the butter in a 10-inch skillet over medium heat. Add the uncooked orzo and the garlic; sauté 2 minutes. Add the broth and bring to a boil. Reduce the heat, cover, and simmer for about 20 minutes, or until the orzo is tender and liquid is absorbed. Add the Myzithra cheese, basil, salt, and pepper; mix well. Garnish with fresh basil sprigs.

NOTE: Myzithra is a hard grating cheese available in Greek markets.

Rogue River Rendezvous, Jackson County, OR

PLANTATION RICE

MAKES 6 TO 8 SERVINGS

8 slices bacon, diced
1 medium onion, chopped
4 tablespoons (½ stick) butter
1 cup coarsely chopped pecans
1¼ cups uncooked long-grain white
    rice
1 teaspoon salt
2¼ cups cold water
2 tablespoons chopped fresh parsley

Sauté the bacon in a large skillet until almost crisp. Add the onion and sauté lightly. Remove the bacon and onion and set aside; drain off all but 2 tablespoons of drippings from the pan. Add the butter to the drippings and sauté the pecans over medium heat until they are fragrant. Remove the pecans and set aside. Stir the rice and salt into the pan, coating the rice well. Add the cold water; stir and bring to a boil. Simmer, covered, for 25 to 30 minutes or until the rice is tender and liquid is absorbed. Stir in the bacon, onions, pecans, and parsley. When heated through, transfer to a serving dish.

A Southern Collection—Then & Now, Columbus, GA

GARDEN LASAGNA

MAKES 6 TO 8 SERVINGS

16 ounces lasagna noodles
1 large sweet onion, chopped
2 cloves garlic, minced
3 tablespoons olive oil
2 large carrots, peeled and coarsely
    chopped
1 red bell pepper, seeded and coarsely
    chopped
8 button mushrooms, coarsely chopped
2 zucchini, 1 coarsely chopped and 1
    sliced
2 yellow squash, 1 coarsely chopped
    and 1 sliced
1 (14-ounce) can diced tomatoes
1 (10-ounce) can tomato purée
1 tablespoon sugar
1½ teaspoons salt or to taste
1 teaspoon freshly ground black
    pepper or to taste
1 tablespoon chopped fresh basil
1 tablespoon chopped fresh oregano
1 tablespoon balsamic vinegar
15 ounces ricotta cheese
1½ cups plus ½ cup shredded
    mozzarella cheese
1 large egg, lightly beaten
1 teaspoon garlic salt
¼ cup grated Parmesan cheese

Cook the noodles following the package directions; drain. Sauté the onion and garlic in the olive oil in a large saucepan for 4 minutes or until the onion is tender. Stir in the carrots, red pepper, mushrooms, coarsely chopped zucchini, and coarsely chopped yellow squash. Sauté for 4 minutes. Add the undrained tomatoes, tomato purée, sugar, salt, and black pepper and mix well. Simmer, covered, 10 minutes, stirring occasionally. Stir in the basil, oregano, and balsamic vinegar. Simmer 5 minutes, stirring occasionally. Remove the sauce from the heat.

Preheat the oven to 350F.

Lightly oil a 13 x 9 x 3-inch baking dish. Combine the ricotta cheese, 1½ cups of the mozzarella, the egg, and garlic salt in a bowl and mix well. Layer one-third of the noodles in the prepared baking dish. Top with half the vegetable sauce and a layer of half the remaining noodles. Spread with all of the cheese mixture, top with the remaining noodles, then the remaining vegetable sauce. Arrange the sliced zucchini and sliced yellow squash over the top. Sprinkle with the remaining ½ cup of mozzarella cheese and the Parmesan cheese. Bake 35 to 40 minutes or until bubbly. Let stand for 15 minutes before serving.

Southern on Occasion, Cobb-Marietta, GA

GREEN RICE

MAKES 8 SERVINGS

3 cups cooked rice
2 large eggs, well beaten
1 cup milk
4 tablespoons (½ stick) butter, softened
¼ cup grated sharp Cheddar cheese
½ tablespoon grated onion
⅓ cup minced parsley
⅔ cup minced raw spinach
1 teaspoon Worcestershire sauce
1¼ teaspoons salt

Preheat the oven to 325F. Combine the rice, eggs, milk, butter, cheese, onion, parsley, spinach, Worcestershire sauce, and salt in a large bowl; mix well. Pour into a greased 2-quart baking dish. Bake uncovered for 45 minutes.

Cooking Through Rose-Colored Glasses, Tyler, TX

MEXICAN RICE

MAKES 4 TO 6 SERVINGS

3 tablespoons bacon drippings
1 cup uncooked rice
1 medium onion, chopped
½ cup minced raw carrots
1½ cups canned tomatoes with juice
1 or 2 cloves garlic, minced
1 teaspoon cumin seed, crushed with
    mortar and pestle
1 (10-ounce) can condensed beef broth
Salt and freshly ground pepper

Heat the drippings in a large cast-iron skillet. Add the rice and brown well. Add the remaining ingredients. Reduce the heat and cook, covered, until the liquid is absorbed, about 25 minutes.

Delicioso, Corpus Christi, TX

PECAN WILD RICE PILAF

MAKES 8 SERVINGS

4 cups chicken broth
1 cup wild rice
2¼ cups water
1¾ cups wheat pilaf (couscous)
1 cup pecan halves
1 bunch green onions, thinly sliced
1 cup currants
½ cup chopped fresh mint leaves
Grated zest of 2 oranges
2 tablespoons olive oil
1 tablespoon fresh orange juice
Freshly ground pepper to taste

Pour the broth into a saucepan and bring to a boil. Stir in the rice. Return to a boil. Reduce the heat to medium-low. Cook, covered, 50 minutes or until the rice is tender. Do not overcook.

While the rice is cooking, pour the water into another saucepan and bring to a boil. Stir in the pilaf. Return to a boil. Simmer, covered, 15 minutes. Let stand 15 minutes. Add to the rice and toss to combine. Add the pecans, green onions, currants, mint, orange zest, oil, and orange juice, stirring to mix well. Season with the pepper.

Dining by Design, Pasadena, CA

WILD RICE AND ALMOND CASSEROLE

MAKES 8 SERVINGS

8 tablespoons (1 stick) butter, melted
½ pound mushrooms, cleaned and
　　sliced
1 clove garlic, minced
2 tablespoons chopped green onions
½ cup almonds, blanched and slivered
1 cup wild rice
3 cups chicken broth
Salt and freshly ground pepper to
　　taste

Preheat the oven to 325F. Melt the butter in a large skillet. Add the mushrooms, garlic, green onions, almonds, and wild rice. Cook, stirring continuously, 5 to 10 minutes or until the rice begins to turn yellow. Add the broth, bring to a boil, and season with salt and pepper to taste. Turn into a 1½-quart baking dish and cover tightly. Bake 1 hour.

Rare Collections, Galveston County, TX

HASH BROWN POTATO CASSEROLE

MAKES 12 SERVINGS

1 (32-ounce) package shredded frozen
    potatoes
2 sticks (½ pound) butter, melted
1 (10-ounce) can cream of chicken
    soup, undiluted
12 ounces American cheese, grated
    (3 cups)
1 (8-ounce) carton sour cream
1 teaspoon salt
½ small onion, chopped
2 cups crushed cornflakes

Preheat the oven to 350F. Place the thawed potatoes in a 13 x 9-inch baking dish. Mix together ½ cup of the melted butter, the soup, cheese, sour cream, salt, and onion in a medium bowl; pour over the potatoes. Top with the crushed cornflakes and drizzle the remaining ½ cup melted butter over the top. Bake, uncovered, for 45 minutes.

Southern Accent, Pine Bluff, AR

ROASTED NEW POTATOES

MAKES 6 TO 8 SERVINGS

2 pounds red new potatoes, unpeeled
    and quartered
¼ cup plus 2 tablespoons fresh lemon
    juice
1½ teaspoons dried oregano
1 teaspoon grated lemon zest
1 teaspoon salt
¼ teaspoon freshly ground black
    pepper
¼–½ cup olive oil
15 bay leaves

Preheat the oven to 375F. Lightly oil a large baking pan. Place the potatoes in the pan. Combine the lemon juice, oregano, lemon zest, salt, pepper, and olive oil in a small bowl; mix well. Pour over the potatoes. Place the bay leaves among the potatoes. Bake 45 minutes or until the potatoes are tender and lightly browned, turning every 10 to 15 minutes. Remove bay leaves before serving.

Very Virginia, Hampton Roads, VA

GOURMET POTATOES

MAKES 6 TO 8 SERVINGS

6 medium potatoes
4 tablespoons (½ stick) butter, melted,
    plus 2 tablespoons butter, softened
1½ cups plus ½ cup grated Cheddar
    cheese
1 cup sour cream
2 green onions, chopped
1 teaspoon salt
¼ teaspoon freshly ground pepper

Cover the potatoes with salted water and bring to a boil in a large saucepan. Reduce the heat and cook about 30 minutes or until tender. Drain and cool slightly. Peel and coarsely shred potatoes; set aside.

Preheat the oven to 300F. Combine the melted butter and the 1½ cups of grated cheese in a heavy saucepan. Cook over low heat, stirring constantly, until the cheese is partially melted. Combine the potatoes, cheese mixture, sour cream, onions, salt, and pepper in a bowl; stir well. Spoon the mixture into a greased 2-quart shallow baking dish. Dot with the 2 tablespoons butter and the remaining ½ cup grated cheese. Bake, covered, for 25 minutes.

Some Like It South!, Pensacola, FL

TOMATO POTATO MELT

MAKES 10 SERVINGS

5 large baking potatoes
12 tablespoons (1½ sticks) butter,
    softened
9 bacon slices, cooked and crumbled
3 small tomatoes, diced
2 green onions with tops, minced
2 cups grated Cheddar cheese
Salt and freshly ground pepper to
    taste

Preheat the oven to 400F. Bake the potatoes 1 hour or until tender. Cool slightly. Reduce the oven temperature to 350F. Cut the potatoes in half lengthwise. Scoop out the pulp into a mixing bowl and reserve the shells. Mash the potatoes in a large bowl. Add the butter to the hot mashed potatoes; blend. Add the bacon, tomatoes, onions, grated cheese, salt, and pepper; mix well. Stuff the mixture into the potato skins. Arrange on a baking sheet and bake 20 minutes or until the cheese melts.

Uptown Down South, Greenville, SC

HOLIDAY MASHED POTATOES

MAKES 8 TO 12 SERVINGS

12 medium potatoes, peeled, quartered

1 (8-ounce) package cream cheese, cubed

4 tablespoons (½ stick) butter, softened

¼ cup sour cream

½ cup milk

2 large eggs, slightly beaten

4 green onions, finely chopped

1 teaspoon salt

¼ teaspoon freshly ground pepper

¼ teaspoon grated nutmeg

Place the potatoes in salted water to cover in a large saucepan. Cover; bring to a boil, and cook over medium heat for 20 to 25 minutes or until tender. Drain the potatoes in a large colander. Place in a large mixing bowl and mash or beat until smooth. Add the cream cheese and butter. Beat until smooth. Stir in the sour cream. In a small bowl, blend the milk, eggs, onions, and seasonings. Add to the potato mixture; whip until the mixture is light and fluffy. Pour into a greased 9-inch round baking pan. (The potatoes can be made in advance up to this point, covered and refrigerated several hours or overnight. They can also be frozen, if desired.) When ready to bake, preheat the oven to 350F. Bake uncovered for 45 to 50 minutes or until puffed and golden brown.

Back Home Again, Indianapolis, IN

GARLIC MASHED POTATOES

MAKES 4 SERVINGS

1 pound (about 4 medium) potatoes, peeled and halved

1 small head garlic, cloves separated and peeled

4 cups chicken stock or water

8 tablespoons (1 stick) butter, softened

Salt and freshly ground pepper to taste

½ cup light cream, heated

Place the potatoes in a saucepan with the garlic cloves and chicken stock. Bring to a boil. Reduce the heat and simmer until the potatoes are soft; drain. With a large spoon or fork, smash the potatoes and garlic and blend in the butter, salt, pepper, and cream. Serve hot.

A Cleveland Collection, Cleveland, OH

MASHED POTATOES WITH TURNIPS

MAKES 8 SERVINGS

4 large potatoes, peeled and cubed
1 medium yellow turnip (rutabaga),
   peeled and cubed
1 medium onion, peeled and cut into
   chunks
2 tablespoons butter, softened
Milk
1 (3-ounce) package cream cheese,
   softened
½ cup sour cream
1½ teaspoons horseradish
Salt and freshly ground pepper to
   taste

Place the potatoes, turnip, and onion in a large saucepan; cover with salted water and bring to a boil. Reduce the heat and simmer until fork tender, about 30 minutes. Meanwhile, preheat the oven to 350F. Grease a 2-quart baking pan.

When the vegetables are tender, drain and mash them with the butter and enough milk to moisten. Stir in the cream cheese, sour cream, and horseradish. Season with salt and pepper. Spoon into a baking dish; bake uncovered for 20 minutes.

Women of Great Taste, Wichita, KS

MASHED POTATO SOUFFLÉ

MAKES 12 SERVINGS

8 large russet potatoes (about 4½ to 5
   pounds)
1 (8-ounce) package cream cheese,
   softened
1 cup sour cream
2 teaspoons garlic salt
½ teaspoon freshly ground pepper
4 tablespoons (½ stick) butter
Paprika to taste

Peel the potatoes and cut into quarters. Cover with boiling salted water in a 5-quart saucepan. Boil for 25 minutes or until tender; drain. Put the potatoes through a food mill or a ricer into a large bowl. Beat the cream cheese and sour cream with an electric mixer until blended. Add the cream cheese mixture, garlic salt, and pepper to the potatoes and mix well. Spoon into a serving dish or a shallow 3- or 4-quart casserole or baking dish. Dot with the butter. Sprinkle lightly with paprika. (To avoid accidentally using too much paprika, hold the shaker 8 inches above the potatoes.)

Serve immediately or cover and refrigerate for up to 2 days. To reheat, bring to room temperature. Bake, covered, at 400F for 50 to 60 minutes or until heated through.

Beyond Burlap: Idaho's Famous Potato Recipes, Boise, ID

GOLDEN PARMESAN POTATOES

MAKES 6 TO 8 SERVINGS

5⅓ tablespoons butter, melted
¼ cup all-purpose flour
¼ cup grated Parmesan cheese
¾ teaspoon salt
¼ teaspoon freshly ground pepper
6 large potatoes, peeled
Chopped fresh parsley to taste

Preheat the oven to 375F. Coat the bottom of a 13 x 9-inch baking dish with the melted butter. Combine the flour, cheese, salt, and pepper in a plastic food storage bag; mix well. Cut each potato into 8 wedges. Moisten the potatoes slightly with water. Shake one-third of the potatoes at a time in the flour mixture, tossing to coat. Arrange the potatoes in the prepared dish. Bake 1 hour or until browned on both sides, turning once. Sprinkle with parsley.

Generations, Rockford, IL

SECRET SPUDS

MAKES 12 SERVINGS

10 medium potatoes, peeled and cut
    up
2 medium onions, coarsely chopped
8 ounces sour cream
8 ounces cream cheese, softened
1 cup heavy cream
1 cup grated Cheddar cheese

Preheat the oven to 350F. Grease a 3-quart casserole.

Boil the potatoes and onions in water to cover in a large saucepan until tender. Drain and mash. Mix in the sour cream and cream cheese. Spoon into the prepared 3-quart casserole. Whip the cream in a small bowl and add the grated cheese; mix well. Spread over the potatoes. Bake uncovered for 45 minutes.

NOTE: Spuds may be prepared one day before serving. Do not freeze.

Dinner on the Diner, Chattanooga, TN

CRAB-STUFFED POTATOES

MAKES 6 SERVINGS

3 large baking potatoes
8 tablespoons (1 stick) butter, softened
½ cup light cream or half-and-half
1 teaspoon salt
½ teaspoon freshly ground pepper
4 teaspoons grated onion
1 cup grated sharp Cheddar cheese
1 (6½-ounce) can crabmeat, drained
½ teaspoon paprika

Preheat the oven to 425F. Scrub the potatoes and poke in several places with a fork. Bake for 1 hour or until tender. Remove the potatoes and reduce the oven temperature to 400F.

Cut the potatoes in half lengthwise. Scoop out the pulp, taking care not to damage the shells. Place the pulp in a large mixing bowl. Add the butter, cream, salt, pepper, onion, and cheese. Whip until smooth. Fold in the crabmeat. Fill the potato shells with the mixture and sprinkle paprika on top. Bake 15 minutes or until the cheese is melted.

Winners, Indianapolis, IN

SOUTHERN HUSH PUPPIES

MAKES 3 DOZEN

Vegetable oil for deep frying
1 onion, chopped
1 large egg, beaten
¾ cup beer
1 cup buttermilk
3¼ cups self-rising cornmeal
1 teaspoon dried sage (optional)

Pour in enough oil to come halfway up a deep, heavy pan and heat to 365F on a deep-fry thermometer.

Combine the onion, egg, beer, buttermilk, cornmeal, and sage in a medium bowl; mix well. The mixture should be fairly thick. Working in batches, drop the batter by spoonfuls into the hot oil. Do not crowd the pan. Fry until golden brown. Remove with a slotted spoon to drain on paper towels.

Beyond Cotton Country, Decatur, AL

New Potatoes and Leeks Dijon

MAKES 4 SERVINGS

½ cup sliced leeks, ¼ inch thick
1½ pounds small new potatoes, cut
    into quarters
1 cup chicken broth
½ cup dry white wine
1 tablespoon Dijon mustard
¼ teaspoon freshly ground black
    pepper

Coat a small skillet with vegetable oil cooking spray and heat to medium. Add the leeks and sauté for 3 to 5 minutes or until tender. Combine the potatoes, broth, wine, and mustard in a medium saucepan. Bring to a boil, reduce the heat, cover, and simmer for 6 minutes. Uncover and simmer for about 15 minutes or until the potatoes are tender. Add the leeks to the potatoes and cook until mixture is thoroughly heated. Season with pepper.

Gold 'n Delicious, Spokane, WA

Praline Sweet Potato Casserole

MAKES 4 TO 6 SERVINGS

1 (16-ounce) can sweet potatoes or
    yams
2 tablespoons butter, melted
3 tablespoons orange juice
6 tablespoons packed dark brown
    sugar
5 tablespoons chopped nuts
¼ teaspoon ground cinnamon

Lightly grease a 1-quart glass baking dish suitable for the microwave oven; set aside. Mash the sweet potatoes. Add the melted butter and orange juice; blend thoroughly. Spoon into the casserole. Combine the brown sugar, nuts, and cinnamon; mix well. Sprinkle over the sweet potato mixture. Cover with plastic wrap. Microwave 6½ minutes at 80 percent power. Let stand 3 minutes before serving.

Treasures of the Smokies, Johnson City, TN

ACAPULCO EGGS WITH CHEESE SAUCE

MAKES 4 SERVINGS

CHEESE SAUCE:
2 tablespoons butter
2 tablespoons all-purpose flour
1 teaspoon salt
⅛ teaspoon paprika
¾ cup milk
¼ cup dry white wine
1 cup shredded Monterey Jack cheese

ACAPULCO EGGS:
Vegetable oil
4 (9-inch) corn tortillas
8 large eggs
Salt and freshly ground pepper
4 teaspoons chopped green chiles

Make the cheese sauce: Heat the butter in a skillet over low heat until melted. Blend in the flour, salt, and paprika. Cook over low heat, stirring until smooth and bubbly. Remove from the heat. Gradually stir in the milk and wine. Heat to boiling, stirring constantly. Boil and stir 1 minute. Stir in the cheese. Cook, stirring constantly, over low heat until the cheese is melted. Cover and keep warm over low heat while preparing the eggs.

Heat ¼ inch of oil in a large skillet until hot. Fry the tortillas until light brown. Remove with tongs to drain on paper towels; keep warm.

Break each egg into a measuring cup. Carefully slip one egg at a time into the same skillet. Immediately reduce the heat. Cook slowly, spooning oil over the eggs until the whites are set and a film forms over the yolks. Add additional oil if needed. Place 2 eggs on each tortilla. Add salt and pepper. Pour the cheese sauce over the eggs and sprinkle with green chiles.

Delicioso, Corpus Christi, TX

EGGS ROYALE CASSEROLE

MAKES 6 SERVINGS

2 cups herb-seasoned croutons
1 cup shredded cheese
4 large eggs, slightly beaten
2 cups milk
½ teaspoon salt
½ teaspoon dry mustard
⅛ teaspoon onion powder
½ teaspoon freshly ground pepper
10 slices bacon, cooked until crisp

Preheat the oven to 325F. Combine the croutons and cheese and sprinkle over the bottom of a greased 2-quart casserole. Mix the eggs with the milk and seasonings in a medium bowl until well blended; pour over the croutons and cheese. Crumble the bacon on top. Bake 55 to 60 minutes.

NOTE: This may be assembled the the night before, and baked for breakfast or brunch. Sprinkle with the crumbled bacon just before baking.

Out of Our League, Greensboro, NC

ANY-KIND-OF-QUICHE

CRUST:

1 (3-ounce) package cream cheese
4 tablespoons (½ stick) butter
1 cup all-purpose flour
½ teaspoon salt

QUICHE MIXTURE:

3 tablespoons chopped shallot or onion
3 tablespoons butter
5 large eggs, beaten
1½ cups half-and-half
1 teaspoon salt
⅛ teaspoon freshly ground pepper
⅛ teaspoon grated nutmeg
Choice of Fillings 1, 2, 3, or 4

FILLING 1:

¾ cup chopped cooked broccoli
1 cup chopped ham
1 cup grated Swiss cheese

FILLING 2:

1 (10-ounce) package frozen spinach,
    thawed and squeezed dry
1 cup crumbled cooked Italian sausage
1 cup mixed grated mozzarella and
    Cheddar cheeses

FILLING 3:

1½ cups sautéed thinly sliced zucchini
1 cup sautéed sliced onion
½ cup diced tomatoes
1 cup grated Monterey Jack cheese

FILLING 4:

1 (6-ounce) can crabmeat, drained and
    flaked
2 cups sliced and sautéed mushrooms
1 cup grated Swiss cheese

For the crust, mix the cream cheese, butter, flour, and salt in a food processor or mixer until the dough just forms a soft ball. Press into a 10-inch quiche dish or pie plate. Flute the edges. Chill while preparing the quiche mixture.

For the quiche mixture, sauté the shallot in butter in a medium skillet for 3 minutes. Preheat the oven to 375F. Choose the filling you will be using and sauté any of the vegetables that require it just until tender. Add the other ingredients. Spread the mixture evenly over the unbaked crust.

Beat together the eggs, half-and-half, salt, pepper, and nutmeg; pour into the crust. Bake 40 to 50 minutes or until set. Let stand 5 minutes before serving.

Brunch Basket, Rockford, IL

BAKED CHEESE GRITS

MAKES 4 TO 6 SERVINGS

6 cups water
2½ teaspoons salt
1½ cups grits
8 tablespoons (1 stick) butter
¼ teaspoon ground red pepper
   (cayenne)
3 large eggs, beaten
1 pound sharp Cheddar cheese, grated
   (4 cups)

Bring the water to a boil, add the salt, and stir in the grits. Cover and cook over low heat, stirring occasionally, until thickened, about 20 minutes. Add the butter, cayenne, eggs, and all but ¼ cup of the cheese, mixing well.

Preheat the oven to 350F. Pour the grits mixture into a buttered 2½-quart baking dish; top with the remaining cheese. Bake 1 hour and 15 minutes.

Plantation Cookbook, New Orleans, LA

CHEESE ENCHILADAS

MAKES 6 TO 8 SERVINGS

1 tablespoon vegetable oil
1 tablespoon chili powder
1 tablespoon all-purpose flour
1 (6-ounce) can tomato paste or purée
4 (6-ounce) cans water
Salt to taste
1 (8-count) package corn tortillas
1 large onion, grated
1 pound Cheddar cheese, grated
   (4 cups)

Preheat the oven to 400F. Heat the oil in a skillet, add the chili powder and flour, and stir until thickened. Add the tomato paste, water, and salt, stirring until the sauce reaches a creamy consistency. Dip the tortillas in the sauce to soften them. Roll some of the onion and cheese in each tortilla and put them in a flat baking pan. Cover with any remaining sauce, cheese, and onion. Bake 10 minutes or until the cheese is melted.

Cooking Through Rose-Colored Glasses, Tyler, TX

MEXICAN CHEESECAKE

MAKES 12 TO 14 SERVINGS

2 cups corn chips, crushed

4 tablespoons (½ stick) butter or
   margarine, melted

2 (16-ounce) cans refried beans

1 package taco seasoning

3 medium avocados, mashed

2 tablespoons lemon juice

½ teaspoon salt

½ teaspoon freshly ground pepper

1 cup sour cream

½ cup mayonnaise

Taco sauce to taste (optional)

1 cup chopped green onions

3 medium tomatoes, chopped and
   drained

1 (6-ounce) can ripe olives, sliced

6 ounces Cheddar cheese, grated (1½
   cups)

6 ounces Monterey Jack cheese, grated
   (1½ cups)

Tortilla chips

Preheat the oven to 350F. Mix the crushed corn chips with the melted butter. Press on the bottom and up the sides of a 9-inch springform pan. Bake for 8 to 10 minutes; cool.

Mix the refried beans and half the taco seasoning in a small bowl. Spread lightly on the corn chip crust. Mash the avocados with the lemon juice, salt, and pepper in a small bowl. Spread over the beans. Mix the sour cream, mayonnaise, and remaining taco seasoning in a small bowl. If spicier flavoring is desired, add taco sauce. Spread the sour cream mixture over the avocado mixture. Sprinkle the onions, tomatoes, olives, and cheeses over the sour cream.

Chill for several hours before serving. To serve, remove the side of the springform. Center the cheesecake on a platter and surround with tortilla chips.

Out of Our League, Too, Greensboro, NC

HOT CURRIED FRUIT

MAKES 10 TO 12 SERVINGS

1 (29-ounce) can peach halves
1 (29-ounce) can pear halves
1 (16-ounce) can apricot halves
1 (8-ounce) can pineapple chunks
About 20 maraschino cherries
4 tablespoons (½ stick) butter, melted
¾ cup packed light brown sugar
3½–4 teaspoons curry powder

Preheat the oven to 325F. Drain all the fruits. Arrange the peaches and pears hollow side up in a 3-quart baking dish. Place the apricots on top. Sprinkle the pineapple and cherries over the other fruit.

Combine the butter, sugar, and curry powder in a small bowl. Sprinkle over the fruit. Bake 1 hour, basting 3 or 4 times. Cool and refrigerate at least 1 day. Heat before serving.

Tea-Time at the Masters, Augusta, GA

CRANBERRY CHUTNEY

MAKES 4 PINTS

1 pound fresh or frozen cranberries
2 Granny Smith apples, cored and
    chopped
2 fresh pears, cored and chopped
1 cup yellow raisins
¼ cup fresh lemon juice
1 teaspoon grated onion
2½ cups packed dark brown sugar
1 cup water
¼ cup chopped candied ginger
Dash of salt
¼ teaspoon ground cloves

Place all the ingredients in a large heavy saucepan. Bring to a boil and cook over medium heat for 1½ to 2 hours or until the mixture is thick; stir occasionally to prevent sticking. Pour into hot sterilized jars and can, or let cool and store in the refrigerator, covered.

Pearls of the Concho, San Angelo, TX

MEAT
AND
GAME

Northern Plains and Canada

There is a saying on the prairies and ranges of Montana: "If it can't moo, it ain't meat." Food on the frontier was plain, hearty, and filling. For the pioneers in North and South Dakota, Montana, and Canada, dinner meant meat and potatoes—and meat usually meant beef. Variety came from the hunt, with ample supplies of venison, antelope, fish, and an array of wild fowl, such as prairie chicken and pheasant.

Way back when, stewing was the preferred approach, in part because the meat was often tough and stringy. The chuck-wagon cooks got imaginative in the preparation of their stews. Consider, for instance, the cowboy specialty "Garbage Can Stew." The updated version of that old favorite goes like this: Have the boys drink about 30 cans of beer (they didn't have beer in cans in the good old days); then fill the cans with water and place them in the bottom of a large garbage can (preferably clean). Throw in lots of beef, vegetables, salt, and sage, and set the garbage can on a grate over an open fire. The water in the beer cans will keep the bottom of the garbage can from burning out. After four or five hours of simmering, enjoy authentic cowboy cooking.

A fine gourmet meal in the mid-1970s consisted of a slab of meat weighing approximately the same as you did at birth and a baked potato. Not too different from what the frontiersmen ate by the campfires. Simple ranch-style cooking was the rule of thumb, and it had been that way for more than 100 years. But in the last 30 years, cuisine in the Northern Plains has seen artistic growth akin to the renaissance, only edible. This didn't mean a drastic culinary culture shock. What it did mean was that foods that are indigenous to the region got dressed up a little bit.

Take the slab of beef. You can still get a nice juicy steak, but now it is offered slathered with tarragon-butter sauce. Seafood that thrives in the waters of Canada isn't just pan-fried anymore. From saffron-poached halibut to Asian-spiced trout and prawns served with pasta, Canadians are experimenting with their seafood bounty as never before. Clearly, cooking methods have undergone some changes.

Lambs don't moo, but a ranch hand might choose a crown roast of lamb instead of beef for dinner. Raised on the finest air, water, and grass, Montana lamb can compete right up there with lamb imported from New Zealand. For dessert, do as the natives do and dig into something sweet made from huckleberries. These berries flourish during the hot summers in Montana and are made into a tempting variety of pies, tarts, jams, confections, and ice cream. In the mood for something more exotic? How about a huckleberry daiquiri or a nightcap made from huckleberry liqueur?

Haute cuisine it ain't, but the Northern Plains and Canadian region's beef, wild game, and seafood have fed generations of folks and fueled their pioneer spirits.

—Bob Zimorino, Executive Chef and contributing food writer for *The Missoula*
Missoula, MT

TUREEN SUPPER

On chilly fall and winter days, inviting the neighbors over for enticing bowls of soups and chilis speaks of true hospitality. Folks tend to stay indoors during colder weather, and this menu will warm them up inside and out.

HOT APPETIZER PIE 23

HOT BUTTERED RUM 56

CRUNCHY ROMAINE SALAD 72

CORN CHOWDER 117

SNOWY DAY WHITE CHILI 130

POTATO MOCHA POUND CAKE 318

GAME FOR DINNER

Plan a special wild game dinner for your family. If there are hunters in your house, they can show off their bounty. If not, the availability of most foods today might allow you to purchase game from your local grocer or even through the Internet. A wild game dinner is a treat the whole family will enjoy.

BACON BISCUIT PUFFS 7

ROAST WILD DUCK 209

VENISON CHORIZO 212

HASH BROWN POTATO CASSEROLE 161

MUSHROOM SOUFFLÉ 140

HEAVENLY APPLE DUMPLINGS 353

RECIPE FOR A BETTER COMMUNITY

JUNIOR LEAGUE OF ROCKFORD, ILLINOIS COMMUNITY PROJECT:

Rock River Discovery Park

Completed in 1991, Rock River Discovery Park is the first community-built science park in the U.S. The Junior League of Rockford, the Rockford Park District, and the Discovery Center were partners in this project.

The cookbooks that helped to make it happen: *Brunch Basket* and *Generations* generate $10,000 to $12,000 annually for the park.

Did you know? In the May 1992 issue of *Child* magazine, the Rock River Discovery Park was featured as one of the "10 Best Playgrounds in America."

FILETS OF BEEF CHASSEUR

MAKES 8 SERVINGS

3 cloves garlic, crushed, divided
1½ teaspoons seasoned salt
¼ teaspoon freshly ground pepper
8 (8-ounce) beef tenderloin filets (filet
    mignon steaks), sliced 1 inch thick
6 tablespoons butter, divided
2 tablespoons brandy
½ pound fresh mushrooms, sliced
3 tablespoons all-purpose flour
2 teaspoons tomato paste
¾ cup dry red wine
1 cup chicken broth
½ cup beef broth
½ cup water
¼ teaspoon Worcestershire sauce
2 tablespoons currant jelly

Combine half the garlic, the seasoned salt, and the pepper. Pat the meat dry and rub with the garlic mixture. Sear the steaks in a large skillet in 2 tablespoons of the butter until brown on the outside with the center raw. Arrange the steaks in a 13 x 9-inch baking dish.

Pour the brandy into the skillet and stir over moderate heat, scraping up the brown bits. Add the remaining 4 tablespoons of butter. When the butter is foaming, add the mushrooms and cook until browned, about 5 minutes. Stir in the flour and reduce the heat to low. Stir in the tomato paste and remaining garlic. Remove from the heat; whisk in the wine, chicken broth, beef broth, and water. Bring to a boil over moderate heat, stirring constantly. Reduce the heat and simmer 10 minutes, until the liquid is reduced by a third. Add the Worcestershire and currant jelly. Adjust seasonings to taste and thin the sauce to a coating consistency. Cool and pour over the steaks. (At this point the steaks may be covered and refrigerated overnight. Allow them to come to room temperature before cooking.)

Preheat the oven to 400F. Bake the filets, uncovered, for 15 to 20 minutes for rare, 20 to 25 minutes for medium to medium-well.

St. Louis Days . . . St. Louis Nights, St. Louis, MO

BEEF FILETS WITH BLUE CHEESE

MAKES 6 SERVINGS

6 slices bacon, partially cooked,
    drained
6 small beef filet mignon steaks, 6 to
    8 ounces each, cut 2 inches thick,
    patted dry
Salt and freshly ground pepper to
    taste
1 tablespoon olive oil
½ cup dry white wine
2 cloves garlic, crushed
2 tablespoons chopped onion
1 tablespoon cornstarch
1 (14-ounce) can beef broth
¼ teaspoon crushed rosemary
2 tablespoons butter, softened
2 tablespoons crumbled blue cheese
Minced parsley to garnish

Wrap a strip of bacon around the outside edge of each steak and secure with a wooden pick. Pat the meat dry and season with salt and pepper. Sear the steaks on both sides in the olive oil in a large heavy skillet. Continue to cook for 6 minutes on each side or until medium-rare. Remove to a warm plate.

Put the wine, garlic, and onion in the skillet. Bring to a simmer. Dissolve the cornstarch in the beef broth in a bowl. Add to the skillet mixture and cook until thickened, stirring constantly. Add the rosemary, butter, and blue cheese. Season with salt and pepper. Cook until melted, stirring constantly.

Spoon small amounts of the sauce onto individual serving plates. Add the steaks and spoon more of the sauce over the top. Garnish with parsley.

NOTE: Sautéed sliced mushrooms and capers may also be added to the sauce.

Bay Tables, Mobile, AL

BEEF TENDERLOIN ROAST WITH MUSHROOM SAUCE

MAKES 6 SERVINGS

1 (3-pound) beef tenderloin roast
1 tablespoon minced onion
3 tablespoons butter
1 cup sliced mushrooms
3 tablespoons all-purpose flour
1 cup beef broth
2 tablespoons Burgundy
1 tablespoon lemon juice
½ teaspoon dried tarragon
1 teaspoon chopped parsley

Preheat the oven to 450F. Pat the meat dry and place it on a rack in a baking pan. Roast for 35 minutes or until the meat registers 125F to 130F on an instant-read thermometer (cook longer if less-rare meat is desired).

Sauté the onion in the butter in a small skillet. Add the mushrooms and cook 5 minutes or until browned. Stir in the flour. Add the remaining ingredients; mix well. Cook over medium heat, stirring until thickened. Serve the sauce with the beef.

First Impressions: Dining with Distinction, Waterloo-Cedar Falls, IA

COLD PEPPERED TENDERLOIN
WITH TARRAGON SAUCE

1½-2 pounds beef tenderloin, room
    temperature
1 teaspoon coarse salt
1 tablespoon coarsely ground black
    pepper
1 tablespoon vegetable oil
Tarragon Sauce (see below)

Preheat the oven to 500F. Pat the tenderloin dry and rub all sides with salt and pepper. In a roasting pan just large enough to hold the tenderloin, brown the meat on all sides in hot oil. Place in the oven and bake 15 to 20 minutes or until the internal temperature reaches 130F for medium-rare. Cool to room temperature. (The tenderloin may be roasted up to 2 days in advance, wrapped in foil and chilled.) Carve the meat in thin slices. Arrange on a serving platter and top with chilled tarragon sauce. Serve remaining sauce on the side.

TARRAGON SAUCE:

2 tablespoons heavy cream
2 tablespoons white wine vinegar
1 teaspoon Worcestershire sauce
1½ teaspoons Dijon mustard
½ cup olive oil
1½ teaspoons minced fresh tarragon
1 tablespoon capers, minced
2 tablespoons thinly sliced green onion
2 tablespoons minced fresh parsley
Salt to taste

Blend the cream, vinegar, Worcestershire sauce, and mustard in a food processor. With the machine running, add the oil in a slow steady stream to form a thin sauce. Transfer the mixture to a small bowl and stir in the tarragon, capers, onion, parsley, and salt. Cover and chill. The sauce may be made 1 day ahead.

Women of Great Taste, Wichita, KS

Beef Wellington

MAKES 8 SERVINGS

BEEF:

*1 whole beef tenderloin, about 5
  pounds, trimmed*
*1 long strip of beef suet, split
  lengthwise*

MARINADE:

2½ cups dry red wine
7 tablespoons Worcestershire sauce
Juice of 1 lemon
*¼ teaspoon freshly ground black
  pepper (several grinds from a
  pepper mill)*

MADEIRA SAUCE:

Pan juices
½ cup beef consommé
½ cup Madeira wine
*Salt and freshly ground pepper to
  taste*
2-3 tablespoons reserved marinade
*2 teaspoons arrowroot or cornstarch
  dissolved in a few tablespoons cold
  water*
*½ pound truffles (available at gourmet
  shops) (optional)*

DUXELLES:

2 tablespoons butter
*1-1½ pounds fresh mushrooms. finely
  diced*
5 green onions, finely minced
1 clove garlic, pressed
¼ cup finely chopped parsley
½ cup Madeira wine
*Salt and freshly ground pepper to
  taste*
*1 (5-ounce) can goose liver pâté (may
  use less if desired)*

Two days before serving, place the beef in a shallow nonaluminum pan. Combine the marinade ingredients and pour over the meat. Cover and refrigerate for 24 hours.

The day before serving, drain the marinade from the meat and reserve. Fold the tail end under the roast and tie securely to form a 12-inch-long piece of meat with uniform thickness. Place one strip of suet on the bottom and one strip of suet on top of the meat. Insert a meat thermometer in the center of the meat. Preheat the oven to 425F. Roast the meat 30 minutes, turning once. Replace the suet after turning. The thermometer will indicate very rare. (If your final measure of doneness is well-done, cook slightly longer at this point.) Remove the meat from the pan. Cool and refrigerate. Reserve the pan juices. Skim the fat from the pan juices and discard. In a medium saucepan, combine all the ingredients for the Madeira sauce, except the arrowroot and the optional truffles. Cook down for about 5 minutes. Adjust the seasonings. Add the dissolved arrowroot, stirring constantly over low heat until thickened. Add the truffles. Cover and refrigerate until ready to reheat.

Make the duxelles: Melt the butter in a large skillet and sauté the mushrooms, green onions, and garlic for 8 to 10 minutes or until the mixture is quite dry. Drain if necessary. Add the parsley, then the wine, and boil down until the wine has almost evaporated. Season with salt and pepper. Blend in the pâté. Cover and refrigerate.

In a medium-sized mixing bowl, mix the flour and salt. Using a pastry blender, cut in the butter and shortening until coarse granules form. Sprinkle with bouillon, small amounts at a time, tossing constantly, until the dough holds together. Wrap in waxed paper and refrigerate.

About three hours before serving, remove the duxelles and meat from the refrigerator. Remove the string. Allow the meat to come to room temperature. When it has reached room temperature, remove the pastry from the refrigerator. When soft enough to roll, roll the pastry out into a 9 x 14-inch rectangle, ¼ inch thick (enough to envelop the meat). Stir the duxelles to soften, and spread them evenly over the pastry, leaving a 1-inch border all

PASTRY:

3 cups all-purpose flour

2 teaspoons salt

14 tablespoons (2 sticks minus 2 tablespoons) butter, chilled

Chilled bouillon mixed with ice water (to total no more than ¾ cup)

1 large egg, beaten with 1 tablespoon water

around. Place the meat in the center and fold the pastry over the meat, sealing the seams well by moistening the edges. Place seam side down on a greased cookie sheet. Decorate the top with pastry cutouts from leftover dough and brush the top with egg and water. Prick on all sides with the tines of a fork. Preheat the oven to 400F. Bake for 15 minutes. Reduce the temperature to 350F and bake for 30 minutes more or until golden brown. Allow to stand 20 minutes before cutting. Gently reheat the sauce. Slice the meat into 1¼-inch portions and serve with Madeira sauce.

Rare Collections, Galveston County, TX

SIRLOIN OF BEEF WITH MADEIRA MUSHROOM SAUCE

MAKES 10 TO 12 SERVINGS

6 tablespoons butter, divided

1 (8- to 10-pound) sirloin strip roast, well trimmed

Salt and freshly ground pepper

2 cups Madeira Mushroom Sauce (see below)

Preheat the oven to 450F. Heat 4 tablespoons of the butter in a shallow roasting pan. Pat the meat dry, then turn in the butter to coat. Sprinkle with salt and pepper. Place in the oven and bake for 25 to 30 minutes, basting frequently, until the meat registers 125F on an instant-read thermometer. Remove the beef and pour off the fat from the pan. Pour in the Madeira sauce and the remaining 2 tablespoons of butter; heat through. Slice the beef and serve with the sauce.

MADEIRA MUSHROOM SAUCE:

1 tablespoon butter

4 large mushrooms, sliced

Salt and freshly ground pepper to taste

2 tablespoons finely chopped shallots

⅓ cup Madeira wine

1½ cups brown sauce or gravy

Heat the butter in a medium skillet. Add the mushrooms. Sprinkle with salt and pepper. Cook until the mushrooms are soft. Add the shallots and cook to soften. Add the wine and cook 1 minute. Stir in the brown sauce; simmer for 15 minutes.

Charlotte Cooks Again, Charlotte, NC

BOEUF BOURGUIGNON

MAKES 10 SERVINGS

7–8 pounds boneless beef chuck,
    rump, or round
3 tablespoons vegetable oil
4 pounds onion, sliced thick
¼ cup all-purpose flour
1 tablespoon salt, or to taste
1 tablespoon thyme
1 tablespoon marjoram
½ fifth of Burgundy wine
2 pounds mushrooms, sliced

Cut the meat into 1- to 2-inch cubes. Heat the oil in a large heavy skillet and add the meat cubes, cooking them in batches, turning to brown well on all sides. As the pieces are browned, transfer them to a Dutch oven. Glaze the onions in the remaining fat in the skillet. Stir in the flour, salt, and spices. Spoon into the Dutch oven.

Pour about 1 cup of the wine over the beef mixture, bring to a boil, lower the heat, and cover tightly. Continue drizzling wine over the mixture while it cooks 2 to 3 hours over low heat. About 1 hour before serving, sauté the mushrooms and add to the meat. Serve over rice.

Holiday Flavors and Favors, Greensboro, NC

RARE ROAST RIBS OF BEEF

MAKES 4 TO 6 SERVINGS

1 (3-rib) roast of beef
Salt and freshly ground pepper
¼–¾ cup red wine, optional
Water

Preheat the oven to 375F. Pat the meat dry and place it, fat side up, on a rack in a shallow roasting pan. Sprinkle with salt and pepper. Bake 1 hour. Turn off the oven. This may be done hours before serving. Do not open the oven door until ready to serve.

Before serving, set the oven to 300F and reheat for 22 minutes. Remove the roast to a heated platter. Let stand a few minutes before slicing and serving. The meat will be rare with juices all the way through.

Drain excess fat from the pan. Pour the red wine or water or a combination of both into the pan; stir to loosen the meat sediment. Cook on top of the stove until the liquid boils. Simmer for 2 minutes. Add salt and pepper to taste. Strain, if necessary. Pour into a heated gravy boat. Serve with the beef.

Nutbread & Nostalgia, South Bend, IN

BISTECCA ALLA DIAVOLA

MAKES 4 SERVINGS

1 tablespoon olive oil
4 steaks (any good cut), ¾ inch thick
Salt and freshly ground pepper to
    taste
½ cup dry Marsala wine
½ cup dry red wine
1½ teaspoons finely minced garlic
1 teaspoon fennel seed
1 tablespoon tomato paste diluted in
    1 tablespoon water
¼ teaspoon Tabasco or crushed hot red
    pepper flakes
2 tablespoons minced parsley

Pour the oil into a skillet large enough to hold all 4 steaks. Place over medium-high heat and tilt the pan so the bottom is well coated. Pat the meat dry and season with salt and pepper. When the oil is hot, cook the steaks about 3 minutes on each side or to the desired doneness. Remove the steaks from the pan.

Pour off most of the oil from the pan and add the Marsala and red wine. On medium-high heat reduce the liquids slightly while scraping the sides and bottom of the pan. Add the garlic, fennel seed, diluted tomato paste, and Tabasco. Cook and stir until the sauce is thick and syrupy, about 1 minute. Add the steaks just long enough to coat with sauce. Transfer the steaks to warm plates and top with the remaining sauce. Add parsley and serve.

Bound to Please, Boise, ID

DELUXE CHERRY BRISKET

MAKES 6 TO 8 SERVINGS

1 (5-pound) beef brisket
Soy sauce to taste
Worcestershire sauce to taste
1 package dry Lipton onion soup mix
Caraway seeds
Celery seeds
Rosemary
1 (20-ounce) can cherry pie filling

Place the brisket in a shallow dish. Season with soy and Worcestershire sauce. Sprinkle the soup mix over the brisket. Add caraway seeds, celery seeds, and rosemary to taste. Cover tightly with plastic wrap and marinate in the refrigerator for 2 days.

Preheat the oven to 325F. Wrap the brisket and seasonings in 2 layers of aluminum foil. Place on a baking sheet and bake for 4 hours. Let cool before unwrapping. Pour the juices into one container and place the meat in another; refrigerate both.

Preheat the oven to 350F. Scrape all the seasonings off the brisket and slice the meat. Put the gravy in the bottom of a baking pan and place the brisket slices over the gravy. Pour the cherry pie filling over the top; bake 30 to 45 minutes.

Rare Collections, Galveston County, TX

GRILLADES

4 pounds ½-inch-thick lean boneless
  rump or round steak, beef or veal
½ cup bacon drippings, divided
½ cup all-purpose flour
1 cup chopped onions
2 cups chopped green onions
¾ cup chopped celery
1½ cups chopped green bell pepper
2 cloves garlic, minced
2 cups chopped tomatoes
½ teaspoon tarragon (optional)
⅔ teaspoon thyme
1 cup water
1 cup red wine
1 tablespoon salt or to taste
½ teaspoon freshly ground black
  pepper
2 bay leaves
½ teaspoon Tabasco
2 tablespoons Worcestershire sauce
3 tablespoons chopped parsley

Remove any fat from the meat. Cut the meat into serving-size pieces. Pound to ¼-inch thickness. Pat the meat dry and brown the pieces over medium-high heat in a Dutch oven in 4 tablespoons of the bacon drippings. Do not crowd the pan; brown the meat in batches. As the meat browns, remove it to a warm plate.

To the fat remaining in the Dutch oven add 4 tablespoons of bacon grease and the flour. Stir and cook over medium heat to make a dark brown roux. Add the onions, green onions, celery, green pepper, and garlic; sauté until tender. Add the tomatoes, tarragon (if desired), and thyme, and cook for 3 minutes. Add the water and wine. Stir well for several minutes; return the meat to the Dutch oven and add the salt, pepper, bay leaves, Tabasco, and Worcestershire sauce. Lower the heat and continue cooking, stirring occasionally. If veal rounds are used, simmer, covered, approximately 1 hour. If beef rounds are used, simmer, covered, approximately 2 hours.

Remove the bay leaves. Stir in the parsley, cool, and let the grillades sit for several hours or overnight in the refrigerator. More liquid may be added. Grillades should be very tender. Serve over grits or rice.

Plantation Cookbook, New Orleans, LA

SALPICÓN

3 pounds beef brisket

2 onions, 1 halved, 1 chopped

1 large carrot, quartered

1 stalk celery, quartered

2 cloves garlic, chopped

1 cup chopped fresh cilantro, divided

1 (12-ounce) can whole tomatoes

Salt and freshly ground pepper to
   taste

1 large ripe tomato, chopped

1 (4-ounce) can chile chipotle, drained
   and chopped (reserve liquid)

¼ cup light olive oil

¼ cup vinegar

½ pound Monterey Jack cheese, cut
   into ¼-inch cubes

2 large avocados, pitted, peeled, and
   sliced lengthwise

Preheat the oven to 325F. Place the brisket in a heavy pot and cover with water. Add the halved onion, carrot, celery, garlic, ½ cup of the chopped cilantro, the canned tomatoes, salt, and pepper. Bring to a boil on top of the stove. Transfer to the oven and bake, covered, for approximately 4 hours or until very tender. Remove the meat from the liquid, cool slightly, and shred thoroughly with a fork.

In a large bowl, combine the shredded beef, chopped onion, chopped tomato, the remaining cilantro, chile chipotle, the cooking liquid to taste, oil, vinegar, salt, and pepper. Let cool in the refrigerator at least 4 hours.

Before serving, toss with the cheese and turn into a decorative bowl. Garnish with sliced avocado. Serve with warm corn or flour tortillas, pinto beans, and guacamole or tossed green salad.

Seasoned with Sun, El Paso, TX

SMOKY BRISKET

MAKES 8 TO 10 SERVINGS

3 tablespoons liquid smoke (or soy sauce)
3 teaspoons garlic salt
2 teaspoons onion salt
2 teaspoons celery salt
1 (4- to 6-pound) beef brisket
Freshly ground black pepper to taste
3 tablespoons Worcestershire sauce

Make a paste with the liquid smoke, garlic salt, onion salt, and celery salt in a small bowl. Paint or rub the brisket with the paste. Wrap the meat tightly in foil and seal. Marinate in the refrigerator overnight.

Preheat the oven to 250F. Unwrap the brisket and sprinkle with pepper to taste; baste with the Worcestershire sauce. Rewrap in foil. Place in a shallow baking pan and bake for 6 hours. Remove the brisket from the foil wrapping; reserve the drippings and chill. When ready to serve, slice the brisket in thin slices. Skim the fat off the top of the chilled drippings; place the drippings in a shallow baking pan. Add the sliced brisket. Heat thoroughly.

NOTE: This dish may be prepared several days in advance.

Some Like It Hot, McAllen, TX

DINOBURGERS

MAKES 6 SERVINGS

1 pound ground beef
¼ cup chopped onion
½ teaspoon salt
¼ teaspoon garlic powder
½ cup ketchup
¼ cup sour cream
6 hamburger buns

In a large skillet, cook the ground beef, stirring to break up lumps, with the onion until the beef is browned. Drain any excess fat.

Stir in the salt, garlic powder, ketchup, and sour cream. Simmer for 2 minutes. Serve on hamburger buns.

Children's Party Book, Hampton Roads, VA

ITALIAN BEEF SANDWICHES

MAKES 15 TO 20 SERVINGS

1 (5-pound) rump roast
2 or more cloves garlic, slivered, plus 1
    clove garlic, minced
Salt and freshly ground pepper to
    taste
1 tablespoon fennel seed
3 cups boiling water
3 beef bouillon cubes
½ cup finely chopped green bell pepper
2 tablespoons Worcestershire sauce
1 teaspoon marjoram
1 teaspoon oregano
1 teaspoon thyme
Dash of Tabasco

Preheat the oven to 325F. Make slashes on the meat on all sides. Stuff garlic slivers into the slashes. Pat the meat dry and sprinkle with salt and pepper. Place on a rack in a shallow roasting pan. Sprinkle the top of the roast with fennel. Roast for 25 to 30 minutes per pound. Remove the meat to cool on a plate.

Pour the boiling water into the roasting pan and dissolve the bouillon cubes. Stir with a wooden spoon to scrape up the pan drippings. Add the bell pepper, minced garlic, Worcestershire sauce, marjoram, oregano, thyme, salt and pepper to taste, and Tabasco. Simmer 15 minutes.

Slice the meat paper thin and marinate in the gravy overnight in the refrigerator. To serve, simmer the mixture on top of the stove until heated through. Serve with sandwich rolls.

Udderly Delicious, Racine, WI

MARINATED BEEF SALAD

*2½-3 pounds cold rare beef (about
    3-4 cups julienned)*
½ red or green bell pepper
½ red onion, sliced
1 green onion, sliced
⅔ cup Garlic Dressing (see below)
¼ cup chopped fresh parsley
Thinly sliced orange rounds

Cut the beef and bell pepper into julienne strips; place in a mixing bowl. Add the red and green onion. Toss with garlic dressing. Add the parsley and orange slices; toss lightly. Cover and refrigerate. Serve at room temperature with pita bread.

GARLIC DRESSING:

MAKES 1½ CUPS

1 large egg yolk
⅓ cup red wine vinegar
2 cloves garlic, minced
Salt to taste
Freshly ground black pepper to taste
1 cup olive oil

Combine the egg yolk, vinegar, garlic, salt, and pepper in a food processor. Process on and off. Add the olive oil in a steady stream with the motor running. Process on and off. Transfer the dressing to a jar and store in the refrigerator.

Celebrations on the Bayou, Monroe, LA

FAJITAS DE TRUETT

MAKES 6 TO 10 SERVINGS

3-5 pounds beef skirt steak
Lemon-pepper seasoning to taste
Seasoned salt to taste
Garlic salt to taste
Fajita Barbecue Sauce (see below)
Commercial Italian dressing
2 tablespoons olive oil
Warm flour tortillas

Remove excess fat, skin, and membrane from the beef. Pat the meat dry and sprinkle both sides with the lemon-pepper seasoning, seasoned salt, and garlic salt. Cover with a damp cloth and keep cool for 1 to 2 hours. Meanwhile, prepare the sauce and keep warm. Approximately 30 minutes before cooking, coat each side of the meat with Italian dressing. Roll the meat into rolls and store in a baking pan covered with a damp cloth until ready to cook.

Heat a large cast-iron skillet over medium-high heat until very hot. Pour in the olive oil. Unroll the meat, pat it dry, and cook for approximately 5 minutes on each side for medium rare (less for rare and longer for medium). Brush the meat on both sides with the barbecue sauce and cook for an additional 30 seconds on each side. Transfer to a carving board, let rest for 4 or 5 minutes, and slice it across the grain into 1-inch strips.

Brush the meat strips with additional sauce if desired and wrap in the warm tortillas.

FAJITA BARBECUE SAUCE:

1 medium onion, diced
4 tablespoons (½ stick) butter
¼ cup Worcestershire sauce
1 (18-ounce) bottle smoky barbecue
  sauce
4 ounces beer
½ cup ketchup
1 tablespoon brown sugar (or to taste)

Sauté the onion in the butter in a medium saucepan. Add the two sauces, the beer, and the ketchup. Simmer on low heat for 45 minutes, adding brown sugar the last 5 minutes. Add more beer if needed for a thinner consistency.

Some Like It Hot, McAllen, TX

STEAK FAJITAS

MAKES 6 SERVINGS

⅓ cup soy sauce
⅓ cup vegetable oil
3 tablespoons wine vinegar
3 cloves garlic, minced
1 small onion, minced
3 pounds skirt steak, cut into strips 4
    to 6 inches long by 2 inches wide
Warm flour tortillas
Garnishes (grilled onions, grilled bell
    peppers, guacamole, salsa, refried
    beans, sour cream)

Combine the soy sauce, oil, vinegar, garlic, and onion. Pour over the steak and marinate for at least 4 hours or overnight, turning several times.

Prepare a medium-hot charcoal fire or preheat a gas-fired grill or the kitchen broiler. Remove the meat, discarding the marinade. Pat the meat dry and grill or broil it for 2 to 3 minutes on each side for medium rare. Wrap the meat strips in a tortilla and garnish as desired.

Delicioso, Corpus Christi, TX

SICILIAN BEEF ROLL

MAKES 8 SERVINGS

2 pounds ground beef
1 cup fresh bread crumbs
½ cup grated Parmesan cheese
1 tablespoon chopped fresh basil or 1
    teaspoon dried
1½ teaspoons fresh oregano or
    ½ teaspoon dried
¼ teaspoon salt
¼ teaspoon freshly ground pepper
2 tablespoons chopped fresh parsley
2 cloves garlic, minced
½ cup tomato juice
2 large eggs, beaten
8 thin slices prosciutto
1½ cups grated mozzarella cheese plus
    6 ounces mozzarella, sliced
Fresh basil leaves for garnish

Preheat the oven to 350F.

Combine the ground beef, bread crumbs, Parmesan cheese, basil, oregano, salt, pepper, parsley, garlic, tomato juice, and eggs in a large bowl; mix well. Place the mixture on a large sheet of wax paper and shape into a 10 x 12-inch rectangle. Top with prosciutto; sprinkle with grated mozzarella. Starting with a short end, roll up jelly-roll fashion. Place, seam side down, in a 13 x 9-inch baking dish. Bake for 1¼ hours. Lay the cheese slices on top of the beef roll. Bake 5 minutes. Let stand 10 minutes before slicing. Garnish with basil leaves. Serve immediately.

Sassafras! Springfield, MO

PICKLED BEEF

1 (2¼-pound) beef round roast
2 tablespoons butter, softened
2 cloves garlic, finely chopped
1 teaspoon ground black pepper
½ medium onion
1 bouquet garni (parsley, thyme, and
   1 bay leaf, tied in a cheesecloth
   bag)

MARINADE:

1 cup olive oil
½ cup vegetable oil
3 cloves garlic, finely chopped
2 tablespoons balsamic vinegar
1½ tablespoons chicken consommé
   powder
½ teaspoon each oregano, marjoram,
   rosemary, dill, garlic salt, lemon-
   pepper
½ teaspoon Worcestershire sauce
½ teaspoon Maggi sauce
Juice from a 3½-ounce can of pickled
   jalapeño peppers

GARNISH:

½ onion, thinly sliced
1 ripe avocado, pitted, peeled, and
   thinly sliced
2 plum tomatoes, thinly sliced
Jalapeño peppers to taste, thinly sliced
Parsley sprigs (optional)

Pat the meat dry. Mix the butter with the garlic and black pepper and rub all over the meat. Brown the meat on all sides in a very hot skillet. Place in a pressure cooker with enough water to cover and add the onion and bouquet garni. Cook according to manufacturer's directions for 1¼ hours. Remove the meat and allow to cool before carving into thin slices. Discard the bouquet garni and reserve the cooking liquid for another use. Place the sliced meat in a bowl.

Mix all the marinade ingredients together and pour over the meat. Cover with plastic wrap and place in the refrigerator for 24 hours or at least overnight.

On a serving platter, interweave the slices of cold meat with the slices of onion, avocado, and tomatoes; cover with the marinade. Decorate with the pickled jalapeño peppers and parsley, if desired.

Behind the Walls, Mexico City, Mexico

LASAGNA

2 pounds ground beef
1 medium onion, chopped
1 clove garlic, crushed
1 teaspoon chopped parsley
2 tablespoons sugar
1 teaspoon basil
1 teaspoon Italian herb seasoning
1 teaspoon salt
¼ teaspoon freshly ground pepper
2 tablespoons salad oil
2 (16-ounce) cans whole peeled
    tomatoes
1 (15-ounce) can tomato sauce
2 (6-ounce) cans tomato paste
¾ cup sliced mushrooms
¼ cup chopped ripe olives
¾ pound lasagna noodles
1 (16-ounce) carton ricotta cheese or
    cottage cheese
2 large eggs, beaten
¾ pound mozzarella cheese, sliced
¾ cup grated Parmesan cheese

Heat a large heavy kettle over medium heat and sauté the beef, onion, garlic, and parsley, stirring to break up lumps of meat. Drain. Add the sugar, basil, Italian seasoning, salt, and pepper; mix well. Then add the tomatoes, tomato sauce, tomato paste, mushrooms, and olives. Bring to a boil, lower the heat, and simmer uncovered for 1 hour or more.

Preheat the oven to 375F. Cook the lasagna noodles according to package directions; drain well. Mix together the ricotta cheese and beaten eggs. In a 13 x 9-inch baking dish, spread 1 cup sauce over the bottom. Arrange a layer of noodles lengthwise over the sauce, spread with some of the ricotta mixture, then with mozzarella slices. Repeat layers, placing the next layer of noodles crosswise. Sprinkle Parmesan cheese on top. Covered tightly and bake for 30 to 40 minutes. Let cool for 10 to 15 minutes before serving. This can be refrigerated and baked later in the day, but allow 15 minutes more baking time. This also freezes well.

Winning Seasons, Tuscaloosa, AL

BASIL SOUR CREAM MEATBALLS

MAKES 8 SERVINGS

3 slices bread, crumbled
¼ cup milk
1 large egg, beaten
5 tablespoons butter, divided
½ cup chopped onion
1 pound ground beef
1 pound ground pork
1 teaspoon salt
½ teaspoon freshly ground pepper
½ teaspoon grated nutmeg
1 clove garlic, crushed
¼ cup all-purpose flour
2 cups beef broth
1 teaspoon tomato paste
1 teaspoon dried basil
8 ounces sour cream

Preheat the oven to 350F. Place the bread in a small bowl and combine with the milk and egg to soak up moisture.

In a small saucepan, melt 2 tablespoons of the butter; sauté the onion until tender. In a large bowl, combine the bread mixture with the onion, beef, pork, salt, pepper, and nutmeg, mixing well; shape into 1½-inch meatballs. Arrange on a lightly greased broiler pan rack; bake 25 minutes or until cooked through.

In a large saucepan, melt the remaining 3 tablespoons of butter; sauté the garlic for 1 minute. Add the flour, stirring well. Cook 1 minute. Gradually add the broth, stirring until smooth; bring to a boil and stir in the tomato paste and basil. Remove from heat; gently stir in the sour cream and meatballs. Place over medium heat, stirring constantly, just until heated. Serve over buttered pasta or in a chafing dish as a first course.

Tampa Treasures, Tampa, FL

MARINATED PORK TENDERLOIN

MAKES 4 TO 6 SERVINGS

1 jalapeño pepper, minced
1 (1-inch) piece fresh gingerroot, minced
⅓ cup honey
1 tablespoon Asian sesame oil
3 tablespoons soy sauce
¼ teaspoon crushed red pepper flakes
2 (1-pound) pork tenderloins

Combine the jalapeño pepper, ginger, honey, sesame oil, soy sauce, and red pepper flakes in a plastic food storage bag. Add the pork tenderloins. Marinate in the refrigerator overnight; drain.

Prepare a medium-hot charcoal fire or preheat a gas-fired grill and oil the rack. Pat the meat dry and grill the whole tenderloins for 8 to 10 minutes on each side, turning once, until just cooked through; do not overcook. Let stand on a carving board, covered loosely, for 5 to 10 minutes. Cut lengthwise into thin slices.

Generations, Rockford, IL

MADISON PARK PORK MEDALLIONS

MAKES 4 SERVINGS

1 (1-pound) pork tenderloin
⅓ cup red wine
⅓ cup chicken stock
2 tablespoons Dijon mustard
1 tablespoon freshly squeezed lemon
  juice
1 tablespoon mustard seed
2 medium cloves garlic, minced
1 teaspoon ground cumin
2 teaspoons Worcestershire sauce
¼ teaspoon salt
¼ teaspoon ground white pepper
⅛ teaspoon crushed red pepper flakes
4 tablespoons (½ stick) cold butter
2 tablespoons chopped fresh chives

Cut the pork into 8 equal slices. Place the slices in a single layer in a shallow baking dish. In a small bowl, mix together the remaining ingredients except the butter and chives. Pour the marinade over the meat; cover and marinate in the refrigerator 2 hours.

Preheat the oven to broil. Remove the pork slices from the marinade and place on an oiled broiler pan. Pour the marinade into a small saucepan and bring to a boil over high heat. Boil the marinade until reduced by half. Turn the heat down to low and swirl in butter a little at a time; do not allow sauce to boil after butter has been added.

Broil the pork slices 3 minutes per side. Transfer the pork to plates, allowing 2 slices per person. Spoon a little sauce over the pork and sprinkle with chives. Serve immediately.

Simply Classic Cookbook, Seattle, WA

RASPBERRY HERB PORK TENDERLOIN

MAKES 4 TO 6 SERVINGS

½ cup raspberry vinegar
2 cloves garlic, minced
1 tablespoon Dijon mustard
1 tablespoon honey
¼ teaspoon dried marjoram
¼ teaspoon dried sage
¼ teaspoon dried thyme
½ teaspoon coarsely ground pepper
2 (1-pound) pork tenderloins, trimmed

Combine the raspberry vinegar, garlic, mustard, honey, and herbs in a small bowl. Pour the marinade into a heavy zipper-lock plastic bag and add the tenderloins, turning to coat the surfaces. Refrigerate for at least 2 hours and up to 24 hours, occasionally turning the bag.

Prepare a medium-hot fire in a charcoal grill or preheat a gas-fired grill and oil the rack. Remove the tenderloins from the marinade and set the marinade aside. Pat the meat dry and place the tenderloins on the grill. Cook over medium heat for 8 to 10 minutes on each side, turning once. Baste often with the remaining marinade. Do not overcook. The meat will look slightly pink but this will fade when removed from the heat. (May check with an instant-read thermometer at 165F.) Let the meat stand for 5 to 10 minutes, loosely covered. To serve, slice thinly across the grain.

Rogue River Rendezvous, Jackson County, OR

PEPPERED PORK TENDERLOINS

MAKES 4 TO 6 SERVINGS

SOUR CREAM GARLIC SAUCE:

¾ *cup mayonnaise*
¾ *cup sour cream*
⅓ *teaspoon salt*
⅓ *teaspoon freshly ground pepper*
1 *clove garlic, put through a press*
1 *tablespoon Dijon mustard*
1 *teaspoon Worcestershire sauce*

MARINADE:

2 *cups vegetable oil*
⅓ *cup soy sauce*
¼ *cup honey*
1 *tablespoon minced onion*
1 *clove garlic, pressed*

4 *(8- to 12-ounce) pork tenderloins*
Seasoned salt to taste
Freshly ground pepper to taste

Make the sauce: Combine the mayonnaise, sour cream, salt, pepper, garlic, mustard, and Worcestershire sauce in a small bowl and mix well. Chill, covered, in the refrigerator. Bring to room temperature before serving.

To make the marinade, combine the oil, soy sauce, honey, onion, and garlic in a large nonaluminum bowl and mix well. Trim the tenderloins and place in the marinade. Marinate in the refrigerator for 6 hours or longer, turning occasionally.

Prepare a medium-hot fire in a charcoal grill or preheat a gas-fired grill and oil the rack. For indoor cooking, preheat the broiler. Drain the tenderloins, discarding the marinade. Pat the meat dry and sprinkle with seasoned salt and pepper. Place on the grill rack or on a rack in the broiler pan. Grill the tenderloins for 3 to 4 minutes per side, turning once. Cut each tenderloin crosswise into 6 to 8 pieces ¾ inch thick. Return the slices to the grill or broiler rack. Grill or broil 4 to 5 minutes longer or until cooked through. To serve, arrange the tenderloin medallions on a serving plate and sprinkle with additional ground pepper to taste. Serve with the sour cream garlic sauce.

Meet Us in the Kitchen, St. Louis, MO

THE KING'S GRILLED TENDERS

MAKES 8 TO 10 SERVINGS

1½ cups vegetable oil
¾ cup soy sauce
½ cup red wine vinegar
⅓ cup fresh lemon juice
¼ cup Worcestershire sauce
2 tablespoons dry mustard
2 tablespoons snipped parsley
1 tablespoon ground black pepper
2 cloves garlic, minced
3 (1-pound) pork tenderloins

Combine the oil, soy sauce vinegar, lemon juice, Worcestershire sauce, dry mustard, parsley, pepper, and garlic in a medium bowl. Cover and refrigerate the marinade for 3 hours. Place the tenderloins into a large zipper-lock plastic bag set into a shallow dish. Pour the marinade over the meat; close the bag. Marinate in the refrigerator overnight, turning the bag occasionally to redistribute the marinade.

When ready to cook, prepare a medium-hot fire in a charcoal grill. Drain the tenderloins and pat dry. Grill, covered, directly over medium coals for 14 to 20 minutes, turning to brown on all sides, or until no pink remains. Allow to rest for 5 to 10 minutes before slicing to serve.

Heart & Soul, Memphis, TN

CRANBERRY PORK TENDERLOIN

MAKES 8 TO 10 SERVINGS

3 cloves garlic, minced
2 teaspoons ground black pepper, divided
2 tablespoons fresh thyme, chopped, or 2 teaspoons dried, divided
3 (1-pound) pork tenderloins
1 fifth (about 3 cups) ruby or tawny port wine
1 cup heavy cream
2 tablespoons minced shallots
½ cup dried cranberries
1 tablespoon vegetable oil

Combine the garlic, 1 teaspoon pepper, and 1 tablespoon fresh or 1 teaspoon dried thyme in a small bowl. Rub the mixture on the pork tenderloins; place in a large shallow dish. Cover and refrigerate for 6 hours or overnight.

Prepare the sauce by pouring the port into a medium saucepan. Bring to a boil and cook for about 25 minutes or until reduced to 1 cup. Add the cream, shallots, the remaining 1 teaspoon pepper, and the remaining thyme. Cook over low heat until the sauce starts to thicken. Add the cranberries and heat thoroughly. (The sauce can be made up to 24 hours in advance and refrigerated. Reheat gently.)

Prepare a medium-hot fire in a charcoal grill, or preheat the broiler. Pat the meat dry and rub with oil. Broil or grill the pork over medium coals for about 15 to 20 minutes, turning so that all sides are brown. Place on a cutting board and let stand, loosely covered, for 5 to 10 minutes. Slice and serve with the port sauce.

Gold 'n Delicious, Spokane, WA

KALUA PORK

MAKES 8 TO 10 SERVINGS

1 (5-pound) bone-in center-cut pork
    loin roast
¼ cup soy sauce
3 tablespoons sherry
1 large clove garlic, crushed
½ teaspoon ground cinnamon
½ teaspoon thyme
⅔ cup peach preserves
¼ cup chili sauce
1 cup water, divided
1 (8-ounce) can water chestnuts,
    drained and sliced
Fresh parsley sprigs for garnish

Marinate the roast in a sauce made from the soy sauce, sherry, garlic, cinnamon, and thyme for 2 to 3 hours, turning often.

Preheat the oven to 450F. Pat the meat dry, reserving the marinade, and place the roast in a shallow roasting pan. Bake for 15 minutes, then reduce oven heat to 325F and continue cooking for about 1½ hours or until the internal temperature reaches 150F on an instant-read thermometer.

Meanwhile, in a small saucepan, combine the reserved marinade, peach preserves, chili sauce, and ½ cup of water. Bring to a boil, stirring constantly. When the meat is done, baste it with the sauce and cook 10 more minutes. Remove to a carving board. Add the remaining ½ cup water to the pan to scrape up the brown bits. Add the pan juices and water chestnuts to the sauce and heat through. To serve, carve the roast and arrange the slices on a platter. Spoon the sauce and water chestnuts around the roast. Garnish with parsley. Pass the remaining sauce.

Tea-Time at the Masters, Augusta, GA

GRILLED APRICOT RIBS

MAKES 4 SERVINGS

1 (17-ounce) can apricot halves
⅓ cup packed dark brown sugar
3 tablespoons vinegar
1 clove garlic, chopped
4 teaspoons soy sauce
⅛ teaspoon ground ginger
1 slab pork ribs (about 3 pounds)
Salt and freshly ground pepper

Prepare a medium hot fire in a charcoal grill. Meanwhile, make the apricot basting sauce: Drain the apricots, reserving ⅓ cup of syrup. Purée the apricots with the reserved syrup in a blender. Pour into a small saucepan. Add the brown sugar, vinegar, garlic, soy sauce, and ginger. Stir and simmer over medium heat, uncovered, 10 to 15 minutes.

Oil the grill rack. Pat the ribs dry and season with salt and pepper. Place on the grill rack and cook slowly about 50 minutes. Baste with apricot sauce the last 30 minutes of cooking.

Hearts and Flour, Waco, TX

SEASONED PORK ROAST WITH MUSHROOM SAUCE

MAKES 6 SERVINGS

2 teaspoons crushed fresh rosemary
1 teaspoon black peppercorns, crushed
½ teaspoon Szechwan peppercorns, (optional)
1½ teaspoons dried leaf sage
¾ teaspoon thyme
1 teaspoon coarse salt
½ teaspoon coriander seed
1 teaspoon minced garlic
1 (4-pound) boneless pork loin roast, rolled and tied
Mushroom Sauce (see below)

Preheat the oven to 425F. Mix all the spices together in a small bowl. Coat the roast with the spices, patting to keep on meat. Insert a meat thermometer in the roast and place the roast on a rack in a shallow baking pan. Roast for 15 minutes. Reduce the temperature to 325F and continue to roast until the center temperature registers 150F, about 1½ hours. Allow the meat to rest for 10 minutes before carving. Serve with mushroom sauce.

MUSHROOM SAUCE:

2 tablespoons olive oil
3 cloves garlic, minced
1 shallot, sliced
1 pound mushrooms, cut into quarters (discard stems)
1 cup dry sherry or Madeira
1 cup chicken stock
1 tablespoon soy sauce
2 teaspoons cornstarch dissolved in 1 tablespoon water
Salt and freshly ground pepper to taste (optional)

Heat the oil in a medium skillet. Sauté the garlic and shallot for 1 minute. Add the mushrooms and sauté over medium-high heat for 4 to 5 minutes or until they start to brown. Add the sherry and simmer until most of the liquid evaporates. Add the chicken stock and soy sauce. Bring to a boil. Stir in the cornstarch mixture and simmer for 2 to 3 minutes. Season with salt and pepper, if desired.

Dining by Fireflies, Charlotte, NC

GRILLED MAPLE-GLAZED BABY BACK RIBS

1½ cups pure maple syrup

1½ cups apple cider vinegar

1 cup peanut, sunflower, or vegetable
oil

½ cup molasses

½ cup soy sauce

3 tablespoons prepared sweet mustard

2 tablespoons juniper berries, crushed
(optional)

4 racks baby back pork ribs, cracked
along backbone

Combine all the ingredients except the ribs in a medium bowl and blend well. Quickly rinse the ribs under cold running water and pat dry with paper towels. Place in a shallow nonaluminum container. Cover with the marinade and turn over to coat thoroughly. Cover and refrigerate at least 12 hours, turning ribs occasionally. Return to room temperature before cooking.

Preheat the oven to 300F. Remove the ribs from the container, reserving the marinade. Place ribs in a large pan and bake for 50 minutes. Prepare a covered charcoal grill for moderate direct-heat cooking. Strain the marinade into a medium saucepan. Bring to a boil and simmer over moderate heat for 1 hour or until the marinade is reduced to about 2½ cups. (This will be used to glaze ribs while they are cooking on the grill.)

When the fire is ready, brush the grill rack with oil. Place ribs on the rack and cover the grill. Brush the ribs frequently with reduced marinade as they cook, turning until the meat is tender and glazed, approximately 30 minutes. Slice the ribs into individual portions and serve piping hot.

Dining by Fireflies, Charlotte, NC

MUSTARD-GLAZED SPARERIBS

MAKES 6 SERVINGS

1 small onion, chopped
2 tablespoons vegetable oil
1 cup honey
1 cup Dijon mustard
½ cup cider vinegar
1 teaspoon ground cloves
Salt
6 pounds (about) baby back rib
    sections
Freshly ground pepper to taste

Sauté the onion in the heated oil in a saucepan over medium heat for 5 minutes or until tender. Add the honey, mustard, vinegar, cloves and ½ teaspoon of salt and mix well. Bring to a boil and reduce the heat. Simmer for 5 minutes, stirring occasionally.

Pat the ribs dry and season them generously on both sides with salt and pepper. Place on an oiled grill rack 4 to 6 inches above a heated grill with a cover. Cover the grill and open the vents halfway. Grill for 40 minutes, turning once, adding coals if necessary to maintain an even heat.

Brush the ribs with the mustard mixture and grill, covered, 10 minutes. Turn the ribs and brush again with the mustard mixture. Grill 10 minutes longer. Cut the ribs into single-rib servings. Heat the remaining basting sauce until bubbly. Serve with the ribs.

Wild Thymes and Other Temptations, Tucson, AZ

ROSEMARY PORK CHOPS

MAKES 8 SERVINGS

¼ cup Dijon mustard
¼ cup balsamic vinegar
¼ cup lemon juice
6 cloves garlic, minced
3 tablespoons fresh rosemary
¾ teaspoon salt
1 teaspoon freshly ground black pepper
½ cup olive oil
8 center-cut loin pork chops, cut 1 to
    1½ inches thick

Combine the mustard, vinegar, lemon juice, garlic, rosemary, salt, black pepper, and oil in a small bowl; mix well. Place the pork chops in a shallow dish or in a large zipper-lock bag. Pour the marinade over the chops and let stand for 2 hours in the refrigerator.

Meanwhile, prepare a medium hot fire in a charcoal grill or preheat a gas-fired grill. Remove the chops from the marinade and pat them dry. Place on the grill rack and cook, turning once, for 5 to 8 minutes on each side.

I'll Cook When Pigs Fly, Cincinnati, OH

PORK CHOPS WITH BROWNED GARLIC BUTTER

MAKES 6 SERVINGS

1½ teaspoons salt

½ teaspoon onion powder

¼ teaspoon garlic powder

¼ teaspoon ground white pepper

¼ teaspoon dry mustard

¼ teaspoon ground sage

¼ teaspoon ground cumin

¼ teaspoon dried thyme, crushed

6 center-cut pork chops, cut ½ inch
    thick

⅔ cup all-purpose flour

3 tablespoons cooking oil

6 tablespoons butter or margarine

2 cloves garlic, minced

1 teaspoon snipped parsley

1 teaspoon hot pepper sauce

1 teaspoon fresh lemon juice

1 teaspoon freshly ground black pepper

Combine the salt, onion powder, garlic powder, white pepper, dry mustard, sage, cumin, and thyme in a small bowl; mix well. Sprinkle each side of the pork chops with ¼ teaspoon of the seasoning mix. Rub the seasonings into the chops with your fingertips. Combine the flour and any remaining seasoning mix in a pie plate. Dip both sides of the pork chops into the flour mixture to coat; shake off excess.

In a large skillet, heat the oil. Cook the chops over medium heat for 4 to 5 minutes per side or until golden brown. Drain on paper towels. Meanwhile, in a 1-quart saucepan, heat the butter until almost melted. Add the garlic and cook over medium-high heat for 2 to 3 minutes or until the foam on the surface is light brown. Stir in the parsley, hot pepper sauce, lemon juice, and black pepper. Cook until the sauce is lightly browned. Immediately drizzle over the pork chops.

Heart & Soul, Memphis, TN

Grilled Smoked Pork Chops with Spinach, Cheese Grits, and Black-Eyed Pea Salsa

MAKES 4 SERVINGS

*4 bone-in smoked pork loin chops,
 thick cut*
½ cup cooked black-eyed peas
2 tablespoons chopped red bell pepper
*2 tablespoons chopped yellow bell
 pepper*
*2 tablespoons chopped green bell
 pepper*
1 large shallot, minced
1 clove garlic, minced
1 tablespoon minced fresh cilantro
1 teaspoon minced jalapeño
Juice of 2 limes
Salt
4 cups chicken or ham stock
1 cup uncooked stone-ground grits
½ cup grated white Cheddar cheese
2 cups blanched fresh spinach
1 tablespoon olive oil
Freshly ground pepper to taste

Grill the pork chops on both sides until cooked through. Keep warm in the oven. Combine the black-eyed peas, bell peppers, shallot, garlic, cilantro, jalapeño, lime juice, and salt to taste in a bowl; mix well and set the salsa aside.

Bring the stock to a boil in a saucepan. Stir in the grits and 1 teaspoon of salt. Simmer for 4 to 6 minutes or until the liquid is absorbed, stirring frequently. Stir in the cheese. Sauté the spinach in heated olive oil in a small sauté pan until heated through. Season with salt and pepper.

Arrange the chops on individual serving plates. Serve with the salsa, cheese grits, and spinach.

True Grits, Atlanta, GA

BEST LAMB I'VE EVER TASTED

MAKES 12 TO 14 SERVINGS

1 (7-pound) leg of lamb, trimmed of
   fat, boned, and butterflied
Olive oil
2 tablespoons soy sauce
Juice of ½ lemon
½ teaspoon rosemary
2 cloves garlic, put through a press

Preheat the oven to 375F. Rub the unboned side of the lamb with olive oil and place oiled side down in a shallow baking pan. Combine 3 to 4 tablespoons of olive oil, the soy sauce, lemon juice, rosemary, and garlic in a small bowl; mix well. Rub the marinade over the other side of the lamb. Roast for 20 minutes. Remove the lamb from the oven and turn the heat up to broil. Push 2 skewers lengthwise through the lamb to secure it; then baste with additional olive oil. Return to the oven and broil the lamb for 2 to 3 minutes or until browned. Let stand 10 minutes before carving.

Mountain Elegance, Asheville, NC

GRILLED BUTTERFLIED LEG OF LAMB

MAKES 8 TO 10 SERVINGS

6 tablespoons fresh lemon juice
¼ cup olive oil
2 teaspoons Worcestershire sauce
2 teaspoons salt
1 teaspoon grated fresh lemon zest
½ teaspoon dried crushed rosemary
½ teaspoon dry mustard
¼ teaspoon freshly ground black
   pepper
1 (5-pound) butterflied leg of lamb,
   trimmed to an even thickness

Combine the lemon juice, oil, Worcestershire, salt, and seasonings in a small bowl; mix well. Place the lamb in a shallow dish and rub the marinade over all surfaces. Cover and refrigerate 6 to 8 hours, turning often.

Preheat the broiler or prepare a medium-hot charcoal fire. Position the broiler rack 4 to 6 inches from the heat source. Remove the lamb from the marinade and pat dry. Reserve the marinade. Place the meat skin side down on the broiler pan or skin side up on the grill rack. Grill for 12 to 15 minutes on each side or to the desired degree of doneness, turning often and basting with the reserved marinade. Let stand 10 minutes before carving.

Very Virginia, Hampton Roads, VA

GOLD RUSH BRUNCH

MAKES 8 SERVINGS

1 (10-ounce) package dry hashed
    brown potatoes with onions
4 tablespoons (½ stick) butter or
    margarine
¼ cup all-purpose flour
Salt and freshly ground pepper
2 cups milk
1 cup sour cream
2 tablespoons minced parsley
8 slices Canadian bacon
8 large eggs

Preheat the oven to 300F. Prepare the potatoes according to the package directions; set aside.

Melt the butter in a medium saucepan. Blend in the flour, ½ teaspoon of salt, and ⅛ teaspoon of pepper. Gradually stir in the milk; cook, stirring, until thick and bubbly. Remove from the heat. Add the sour cream, parsley, and hashed browns, mixing well. Spoon into a 13 x 9-inch baking pan; arrange the bacon on top. Bake for 20 minutes. Break the eggs in depressed areas made with a spoon; sprinkle with salt and pepper to taste. Bake 15 to 25 minutes or until the eggs are set.

Brunch Basket, Rockford, IL

BACON-AND-ONION CRUSTLESS QUICHE

MAKES 6 TO 8 SERVINGS

4 tablespoons (½ stick) butter
¾ pound bacon, fried crisp
2 onions, chopped
4 large eggs
1½ cups milk
Salt and freshly ground pepper to
    taste
½ pound Swiss cheese, grated

Preheat the oven to 400F. Spread 1 tablespoon of butter evenly in a 9-inch tart pan or pie pan.

Cook the bacon in a heavy skillet over medium heat until crisp. Remove to drain on paper towels; pour off the fat. Melt the remaining 3 tablespoons of butter in the skillet, add the onions, and sauté until soft but not browned, about 6 minutes. Beat the eggs in a medium bowl, add the milk and beat to combine. Season with salt and pepper.

Line the bottom of the tart pan with bacon strips and scatter the cheese on top. Pour in the egg mixture. Bake for 25 to 30 minutes or until the custard is browned and set.

NOTE: This easy, crustless quiche can be frozen after baking.

California Sizzles, Pasadena, CA

SCRAMBLED EGG CASSEROLE

MAKES 8 TO 10 SERVINGS

1 cup cubed ham or diced Canadian
    bacon
¼ cup chopped green onion
3 tablespoons butter
1 dozen large eggs, beaten
1 (14-ounce) can sliced mushrooms,
    drained
Cheese Sauce (see below)
¼ cup melted butter
2¼ cups fine soft bread crumbs
⅛ teaspoon paprika

Sauté the ham and green onion in the 3 tablespoons of butter in a large skillet for 5 minutes or until onion is tender. Add the eggs and cook over medium-high heat, stirring gently to form large, soft curds. When the eggs are set, stir in the mushrooms and the cheese sauce. Spoon the eggs into a greased 13 x 9-inch baking pan. Combine the melted butter and bread crumbs, mixing well; spread evenly over the egg mixture. Sprinkle with the paprika.

(The casserole can be prepared up to this point, covered, and chilled overnight for serving the next day.) Preheat the oven to 350F. Bake, uncovered, 30 minutes.

CHEESE SAUCE:

2 tablespoons butter
2½ tablespoons all-purpose flour
2 cups milk
½ teaspoon salt
⅛ teaspoon freshly ground pepper
1 cup shredded American cheese

Melt the butter in a heavy saucepan over low heat; blend in the flour and cook 1 minute. Gradually add the milk; cook over medium heat until thickened, stirring constantly. Add the salt, pepper, and cheese and continue stirring until the cheese melts and the mixture is smooth.

Quail Country, Albany, GA

HAM SANDWICHES

MAKES 8 SERVINGS

8 tablespoons (1 stick) butter, softened
8 onion rolls or hamburger buns, split
1 small onion, chopped
2 tablespoons poppy seeds
1 teaspoon dry mustard
1 pound shaved ham
8 ounces Swiss cheese, sliced

Preheat the oven to 350F. Spread the butter on the cut sides of the rolls, reserving 1 tablespoon of butter. Sauté the onion in the reserved butter in a skillet until softened, about 5 minutes. Add the poppy seeds and dry mustard; mix well. Remove from the heat.

Layer the ham, a cheese slice, and some of the onion mixture on half of each roll. Replace the roll tops; wrap in foil. Place on a baking sheet. Bake 20 minutes.

Dining in the Smoky Mountain Mist, Knoxville, TN

STUFFED WHITEWING DOVE BREASTS

MAKES 6 TO 8 SERVINGS

30 whitewing doves (squab)
6 ounces Cheddar cheese
5 pickled jalapeño peppers
15 slices bacon, cut in half

Preheat the oven to 350F. Remove the skin and legs from the doves; carefully fillet each dove breast. Cut the cheese into 30 strips. Wash and seed the peppers; slice each pepper into 6 strips. Stuff each dove breast with a slice of pepper and a slice of cheese. Wrap each breast in a half slice of the bacon; secure with a toothpick. Place the breasts in a 13 x 9-inch baking pan. Bake for 15 to 20 minutes, turn the breasts, and bake 10 minutes more or until the bacon is crisp.

Some Like It Hot, McAllen, TX

MADISON COUNTY BARBECUED DOVE

MAKES 4 SERVINGS

8 doves (squab)
2 onions, cut into quarters
2 jalapeños, seeded, cut into quarters
8 slices bacon
8 tablespoons (1 stick) butter
¼ cup vinegar
¼ cup Worcestershire sauce
¼ cup sugar or ½ cup honey
1 clove garlic, crushed
1 tablespoon prepared mustard
2 cups ketchup
¼ cup lemon juice
½ cup water
2 tablespoons Tabasco

Prepare a medium-hot fire in a charcoal grill.

Rinse the doves and pat dry. Place 1 onion quarter and 1 jalapeño quarter in each dove cavity; wrap with the bacon. Combine the butter, vinegar, Worcestershire sauce, sugar, garlic, mustard, ketchup, lemon juice, water, and Tabasco in a saucepan. Simmer for 20 minutes, stirring occasionally.

Brush the doves with the sauce. Arrange breast side down on the grill rack and grill over medium-high coals, turning to brown the bacon on all sides, for 10 minutes or until cooked through. Remove to a serving platter; drizzle with the sauce.

Sweet Home Alabama, Huntsville, AL

ROAST WILD DUCK

MAKES 8 SERVINGS

4 wild ducks, cleaned
¼ cup bacon drippings
2 teaspoons salt
½ teaspoon freshly ground pepper
2 oranges, sliced very thick
3 carrots, sliced very thin
1 onion, halved
1½ cups grape wine
Water
3 tablespoons all-purpose flour

Preheat the oven to 325F. Pat the ducks dry and rub the breasts with bacon fat. Salt and pepper the ducks inside and out. Place the birds breast side up in a roasting pan. Put a thick orange slice on top of each duck. Put carrots and onion in the roaster. Combine the wine and 1½ cups of water and pour into the roaster, being careful not to pour onto the seasoned ducks. Bake, covered, for 1½ hours, basting every 30 minutes. Discard the orange slices and the onion and turn the ducks breast side down. Bake, covered, an additional 30 minutes.

Remove the ducks to a warm platter. With a fork, mash the carrots in the broth. Make a gravy by adding the flour mixed with 3 tablespoons of water to the broth; stir until thick. Pass in a gravy boat.

Cotton Country Cooking, 25th Anniversary Edition, Morgan County, AL

DUCK AND WILD RICE CASSEROLE

MAKES 6 SERVINGS

*2 medium-size wild ducks (3 cups
    cubed cooked meat)*
3 stalks celery, cut into chunks
*1 onion, halved, plus ½ cup chopped
    onion*
Salt and ground black pepper to taste
*1 (6-ounce) package seasoned wild
    and long-grain rice*
8 tablespoons (1 stick) butter
¼ cup all-purpose flour
1 (4-ounce) can sliced mushrooms
1½ cups half-and-half
1 tablespoon chopped parsley
Slivered almonds

Place the ducks in a large stockpot; cover with water and add the celery, onion halves, salt, and pepper. Bring to a boil, reduce the heat, and simmer, covered, for 1 hour (or until tender). Remove the ducks and, when they are cool enough to handle, skin and bone them and cube the meat. Reserve and strain the broth. Cook the rice according to the package directions.

Preheat the oven to 350F. Melt the butter in a large skillet; sauté the chopped onion, then stir in the flour. Drain the mushrooms, reserving the liquid. Add the mushrooms to the onion mixture. Add enough duck broth to the mushroom liquid to make 1½ cups; stir this into the onion mixture. Add the half-and-half, parsley, rice, 1½ teaspoons of salt, and ¼ teaspoon of pepper. Stir in the cubed duck meat. Pour the mixture into a greased 2-quart casserole. Sprinkle almonds on top.

Bake, covered, for 15 to 20 minutes. Uncover and bake for 5 to 10 minutes longer or until very hot. (If the casserole has been refrigerated it will take longer to heat.)

NOTE: If you don't have ducks, try substituting chicken.

Southern Accent, Pine Bluff, AR

ROAST DUCK WITH ORANGE JUICE AND WINE

MAKES 4 SERVINGS

1 (4- to 5-pound) wild duck, cleaned
Salt and freshly ground pepper
6 onions, cut in small chunks
6 apples, peeled and chopped
8 to 10 stalks celery, cut in short
    lengths
1 cup coarse bread crumbs
8 tablespoons (1 stick) butter, melted
1 cup orange juice
1 cup dry red wine
6 bay leaves
10 whole cloves
2 tablespoons all-purpose flour

Wash the duck inside and out, and dry well. Rub the inside of the duck with salt and pepper. Combine the onions, apple, celery, and bread crumbs to make a very coarse dressing. Stuff this inside the duck, and sew it up for roasting. Rub the outside with salt and pepper; if duck is fatty, score the outer surface.

Preheat the oven to 450F. Place the duck in an uncovered roasting pan with the butter. Turn until the bird is brown. Then reduce the temperature to 400F. Bake, covered, for 20 to 25 minutes per pound. Combine the orange juice, wine, bay leaves, and cloves in a small bowl. After the duck is brown, baste frequently with the orange juice mixture.

When the duck is done, transfer it from the roasting pan to a serving dish. Remove the stuffing, which is not intended to be eaten. Strain the bay leaves and cloves from the pan juices. Place the juices in a small saucepan. Stir in the flour and any remaining orange juice and wine sauce. Add salt and pepper to taste if necessary. Cook until the mixture begins to thicken, stirring constantly. Serve this sauce in a separate gravy boat at the table.

Smoky Mountain Magic, Johnson City, TN

MRS. STONEWALL JACKSON'S STUFFED PARTRIDGES

Partridges
Bacon, in strips
Salt and pepper
Butter

(An original recipe from *Old North State Cookbook*)

Select firm, plump birds. Do not split and then draw them down the back, but draw them, stuff them, and bake them in a moderate oven as you would a hen. Lay a strip of bacon across the breast of each. Season with salt, pepper and lumps of butter. Baste frequently. Serve on small triangles of toast which have been buttered on both sides.

The Charlotte Cookbook, Charlotte, NC

VENISON CHORIZO

MAKES 6 POUNDS

6 whole dried red chile peppers, seeded
4 ounces ground red chiles (hot)
2 whole heads of garlic, separated, peeled, and minced
3 tablespoons dried oregano
2 tablespoons distilled white vinegar
5 teaspoons salt
1 teaspoon ground black pepper
½ teaspoon ground cloves
6 pounds ground venison

In a saucepan, cover the dried chiles with water and boil until soft. Drain, reserving liquid. Purée the chiles with enough liquid to form a smooth paste. Combine the dried chile paste with the ground chiles, the garlic, oregano, vinegar, salt, pepper, and cloves in a small bowl. Mix with the venison and fry a small piece to check the seasoning. Refrigerate for 3 days or freeze until ready to use. Make into patties and fry in hot oil.

¡Viva! Tradiciones, Corpus Christi, TX

FISH

AND

SEAFOOD

SOUTHWEST

Think Southwest and you might think heat: hot land, hot food. But just as the Southwest is more than endless desert under a watercolor sky, so too is its food diverse and infused with history and tradition.

In the spirit of America's melting-pot cuisine, Southwestern food reflects the diversity of the people who settled this rugged corner of the country: the hearty game of Colorado mountain men, the beans and grains of the Pueblo Indians, the seasonings of the Spanish, and the smoked meats and sausage of the Germans.

Blame it on the size of the Lone Star State, but Texans think big—big parties, big portions, and big, bold, intensely flavored food. Take the Texas barbecue. This state is so big that depending where you are, you'll hear four different approaches to barbecuing. East Texans swear by thick, sweet, and tangy barbecue sauce brushed on the meat before cooking. In south Texas, they love their sauce hot and spicy and the result is robust-flavored meat with just enough heat to go perfectly with a swig of icy cold beer. Go to central Texas and they rely on mesquite, hickory, and oak to impart a rich and smoky flavor to their meats, which they consider to be the true essence of outdoor barbecue. In west Texas, diced juicy tomatoes cool the heat of New Mexico chile peppers in their barbecue sauce. What they all agree on is the barbecue meats, which are usually large sides of beef or a whole suckling pig, cooked for up to 14 to 18 hours.

What is eaten with the barbecued meats? Huge bowls of Texas caviar—otherwise known as black-eyed peas—and beans with pico de gallo, a condiment consisting of tomatoes, onions, garlic, jalapeños, and cilantro. And a Texan gathering wouldn't be complete without chili—another dish that inspires heated discussions on the best method of cooking it.

Tex-Mex cooking came out of Texas cities that border close to Mexico. This style of cooking started out using generous amounts of spices to smother the inferior cuts of shredded chicken, beef, and pork. And it works—the corn tortillas filled with the highly seasoned meat topped with melted cheese and chili sauce taste wonderful. Served with rice and beans, they make a complete, filling, and inexpensive meal. New Mexican cooks take the same tortillas, onions, and cheese and stack them like a multilayered sandwich, then blanket the whole thing in chile sauce. That would be a sauce made from chile, the pepper—and it's the diner's call whether that sauce will be red or green. Meanwhile, in Arizona, they're serving chimichangas, a local creation that's essentially a fried burrito.

The most exciting news that's hit the Southwest cooking scene since chile is the inspiring influx of Southeast Asian and Indian home cooks. These cooks immigrated from hot countries and know a thing or two about eating spicy hot dishes to cool off. They have generously shared ancient methods of controlling fiery ingredients without compromising the heat of the dish. From the Thais, the Southwest has learned that creamy coconut milk can temper red-hot chile pastes beautifully. They've learned from the Vietnamese that when eaten with cool salads and fresh vegetables, sauces laced with super-hot chiles can be invigorating and refreshing. And the Indians have shared that the key to eating mouth-burning curries is plenty of rice, sweet chutney, and cool and tangy yogurt-based raita.

However it is cooked, in the Southwest you'll find a hungry crowd with margaritas in hand ready to feast and celebrate, which adds up to a unique fiesta.

—Cathy Barber, *Dallas Morning News*
Dallas, TX

EARLY SUMMER COOKOUT

Everyone relishes the idea of getting together in the backyard for a cookout when the weather permits. Where there are good food and good friends (and maybe even some tasty margaritas), the outing might last into the wee hours.

NEW WAVE MARGARITAS 56

EASY SHRIMP DIP 28

CORNBREAD MEXICANA 283

MUSTARD-GLAZED SPARERIBS 202

GRILLED MIXED VEGETABLES 155

STRAWBERRY-RHUBARB SLUMP 357

COASTAL BEND DINNER

Seafood is a focal point of life in the Coastal Bend region of Texas. Saltwater fishing is a pastime for many South Texans and for the thousands of tourists who travel to the region annually in search of the prize-winning catch. Snapper reigns as a must for any celebration. Serve your fish dinner with veggies and pasta, and top it off with delicious brownies for a Corpus Christi favorite.

Submitted by *¡Viva! Tradiciones,* Corpus Christi, TX

SNAPPER WITH HERB CRUST 224

CAULIFLOWER AND BROCCOLI SPECIAL 141

DIVINE WISDOM FETTUCCINE 155

EDIE'S BROWNIES 344

RECIPE FOR A BETTER COMMUNITY

JUNIOR LEAGUE OF HONOLULU, HAWAII COMMUNITY PROJECT:

The Hawaii Children's Discovery Center

From 1986 to 1988, the Junior League of Hawaii assisted in developing the master plan for a participatory museum for children and families. In the 1988–1989 League year, a docent and group tour program was put into service. Although the Junior League of Honolulu is no longer actively involved, the League is recognized in the community for having established the museum.

The cookbook that helped to make it happen: *Another Taste of Aloha* funded $41,000 of The Hawaii Children's Discovery Center.

Did you know? *Another Taste of Aloha* sold out on QVC!

GRILLED KING MACKEREL STEAKS

MAKES 6 SERVINGS

2 pounds fresh or frozen king
    mackerel steaks
¼ cup orange juice
¼ cup soy sauce
2 tablespoons ketchup
2 tablespoons vegetable oil
2 tablespoons chopped parsley
1 tablespoon lemon juice
1 clove garlic, crushed
½ teaspoon oregano
½ teaspoon freshly ground pepper

Cut the fish steaks into serving-size portions and place in a single layer in a shallow baking dish. Combine the orange juice and the remaining ingredients in a small bowl. Pour over the fish. Let stand for 30 minutes, turning once. Remove the fish, reserving the sauce for basting. Place the fish in well-greased, hinged wire grills. Grill about 4 inches from moderately hot coals for 8 minutes. Baste with the sauce. Turn and cook 7 to 10 minutes longer or until the fish flakes easily when tested with a fork.

Some Like It South!, Pensacola, FL

LEMON THYME SWORDFISH

MAKES 6 SERVINGS

6 (6-ounce) swordfish steaks, ½ inch
    thick, skin removed
Juice of 2 lemons
2 shallots, thinly sliced
2 cloves garlic, crushed
2 tablespoons coarse mustard
¼ cup olive oil
3-4 sprigs of fresh thyme, minced
Freshly ground pepper

Place the swordfish in a shallow bowl. Whisk the lemon juice, shallots, garlic, mustard, oil, and thyme in a small bowl. Season with the pepper. Pour over the swordfish. Marinate, covered, at room temperature for 30 minutes, or in the refrigerator for several hours.

Fire up the grill. Brush the grill rack with oil. Arrange the swordfish on the rack. Grill for 3 to 4 minutes per side or until seared on the outside and cooked through.

Dining by Design, Pasadena, CA

TENNESSEE RIVER CATFISH WITH JALAPEÑO TARTAR SAUCE

MAKES 8 SERVINGS

Vegetable oil
¾ cup beer
3 tablespoons mustard
½ teaspoon salt
½ teaspoon freshly ground pepper
½ cup self-rising cornmeal
½ cup plain cornmeal
2 pounds catfish fillets
Jalapeño Tartar Sauce (see below)

Begin heating 2 inches of oil over medium-high heat in a deep heavy pot to 375F.

Meanwhile, combine the beer, mustard, 2 tablespoons of oil, salt, and pepper in a shallow bowl; mix well. Stir in the self-rising cornmeal. Put the plain cornmeal in another shallow bowl. Dip the catfish into the plain cornmeal, then into the beer mixture. Add to the hot oil one piece at a time, cooking in batches if necessary; do not crowd the pan. Fry until crispy and golden brown. Serve with jalapeño tartar sauce.

JALAPEÑO TARTAR SAUCE:

MAKES 4½ CUPS

3 cups mayonnaise
⅔ cup finely chopped onion
3 green onions, finely chopped
½ cup chopped parsley
⅓ cup vinegar
Grated zest and juice of 1 lemon
1 tablespoon Tabasco
¼ teaspoon ground red pepper
  (cayenne)
¼ cup Creole mustard
½ cup chopped dill pickles
8 jalapeño peppers, seeded (if desired)
  and chopped

Mix all the ingredients in a small bowl. Chill, covered, until ready to serve.

Beyond Cotton Country, Decatur, AL

HEART AND SOLE

MAKES 4 SERVINGS

6 fillets of sole or flounder
Salt and freshly ground pepper to
    taste
3-4 tomatoes, thinly sliced
½ cup fine bread crumbs
¼ cup white wine
6 tablespoons (¼ stick) butter
2 teaspoons fresh lime juice
¼ cup grated Parmesan cheese

Preheat the oven to 400F.

Rinse the fillets, pat them dry, and season with salt and pepper. Cover the bottom of a 13 x 9-inch baking dish with the tomato slices. Sprinkle with bread crumbs. Arrange the fillets on top. Combine the wine, butter, and lime juice in a saucepan. Simmer until butter is melted. Pour over the fillets and sprinkle with the cheese. Bake 10 to 15 minutes or until the fillets flake easily when tested with a fork. Do not overcook.

Hearts and Flour, Waco, TX

MARINATED TUNA ORIENTAL STYLE

MAKES 4 SERVINGS

¼ cup sherry wine vinegar
¼ cup soy sauce
2 teaspoons Dijon mustard
Freshly ground pepper
6 tablespoons Asian sesame oil
6 tablespoons vegetable oil
4 tuna steaks, approximately 1 inch
    thick
Lime slices and coriander sprigs for
    garnish

Combine the vinegar, soy sauce, mustard, and pepper in a blender or food processor. With the motor running, add the oils in a steady stream and blend until emulsified. Pour the mixture over the tuna steaks and let them marinate for 2 hours in the refrigerator.

Prepare a medium-hot charcoal fire or preheat the broiler and place the oven rack about 3 inches from the heat source.

Grill or broil the tuna for 3 to 5 minutes per side, basting frequently with marinade. Do not overcook. Garnish with lime slices and coriander.

Settings . . . From Our Past to Your Presentation, Philadelphia, PA

GRILLED SALMON WITH YOGURT DILL SAUCE

MAKES 6 SERVINGS

2 cups plain nonfat yogurt
1 tablespoon lemon juice
2 cloves garlic, minced
1 tablespoon chopped fresh dill, or 1
   teaspoon dried
⅛ teaspoon salt
⅛ teaspoon ground black pepper
Dash of hot pepper sauce
½ cucumber, peeled and thinly sliced
6 (8-ounce) salmon steaks or fillets

Combine the yogurt with the lemon juice, garlic, dill, salt, pepper, and hot pepper sauce in a medium bowl. Gently stir in the cucumber.

Prepare a medium-hot charcoal fire or preheat the broiler, placing the oven rack about 3 inches from the heat source. Broil or grill the salmon over medium-hot coals for 10 to 20 minutes, or until the fish flakes easily, turning once. Cooking time will depend on thickness; do not overcook. Spread the yogurt dill sauce over the salmon before serving.

Gold 'n Delicious, Spokane, WA

GRILLED CITRUS SALMON

MAKES 6 SERVINGS

1½ tablespoons fresh lemon juice
2 tablespoons olive oil
1 tablespoon butter or margarine
1 tablespoon Dijon mustard
4 cloves garlic, minced
2 dashes ground red pepper (cayenne)
2 dashes salt
1 teaspoon dried basil
1 teaspoon dried dill
2 teaspoons capers
3 pounds salmon fillets

In a small sauté pan over medium heat, combine the lemon juice, olive oil, butter, mustard, garlic, red pepper, salt, basil, dill, and capers. While stirring, bring to a boil. Reduce the heat and simmer for 5 minutes.

Place the salmon fillets skin side down on a piece of heavy-duty foil with the edges folded up, to make a pan. Pour the sauce evenly over the fish.

Prepare a medium-hot charcoal fire. Place the fish on the grill and cover with a lid. Barbecue over medium-hot coals for 10 to 12 minutes, depending on thickness of fillets. The fish will be flaky and light pink in color when cooked.

From Portland's Palate, Portland, OR

SALMON WITH SUN-DRIED TOMATO SALSA

MAKES 6 SERVINGS

½ cup white wine
3 tablespoons olive oil
Salt and freshly ground pepper to
*   taste*
6 (1-inch-thick) salmon steaks
4 small ripe tomatoes
¼ cup diced sun-dried tomatoes
3 shallots, diced
2 tablespoons chopped cilantro
2 tablespoons minced garlic
¼ cup diced green bell pepper
2 teaspoons lemon juice

Whisk together the wine, oil, ½ teaspoon of salt, and ½ teaspoon of pepper in a small bowl. Place the salmon steaks in a shallow glass pan and pour the wine mixture over the fish, turning to coat. Cover with plastic wrap and marinate 1 hour, turning once.

To make salsa, drop the ripe tomatoes into a boiling-water bath for 1 minute. Remove. Peel, core, and cut into halves. Squeeze to remove seeds. Dice the tomatoes and place in a large bowl. Add the remaining ingredients and stir to mix. Cover and set aside.

Prepare a medium-hot charcoal fire or preheat the broiler, with the oven rack about 3 inches from the heat source. Broil or grill the salmon for 5 to 7 minutes on each side. Serve immediately, topped with salsa.

Rogue River Rendezvous, Jackson County, OR

GOLDEN TEQUILA SAUCED WHITE FISH FILLETS

MAKES 2 SERVINGS

Zest and juice of 1 small lime
½ cup seeded and diced tomato
4 green onions, thinly sliced
1 tablespoon tequila
½ teaspoon salt, divided
¼ teaspoon pepper, divided
1 to 2 tablespoons butter
¼ cup all-purpose flour
1 pound firm white fish fillets

Combine the lime juice, tomato, onions, tequila, ¼ teaspoon of the salt, and ⅛ teaspoon of the pepper in a small bowl. Cover and refrigerate the tequila sauce for 2 to 3 hours.

Preheat the oven to 350F. Heat the butter in an ovenproof sauté pan. Season the flour with the remaining ¼ teaspoon of salt and ⅛ teaspoon of pepper. Lightly flour the fish, shaking off excess, and brown on one side over medium-high heat. Turn the fish over, cover with tequila sauce, and place in the oven. Bake for 10 to 15 minutes or until the fish flakes in the center. Top the fish with the lime zest and serve immediately.

Gold 'n Delicious, Spokane, WA

RED SNAPPER EN PAPILLOTE

10 tablespoons (1 stick plus 2
    tablespoons) butter, melted, divided
1 onion, chopped fine
1 cup all-purpose flour
2 cups milk, brought to a boil
Salt and freshly ground pepper to
    taste
2 large eggs
Dash of grated nutmeg
Dash of Tabasco
2 tablespoons sauterne wine
½ pound fresh shrimp, cooked, shelled,
    and chopped
½ pound crawfish meat, cooked and
    chopped
2 (1-pound) red snapper fillets,
    skinned

Preheat the oven to 350F. Butter a 1-foot-square piece of cooking parchment or aluminum foil.

In a large saucepan, melt 1 stick of the butter; sauté the onion for 5 minutes. Slowly add the flour to form a paste; cook, stirring constantly, over low heat until the mixture is dry. Graduallly whisk in the milk. Season with salt and pepper. Cook over medium heat, stirring constantly, until thickened and bubbly; remove the sauce from the heat.

In a small bowl, beat the eggs with the nutmeg, Tabasco, and sauterne; fold into the sauce. Add the shrimp, crawfish, and salt. On the prepared piece of parchment paper, spread one-third of the sauce; top with 1 red snapper fillet. Top, in order, with one-third of the sauce, the other red snapper fillet, and the remaining sauce. Fold the paper to form a bag with crimped edges and fold the edge to seal. Brush the paper with the remaining 2 tablespoons of melted butter. Place the package on a baking sheet and bake for 30 minutes; halfway through the cooking, turn the pan in the oven to ensure even doneness. Transfer the package to a serving platter and open at the table.

Tampa Treasures, Tampa, FL

SNAPPER WITH HERB CRUST

6 red snapper fillets
¼ cup olive oil
½ loaf French bread, cubed
2 strips bacon, cooked until crisp
2 teaspoons dried basil
2 teaspoons chopped chives
2 teaspoons dried parsley

Preheat the oven to 400F. Coat the fish with the oil. Process the bread, bacon, basil, chives, and parsley in a food processor until crumbly. Roll the fish in the bread mixture. Arrange the fillets in a greased 13 x 9-inch baking dish. Bake 15 minutes.

¡Viva! Tradiciones, Corpus Christi, TX

SNAPPER WITH SOUR CREAM STUFFING

MAKES 6 SERVINGS

3-4 pounds red snapper, cut into fillets
1½ teaspoons salt
Sour Cream Stuffing (see below)
2 tablespoons butter, melted, or olive
  oil

Preheat the oven to 350F. Cut a pocket in each fillet. Sprinkle the fish inside and out with salt. Stuff the fish loosely with the sour cream stuffing. Close the opening with skewers or wooden picks. Place the fish in a shallow greased baking pan. Brush with the butter or oil. Bake 40 to 60 minutes, or until the fish flakes easily. Baste with the pan juices while cooking.

SOUR CREAM STUFFING:

¾ cup chopped celery
½ cup chopped onion
4 tablespoons (½ stick) butter, melted
4 cups dry bread cubes
½ cup sour cream
2 tablespoons lemon zest
¼ cup peeled and diced lemon
1 teaspoon paprika
1 teaspoon salt

Sauté the celery and onion in the butter in a medium skillet. Add all the other ingredients and mix thoroughly.

Sugar Beach, The Emerald Beaches, FL

CHAMPAGNE SNAPPER

MAKES 4 SERVINGS

4 red snapper fillets
1 teaspoon salt
½ teaspoon freshly ground pepper
1 cup Champagne or dry white wine
2 tablespoons butter
1 bay leaf
1 tablespoon chopped onion
1 tablespoon finely chopped celery
    with leaves
2 teaspoons finely chopped fresh
    parsley
2 tablespoons cream
⅓ cup sliced sautéed mushrooms
3 tablespoons freshly grated Parmesan
    cheese

Preheat the oven to 325F. Sprinkle both sides of the fillets with the salt and pepper. Arrange in a single layer in a greased 13 x 9-inch baking dish.

Combine the Champagne, butter, bay leaf, onion, celery, and parsley in a saucepan. Bring to a boil; reduce the heat. Simmer until reduced by half, stirring frequently. Discard the bay leaf. Stir in the cream. Remove from heat. Add the mushrooms to the sauce. Pour over the fillets. Sprinkle with the cheese. Bake 25 to 30 minutes or until brown and bubbly.

Sunny Side Up, Greater Fort Lauderdale, FL

LINGUINE WITH SCALLOPS AND SNOW PEAS

MAKES 4 TO 6 SERVINGS

¾ pound fresh linguine
4 tablespoons (½ stick) butter, melted,
    plus 5 tablespoons cold butter
2 cloves garlic, minced
½ pound bay scallops
½ pound medium shrimp, shelled and
    deveined
1 teaspoon salt
1 teaspoon freshly ground pepper
2 cups snow peas, blanched
¾ cup grated Parmesan cheese

Cook the linguine according to the package directions; drain. Toss with the melted butter. Heat the remaining 5 tablespoons of butter in a large skillet. Add the garlic and sauté until softened. Add the scallops, shrimp, salt, and pepper. Sauté for 3 to 4 minutes, or until the shrimp and scallops are opaque. Add the snow peas and heat through. Toss the mixture with the linguine. Add the cheese and serve at once.

Settings . . . From Our Past to Your Presentation, Philadelphia, PA

GRILLED RED SNAPPER WITH MANGO SALSA

MAKES 4 SERVINGS

¼ cup fresh lime juice
4 tablespoons chopped fresh cilantro,
    divided
2 teaspoons olive oil
4 red snapper fillets (see Note)
¾ teaspoon each salt and freshly
    ground pepper
Mango Salsa (see below)

Combine the lime juice, 2 tablespoons of the cilantro, and the olive oil in a large shallow dish and mix well. Place the fish in the marinade, turning to coat. Marinate, covered, in the refrigerator for 30 minutes, turning once. Meanwhile, prepare a medium-hot fire in a charcoal grill or preheat a gas-fired grill to 350F to 400F.

Drain the fish, discarding the marinade. Sprinkle with salt and pepper. Place in a grilling basket sprayed with vegetable oil cooking spray. Grill for 10 minutes on each side or until the fish flakes easily when tested with a fork. Place the fish on a serving platter. Spoon mango salsa evenly over the top. Sprinkle with the remaining 2 tablespoons of cilantro.

NOTE: Grouper, mahi mahi or your favorite fish may be used instead of red snapper.

MANGO SALSA:

1 cup chopped Roma tomatoes
1 cup chopped mango
1 tablespoon chopped red onion
1 tablespoon chopped fresh cilantro
½ teaspoon sugar
½ teaspoon ground cumin
⅛ teaspoon salt
⅛ teaspoon freshly ground pepper
Dash of hot sauce
2 tablespoons fresh lime juice

Mix the tomatoes, mango, red onion, cilantro, sugar, cumin, salt, pepper, hot sauce, and lime juice in a medium bowl. Serve at room temperature.

Bay Tables, Mobile, AL

SEAFOOD RISOTTO

MAKES 4 SERVINGS

½ pound medium-size fresh shrimp,
  shelled, deveined, and cut in half
  lengthwise
½ pound sea scallops, cut in half
6 cloves garlic, minced
4 tablespoons olive oil, divided
1 cup minced onion
1½ cups Arborio rice
½ cup dry white wine
1 cup clam juice, heated
2 cups hot water
2 tablespoons brandy or cognac
1 teaspoon salt
2 tablespoons minced fresh parsley
Freshly grated Parmesan cheese

Heat 2 tablespoons of the oil in a heavy saucepan over medium heat. Sauté the shrimp, scallops, and three-fourths of the garlic 2 minutes or until the shrimp turn pink and the scallops are opaque.

Sauté the onion and the remaining garlic in the remaining 2 tablespoons oil in a separate saucepan over medium heat until golden. Add the rice and stir until the grains are coated. Stir in the wine, and cook until all the liquid is absorbed. Mix the clam juice with the 2 cups of hot water. Add ½ cup of this mixture to the rice and cook until all liquid is absorbed. Continue to add in liquid by the half cup, stirring occasionally after each addition. Add the brandy; cook, stirring constantly, until almost all liquid is absorbed, the mixture is creamy, and the rice is tender. Add the seafood mixture, salt, and parsley; heat until hot. Serve immediately with the Parmesan cheese.

Victorian Thymes & Pleasures, Williamsport, PA

NEWPORT MEDLEY

1 pound small hard-shell clams
1 pound mussels
1 medium onion, finely chopped
2 tablespoons butter
2 tablespoons all-purpose flour
½ teaspoon salt
½ teaspoon ground black pepper
¼ teaspoon ground red pepper
* (cayenne)*
2 teaspoons curry powder
2 teaspoons turmeric
2 cloves garlic, minced
1-1½ cups milk
¾ cup cooking broth from mussels and
* clams*
Juice of 2 lemons
¼ cup dry sherry
¾ cup heavy cream
¾ pound cooked shrimp, shelled and
* deveined*
Freshly chopped parsley

Scrub the clams and mussels and soak in cold water for 1 hour. Drain and rinse. Place in a pot with ½ cup of water, bring to a boil over high heat, and cook 5 to 8 minutes or until the shells open. Remove with a slotted spoon and take the clams and mussels from their shells; save the cooking liquid and strain through a paper-towel-lined sieve.

In a frying pan, sauté the onion in the butter until golden. Stir in the flour, salt, pepper, cayenne, curry powder, turmeric, and garlic. Cook and stir until a paste forms. Gradually add the milk and broth. Stir to make a smooth sauce. Add the lemon juice, sherry, cream, shellfish, and shrimp. Cook about 5 minutes until heated through. Transfer to a serving bowl and top with parsley.

A Taste of New England, Worcester, MA

CAPE SHORE LOBSTER BAKE

MAKES 6 TO 8 SERVINGS

*6-8 pounds clams, washed and
   wrapped in cheesecloth in 1-pound
   packages*
6-8 (1¼-pound) lobsters
*6-8 ears of corn, husks intact but silk
   removed*
1 pound hot dogs (optional)
½ dozen eggs (optional)
Melted butter
Lemon slices

Fashion an outdoor fireplace out of cement blocks or rocks. A metal trash can with a cover, lined with about 2 inches of stone, provides a simple and convenient means of preparing a small lobster bake. With an abundant supply of dry wood, start a fire and establish a good base of hot coals. Cover the stones in the bottom of the container with salt water. Spread with about 3 inches of fresh seaweed. Cover the seaweed with the clams; add a layer of seaweed. (None of the food layers should be packed too tightly.) Add the lobsters; cover with seaweed. Add the corn; cover with seaweed. Add the hot dogs and eggs, if desired; cover with seaweed. Place a cover on the container and place the container over the coals. Cook for 50 minutes after steam starts coming out from under the cover. Serve with melted butter and lemon slices.

NOTE: Heatproof gloves help when removing the steamed food.

RSVP, Portland, ME

SEAFOOD ENCHILADAS

MAKES 6 SERVINGS

ENCHILADAS:

½ onion, chopped

2 cloves garlic, chopped

½ red bell pepper, diced

½ green bell pepper, diced

2 tablespoons vegetable oil

½ pound drumfish, redfish, or red snapper, cut into ½-inch pieces

½ pound shrimp, shelled, deveined, and cut into ½-inch pieces

½ pound bay scallops, cut into ½-inch pieces

1 cup chopped tomato

Salt and ground black pepper to taste

12 corn tortillas

½ cup grated Monterey Jack cheese

TOMATILLO SAUCE:

2 cloves garlic, minced

½ onion, chopped

1 tablespoon vegetable oil

2 jalapeños, seeded

2 serrano peppers, seeded

10 tomatillos, husks removed

1 cup chicken broth

1 tablespoon chopped cilantro

To prepare enchiladas, sauté the onion, garlic and bell peppers in the oil in a medium skillet until soft. Add the fish and cook over medium heat for 1 minute. Add the shrimp, scallops, and tomato; cook until the shrimp turn pink, about 5 minutes. Season with salt and pepper. Spray each tortilla with vegetable oil cooking spray and warm on a griddle until soft. Fill each tortilla with some of the filling and sprinkle with cheese. Roll and place seam side down in a 3-quart baking dish.

Preheat the oven to 350F. For the sauce, sauté the garlic and onion in the oil until tender. Place in a blender with the remaining ingredients; process until smooth. Pour over the enchiladas and bake, uncovered, 10 minutes. (For a creamy sauce, add 8 ounces sour cream before baking.)

!Viva! Tradiciones, Corpus Christi, TX

SEAFOOD TETRAZZINI

8 tablespoons (1 stick) butter

¾ cup chopped onion

¾ cup chopped green bell pepper

½ cup all-purpose flour

4 cups milk

2 teaspoons salt

¼ teaspoon freshly ground pepper

1½ cups grated Cheddar cheese

1 teaspoon lemon juice

1 teaspoon prepared mustard

½ teaspoon Worcestershire sauce

1 (6-ounce) can sliced mushrooms,
   with their juice

2 cups lobster meat

1 pound lump crabmeat, picked over well

½ pound shrimp, cooked, shelled, and
   cut in half crosswise

1 pound thin spaghetti, broken and
   cooked

½ cup grated Parmesan cheese

Melt the butter in a large heavy saucepan and sauté the onion and bell pepper for 5 minutes or until softened. Add the flour and stir well; gradually stir in the milk and bring to a boil. Simmer for 5 minutes, then stir in the salt and pepper. Add the Cheddar cheese, then the lemon juice, mustard, and Worcestershire sauce, and continue stirring until the cheese melts. Add the mushrooms and their liquid.

Break the lobster and crab into bite-size pieces and fold carefully with the shrimp into the sauce. Cool and refrigerate (can be made the day before). When ready to serve, warm the sauce and pour over freshly cooked spaghetti in a buttered ovenproof serving dish. Cover with Parmesan cheese and brown in the oven.

Udderly Delicious, Racine, WI

YBOR CITY DEVILED CRAB

CROQUETTE DOUGH:

3 loaves stale white bread, crusts
removed
1 loaf stale Cuban, French, or Tuscan
bread, ground very fine and sifted
through a coarse sieve
1 tablespoon paprika
1 teaspoon salt

CRABMEAT FILLING:

3 tablespoons olive or vegetable oil
3 onions, finely chopped
½ red or green bell pepper, finely
chopped
4 cloves garlic, mashed or finely
chopped
1 teaspoon crushed hot red pepper
flakes
2 bay leaves
½ teaspoon sugar
1 teaspoon salt
1 (6-ounce) can tomato paste
1 pound fresh claw crabmeat, shell
and cartilage removed, shredded

CROQUETTES:

2 large eggs, well beaten
½ cup milk
Salt to taste
Pinch freshly ground black pepper
1 cup crushed cracker crumbs
½ cup all-purpose flour
Vegetable oil for deep frying

About 4 hours before serving, make the dough: Break the white bread into pieces; place in a large bowl, cover with water, and soak 15 minutes. Drain the water and squeeze the soaked bread until almost dry; return to the bowl. Gradually add the sifted Cuban bread until the mixture reaches dough consistency. Add the paprika and salt; mix thoroughly. Form the dough into a ball; refrigerate about 2 hours.

Make the filling: Heat the olive oil in a large skillet; reduce heat to low. Add the onion, bell pepper, garlic, and hot red pepper; sauté very slowly for 15 minutes. Add the bay leaves, sugar, salt, and tomato paste; stir. Cook, covered, 15 minutes over low heat. Add the crabmeat. Cook, uncovered, 10 minutes; remove the bay leaves. Place the mixture on a platter; refrigerate 2 hours.

After the dough and filling have chilled, make the croquettes: With your hands, take about 3 tablespoons of bread dough; press flat. Add 1 tablespoon crab filling; seal the dough around the filling like a croquette with pointed ends. In a small bowl, mix the eggs, milk, salt, and pepper. In another small bowl, mix the cracker crumbs and flour. Roll the croquettes first in the cracker mixture, then in the egg mixture, then in the cracker mixture again. Refrigerate 2 hours.

When ready to cook: Pour enough oil to come halfway up a deep, heavy saucepan or deep-fat fryer and heat to 375F. Place the croquettes, a few at a time, in hot oil; fry until light brown. Remove with a slotted spoon and drain on paper towels.

Tampa Treasures, Tampa, FL

GULF COAST CASSEROLE

¾ cup ripe olives, quartered

2 (4½-ounce) cans medium deveined
   shrimp (or fresh cooked shrimp
   equivalent)

1 cup raw rice

1 (10-ounce) can condensed consommé

1 cup water

2 teaspoons instant minced onion

1 tablespoon lemon juice

½ teaspoon Worcestershire sauce

¼ teaspoon salt

⅛ teaspoon garlic powder

1½ cups diced American cheese

1 (10-ounce) package frozen green peas

Preheat the oven to 350F. Combine the olives, shrimp, rice, and consommé in a 1½-quart baking dish; mix well. Combine the water, onion, lemon juice, Worcestershire sauce, salt, and garlic powder in a measuring cup or bowl. Stir into the shrimp mixture along with ½ cup of the cheese. Bake, covered, 1 hour. Stir in the remaining 1 cup of cheese and the peas. Bake, uncovered, 10 minutes.

Fiesta, Corpus Christi, TX

PIERSIDE MARYLAND STEAMED CRABS

MAKES 3 DOZEN SERVINGS

1 cup beer or water
1 cup vinegar, or as needed
3 dozen Maryland blue crabs
1 cup Chesapeake-style seafood
  seasoning, or as needed
Melted butter

Have ready a large crab pot with a rack. Pour enough beer and vinegar in the pan to come just level with the bottom of the rack. If more liquid is needed, add more until the level is reached. Layer 6 crabs on the rack and sprinkle with 2 tablespoons of the crab seasoning. Repeat until all of the crabs are in the pot. Bring to a boil over high heat. Reduce the heat and simmer for 20 minutes, covered. The crabs are done when they turn bright pink and their legs can be pulled from their sockets.

Serve hot on a table covered with newspaper. Eat the crab pieces plain or dip them in vinegar or melted butter. Sprinkle on extra crab seasoning if desired.

Of Tide & Thyme, Annapolis, MD

GALVESTON CRAB CAKES

1 pound fresh lump crabmeat, picked
    over well
¾ cup Italian-flavored bread crumbs
1 large egg, beaten
¼ cup mayonnaise
1 teaspoon Worcestershire sauce
1 teaspoon dry mustard
½ teaspoon salt
¼ teaspoon freshly ground pepper
2 tablespoons chopped fresh parsley
¼ teaspoon ground red pepper (cayenne)
1 teaspoon prepared horseradish
1 tablespoon fresh lemon juice
2 tablespoons unsalted butter
2 tablespoons olive oil
Lemon wedges
Roasted Corn and Tomato Tartar
    Sauce or Gulf Coast Tartar Sauce
    (see below)

Place the crabmeat in a large bowl. Add the bread crumbs and mix gently. In a separate bowl, combine the egg, mayonnaise, Worcestershire sauce, mustard, salt, pepper, parsley, cayenne, horseradish, and lemon juice. Mix well. Gently blend into the crabmeat mixture.

Form the mixture into 6 large cakes. Heat the butter and oil in a large skillet. Add the crab cakes and sauté for 4 to 5 minutes on each side or until golden brown. Garnish with lemon wedges. Serve with your choice of tartar sauce.

ROASTED CORN AND TOMATO TARTAR SAUCE:

1 (15-ounce) can corn kernels, drained
¼ cup mayonnaise
2 Roma tomatoes, peeled, seeded, and
    diced
2 green onions, minced
½ teaspoon Creole seasoning
¼ teaspoon salt
Freshly ground pepper

Preheat the oven to 350F. Place the corn in one layer on a baking sheet and roast in the oven 15 minutes. Combine the corn, mayonnaise, tomatoes, onions, Creole seasoning, and salt in a bowl. Season with pepper. Cover and refrigerate until ready to use.

Stop and Smell the Rosemary, Houston, TX

GULF COAST TARTAR SAUCE:

3 tablespoons fresh lemon juice

2 tablespoons Dijon mustard

½ teaspoon ground red pepper (cayenne)

1 large egg plus 1 large egg yolk

¼ teaspoon salt

Pinch freshly ground pepper

½ cup vegetable oil

½ cup chopped green onions

¼ cup chopped fresh parsley

½ teaspoon soy sauce

1 teaspoon Worcestershire sauce

2 tablespoons minced dill pickle

2 tablespoons chopped fresh dill

1 tablespoon capers, rinsed and
   drained

1 teaspoon Tabasco

Blend the lemon juice, mustard, cayenne, egg, egg yolk, salt, and pepper in a food processor until smooth. With the machine running, add the oil in a thin stream, blending until thickened. Add the green onions, parsley, soy sauce, Worcestershire sauce, pickle, dill, capers, and Tabasco. Pulse several times until well combined.

SHRIMP CREOLE

MAKES 4 SERVINGS

⅓ cup vegetable oil

¼ cup all-purpose flour

½ cup green onions and tops, chopped

¼ cup chopped green bell pepper

1 (8-ounce) can tomato sauce

1 cup hot water

4 cloves garlic, pressed

½ cup chopped fresh parsley

1½ teaspoons salt

Ground red pepper (cayenne) to taste

2 whole bay leaves

½ teaspoon crushed thyme

1-1½ pounds medium shrimp, shelled
   and deveined

2-3 cups hot cooked rice

In a large skillet, heat the shortening. Blend in the flour, stirring constantly over low heat until the mixture is brown. (Be careful not to burn. If black specks appear you must discard the ingredients and start over.)

Add the onion and bell pepper to the roux and cook about 10 minutes, or until softened. Stir in the tomato sauce mixed with the hot water; add the garlic, parsley, salt, cayenne, bay leaves, and thyme. Bring to a boil, lower the heat, cover, and simmer the sauce for 20 to 25 minutes.

Stir the shrimp into the simmering sauce and remove from the heat. Let stand, covered, for 5 to 10 minutes until the shrimp turn pink. Remove bay leaves and serve the shrimp over rice.

Rare Collections, Galveston County, TX

CRÊPES DE LA MER

MAKES 8 SERVINGS

½ cup all-purpose flour
12 tablespoons (1½ sticks) butter,
    divided
1 cup chopped green onions
2 teaspoons minced garlic
2 tablespoons tomato paste
1½-3 teaspoons curry powder
    (optional)
2½ teaspoons salt
½ teaspoon ground white pepper
1 cup shrimp stock or clam juice, plus
    ½ cup water
2 cups heavy cream, divided
3 pounds small raw shrimp, shelled
    and deveined, or 2 pounds
    crabmeat, picked over well, or a
    combination
¼ cup lemon juice, divided
3 cups sliced fresh mushrooms
⅓ cup minced parsley
1 teaspoon Tabasco
16 (6-inch) crêpes

Make a roux by slowly cooking the flour in 1 stick of the butter in a large skillet until the mixture is light brown. Add the onions and garlic and cook until wilted, about 5 minutes. Add the tomato paste and cook 5 minutes. Stir in the curry powder, salt, and white pepper, and gradually add the stock plus water, and 1½ cups of cream. Bring to a boil. Add the shrimp. Reduce the heat and cook them slowly until they turn pink, about 3 to 5 minutes. Remove the skillet from the heat. (When using crabmeat, do not cook it, just stir it into the sauce after the sauce has simmered for 3 minutes.)

In a separate 12-inch skillet, melt the remaining ½ stick of butter; add 1 teaspoon of the lemon juice and the mushrooms; stir until well coated. Sauté the mushrooms until their juices have evaporated, about 5 to 7 minutes, then add them to the sauce along with the remaining lemon juice, parsley, and Tabasco.

Using a slotted spoon, place some of the mixture in the middle of a crêpe and fold two sides toward the center. Place seam side down in a greased 13 x 9-inch shallow baking dish, or you may use individual ramekins, allowing 2 crêpes for each one. Reserve extra sauce. This much may be done ahead. Cover and refrigerate.

When ready to serve, preheat the oven to 325F. Bring the crêpes to room temperature. Mix the lightly whipped cream with the remaining sauce, and spoon generously over the crêpes. Bake on the middle shelf of the oven only until heated through, then place under a medium broiler just long enough to form a light-brown crust.

Plantation Cookbook, New Orleans, LA

ANNAPOLIS HARBOR BOIL

¾ cup Chesapeake-style seafood
  seasoning
8 lemons, 4 thinly sliced, 4 cut into
  wedges for garnish
1 large yellow onion, sliced into rings
  and separated
1 large bell pepper, sliced lengthwise
  into ½-inch strips
5 pounds red potatoes, scrubbed and
  halved if necessary to make no
  larger than 4-inch circumference
1½ pounds smoked sausage, cut into 3
  lengths and browned
2 pounds medium unshelled shrimp,
  rinsed
8 small ears of corn, halved
1 pound drawn butter
1½ cups cocktail sauce

Fill a 5-gallon crab pot three-fourths full of hot water. Add the seafood seasoning and the 4 sliced lemons. Bring to a rolling boil. Add the onion, bell pepper, and potatoes; boil for 20 minutes. Add the sausage and boil an additional 20 minutes. Add the shrimp and corn and allow to boil for 4 minutes, then turn off the heat and leave for an additional 5 minutes in the water.

Drain the entire mixture and ladle all the items into one or two very large serving bowls. Garnish with lemon wedges. Serve immediately with butter and cocktail sauce.

Of Tide & Thyme, Annapolis, MD

SHRIMP GEORGIADES

MAKES 2 SERVINGS

2 cloves garlic, peeled and sliced
4 green onions, sliced
2 small yellow onions, peeled and
    chopped
Olive oil, enough to cover bottom of
    frying pan
1 tablespoon sherry
2 ripe tomatoes, peeled and diced
Oregano
Salt and freshly ground pepper
2 dozen medium shrimp, shelled and
    deveined
1 cup crumbled feta cheese

Sauté the sliced garlic, the green onions and chopped onions in olive oil in a large skillet for 5 minutes or until clear. Add the sherry and tomatoes; sauté until the mixture begins to bubble. Stir in the dry seasonings to taste. Add the shrimp and cook 7 minutes or until shrimp turn red. Stir in the cheese and simmer until it begins to melt. Serve hot.

Sugar Beach, The Emerald Beaches, FL

DIRTY SHRIMP

MAKES 2 SERVINGS

5 tablespoons butter
1 teaspoon Worcestershire sauce
1 clove garlic, minced
¼ teaspoon ground red pepper
    (cayenne)
½ teaspoon freshly ground black
    pepper
½ teaspoon salt
½ teaspoon dried thyme
1 teaspoon dried basil
½ teaspoon dried oregano
1 pound medium shrimp, shelled and
    deveined
¼ cup beer

Melt the butter in a heavy skillet. Add the Worcestershire sauce, garlic, red and black pepper, salt, thyme, basil, and oregano. Cook for 1 minute. Add the shrimp. Cook for 2 to 3 minutes, stirring to coat shrimp evenly. Add the beer. Cover and cook 1 minute. Serve with French bread to dip in the sauce, or serve this spicy shrimp over rice.

Second Round: Tea-Time at the Masters, Augusta, GA

BASS ALE SHRIMP

MAKES 8 SERVINGS

2 (12-ounce) cans dark beer
1 bay leaf
1½ tablespoons mustard seed
½ teaspoon dill seed
¼–½ teaspoon dried red pepper flakes
¼ teaspoon salt
4 whole peppercorns
1½ pounds medium shrimp, in the
   shell
¼ cup vinegar
2 cloves garlic, crushed
Lettuce leaves and black olives, for
   garnish

Combine the beer, bay leaf, mustard seed, dill seed, pepper flakes, salt, and peppercorns in a saucepan. Bring to a boil and reduce the heat. Simmer for 5 minutes. Add the shrimp. Cook for 2 to 4 minutes or until the shrimp turn pink. Pour into a glass bowl. Add the vinegar and garlic. Chill in the refrigerator for 2 hours or longer. Drain the shrimp, discarding the bay leaf. Mound in the center of a lettuce-lined serving plate. Garnish with a circle of black olives.

Wild Thymes and Other Temptations, Tucson, AZ

SHRIMP AND LINGUINE WITH SHERRY CREAM SAUCE

MAKES 3 SERVINGS

3 tablespoons butter
1 pound medium shrimp, peeled,
   shelled and deveined
1 tablespoon chopped garlic
2 teaspoons chopped shallot
6 tablespoons cream sherry
1 cup heavy cream
3 tablespoons chopped fresh parsley
Salt and freshly ground pepper to
   taste
8 ounces linguine, cooked al dente,
   drained
3 radicchio leaves (optional)
3 lemon slices (optional)
Sprigs of parsley (optional)

Heat the butter in a large skillet over medium heat until melted. Increase the heat to medium-high. Add the shrimp, garlic, and shallot. Sauté for 15 to 20 seconds. Stir in the sherry. Add the cream, parsley, salt, and pepper and mix well. Cook until the shrimp turn pink, stirring constantly. Remove the shrimp with a slotted spoon to a bowl. Cover to keep warm.

Cook the sauce until reduced by one-quarter to one-half, depending on the desired consistency, stirring constantly. Return the shrimp to the skillet. Cook just until heated through.

To serve, spoon the hot pasta onto 3 dinner plates. Divide the shrimp evenly between the servings. Drizzle with the sauce. Top each serving with a radicchio leaf, a lemon slice, and parsley.

Made in the Shade, Greater Fort Lauderdale, FL

Oysters Rockefeller Casserole

3 sticks (¾ pound) butter

1 teaspoon dried thyme

1⅔ cups chopped green onions

1 cup chopped celery

1 large clove garlic, pressed

1 tablespoon Worcestershire sauce

1 teaspoon anchovy paste

1½ cups seasoned bread crumbs

8 cups shucked oysters, drained, liquid
    reserved

¾ cup chopped fresh parsley

½ cup grated Parmesan cheese

2 tablespoons Pernod or other anise-
    flavored liqueur

3 (10-ounce) packages frozen chopped
    spinach, cooked and drained

½ teaspoon salt

¼ teaspoon freshly ground black pepper

¼ teaspoon ground red pepper (cayenne)

Preheat the oven to 375F. Melt the butter in a large skillet. Add the thyme, onions, celery, and garlic. Sauté for 5 minutes. Add the Worcestershire sauce, anchovy paste, and bread crumbs. Cook and stir for 5 minutes or until the bread crumbs are toasted. Fold in the oysters, ½ cup of the oyster liquid, and the parsley, Parmesan and Pernod. Cook 3 minutes or until the oysters curl. Add the spinach, salt, and black and red pepper. Place in a 3-quart casserole dish and bake uncovered for 20 to 25 minutes.

Jambalaya, New Orleans, LA

Conch Fritters

1¼ pounds conch (whelk)
8 slices white bread, cut into ½-inch
  cubes
½ large onion, chopped
2 large eggs
Tabasco to taste
2 tablespoons lime juice
1 teaspoon dry mustard
¼ teaspoon salt
¼ teaspoon freshly ground pepper
¼ teaspoon thyme
1 clove garlic, minced
1½ cups cracker meal
Vegetable oil for deep-frying
Cocktail Sauce (see below)

Cut the orange fin and foot from the conch and discard. Chop the conch. Combine the conch, bread, onion, eggs, Tabasco, lime juice, dry mustard, salt, pepper, thyme, and garlic in a food processor container or a meat grinder. Process until ground. Shape into 1½- to 2-inch balls with moist hands. Coat with the cracker meal.

Pour enough oil to come halfway up a deep, heavy pan and heat it to 356F on a deep-fry thermometer. Fry the fritters in batches in the hot oil for 5 minutes or until golden brown; drain on paper towels. Serve with the cocktail sauce.

COCKTAIL SAUCE:

2 cups ketchup
2 tablespoons horseradish

Combine the ketchup and horseradish in a bowl and mix well. Taste and add additional horseradish, if desired.

Made in the Shade, Greater Fort Lauderdale, FL

Seafood Elegante

Makes 6 to 8 servings

8 tablespoons (1 stick) butter

1 pound mushrooms, sliced

⅓ cup all-purpose flour

1 (10-ounce) can chicken broth

1½ cups heavy cream

1 pound lump crabmeat, picked over
   well

½ pound medium shrimp, cooked,
   shelled, and deveined

¾ pound bay scallops, poached 2-3
   minutes and drained

1 cup buttered fine bread crumbs

8 ounces mozzarella cheese, shredded

Salt and freshly ground pepper to
   taste

Preheat the oven to 350F.

Melt 2 tablespoons of butter in a skillet. Sauté the mushrooms for 5 to 7 minutes or until soft. Remove from the pan and set aside. Melt the remaining 6 tablespoons of butter in the same skillet and blend in the flour, stirring constantly. Gradually stir in the chicken broth and cream. Cook until thickened.

Combine the crabmeat, shrimp, and scallops in a medium bowl. In a 3-quart casserole, alternate layers of the seafood and the mushrooms. Pour the sauce over the layers, allowing it to seep to the bottom. Top with buttered bread crumbs. Sprinkle shredded cheese on top and add salt and pepper to taste. Bake for 30 minutes or until bubbly.

Settings . . . From Our Past to Your Presentation, Philadelphia, PA

POULTRY

WEST COAST

Folks on the West Coast have been creating their own flavors since Spanish missionaries first brought chile, chocolate, and beans from Mexico to California in the eighteenth century. Since then, our food has continued to evolve. Cooks from Santa Barbara to Portland to Seattle take the plentiful gifts from the Pacific Ocean and the fertile valleys and blend them with the influences of Mexico, American Indians, China, Japan, Europe, and the many newcomers who continue to add to the region's diversity.

Some label the West Coast's casual lifestyle "laid back," which suggests that we don't give good eating much thought. Nothing could be further from the truth. Rather, this relaxed attitude encourages everyone from the most ambitious chef to the thriftiest homemaker to adopt, redefine, and improvise anything that piques their curiosity and their taste buds.

Like most Americans, Westerners embraced certain dishes brought by immigrants—such as pizza, tacos, and stir-fry—and then made them their own. But starting in the 1970s, California chefs began to take the cooking techniques and flavors of ethnic cuisine and marry them with fresh regional ingredients. The result was a light, healthful, and refreshing style that became known as California cuisine. This cooking style influenced other areas of the West Coast, and it wasn't long before the rest of the country caught on to California cuisine.

Leading the way were creative chefs, who took full advantage of California's incredible bounty of fruits and vegetables. Meats were marinated and simply grilled or roasted in wood-fired ovens. What made it new and special were the marinade ingredients that were seldom used before—Indian curry powder, Thai chile pastes, sesame oil, mustard seeds, and garlic pesto just to name a few. It was in this spirit of experimentation that cooks discovered that pasta took beautifully to Asian flavors and that mangoes made delicious salsas. "Designer" California pizzas came out in full force and paired ingredients like sun-dried tomatoes and buffalo mozzarella cheese with toppings ranging from fresh seafood to smoked duck breast. And then there was the California roll. Sun-ripened Haas avocados rolled with rice and crabmeat—a match made in heaven.

Meanwhile, the state's wineries overcame their image as "jug wine" producers and earned the respect of skeptics the world over. The enormous popularity of farmers' markets has also had an impact, stimulating new appreciation for locally grown and organic produce.

Not long after California made its mark, the Pacific Northwest came into its own, as food lovers began to celebrate what was in their own backyard: Salmon, hazelnuts, Walla Walla sweet onions, Dungeness crabs, Marionberries, cherries, Hood River pears, wild chanterelle and morel mushrooms. Microbreweries and coffeehouses took off, and people began demanding hearth-style breads and artisanal cheeses. Oregon and Washington wines, once overshadowed by California's, emerged as world-class contenders in their own right—notably those made from the pinot noir grape, which loves the Willamette Valley's damp, cool climate.

Up and down the coast, chefs and home cooks have tapped into life's simple pleasures. The cuisine feeds a yearning for the connection and well-being that come from sharing good, wholesome food with family and friends.

—Katherine Miller, *The Oregonian*
Portland, OR

SPRINGTIME IN THE PACIFIC NORTHWEST

When the snow melts in the mountains of the Pacific Northwest and the waters of the many rivers rush to the ocean, Pacific Coast salmon are plentiful and at their best! This is the time to enjoy not only the best salmon the year will offer, but also the tender crop of new potatoes and springtime asparagus that grow in abundance. Restaurants and home cooks throughout the region team up this winning combination—salmon, new potatoes, asparagus—for the weeks that surround the salmon runs. Huckleberries are found in the mountains of the Pacific Northwest, so they provide the salad that uses a huckleberry syrup. And the light dessert features apples grown in Washington State.

Submitted by *Gold 'n Delicious,* Spokane, WA

GRILLED SALMON WITH YOGURT DILL SAUCE 222

NEW POTATOES AND LEEKS DIJON 167

ORANGE-GLAZED ASPARAGUS 143

HUCKLEBERRY DRIZZLE SALAD 92

SURPRISE PACKAGES 359

CALIFORNIA BRUNCH

From the miles of sun-drenched beaches to the bright lights of Hollywood, to the world-class museums and gardens, Southern California sizzles with energy and excitement. This busy lifestyle demands stylish yet healthful recipes that are easy and quick to prepare. With an abundance of fresh ingredients, cooks can create the distinctive flavors of trend-setting Southern California.

Submitted by *California Sizzles,* Pasadena, CA

RECIPE FOR A BETTER COMMUNITY

JUNIOR LEAGUE OF PASADENA, CALIFORNIA COMMUNITY PROJECT:

James Madison Elementary School

With 97 percent of its families living below the poverty level, James Madison Elementary School became the exclusive recipient of the Junior League of Pasadena's services and funding in 1995. This project has a budget of $280,000, with over 90 volunteers providing 20,000 service hours. Completion of an $80,000 library renovation and a state-of-the-art computer lab has transformed the school into a viable community center. The League is actively involved in all aspects of the James Madison Elementary School community project.

The cookbooks that made it happen: *California Sizzles* and *Dining by Design*.

Did you know? Since enrollment dropped at Madison during the rainy season due to the lack of rain gear, a project called Ponchos for Los Niños was initiated. League members provided 750 rain slickers for students at Madison.

CHICKEN CRABMEAT SUPREME

8 skinless, boneless chicken breast
    halves
4 tablespoons (½ stick) butter, divided
¼ cup all-purpose flour
¾ cup milk
¾ cup chicken broth
⅓ cup dry white wine
1 small onion, chopped
6 ounces fresh or frozen crabmeat,
    picked over well
1 (3-ounce) can chopped mushrooms,
    drained
½ cup cracker crumbs
2 tablespoons chopped parsley
Salt and freshly ground pepper to
    taste
½ cup grated Parmesan cheese
Paprika

Preheat the oven to 350F. Rinse the chicken and pat dry with paper towels. Place the chicken pieces, one at a time, between 2 sheets of waxed paper and pound gently with a mallet into 8 x 5-inch pieces; set aside.

In a saucepan, melt 3 tablespoons of the butter and blend in the flour. Gradually stir in the milk, chicken broth, and wine. Stir over medium-low heat until the mixture is thickened and bubbly. Set the sauce aside.

In a skillet, sauté the onion in the remaining tablespoon of butter until tender, about 5 minutes. Stir in the crabmeat, mushrooms, cracker crumbs, parsley, salt, and pepper. Add 2 tablespoons of the sauce and stir. Spoon some of the crabmeat filling onto the center of a piece of chicken; fold in the sides and roll up. Place seam side down in a buttered 13 x 9-inch baking dish. Continue with the remaining filling and chicken. Cover with the sauce. Bake, covered, 1 hour. Uncover, and sprinkle with cheese and paprika. Bake until the cheese is lightly browned.

Plain and Fancy, Richardson, TX

CREOLE CHICKEN PIE

MAKES 6 SERVINGS

CHICKEN AND BROTH:
1 (3-pound) frying chicken, cut up
4 cups water
½ teaspoon poultry seasoning
½ teaspoon salt
¼ teaspoon freshly ground black
    pepper
1 onion, quartered
2 stalks celery, sliced

PASTRY:
2 cups all-purpose flour
1 teaspoon salt
⅔ cup solid vegetable shortening
5 tablespoons ice water

SAUCE:
⅓ cup vegetable oil
½ cup all-purpose flour
¾ cup chopped celery
¼ cup chopped green bell pepper
¾ cup chopped onion
½ cup chopped green onions
1 clove garlic, minced
1½ cups reserved chicken broth, heated
1 bay leaf
¼ teaspoon Tabasco
1½ teaspoons salt
¼ teaspoon freshly ground black
    pepper
¼ teaspoon dried thyme
1 teaspoon Worcestershire sauce
1 pound mushrooms, sliced
2 tablespoons butter
¼ cup finely chopped fresh parsley
2 teaspoons chopped pimiento

1 large egg yolk, beaten

Combine the chicken with the water, seasonings, onion and celery in a large saucepan. Bring to a boil, lower the heat, and simmer, skimming frequently, for 45 to 60 minutes or until tender. When cool enough to handle, remove the chicken meat from the bone, dice, and reserve. Discard the skin and bones. Strain the broth, skim the fat, and reserve.

To make the pastry, whisk together the flour and salt in a bowl. Cut in the shortening with a pastry blender or with 2 knives until the mixture resembles cornmeal. Sprinkle with the ice water and toss lightly with a fork. Add extra ice water if needed for the dough to bind together. Wrap in waxed paper and chill.

To prepare the sauce, first make a roux: Heat the vegetable oil in a large skillet. Gradually add the flour; cook and stir over very low heat until dark brown. (Be careful not to burn. If black specks appear you must discard the ingredients and start over.) Add the celery, bell pepper, chopped onion, green onions, and garlic. Cook for 5 minutes, stirring frequently. Slowly stir in the broth until smooth. Add the bay leaf, Tabasco, salt, pepper, thyme, and Worcestershire sauce. Simmer for 20 minutes, stirring occasionally. In a separate skillet, sauté the mushrooms in the butter for 5 to 7 minutes. Add the mushrooms, parsley, pimiento, and reserved diced chicken to the sauce. Simmer for 20 minutes. Remove the bay leaf.

Preheat the oven to 425F. To assemble the pie, divide the chilled dough in half. Roll each half between 2 sheets of waxed paper until the dough is ½ inch larger than a 9-inch pie pan. Line the pan with 1 sheet of dough and trim excess. Fill with the sauce mixture. Top with the second sheet of dough and slash in the center to allow steam to escape. Trim excess dough and pinch the edges to seal. Brush the top crust with the beaten egg yolk and place the pie on a baking sheet. Bake for 30 minutes or until the crust is golden brown.

Jambalaya, New Orleans, LA

Chicken and Wild Mushroom Strudel with Dried Cherries

Makes 6 to 8 servings

12 tablespoons (1½ sticks) butter
¼ cup all-purpose flour
2 cups chicken stock
½ cup heavy cream
1 teaspoon crushed fresh rosemary or
    sage
2 cups chopped cooked chicken
½ cup chopped sautéed wild
    mushrooms
½ cup dried cherries
1 package phyllo dough, thawed
    according to package directions
Sour cream (optional)
Sprigs of fresh rosemary

Melt 4 tablespoons of the butter in a large saucepan and stir in the flour. Cook over low heat for 5 minutes or until smooth, stirring constantly. Gradually stir in the chicken stock, cream, and rosemary. Simmer 10 minutes or longer. Add the chicken, mushrooms, and cherries. Cook until heated through.

Preheat the oven to 350F. Melt the remaining 8 tablespoons of butter in a small saucepan. Remove the phyllo from its package and place on a work surface. Keep the dough covered with waxed paper and a damp towel to prevent it from drying out.

Working with 3 sheets of phyllo at a time, brush each sheet with melted butter and layer one over the other. Spread a 1 x 2-inch layer of chicken mixture over the dough, about 3 inches from the left side, leaving 1½ inches at the top and bottom ends of the dough. Fold dough from the top and sides like an envelope over the filling. Roll into a log, brushing lightly with melted butter to seal as needed. Repeat the procedure with the remaining dough and chicken mixture. Arrange on a baking pan. Bake 15 to 20 minutes or until golden brown. Top each serving with sour cream, if desired, and a sprig of rosemary.

Celebrate Chicago: A Taste of Our Town, Chicago, IL

BAKED CHICKEN GARIBALDI

MAKES 2 SERVINGS

1 (2½-pound) chicken, cut up
Salt and pepper to taste
⅓ cup Spanish olive oil
2 cloves garlic, minced
1 onion, cut into half rings
1 green bell pepper, cut into half rings
2 cups chicken gravy
¼ cup red wine
20 buttons or slices of mushrooms
¼ cup grated Parmesan cheese
Parsley leaves
¼ cup grated toasted almonds

Preheat the oven to 350F. Rinse the chicken and pat dry. Season with salt and pepper and arrange in a baking pan. Bake for 20 minutes or until half done. Remove from the oven and set aside to cool.

Heat the olive oil in a skillet, and simmer the garlic, onion, and green pepper until slightly tender. Add the chicken gravy and salt to taste. Bring to a boil and add the red wine and mushrooms.

Remove the chicken skin and bones and place the meat in a 1½-quart casserole dish. Cover the chicken with the sauce and sprinkle with Parmesan cheese. Bake uncovered for 30 minutes or until the cheese is golden brown. Garnish with parsley and toasted almonds.

Gasparilla Cookbook, Tampa, FL

CHICKEN 'N' DUMPLINGS

MAKES 4 TO 6 SERVINGS

1 (3- to 4-pound) chicken, cut up
2 carrots, sliced
2 stalks celery with leaves, halved
1 onion, quartered
Salt and freshly ground pepper to taste
Butter
1½ cups all-purpose flour, or as needed
1 large egg, beaten
3 tablespoons solid vegetable shortening

Put the chicken in a large stockpot with the carrots, celery, onion, salt, and pepper. Add water to cover, bring to a boil, and lower the heat. Skim off foam. Cook for about an hour, until very tender. Remove the chicken from the broth. Strain the broth and discard the vegetables. Return the broth to the pot and add 2 tablespoons of butter for each 5 cups of broth; set aside.

Combine the flour, egg, shortening, ½ teaspoon of salt, and 5 tablespoons of water. Mix well. Divide the dough into three parts; roll each third very thin on a floured board. Let the dough dry for 20 minutes. While the dough is drying, skin and debone the chicken. Cut the dough into strips or squares and drop into the boiling broth. Boil uncovered for 10 minutes. Remove the dumplings with a slotted spoon. Thicken the broth with additional flour, if necessary, to make a gravy. Return chicken and dumplings to gravy; heat through.

Sassafras! Springfield, MO

CHICKEN WITH FETA AND PINE NUTS

MAKES 4 SERVINGS

1 cup finely chopped red onion
2 tablespoons olive oil, divided
1½ teaspoons minced garlic
½ cup pitted olives, cut into thin strips
¼ cup pine nuts, lightly toasted
½ cup oil-packed sun-dried tomatoes, drained and cut into thin strips
¼ pound (about 1 cup) feta cheese, crumbled
2 tablespoons freshly grated Parmesan cheese
1 tablespoon fresh marjoram or 1 teaspoon dried
Salt and freshly ground pepper
2 whole boneless chicken breasts, with skin, halved, rinsed, and patted dry

Preheat the oven to 350F. Cook the onion in 1 tablespoon of the oil in a large ovenproof skillet over medium heat, stirring until softened, about 5 minutes. Add the garlic and cook, stirring, 1 minute. Transfer the mixture to a bowl and let cool. Stir in the olives, pine nuts, tomatoes, cheeses, marjoram, salt, and pepper to taste. Stir to combine.

Insert a sharp paring knife into the thicker end of each chicken breast half and cut lengthwise to make a pocket. Fill each breast half with one-fourth of the filling. In a clean skillet, heat the remaining tablespoon of oil over moderate heat until hot but not smoking; brown the chicken, skin side down. Transfer the chicken, skin-side down, to the oven and bake about 12 minutes or until just cooked through.

Treasures of the Great Midwest, Wyandotte and Johnson Counties, KS

YBOR CHICKEN

MAKES 4 SERVINGS

1 (3½-pound) chicken, cut up
½ cup all-purpose flour
Salt and freshly ground pepper to taste
2 tablespoons olive oil
1 green bell pepper, cut into large pieces
1 large onion, cut into large pieces
1 large clove garlic, minced
1 large ripe tomato, chopped
1 bay leaf
1 cup raisins
2 cups pimiento-stuffed green olives, sliced
1 cup dry red wine
1 chorizo (Spanish sausage), chopped

Preheat the oven to 325F. Rinse the chicken pieces and pat dry with paper towels. Combine the flour, salt, and pepper on a flat plate; coat the chicken in the mixture. Heat the olive oil in a large skillet over medium heat; brown the chicken slowly. Place the chicken in a 1½-quart casserole dish. In the oil remaining in the skillet, sauté the green pepper, onion, garlic, and tomato. Add the bay leaf, raisins, and olives. Stir in the wine; simmer for 5 minutes. Pour over the chicken and scatter the chorizo on top. Bake, covered, 1¼ to 1½ hours or until the chicken is tender. Serve with white rice.

Tampa Treasures, Tampa, FL

CHICKEN GILLESPIE

MAKES 4 SERVINGS

½ cup all-purpose flour
½ teaspoon salt
½ teaspoon freshly ground pepper
2 large eggs
⅓ cup grated Parmesan cheese
4 skinless, boneless chicken breast
  halves
4 tablespoons (½ stick) butter
½ cup white wine
4 slices mozzarella cheese
Parsley for garnish

In a shallow dish, combine the flour, salt, and pepper. In a separate shallow dish, beat the eggs. Place the Parmesan cheese in a third shallow dish. Rinse the chicken and pat dry. Dip the chicken into the seasoned flour, then into the egg, and finally into the Parmesan cheese (repeat process if a thicker crust is desired).

In a large sauté pan over medium heat, melt the butter. Add the chicken and sauté, turning once, until golden brown. Add the wine and cook until chicken is no longer pink in the middle, 8 to 10 minutes. Place mozzarella slices on top, cover, and cook until cheese is melted, about 3 minutes. Sprinkle with parsley and serve.

From Portland's Palate, Portland, OR

COUNTRY CAPTAIN

MAKES 4 SERVINGS

1 (3- to 3½-pound) fryer or 3 pounds
  chicken parts
Salt and freshly ground black pepper
  to taste
3 tablespoons vegetable oil
2 onions, finely chopped
2 green bell peppers, chopped
1-2 garlic cloves, crushed
½ teaspoon white pepper
2 teaspoons curry powder
2 (16-ounce) cans tomatoes
1 teaspoon chopped fresh parsley
½ teaspoon dried thyme
2 cups hot cooked rice
3 or more tablespoons currants
¼ pound slivered almonds, toasted

Preheat the oven to 350F. Cut the chicken into serving pieces, rinse well, and dry with paper towels. Season the chicken well with salt and pepper and fry in vegetable oil in a large skillet until browned. Remove from the pan but keep the chicken hot. Pour off most of the grease; add the onions, green peppers, and garlic. Cook very slowly, stirring constantly, until tender. Season with 1 teaspoon of salt, the white pepper, and the curry powder. Add the tomatoes, chopped parsley, thyme, and black pepper to taste.

Arrange the chicken in a roasting pan and top with the sauce. Bake, covered, for 45 minutes. Place the chicken in the middle of a serving platter and pile the rice around it. Mix the currants with the sauce and pour over the rice. Scatter the almonds over the top.

A Southern Collection—Then & Now, Columbus, GA

CHIC CHICKEN

MAKES 4 SERVINGS

¼ pound fresh mushrooms, cut into
    halves
2 tablespoons olive oil, divided
4 large skinless, boneless chicken
    breast halves
1 tablespoon Italian herb seasoning
½ teaspoon salt
1 teaspoon chicken bouillon granules
1 teaspoon cornstarch
¾ cup water
1 (14-ounce) can artichoke hearts,
    drained and cut into quarters
Freshly grated Parmesan cheese

Sauté the mushrooms in 1 tablespoon of the olive oil in a medium skillet until the mushrooms are tender, 5 to 8 minutes. Remove to a small bowl and set aside.

Rinse the chicken breasts and pat dry with paper towels. Sprinkle the chicken with Italian seasoning and salt. In the same skillet, heat the remaining tablespoon of olive oil and cook the chicken breasts, turning once, until the juices run clear when the chicken is pierced with a fork, 8 to 10 minutes. Remove the chicken to individual plates or a shallow serving dish and keep warm.

Stir together the bouillon, cornstarch, and water until smooth. Pour into the skillet and cook over high heat, stirring constantly until sauce thickens. Add the artichoke hearts and mushrooms. Stir until thoroughly heated. Spoon the mixture over the chicken and sprinkle with cheese.

Women of Great Taste, Wichita, KS

CHICKEN WITH BRIE AND WALNUTS

MAKES 4 TO 6 SERVINGS

4 whole chicken breasts, halved,
    boned, and skinned
Salt to taste
⅛ teaspoon freshly ground pepper
½ cup all-purpose flour
½ cup vegetable oil
8 tablespoons (1 stick) butter
½ pound fresh mushrooms, quartered
1 cup walnut halves
1 cup dry vermouth or dry white wine
10 ounces Brie cheese, sliced, rind
    removed

Rinse the chicken and pat dry with paper towels. Cover the chicken breasts with plastic wrap and pound gently with a mallet to a uniform ¼-inch thickness. Sprinkle with salt and pepper. Dredge the chicken in the flour to coat all sides; shake off excess.

In a large skillet, heat the oil over medium heat until hot but not smoking. Sauté the chicken, turning once, about 10 minutes or until light brown. Remove the chicken from the pan and keep warm. Drain off the oil. Melt the butter in the same pan and sauté the mushrooms and walnuts for 2 minutes. Stir in the vermouth and Brie. Simmer over low heat until slightly thickened. Arrange the chicken on a heated platter. Pour the sauce over the chicken and serve.

A Cleveland Collection, Cleveland, OH

CHICKEN DIJON

MAKES 4 TO 6 SERVINGS

6 skinless, boneless chicken breast
    halves
1 (8-ounce) jar Dijon mustard
1 (8-ounce) carton sour cream
Seasoned bread crumbs
8 tablespoons (1 stick) butter

Preheat the oven to 400F. Rinse the chicken and pat dry. Spread both sides liberally with the mustard, dip in the sour cream, and roll heavily in the bread crumbs.

Line a baking dish with foil. Arrange the chicken in the dish in one layer and dot with the butter. Cover the chicken with foil and bake 30 minutes. Take off the top layer of foil. Increase the oven temperature to 450F. Bake 15 minutes to brown.

Magic, Birmingham, AL

CHICKEN DIJON IN PHYLLO

MAKES 6 SERVINGS

3 whole chicken breasts
1 teaspoon salt
¼ teaspoon ground white pepper
4 tablespoons (½ stick) butter plus
    12 tablespoons (1½ sticks) butter,
    melted
½ cup Dijon mustard
2 cups heavy cream
8 phyllo pastry sheets, thawed
    according to manufacturer's
    instructions
¼ cup fine dry bread crumbs
1 large egg
1 teaspoon water

Preheat the oven to 450F. Rinse the chicken, skin and bone it, and cut the meat into 1-inch strips. Sprinkle with salt and white pepper. Sauté in the 4 tablespoons of butter until the strips are no longer pink, about 5 minutes. Transfer to a platter and keep warm.

Add the mustard to the skillet, scraping the pan. Whisk in the cream, blending thoroughly. Lower the heat and simmer until the sauce is slightly thickened and reduced. Stir in any juices from the chicken. Strain the sauce over the chicken.

Lay 1 sheet of phyllo on a damp dish towel, covering the remaining phyllo with waxed paper and a damp towel. Brush liberally with melted butter and sprinkle with 1–2 pinches of the bread crumbs. Layer 6 more sheets of phyllo on top, preparing each with butter and bread crumbs. Top with the last sheet of phyllo, brushing only the borders with melted butter. Arrange the chicken over the lower third of a long side of the dough, leaving a 2-inch border along outside edges. Turn up the bottom edge, then fold in the side edges, partially enclosing the chicken. Roll up jelly-roll fashion. Place seam side down on a lightly greased baking sheet. Beat the egg with the water and brush the egg wash over the dough to glaze. Bake about 12 to 15 minutes, or until the phyllo is crisp and golden brown. Cut into 2-inch slices.

Purple Sage and Other Pleasures, Tucson, AZ

MALLET CHICKEN MEDALLIONS

MAKES 8 SERVINGS

2 (10-ounce) packages frozen chopped
   spinach, thawed
½ sweet onion, finely chopped
2 cloves garlic, minced
2 tablespoons olive oil
6-8 button mushroom caps, finely
   chopped
1 large egg, beaten
¼ teaspoon grated nutmeg
Salt and freshly ground pepper to
   taste
8 skinless, boneless chicken breast
   halves, rinsed and patted dry
¾ cup shredded Swiss cheese
8 tablespoons (1 stick) butter, melted
Seasoned bread crumbs

Preheat the oven to 375F. Squeeze the moisture from the spinach. Sauté the onion and garlic in the olive oil in a skillet for 5 minutes or until the onion is tender. Stir in the mushrooms. Sauté for 3 minutes. Add the spinach. Sauté for 3 minutes longer; transfer to a colander to drain. Let stand until it reaches room temperature. Stir in the egg, nutmeg, salt, and pepper.

Place the chicken breasts one at a time between sheets of waxed paper and pound with a meat mallet or other heavy object until about ⅜ inch thick. Spread a thin layer of the spinach mixture onto the chicken and sprinkle with the cheese. Roll as for a jelly roll to enclose the filling; secure with a wooden pick.

Brush the chicken rolls generously with the butter and coat with the bread crumbs. Place in a baking dish. Bake 45 minutes. Let stand for 10 minutes. Cut into ½-inch medallions. Serve warm from a chafing dish.

Southern on Occasion, Cobb-Marietta, GA

CUMIN CHICKEN

MAKES 8 SERVINGS

4 small (2- to 3-pound) chickens,
   split in half, backbones removed
1 dozen lemons
Salad oil
½ cup ground cumin
3½ tablespoons celery salt
1 teaspoon ground red pepper
   (cayenne)
¼ cup freshly ground black pepper
½ cup salt

Rinse the chickens and pat dry with paper towels. Place the chicken halves in plastic bags (2 chicken halves and the juice of 3 lemons in each bag). Turn occasionally. Marinate for about 12 hours. Remove the chicken from the bags and pat dry; rub with salad oil. Combine the cumin, celery salt, red pepper, black pepper, and salt in a small bowl; mix well. Rub over the chicken halves.

Prepare a medium-hot charcoal fire or preheat a gas-fired grill. Or, if preferred, preheat the oven to 350F. Grill the chicken 30 minutes on each side or arrange in a baking pan and bake for 1 hour.

Huntsville Heritage Cookbook, Huntsville, AL

Chicken Maria

MAKES 3 TO 4 SERVINGS

4 skinless, boneless chicken breast
    halves
3 large eggs, beaten
1 cup fine dry bread crumbs, or as
    needed
2 to 3 tablespoons butter, melted
½ cup sliced mushrooms
2 tablespoons lemon juice
⅓ cup white wine
⅔ cup chicken broth
6 (¼-inch-thick) slices Monterey Jack
    or Muenster cheese

Rinse the chicken breasts and pat dry with paper towels. Soak the chicken in the eggs at least 1 hour. Drain and roll the chicken in bread crumbs. In a large skillet over medium heat, brown the chicken in melted butter and place in an 8 x 8-inch baking dish.

Preheat the oven to 350F. Combine the mushrooms, lemon juice, wine, and broth in a medium bowl. Pour the mixture over the chicken. Top with the slices of cheese. Cover the dish with foil and bake for 45 to 60 minutes or until tender.

Bound to Please, Boise, ID

Fourth of July Barbecued Chicken

MAKES 12 SERVINGS

1 (12-ounce) can frozen orange juice
    concentrate, thawed
⅓ cup dry white wine
⅓ cup Dijon mustard
1 tablespoon honey
2 tablespoons finely chopped fresh
    rosemary
4 teaspoons soy sauce
2 teaspoons hot pepper sauce
1 large clove garlic, chopped
4 chicken breasts
4 chicken legs
4 chicken thighs
4 chicken wings
Salt and freshly ground pepper to
    taste

Combine the orange juice concentrate, wine, mustard, honey, rosemary, soy sauce, hot pepper sauce, and garlic in a food processor bowl. Process until smooth.

Rinse the chicken pieces and pat them dry. Season the chicken with salt and pepper.

Coat a grill rack with vegetable oil cooking spray. Place on the grill. Fire up the grill. When the coals are moderately hot, arrange the chicken on the rack. Grill for 5 minutes on each side or until golden. Brush the orange mixture over the chicken. Cook for 25 minutes more or until cooked through and the juices are clear, brushing with the orange mixture and turning occasionally.

Dining by Design, Pasadena, CA

OVEN-BARBECUED CHICKEN

MAKES 4 TO 6 SERVINGS

3 tablespoons ketchup
2 tablespoons vinegar
1 tablespoon lemon juice
2 tablespoons Worcestershire sauce
¼ cup water
1 teaspoon paprika
3 tablespoons dark brown sugar
1 teaspoon salt
1 teaspoon chili powder
½ teaspoon ground red pepper
    (cayenne)
2 tablespoons butter, melted
1 teaspoon dry mustard
1 (2½- to 3-pound) chicken, cut into
    serving pieces, rinsed and patted
    dry

Preheat the oven to 500F. Combine the ketchup and the next 11 ingredients in a medium bowl. Dip the chicken pieces in the sauce. Arrange in one layer in a large baking dish and pour any remaining suce over the chicken. Bake, covered with aluminum foil, for 15 minutes. Reduce the oven temperature to 350F and bake 1 hour. Remove the foil so the chicken can brown. Bake, uncovered, 15 minutes.

Cotton Country Collection, 25th Anniversary Edition, Rockford, IL

POULET DE BROCCOLI

MAKES 6 TO 8 SERVINGS

6-8 chicken breasts or thighs, poached,
    skinned and deboned, cut into
    chunks
2 (10-ounce) packages frozen broccoli
    spears
2 (10-ounce) cans cream of chicken
    soup
1 cup mayonnaise
1 teaspoon lemon juice
½ teaspoon curry powder
1¼ cups shredded sharp Cheddar
    cheese
1¼ cups soft bread cubes
2 tablespoons butter, melted

Preheat the oven to 350F. Layer the cooked chicken and broccoli in a greased 13 x 9-inch baking pan. Combine the soup, mayonnaise, lemon juice, and curry powder in a medium bowl. Pour over the chicken and broccoli. Cover with the cheese. Mix the bread cubes and butter and scatter on top. Bake for 30 minutes.

NOTE: If desired, generously sprinkle tarragon leaves across the top before baking.

Some Like It Hot, McAllen, TX

CHICKEN-STUFFED SHELLS
WITH SPINACH BÉCHAMEL SAUCE

MAKES 4 SERVINGS

12 large seashell-shaped pasta

FILLING:

3 tablespoons butter
1 teaspoon finely chopped shallots
1 cup chopped mushrooms
3 slices prosciutto, chopped fine
2 cups shredded cooked chicken
2 tablespoons chopped parsley
15 ounces ricotta cheese
1 large egg, beaten
¼ cup grated Parmesan cheese

SAUCE:

3 tablespoons butter
3 tablespoons all-purpose flour
2 cups milk, heated
10 ounces frozen chopped spinach,
    drained and squeezed dry
1 teaspoon fresh lemon juice
1 teaspoon salt
Pinch of grated nutmeg
Freshly ground pepper to taste
¼ cup grated Parmesan cheese

Cook the pasta shells in plenty of boiling salted water in a large saucepan until barely cooked, about 7 minutes; drain. Let stand in a bowl of cool water until ready to use.

For the filling, heat the butter in a medium skillet. Add the shallots and mushrooms; sauté until tender, about 10 minutes. Add the prosciutto; sauté 2 minutes. Stir in the chicken and parsley. In a large bowl, combine the ricotta, egg, and Parmesan cheese. Fold in the chicken mixture until well blended; set aside.

For the sauce, heat the butter in a small saucepan; gradually stir in the flour. Cook, stirring constantly, until smooth, about 3 minutes. Gradually stir in the milk and cook, stirring constantly, until smooth and thickened, about 10 minutes. Purée the spinach with half the white sauce in a food processor or blender. Add the remaining sauce and the lemon juice. Season with salt, nutmeg, and pepper; set aside.

Preheat the oven to 350F. Lightly butter a 13 x 9-inch baking dish. Fill the shells with the chicken mixture. Arrange in the baking dish. Pour the béchamel sauce over the top. Sprinkle with the ¼ cup Parmesan cheese. Cover with foil and bake 30 minutes. Let stand 10 minutes before serving.

Gracious Gator Cooks, Gainesville, FL

TOMATO, BASIL, AND CHICKEN RISOTTO

MAKES 4 SERVINGS

1 (14-ounce) can chicken broth
1 cup dry white wine
¾ cup water
2 cloves garlic, minced
3 tablespoons olive oil, divided
1 pound skinless, boneless chicken
    breasts, rinsed, dried, and cut into
    bite-size pieces
Salt and freshly ground pepper to
    taste
1 cup uncooked arborio rice
1 medium onion, chopped
1 large tomato, chopped
½ cup shredded Asiago cheese
¼ cup finely shredded fresh basil

Combine the broth, wine, and water in a medium saucepan and place over medium heat until the mixture is almost boiling. Reduce the heat. Keep the mixture hot, but not boiling. Put the garlic in 1 tablespoon of the olive oil in a heavy 2-quart saucepan over medium-high heat. Add half the chicken. Season with salt and pepper. Cook, stirring frequently, for 4 minutes or until the chicken is cooked through. Remove the chicken to a bowl. Repeat with the remaining chicken and 1 tablespoon of the remaining olive oil; remove the chicken to the bowl and set aside.

Put the remaining 1 tablespoon olive oil in the saucepan. Stir in the rice and onion. Cook for 2 minutes, stirring to coat the rice grains. Stir in 1 cup of the hot broth mixture. Reduce the heat to medium-low and simmer until the broth is absorbed. Continue adding the remaining broth mixture 1 cup at time and cooking until absorbed after each addition, stirring frequently. The rice should be tender and the mixture should have a creamy texture. Stir in the tomato and chicken. Cook until heated through. Stir in the cheese and basil. Serve immediately.

Meet Us in the Kitchen, St. Louis, MO

GRILLED TERIYAKI CHICKEN

MAKES 4 TO 6 SERVINGS

1½-2 pounds chicken parts, skinned
½ cup soy sauce
¼ cup dry sherry
2 tablespoons sugar
2 tablespoons grated fresh gingerroot
4 cloves garlic, crushed
2 tablespoons vegetable oil

Rinse the chicken and pat dry. Arrange in a nonaluminum dish. Combine the soy sauce, sherry, sugar, ginger, garlic, and oil; pour over the chicken, tossing to coat. Marinate, covered, in the refrigerator 6 hours or longer, turning occasionally; drain.

Prepare a medium-hot fire in a charcoal grill or preheat a gas-fired grill. Oil the rack. Pat the chicken dry and place on the rack. Grill, turning occasionally, for 30 minutes or until the chicken is tender. Serve hot or cold.

Generations, Rockford, IL

GRILLED CHICKEN WITH CORN SALSA

CORN SALSA:

1¼ cups frozen corn kernels, thawed
   and drained
¼ cup chopped red onion
¼ cup chopped red bell pepper
¼ cup chopped fresh cilantro
1½ tablespoons fresh lime juice
2 teaspoons seeded and chopped
   jalapeño pepper

MARINADE:

½ cup light beer
1 tablespoon low-sodium soy sauce
2 teaspoons lime juice
2 teaspoons seeded and chopped
   jalapeño pepper
1 tablespoon chopped fresh cilantro

4 skinless, boneless chicken breast
   halves, rinsed and patted dry
Salt and freshly ground pepper to taste

Combine all the salsa ingredients in a small bowl; mix well. Refrigerate, covered, for 4 hours.

To make the marinade, mix the beer, soy sauce, lime juice, jalapeño, and cilantro in a small bowl. Pour over the chicken. Refrigerate, covered, 1 to 4 hours, turning occasionally.

Build a medium-hot fire in a charcoal grill, or preheat a gas-fired grill or the kitchen broiler. Drain the chicken and pat dry. Season with salt and pepper. Grill or broil for 4 to 8 minutes per side or until thoroughly cooked. Cut the breasts into diagonal slices. Top with salsa.

Women Who Can Dish It Out, Springfield, MO

CHICKEN FAJITAS

MAKES 16 SERVINGS

½ cup Best Vinaigrette Dressing (see
    below)
½ cup soy sauce
½ cup red or white wine
4½ pounds skinless, boneless chicken
    breasts, rinsed and patted dry
Oregano
Chopped garlic
Coarsely ground black pepper
2 avocados, pitted, peeled, and sliced
Lemon juice
Lemon-pepper seasoning
Pita bread or warm flour tortillas
Alfalfa sprouts

For the marinade, combine the vinaigrette, soy sauce, and wine in a medium bowl. Season the chicken with oregano, garlic, and black pepper to taste. Place the chicken in a shallow container. Pour the marinade over and turn the pieces to coat throughly. Cover and refrigerate for 4 to 6 hours.

Build a medium-hot fire in a charcoal grill, or preheat a gas-fired grill and oil the rack. Remove the chicken and pat dry; discard the marinade. Place the breasts approximately 6 inches from the heat source. Grill for 4 to 8 minutes on each side. Cut the chicken into strips. Toss the avocado slices with the lemon juice and lemon-pepper seasoning. Stuff the chicken strips into the pita bread or fold into tortillas. Garnish with alfalfa sprouts and avocado slices.

BEST VINAIGRETTE DRESSING:

½ cup olive oil
½ cup vegetable oil
⅓ cup wine vinegar
2-3 cloves garlic
1 teaspoon Dijon mustard
1 teaspoon salt
1 teaspoon coarsely ground black
    pepper

Place all the ingredients in a food processor or blender. Blend until the mixture is creamy and the garlic is shredded, about 1 minute. Store in the refrigerator.

Celebrations on the Bayou, Monroe, LA

CHICKEN BOZADA

8 (6-ounce) skinless, boneless chicken
    breast halves
Olive oil
2 tablespoons chopped fresh garlic
2 cups medium dry sherry
1 (3-inch) sprig fresh rosemary
½ cup lemon juice
4 cups heavy cream
Salt and freshly ground pepper to
    taste
1 to 1½ cups Italian-seasoned bread
    crumbs
¼ cup toasted pine nuts
8 sprigs fresh rosemary, or other
    garnish of choice

Rinse the chicken and pat dry with paper towels. Coat the chicken lightly with olive oil. Place on a preheated grill rack. Grill until the chicken is cooked through. Cover and keep warm.

Sauté the garlic in ¼ cup of olive oil in a medium saucepan; do not brown. Add sherry. Boil until reduced by half. Add the rosemary, lemon juice, and cream. Boil until thick and creamy, scraping the side of the pan with a spatula. Remove rosemary; season the sauce with salt and pepper.

Place the chicken in a baking pan. Sprinkle with the bread crumbs. Broil until slightly brown. Spoon the sherry sauce onto individual serving plates; place the chicken in the sauce. Sprinkle with the pine nuts and garnish with rosemary.

Meet Us in the Kitchen, St. Louis, MO

CHICKEN ENCHILADAS

4 skinless, boneless chicken breasts,
    baked or broiled
1 (8-ounce) package cream cheese
1 cup sour cream
1 (4-ounce) can chopped green chiles
1 diced medium onion, sautéed in
    butter
Pinch of ground red pepper (cayenne)
Salt to taste
Hot pepper sauce to taste
8-12 flour tortillas
1 pound mozzarella cheese, grated
½ cup heavy cream
Salsa

Preheat the oven to 350F. Shred the chicken and mix with the cream cheese, sour cream, green chiles, onion, pepper, salt, and hot pepper sauce. Warm the tortillas over low heat in an ungreased frying pan. Fill the tortillas with the chicken mixture, roll up, and place in a 13 x 9-inch baking pan. Cover with the grated cheese. Pour the cream evenly over the tortillas. Bake uncovered for 30 minutes or until the cheese is bubbly. Serve with salsa.

Texas Sampler, Richardson, TX

BUTTERMILK FRIED CHICKEN

MAKES 4 SERVINGS

4 cups self-rising flour, divided
2 cups buttermilk
1 teaspoon salt
Freshly ground black pepper
4 skinless, boneless chicken breast
    halves, rinsed and patted dry
Solid vegetable shortening
½ cup white wine
½ cup heavy cream
Ground white pepper
4 fresh basil leaves, sliced
4 tablespoons (½ stick) butter, melted
Juice of ½ lemon

Combine 2 cups of the flour and the buttermilk in a bowl. Stir until the mixture has a pastelike consistency. In a paper bag, combine the remaining 2 cups flour, salt, and black pepper to taste. Shake the chicken in the seasoned flour, then dredge in the buttermilk mixture and shake in the flour again.

Heat ½ inch of shortening in an iron skillet to between 350F and 375F. Fry the chicken, turning once, for approximately 20 to 25 minutes or until golden brown. Remove to a rack set over a baking sheet and keep it warm while you make the sauce.

Heat the wine in a small saucepan until it's reduced by two-thirds. Add the cream and boil for 20 seconds. Lower the heat and simmer for 2 minutes. Remove from the heat. Add salt and white pepper to taste, and stir in the basil. Add the butter slowly, whisking constantly. Stir in the lemon juice. Serve sauce over each chicken breast.

Food for Thought, Birmingham, AL

SESAME FRIED CHICKEN

MAKES 4 SERVINGS

1 large egg, beaten
¼ cup milk
¾ cup all-purpose flour
¾ teaspoon baking powder
1½ teaspoons salt
1 teaspoon paprika
¼ teaspoon freshly ground pepper
¼ cup sliced almonds
2 tablespoons sesame seeds
4 tablespoons (½ stick) butter
2 tablespoons vegetable oil
2 whole chicken breasts, split, rinsed,
    and patted dry

Preheat the oven to 350F. Combine the egg and milk in a shallow bowl; set aside. Mix the flour, baking powder, salt, paprika, pepper, almonds, and sesame seeds in another shallow bowl. Melt the butter in a 13 x 9-inch baking dish. Add the oil.

Dip the chicken into the egg mixture and then into the flour mixture, coating well. Place in the baking dish, turning each piece once to coat with the butter mixture. Bake skin side down for 20 minutes. Turn the chicken pieces and bake 20 minutes longer or until done.

Nuggets, Colorado Springs, CO

MRS. MITCHELL'S HOT TAMALES

MAKES 60 TAMALES

1 (3½-pound) chicken, cut up, or 3
   pounds chicken parts
1 (3½-pound) pork shoulder roast (if
   boneless, 2 pounds), cubed
6 cloves garlic, chopped, divided
2 large onions, chopped, divided
2½ pounds corn husks
1½ pounds plus 2 tablespoons lard
   (do not substitute)
3 cups meat broth from meat cooked
   for filling, divided
4 cups Red Chile Sauce, divided (see
   opposite page)
7 tablespoons salt, divided
5 pounds masa harina (ground corn
   for tamales)
5 tablespoons baking powder

Place the chicken and pork roast together in a large stockpot; add 3 cloves of the garlic and 1 onion. Cover with water and cook over low heat for at least 1 hour or until the meat falls off the bones. Remove from the stove and let cool. Discard the fat. Drain meat and strain the broth; shred meats, discarding skin and bones.

Clean and dry corn husks. Corn silks brush off easier when husk is dry. Wash in warm water and leave to soak until ready to use. Sauté the remaining onion and garlic in the 2 tablespoons lard; add 1 cup of broth, 2 cups of the red chile sauce, 2 tablespoons of the salt, and the shredded meats to make the filling. Let simmer 20 minutes, adding more broth if needed.

Whip the 1½ pounds of lard to the consistency of whipped cream. Mix with the masa, adding baking powder and the remaining 5 tablespoons of salt. Beat until the mixture is very fluffy. A bit of masa should float on top when dropped into a cup of cold water. Add the 2 remaining cups of chile sauce and the remaining 2 cups of broth to the masa and mix well. More broth can be added if the masa seems too thick to spread easily.

Place 1 heaping tablespoon of masa in the middle of a husk, spreading toward outside edges, top and bottom. Spread closer to the top of the husk than to the bottom. Spread 2 tablespoons of filling in the middle of the masa lengthwise. Overlap the husk in a roll and fold the bottom of the husk up 1½ inches. Place on a flat surface with the fold underneath. Repeat until all the masa and filling have been used.

Steam the tamales by placing them upright on a folded end in a steamer. Place husks or foil on top; cover tightly and steam 2 to 3 hours. If no steamer is available, use a large cooking vessel such as a cold-pack canner. Line the bottom with foil, as the husks scorch easily. Place the tamales on a rack or pan inside the cooker and put a tin can, which has had both ends opened, in the center. Stack the tamales around the can and pour 4 or 5 inches of water in the cooker. Steam 2 to 3 hours tightly covered. Tamales are done when one can be rolled clear and free of the husk.

RED CHILE SAUCE:

24 pods dried red chiles
4 cups water

Wash the chile pods and remove the stems and seeds. Bring the chiles and water to a boil in a saucepan; reduce heat and simmer 10 minutes or longer. Pour the liquid into a blender; strain the sauce through a colander or sieve if there are chile skins remaining after blending. The yield should be approximately 4 cups of sauce.

Seasoned with Sun, El Paso, TX

JALAPEÑO SOUTHERN FRIED CHICKEN

MAKES 10 TO 12 SERVINGS

5 cups buttermilk
2 large cloves garlic, minced
2 medium jalapeño peppers, minced, divided
5-6 pounds skinless boneless chicken breast halves, rinsed and patted dry
1½ cups self-rising flour
2 teaspoons finely shredded orange zest
1 teaspoon salt
½ teaspoon dried basil, crushed
¼ teaspoon ground red pepper (cayenne)
8 tablespoons (1 stick) butter
½ cup honey
Vegetable oil for frying
Jalapeño pepper slices for garnish

Combine the buttermilk, garlic, and half the minced jalapeño pepper. Place the chicken pieces in a large bowl; pour the buttermilk mixture over. Cover and chill for ½ to 2 hours.

In a medium bowl, combine the flour, orange zest, salt, basil, and red pepper. Drain the chicken. Coat the chicken in the flour mixture, shaking off excess. Place the coated chicken pieces on waxed paper; let stand at room temperature for 20 minutes.

Meanwhile, in a small heavy saucepan, melt the butter over low heat. Add the remaining minced jalapeño pepper. Cook and stir for 1 minute. Stir in the honey. Bring to boiling; reduce heat. Simmer for 15 minutes. Remove from the heat, cover the sauce and keep warm.

In a large heavy skillet, heat ½ to ¾ inch of vegetable oil to 350F to 375F. Add the chicken in batches (do not crowd) and fry for 5 to 7 minutes per side or until crisp and golden brown. Drain on paper towels. Transfer to a platter. Garnish with jalapeño slices. Pass honey–jalapeño sauce.

Heart & Soul, Memphis, TN

BUFFALO CHICKEN WINGS

MAKES 20 TO 25 WINGS

20 to 25 chicken wings
Vegetable oil for deep frying
4 tablespoons (½ stick) butter, melted
1 bottle hot sauce
Blue Cheese Dressing (see below)
Celery sticks

Disjoint the chicken wings and discard the tips. Rinse and pat dry. The wings must be completely dry to fry properly since there is no batter or breading. Preheat the oil in a deep fryer or a heavy pan to 365F. Add the chicken wings a few at a time to the hot oil. Do not allow the oil to cool as the chicken is added. Deep-fry without crowding for 6 to 10 minutes or until crisp and golden brown. Drain well by shaking in the fryer basket or a strainer.

Blend the butter with ½ bottle of the hot sauce for medium-hot wings. Add additional hot sauce for hotter wings or additional butter for milder wings. Combine the wings and the hot sauce in a large container. Let stand, covered. Serve the wings with blue cheese dressing and celery sticks.

BLUE CHEESE DRESSING:

MAKES 3 1/2 CUPS

2 cups mayonnaise
3 tablespoons cider vinegar
1 tablespoon dry mustard
½ teaspoon ground white pepper
¼ teaspoon salt
8 ounces blue cheese, crumbled
¼ to ½ cup cold water

Combine the mayonnaise, vinegar, dry mustard, pepper, and salt in a large bowl and beat until well blended. Mix in the blue cheese. Add enough cold water gradually to make the dressing of the desired consistency, whisking constantly. Store in an airtight container in the refrigerator.

Great Lake Effects, Buffalo, NY

ELEGANT CHICKEN LIVERS

MAKES 4 SERVINGS

6 strips bacon
6 green onions, chopped
1 (2½-ounce) can mushroom pieces,
    drained
1 pound chicken livers
1 beef bouillon cube
½ cup water
½ cup white wine

Cook the bacon in a medium skillet until crisp; remove from the pan and crumble. Sauté the onions and mushrooms in the bacon drippings for 1 minute. Add the livers and sauté 5 minutes more. Dissolve the bouillon cube in the water; add to the livers along with the wine. Stir in the bacon and heat through. Serve over hot cooked rice.

Hearts and Flour, Waco, TX

UPPER CRUST CORNISH HENS

½ cup long-grain rice
¼ cup wild rice
2½ cups boiling water
4 tablespoons (½ stick) butter, melted
1½ cups blackberries
1 apple, chopped
¼ cup packed dark brown sugar
4 green onions, chopped
½ cup pecans, broken
½ teaspoon thyme
½ teaspoon marjoram
½ teaspoon ground white pepper
4 Cornish hens
Salt and freshly ground black pepper
1½ cups dry white wine

SAUCE:
2 sticks (½ pound) butter, melted
½ cup pecans, ground

Boil both rices in the boiling water for 15 minutes over high heat in a large saucepan. Cook longer if you do not want crunchy wild rice. Drain the rice and combine with the butter, blackberries, apple, sugar, onions, pecans, thyme, marjoram, and white pepper in a large bowl. Stir gently until well mixed.

Preheat the oven to 350F. Remove the giblets from the Cornish hens and rinse the hens. Rub salt and pepper in the cavity of each hen and stuff each loosely with some of the rice mixture. Close the cavities, truss, and secure with wooden picks. Place the hens, breast side up, in an uncovered roaster. Pour wine over each hen. Combine the melted butter and pecans for the sauce. Spread on each hen, coating completely. Bake 1 hour, basting frequently with the drippings.

Treasures of the Smokies, Johnson City, TN

CORNISH HENS
WITH DRIED CRANBERRY CHUTNEY

MAKES 2 SERVINGS

2 cloves garlic, chopped
¼ teaspoon dried oregano
1 tablespoon minced shallots
¼ cup olive oil
¾ cup commercial balsamic vinegar
¼ teaspoon crushed red pepper flakes
1 teaspoon chopped fresh rosemary
Dash of ground white pepper
2 Cornish hens, halved
4 fresh rosemary stalks
½ cup Dried Cranberry Chutney (see
   below)

Mix the garlic, oregano, shallots, oil, vinegar, red pepper, rosemary, and white pepper together in a small bowl. Pour over the Cornish hens. Marinate in the refrigerator for 2 hours or longer.

Prepare a medium-hot charcoal fire or preheat a gas-fired grill. Clean the rosemary stalks, keeping about 1½ inches of rosemary leaves on top of the stems. Soak in water to keep stalks from burning on the grill. Split the backbones of the hens so they will lie flat. Grill bone side down for 10 minutes; turn and grill for 8 minutes longer or until the thigh juices run clear when pricked with a fork. Serve with the chutney.

DRIED CRANBERRY CHUTNEY:

1 cup dried cranberries
½ cup raisins
½ cup brandy
1 teaspoon peeled and chopped fresh
   gingerroot
1 clove garlic, crushed
Ground cumin to taste
1 shallot, minced
½ cup chopped onion
½ teaspoon chopped fresh rosemary
1 tablespoon chopped chives
1 teaspoon salt
2 tablespoons butter
⅛ teaspoon dry mustard
2 tablespoons sun-dried tomato paste
¼ cup commercial balsamic vinegar
¼ cup packed dark brown sugar

Soak the cranberries and raisins in the brandy in a small bowl for at least 4 hours. Sauté the ginger, garlic, cumin, shallot, onion, rosemary, chives, and salt in the butter in a small skillet. Add the dry mustard, tomato paste, vinegar, and brown sugar; stir well. Drain the cranberries and raisins, reserving the brandy. Add the fruit to the skillet, stirring well. Then add the brandy. Cook for 1½ hours or until thickened, adding water as needed. Check seasoning.

Pearls of the Concho, San Angelo, TX

ARROZ CON POLLO

MAKES 6 SERVINGS

1 (3- to 4-pound) chicken, cut up
Vegetable oil
1½-2 cups raw rice
1 large onion, chopped
1½ jalapeños or 3 serrano peppers,
    seeded and diced
1 (8-ounce) can tomato sauce
2 teaspoons salt
1 teaspoon garlic powder
1 teaspoon ground cumin
Juice of ½ lemon or lime

Rinse the chicken and pat dry with paper towels. Brown the chicken pieces in ¼ inch of vegetable oil in a large skillet; set aside. Use this oil in a large cooking pot to brown the rice, onion, and peppers. (Add extra oil, if needed.) When the rice is brown, add the browned chicken, tomato sauce, salt, spices, and 2 to 3 cups of water. Stir well. Simmer, covered, 35 to 45 minutes, or until the chicken is tender and most of the water is absorbed. Squeeze the lemon or lime juice over it and serve.

Delicioso, Corpus Christi, TX

Breads and Breakfast Cakes

SEASONAL AND HOLIDAY CELEBRATIONS

America loves a party! Whether it's a Christmas dinner, a Mother's Day brunch, or a Fourth of July picnic, our holidays and seasonal celebrations tie us together with shared traditions and communal values. And more often than not, it's food that forms the common thread running through these special times.

Every family, every community, every region has its treasured dishes that denote various holidays and reflect the changing seasons. And America's community cookbooks have long been an important repository for these cherished recipes.

As the calendar turns to a new year, Southerners may be celebrating with hoppin' John, a traditional dish of black-eyed peas and collard greens. Come February, it's all hearts and flowers—from Valentine cupcakes for school parties to rich chocolate concoctions shared with that special someone. Along the Gulf Coast from New Orleans to Mobile, they'll be celebrating Mardi Gras with fun and feasting. Gumbo, jambalaya, crawfish étouffée—let the good times roll!

After a long winter, there's no more welcome sight than the first local asparagus or strawberries in the market. And the arrival of these fresh foods coincides with the festivities, both joyful and solemn, of the season. At America's Easter tables, ham and lamb have pride of place—be it a traditional Yankee roast lamb with mint jelly, a Southern country ham, or a California-style leg of lamb with fresh herbs and plenty of garlic. For Passover, there are both special dishes and dietary restrictions that challenge the cook. In either case, we turn to community cookbooks; in our increasingly mobile society, it's there that we find continuity and the traditional dishes that are just like grandma's.

Memorial Day means breaking out the grill, and every region has its own way of greeting the outdoor-cooking season. Later, on July Fourth, we celebrate our nation's independence by declaring our own independence from the confines of the kitchen. It's picnic time, either in the park after the parade or under the stars before the fireworks. New Englanders traditionally enjoy salmon and peas—an old custom that lives on in many communities, and in community cookbooks.

All too soon, the lazy days of summer give way to Labor Day—often the last cookout of the season—and shortly thereafter, the holidays begin in earnest. Blink your eyes and it's Halloween; blink again and it's Thanksgiving, perhaps the most unifying day of the year for Americans. Who doesn't eat turkey on the fourth Thursday of November? But that's not to say you won't find regional differences on America's tables, from the gelatin molds of the Midwest to the oyster stuffing of New England to the spicy cornbread of the Southwest.

At Christmas, we pull out all the stops—and we pull out those old, tattered cookbooks whose stained pages speak volumes. Chanukah celebrations bring latkes; for African-American families, Kwanzaa means old-fashioned soul food and dishes with roots in African cuisine.

There are as many ways to celebrate as there are cooks—and that's what makes our community cookbooks such a vital resource. It's where so many of our priceless holiday recipes, handed down orally for generations, are preserved for posterity.

—Jane Dornbusch, *Boston Herald*
Boston, MA

CHRISTMAS EVE TAMALE SUPPER BUFFET

Tamales are served on Christmas Eve in many El Paso homes that have their traditional dinner on Christmas Day. This custom may have gained popularity because it is a simple way of entertaining at such a busy time. Legend has it that the tamale tradition began in Mexico. The grandmothers usually lived with their families. To give themselves something to do in the midst of all the Christmas preparation, they made tamales to be eaten on Christmas Eve. Tamales go well with some of the following traditional foods and lots of eggnog and hot spiced wine to drink.

Submitted by *Seasoned with Sun,* El Paso, TX

JALAPEÑO CHILE SALSA 27

TORTILLA SOUP 110

GAZPACHO SALAD 77

ALMOND EMPANADITAS 358

MEXICAN HOLIDAY COOKIES 348

CELEBRATING MARDI GRAS

Mardi Gras is celebrated in various cities throughout the Southern states. Galveston's Mardi Gras began in 1871 and is celebrated every February. Krewes have "Grand" Balls, and day and night parades. The town is decorated in purple, green, and gold. And good food, served with plenty of Champagne or wine coolers, abounds throughout the region.

Submitted by *Rare Collections,* Galveston County, TX

CAVIAR AND EGG HORS D'OEUVRES 35

CRUNCHY SPINACH DIP 34

SHRIMP CREOLE 237

CAESAR SALAD WITH DRESSING 70

GRASSHOPPER CRÊPES 356

LEMON CURD BARS 341

RECIPE FOR A BETTER COMMUNITY

JUNIOR LEAGUE OF WATERLOO-CEDAR FALLS, IOWA
COMMUNITY PROJECT:

Grin and Grow Daycare

In 1978, the Junior League of Waterloo–Cedar Falls initiated Grin and Grow, a daycare center for at-risk children. In 1993, the League helped to renovate the daycare center by volunteering over 300 hours and donating $30,000.

The cookbooks that helped to make it happen: *Buttercups and Brandy* and *Pig-Out* have generated over $100,000.

Did you know? To market *Pig-Out* the Junior League of Waterloo-Cedar Falls sold paraphernalia such as pig-themed aprons, notebooks, and chip clips at community fairs.

SALLY LUNN HOT BREAD

MAKES 12 TO 15 SERVINGS

2 packages active dry yeast
¼ cup warm water
4 large eggs
1 cup warmed milk
8 tablespoons (1 stick) butter, melted
3 tablespoons sugar
1 teaspoon salt
4 cups sifted all-purpose flour

Dissolve the yeast in the warm water and let stand until creamy, about 5 minutes. Beat the eggs in a large bowl until light in color. Add the milk, butter, sugar, salt, and yeast. Stir in the flour and beat until smooth and elastic in a standing mixer fitted with a dough hook. Let rise in the bowl, covered with a towel, until double in size, about 1½ to 2 hours. Beat well and pour into a greased angel food cake pan. Cover with a towel and allow to rise 1¼ hours.

Preheat the oven to 350F. Bake for 40 minutes. Serve hot.

Smoky Mountain Magic, Johnson City, TN

EASTER BREAD

MAKES 1 LOAF

1 package active dry yeast
¼ cup water, heated to 105F-115F
⅓ cup sugar
4 tablespoons (½ stick) butter, softened
½ teaspoon salt
½ cup scalded milk
¼ teaspoon anise flavoring
5 drops cinnamon oil
2¾ to 3 cups all-purpose flour
2 large eggs
1 tablespoon water
3 tablespoons sesame seeds

Sprinkle the yeast over the warm water; let stand about 5 minutes, until creamy. In a large bowl combine the sugar, butter, and salt. Add the scalded milk. Stir until the butter melts. Cool to luke-warm. Add the anise and cinnamon oil. Stir in 1 cup of the flour and beat well. Add 1 beaten egg and the dissolved yeast. Beat well. Gradually mix in enough remaining flour to make a soft dough. Place the dough on a floured surface and cover with a kitchen towel. Let rest 10 minutes. Knead for 8 to 10 minutes or until smooth and elastic. Shape the dough into a ball. Place in a lightly oiled bowl and turn to grease all sides. Cover with a towel and set in a warm place for about 1½ hours or until doubled in size. Punch down the dough and cover the bowl. Return to a warm place and let rise until doubled again.

Turn the dough out onto a floured surface; divide into three equal parts and shape each into a ball. Let rest 10 minutes. Grease a baking sheet and set aside. Roll each dough ball into an 18-inch rope, tapering the ends. Line up the ropes 1 inch apart on the baking sheet. Working from the middle to each end, loosely braid the ropes. Pinch the ends together and tuck under slightly. Cover the braid and let rise in a warm place about 45 minutes or until doubled.

Preheat the oven to 375F. Beat together the 1 tablespoon water and the remaining egg in a small bowl. Brush over the braid. Sprinkle with sesame seeds. Bake about 25 minutes or until deep brown. Cool slightly before serving.

Sugar Beach, The Emerald Beaches, FL

CORNBREAD

¾ cup cornmeal
1¼ cups all-purpose flour
1 cup sugar
½ teaspoon salt
1 tablespoon baking powder
¼ cup powdered milk
1 large egg
¾ cup warm water
4 tablespoons (½ stick) butter, melted

Preheat the oven to 425F. Combine the cornmeal, flour, sugar, salt, baking powder, and powdered milk in a large bowl. Beat the egg until thick in a small bowl; add the warm water and the butter. Pour into the dry ingredients; mix well. Pour into a greased 8-inch baking pan. Bake for 25 minutes.

RSVP, Portland, ME

CORNBREAD MEXICANA

MAKES 20 TO 30 SERVINGS

1 cup all-purpose flour
1 cup cornmeal
¼ teaspoon salt
4 teaspoons baking powder
2 sticks (½ pound) butter, softened
1 cup sugar
4 large eggs
1 (16-ounce) can cream-style corn
½ cup grated Monterey Jack cheese
½ cup grated Cheddar cheese
1 (4-ounce) can diced green chiles,
    drained (optional)

Preheat the oven to 375F. Whisk together the flour, cornmeal, salt, and baking powder in a large bowl

In another bowl, cream the butter and sugar; beat in the eggs one at a time. Add the corn, cheeses, chiles, and flour mixture; stir until blended. Pour the batter into a greased 13 x 9-inch pan. Place in the oven. Immediately lower the oven temperature to 325F. Bake for 1 hour.

St. Louis Days . . . St. Louis Nights, St. Louis, MO

SOUR CREAM CORNBREAD

MAKES 6 TO 8 SERVINGS

8 tablespoons (1 stick) butter
1 cup canned cream-style corn
1 cup sour cream
1 cup self-rising cornmeal
2 large eggs, beaten
½ medium onion, grated, optional

Preheat the oven to 350F and melt the butter in an 8 x 8-inch square pan or an 8-inch iron skillet in the oven. Combine the corn, sour cream, cornmeal, eggs, and onion in a medium bowl. Pour the melted butter into the batter and mix well. Pour the batter into the hot pan. Bake for 35 to 40 minutes.

Cotton Country Cooking, 25th Anniversary Edition, Morgan County, AL

CORN SPOON BREAD

MAKES 6 SERVINGS

3 large eggs, separated
¼ cup cornmeal
¼ teaspoon salt
1¼ cups milk, scalded
2 tablespoons butter
1 (16-ounce) can cream-style corn
¼ teaspoon baking powder

Preheat the oven to 375F. Grease a medium baking dish. Beat the egg whites until stiff in a large bowl. In a separate bowl, beat the egg yolks until thick and lemon-colored.

Stir the cornmeal and salt into the milk in a medium saucepan; beat well. Cook over low heat, stirring, until the mixture has the consistency of thick mush. Blend in the butter and corn, then the baking powder. Fold in the egg yolks, then the whites. Pour into the prepared baking dish. Bake about 35 minutes or until puffy and golden brown (a knife inserted in center should come out clean). Serve immediately with butter or gravy.

Huntsville Heritage Cookbook, Huntsville, AL

HOT CORNBREAD STICKS

MAKES 8 SERVINGS

1½ cups cornmeal
1 cup all-purpose flour
½ cup sugar
1 tablespoon baking powder
½ teaspoon salt
1½ cups half-and-half
⅓ cup solid vegetable shortening,
    melted
2 large eggs, beaten
4 tablespoons (½ stick) butter, melted

Preheat the oven to 350F. Combine the cornmeal with the flour, sugar, baking powder, and salt in a large bowl and mix well. Combine the half-and-half with the shortening, eggs, and butter in a medium bowl and mix well. Add the liquid mixture to the dry ingredients, stirring until smooth.

Pour the batter into greased corn-stick pans, filling the cups two-thirds full, or a greased 9 x 5 x 3-inch loaf pan. Bake for 15 to 20 minutes for corn sticks or 55 minutes for the loaf or until a toothpick inserted in the center comes out clean. Cool in the pans for 10 minutes and invert on a wire rack. Serve warm or cool completely. (Can be frozen several months and reheated before serving.)

Dining by Fireflies, Charlotte, NC

APPLE CHEESE BREAD

MAKES 1 LOAF

8 tablespoons (1 stick) butter, softened
½ cup sugar
2 large eggs
2 cups all-purpose flour
1 teaspoon baking powder
½ teaspoon baking soda
½ teaspoon salt
1½ cups grated Granny Smith or
    McIntosh apples
¾ cup grated Cheddar cheese
½ cup chopped walnuts

Preheat the oven to 350F. Grease a 9 x 5 x 3-inch loaf pan. In a large bowl, cream the butter and sugar together until fluffy. Beat in the eggs one at a time. In a medium bowl, whisk the flour with the baking powder, baking soda, and salt. Add the flour to the butter mixture and stir until well mixed. Stir in the apple, Cheddar cheese, and walnuts. Spoon the mixture into the prepared pan. Bake 1 hour or until a wooden pick inserted near the center of the loaf comes out clean. Cool in the pan for 10 minutes before removing to a rack to cool completely.

Sound Seasonings, Westchester on the Sound, NY

PEAR TEA CAKE

MAKES 1 LOAF

½ cup dried pears, chopped
½ cup dried apricots, chopped
½ cup golden raisins
2 tablespoons pear brandy or apricot
  brandy
4 tablespoons (½ stick) butter, softened
1 cup sugar
2 large eggs
2 cups all-purpose flour
2½ teaspoons baking powder
½ teaspoon salt
1 cup milk
¾ cup chopped skinned and toasted
  hazelnuts

Soak the pears, apricots, and raisins in the brandy in a medium bowl for at least 1 hour.

Preheat the oven to 350F. Grease and flour a 9 x 5 x 3-inch loaf pan. Cream the butter and sugar together in a mixing bowl. Add the eggs; beat well. In a separate bowl, whisk together the flour, baking powder, and salt. Add the flour mixture to the egg mixture, alternating with milk, and mixing just until blended. Fold in the fruit and nuts. Pour into the prepared pan. Bake 1 hour or until a toothpick inserted near the center of the loaf comes out clean. Cool for 10 minutes in the pan and turn out onto a wire rack to cool completely.

Rogue River Rendezvous, Jackson County, OR

ORANGE POPPY SEED BREAD

MAKES 2 LOAVES (18 SERVINGS)

3 cups all-purpose flour
2¼ cups sugar
2 tablespoons poppy seed
1½ teaspoons baking powder
½ teaspoon salt
3 large eggs
1½ cups milk
1 cup vegetable oil
2 tablespoons finely shredded orange
  zest
1½ teaspoons vanilla extract, divided
1 teaspoon almond extract, divided
¾ cup powdered sugar
¼ cup orange juice

Preheat the oven to 350F. Grease two 8 x 4-inch loaf pans.

In a large bowl, whisk together the flour, sugar, poppy seed, baking powder, and salt. In another bowl, whisk together the eggs, milk, oil, orange zest, 1 teaspoon of the vanilla, and ½ teaspoon of the almond extract. Add to the flour mixture and beat with an electric mixer on medium speed for 2 minutes. Scrape the batter into the prepared pans. Bake for about 1 hour or until a toothpick inserted near the center comes out clean.

Meanwhile, make the glaze. In a medium bowl, stir together the powdered sugar, orange juice, the remaining ½ teaspoon vanilla, and remaining ½ teaspoon almond extract until smooth. Using a long-tined fork, poke holes in the tops of the baked loaves. Pour the glaze over the loaves. Cool the loaves in the pans for 10 minutes. Remove the bread from the pans and cool thoroughly on wire racks.

Heart & Soul, Memphis, TN

HARVEST LOAF

MAKES 1 LOAF

8 tablespoons (1 stick) butter, softened
1 cup sugar
2 large eggs
1 cup canned pumpkin purée
1¾ cups all-purpose flour
1 teaspoon baking soda
½ teaspoon salt
1 teaspoon ground cinnamon
½ teaspoon ground cloves
¼ teaspoon ground ginger
¾ cup semisweet chocolate chips
¾ cup chopped pecans
Spice Glaze (see below)

Preheat the oven to 375F. Grease a 9 x 5 x 3-inch loaf pan and set aside.

Cream the butter and sugar in a large bowl until fluffy. Add the eggs, one at a time, beating well after each addition. Add the pumpkin and mix well. Whisk the flour, baking soda, salt, and spices together in a medium bowl. Stir into the creamed mixture and mix well. Fold in the chocolate chips and pecans. Pour the batter into the prepared loaf pan. Bake for 70 to 75 minutes or until a wooden pick inserted near the center of the loaf comes out clean. Cool in the pan for 10 minutes. Then turn out of the pan onto a rack. Pour spice glaze over the top of the loaf and let cool completely.

SPICE GLAZE:

½ cup powdered sugar
½ teaspoon ground cinnamon
⅛ teaspoon grate nutmeg
1-2 tablespoons cream or milk

Combine the sugar and spices in a small bowl. Add enough cream to make of spreading consistency.

Celebrations on the Bayou, Monroe, LA

FLORIDA ORANGE BREAD

MAKES 1 LOAF

4 cups all-purpose flour
4 teaspoons baking powder
2 teaspoons salt
½ teaspoon baking soda
1½ cups sugar
⅓ cup water
¾ cup slivered orange zest
3 tablespoons butter
1⅓ cups orange juice
3 large eggs, beaten

Preheat the oven to 325F. Grease a 10 x 5-inch loaf pan and line with waxed paper.

Whisk the flour, baking powder, salt, and baking soda together. Combine the sugar and water in a saucepan. Stir in the orange zest. Cook over medium heat until the sugar dissolves, stirring constantly. Remove from the heat. Cool 5 minutes. Add the butter, stirring until blended. Stir in the orange juice and eggs.

Add the wet ingredients to the dry ingredients, stirring just until moistened; the batter will be lumpy. Spoon into the prepared loaf pan. Bake 1¼ hours or until a wooden pick inserted near the center of the loaf comes out dry. Cool in the pan for 10 or 15 minutes, then turn out on a rack and cool completely.

Sunny Side Up, Greater Fort Lauderdale, FL

ZUCCHINI CHOCOLATE BREAD

MAKES 2 LOAVES

3 large eggs
1 cup vegetable oil
2 teaspoons vanilla extract
2 cups sugar
3 cups grated zucchini
2⅓ cups all-purpose flour
½ cup unsweetened cocoa powder
2 teaspoons baking soda
1 teaspoon ground cinnamon
1 teaspoon salt
¼ teaspoon baking powder
½ cup chopped nuts (optional)
1 cup chocolate chips

Preheat the oven to 350F. Grease and flour two 9 x 5 x 3-inch loaf pans.

Mix the eggs, oil, vanilla, sugar, and zucchini in a medium bowl. Whisk together the flour, cocoa, soda, cinnamon, salt, and baking powder in a large bowl. Stir in the nuts and chocolate chips. Add the zucchini mixture and stir well. Pour into the prepared pans.

Bake 45 minutes or until a wooden pick inserted near the center of a loaf comes out clean. Cool the bread in the pans for 10 minutes, then turn out and finish cooling on a rack.

Texas Sampler, Richardson, TX

ZUCCHINI-PINEAPPLE BREAD

MAKES 2 LOAVES

3 large eggs
1 cup vegetable oil
2 cups sugar
2 teaspoons vanilla extract
3 cups all-purpose flour
2 teaspoons baking soda
¼ teaspoon baking powder
2 teaspoons ground cinnamon
1 teaspoon grated nutmeg
1 teaspoon salt
2 cups coarsely shredded unpeeled
   zucchini
1 (8-ounce) can crushed pineapple,
   well drained
1 cup chopped dates
1 cup chopped pecans

Preheat the oven to 350F. Grease two 9 x 5 x 3-inch loaf pans. Beat the eggs, oil, sugar, and vanilla together until thickened.

Whisk the flour, baking soda, baking powder, spices, and salt in a large bowl until thoroughly combined. Add the zucchini and toss to separate and coat with flour.

Add the egg mixture and the pineapple to the flour mixture; stir until just combined. Fold in the dates and pecans.

Scrape the batter into the prepared pans and bake for about 1 hour or until a wooden pick inserted near the center of a loaf comes out clean. Let the bread cool in the pans for 10 minutes, then turn out of the pans and cool on a rack.

Nutbread & Nostalgia, South Bend, IN

PUMPKIN-CHOCOLATE CHIP LOAF

MAKES 2 LOAVES

3 cups all-purpose flour
3 cups sugar
2 teaspoons baking soda
½ teaspoon baking powder
1 teaspoon salt
1 teaspoon ground cloves
1 teaspoon ground allspice
1 teaspoon ground cinnamon
1 cup vegetable oil
4 large eggs
⅔ cup water
2 cups canned pumpkin purée
1 (12-ounce) package chocolate chips

Preheat the oven to 325F. Grease and flour two 9 x 5 x 3-inch loaf pans.

Mix together all ingredients except the pumpkin and chocolate chips in a large bowl; blend well. Add the pumpkin to the mixture and then fold in the chocolate chips. Divide the mixture between the prepared pans. Bake 1 hour and 15 minutes or until a wooden pick inserted near the center of a loaf comes out clean. Remove the loaves to a rack and let cool in the pans for 10 minutes. Turn out of the pans and let cool completely.

Purple Sage and Other Pleasures, Tucson, AZ

LEMON LOAF

MAKES 1 LOAF

12 tablespoons (1½ sticks) butter,
   softened
2 cups sugar, divided
3 large eggs
2¼ cups plus 2 tablespoons all-
   purpose flour
¼ teaspoon salt
¼ teaspoon baking soda
¾ cup buttermilk
Grated zest of 1 lemon
¾ cup chopped nuts (optional)
Juice of 1 lemon

Preheat the oven to 350F. Grease and flour a 9 x 5 x 3-inch loaf pan.

Cream the butter and 1½ cups of the sugar in a large bowl until fluffy and beat in the eggs. Whisk the dry ingredients together and add to the batter, alternating with the buttermilk; mix well. Stir in the lemon zest and nuts, if desired; mix well. Pour into the prepared loaf pan. Bake 1 hour.

While the loaf is baking, stir together the lemon juice and the remaining ½ cup of sugar. Allow the mixture to stand until the sugar dissolves.

Let the bread cool in the pan for 10 minutes, then remove from the pan, pierce the top of the loaf with a cake tester in several places, and spoon the lemon glaze over the loaf. Allow to cool; then slice to serve.

Treasures of the Great Midwest, Wyandotte and Johnson Counties, KS

BLUEBERRY-LEMON BREAD

MAKES 1 LOAF

¾ cup sugar
2 tablespoons butter, softened
½ cup plain fat-free yogurt
½ cup egg substitute
1 teaspoon lemon juice
2 cups all-purpose flour
1 tablespoon baking powder
¼ teaspoon baking soda
¼ teaspoon salt
¾ cup skim milk
1 cup blueberries
4 teaspoons lemon zest, finely
   shredded

Preheat the oven to 350F. Coat a 9 x 5 x 3-inch loaf pan with vegetable oil cooking spray.

Cream the sugar and butter in a large bowl. Add the yogurt, egg substitute, and lemon juice. In a separate bowl, whisk together the flour, baking powder, baking soda, and salt. Stir into the yogurt mixture. Add the milk and mix until just combined Fold in the blueberries and lemon zest.

Pour the batter into the prepared pan and bake 40 to 45 minutes, or until a wooden pick inserted near the center of the loaf comes out clean. Let the loaf cool in the pan for 10 minutes, then turn out onto a rack and cool completely.

Women Who Can Dish It Out, Springfield, MO

Lin's Tropical Banana Bread

Makes 1 loaf

1½ cups sugar
½ cup vegetable oil
¼ cup dark rum
2 ripe bananas, mashed
2 large eggs
1 tablespoon milk
1 teaspoon vanilla extract
1¼ cups unbleached flour
2 tablespoons dry buttermilk blend
1 teaspoon baking soda
½ teaspoon salt
½ cup finely chopped walnuts
½ cup coarsely chopped pecans
¼ cup finely grated coconut (optional)
Rum Glaze (see below)

Preheat the oven to 325F. Grease a 9 x 5 x 3-inch loaf pan.

Combine the sugar, oil, rum, bananas, eggs, milk, and vanilla in a mixer bowl. Beat until blended, scraping the bowl occasionally. Mix the flour, buttermilk blend, baking soda, and salt in a small bowl. Add to the banana mixture, stirring just until moistened; do not overmix.

Spoon the batter into the prepared pan. Sprinkle the walnuts, pecans, and coconut over the top. Bake 45 minutes or until the edges pull from the sides of the pan. Let cool in the pan for 10 minutes, then remove the bread from the pan (pecans and co-conut should be on top). Drizzle with the warm rum glaze. Serve warm or chill for later use.

Rum Glaze:

¼ cup sugar
2 tablespoons butter
2 tablespoons water
¼ cup dark rum

Combine the sugar, butter, and water in a microwave-safe bowl. Microwave until boiling. Boil for 1 to 2 minutes. Stir in the rum. (Or you may boil in a saucepan for 5 minutes, then add the rum.)

Made in the Shade, Greater Fort Lauderdale, FL

BUTTERNUT ROLLS

MAKES 24 LARGE OR 46 SMALL ROLLS

¼ cup lukewarm water (105F to 115F)
1 teaspoon sugar
2 packages active dry yeast
1 cup milk
1 cup raisins
1 cup Butternut Squash Purée (see below)
⅓ cup firmly packed light brown sugar
5 tablespoons unsalted butter, melted and cooled
2 large eggs plus 1 egg yolk, lightly beaten, divided
1 tablespoon grated lemon zest
2 teaspoons salt
1 teaspoon ground cinnamon
6-7 cups all-purpose flour
Pinch of salt

In a large bowl, combine the warm water and sugar. Dissolve the yeast in this water and let stand for 15 minutes or until it is foamy. In a medium saucepan, scald the milk. Add the raisins and let the mixture cool to lukewarm. Combine the milk mixture in a large bowl with the squash purée, brown sugar, butter, 1 of the eggs and the egg yolk, lemon zest, salt, and cinnamon. Add the yeast mixture. Stir in 5 cups of the flour with a wooden spoon. Turn the dough out onto a floured surface and knead for 8 to 10 minutes, or until smooth and elastic. More flour may be added if dough is too sticky. Place the dough in a greased bowl, turning once. Cover the dough loosely with a kitchen towel. Let rise in a warm place until doubled in bulk, about 1½ hours.

Punch down the dough, divide in half, and roll each half into a 24-inch log. Cut each log into 12 pieces. Form each piece into a smooth ball and arrange the balls 2 inches apart on lightly greased baking sheets. (For smaller rolls, cut the logs into 24 pieces.) Cover the rolls loosely. Let rise in a warm place for 45 to 50 minutes, or until almost doubled in bulk.

Preheat the oven to 375F. Brush the rolls with the remaining egg, which has been beaten lightly with a pinch of salt. Bake 15 minutes or until golden. Allow to cool on a rack (rolls may be frozen at this point).

BUTTERNUT SQUASH PURÉE:

1 (2½-pound) butternut squash

Preheat the oven to 350F. Place the squash on a lightly greased baking sheet; bake 35 to 40 minutes or until tender.

Allow the squash to cool. Peel and seed. Cut into small pieces and purée in a blender. Squash purée may be refrigerated or frozen until ready to use.

Second Round: Tea-Time at the Masters, Augusta, GA

HOMEMADE ROLLS (ANGEL BISCUITS)

MAKES 5 DOZEN

5 cups sifted all-purpose flour
¼ cup sugar
1 teaspoon baking soda
3 teaspoons baking powder
1½ teaspoons salt
¾ cup solid vegetable shortening
1½ packages active dry yeast
2 tablespoons warm water
2 cups buttermilk

Sift together the flour, sugar, baking soda, baking powder, and salt in a large bowl. Cut in the shortening with a pastry blender until the mixture resembles coarse meal. Meanwhile, dissolve the yeast in the warm water. Add the buttermilk. Combine with flour mixture and toss with a fork until the dough just holds together. Turn out on a well-floured board and knead for 1 minute. Roll out to ½-inch thickness and cut into 2-inch biscuits. Place close together on an ungreased baking sheet and cover with a clean towel. Let rise about 1 hour.

Preheat the oven to 400F. Bake the rolls for 15 minutes, or until they are a pale tan. Serve at once.

Holiday Flavors and Favors, Greensboro, NC

EXA'S ROLLS

MAKES 2 DOZEN

1 cup milk, scalded
1 cup potato water (water in which a
    potato has been cooked without
    salt)
½ cup solid vegetable shortening
8 tablespoons (1 stick) butter, softened
1 large egg, beaten
½ cup plus 1 teaspoon sugar
2 teaspoons salt
1 package active dry yeast
¼ cup warm water
5½ cups all-purpose flour, or as needed

Combine the scalded milk, potato water, shortening, and butter in a large bowl. Stir to melt the shortening and butter; cool to room temperature. Add the egg, ½ cup of the sugar, and the salt. In a small bowl, dissolve the yeast in the ¼ cup warm water and the remaining 1 teaspoon sugar. Add to the batter. Stir in 2 cups of the flour; beat well. Cover the sponge with a kitchen towel and let rise 1 hour.

Beat in the remaining flour (or as much of the flour as you need to make a medium soft dough). Turn out on a floured board and knead for 8 to 10 minutes, or until smooth and elastic. Place in a greased bowl, turn to coat the dough, and cover with a towel. Let rise until double in bulk, about 1 to 1½ hours.

Punch the dough down and divide equally into 24 pieces. Form the pieces into balls and arrange 2 inches apart on greased baking sheets. Cover lightly with kitchen towels and let rise until doubled, about 45 minutes.

Preheat the oven to 375F. Bake the rolls about 12 to 15 minutes.

Pearls of the Concho, San Angelo, TX

SWEET POTATO ROLLS

MAKES 32 ROLLS

2 packages active dry yeast
1½ cups warm water (105F-115F)
3 cups whole wheat flour
3 cups all-purpose flour
⅓ cup packed light brown sugar
1¼ teaspoons salt
¼ cup fat-free plain yogurt
4 tablespoons extra-light margarine
½ cup egg substitute
1 (16-ounce) can cut sweet potatoes, drained

Combine the yeast and water in a food processor or blender. Process for 30 seconds. Let stand for 5 minutes. In a large bowl, combine the flours. Add 1 cup of the flour mixture, the brown sugar, salt, yogurt, margarine, egg substitute, and sweet potatoes to the yeast mixture. Process until smooth.

Stir the yeast mixture into the remaining flour mixture. Knead the dough for 5 minutes. Place in a bowl coated with vegetable oil cooking spray. Cover and let rise until doubled, about 1 hour. Punch the dough down and divide in half. Roll each half into a 16-inch circle and cut each into 16 wedges. Roll up the wedges. Place on baking sheets coated with cooking spray. Cover lightly with a clean towel and let rise until doubled, about 45 minutes. Preheat the oven to 350F. Bake 15 minutes.

Women Who Can Dish It Out, Springfield, MO

GINGER SCONES

MAKES 6 DOZEN

6 cups cake flour
½ cup sugar
3 tablespoons baking powder
3¼ cups (6½ sticks) butter or
    margarine, cut into ½-inch pieces
1½ cups chopped crystallized ginger
3 cups heavy cream, divided

Preheat the oven to 350F. Combine the flour, sugar, and baking powder in a large bowl and mix well. Cut in the butter until crumbly. Add the ginger and 2½ cups of the cream and mix well; do not overmix. Pat the dough to ¾-inch thickness on a lightly floured surface. Cut with a biscuit cutter. Arrange on ungreased baking sheets. Freeze for 15 to 20 minutes. Brush the tops with the remaining ½ cup cream. Bake 30 minutes.

Wild Thymes and Other Temptations, Tucson, AZ

LEMON MUFFINS WITH WALNUTS

MAKES 12 TO 16 MUFFINS

8 tablespoons (1 stick) unsalted butter,
    softened
1 cup plus 4 teaspoons sugar, divided
2 large eggs
1 teaspoon baking soda
2 teaspoons freshly grated lemon zest
2 cups all-purpose flour, divided
1 cup buttermilk, divided
½ cup chopped walnuts
¼ cup freshly squeezed lemon juice

Preheat the oven to 375F. Have ready muffin tins that have been greased or lined with baking cups.

Beat the butter and 1 cup of the sugar with a mixer in a large bowl until creamy. Add the eggs and beat well. Stir in the baking soda and lemon zest. Fold in 1 cup of the flour and then ½ cup of buttermilk. Fold in the remaining flour and the remaining buttermilk; stir in the walnuts.

Pour ¼ cup of batter for each muffin into the prepared tins. Bake for 20 to 25 minutes or until browned. Remove from the oven and brush the lemon juice over the hot muffins. Sprinkle with the remaining 4 teaspoons sugar.

Gold 'n Delicious, Spokane, WA

MANGO MUFFINS

MAKES 2 DOZEN

2 cups all-purpose flour
2 teaspoons baking soda
2-3 teaspoons ground cinnamon
¼ teaspoon salt
1½ cups sugar
¾ cup vegetable oil
2 cups finely chopped ripe mango or
    1 (800-gram) can mangoes, finely
    chopped
2 teaspoons vanilla extract
3 large eggs, beaten
½ cup raisins (optional)
½ cup walnuts, chopped (optional)
½ cup shredded coconut (optional)

Preheat the oven to 350F. Grease muffin tins or line with paper baking cups.

In a bowl sift the flour, baking soda, cinnamon, and salt together and add the sugar. Make a well in the center of the flour mixture and pour in the oil, mangoes, vanilla, and eggs; mix until well combined. Stir in the raisins, nuts, and coconut, if you desire. Let the batter stand for 15 minutes; then pour into the prepared pans. Bake the muffins for approximately 30 minutes, or until a knife inserted into the center comes out clean.

Behind the Walls, Mexico City, Mexico

PECAN MINI MUFFINS

MAKES 24 MINIATURE MUFFINS

8 tablespoons (1 stick) butter
2 large eggs, beaten
1 cup packed dark brown sugar
½ cup all-purpose flour
1 teaspoon vanilla extract
1½ cups chopped pecans

Preheat the oven to 350F. Spray miniature muffin tins with vegetable oil cooking spray.

Melt the butter in a small skillet; place in a medium bowl and cool. Add the eggs and brown sugar and mix with a spoon. Stir in the flour, vanilla, and pecans; mix well. Fill the prepared muffin tins to the top with batter. Bake for 20 minutes.

St. Louis Days . . . St. Louis Nights, St. Louis, MO

MARTHA'S "MEANT TO BE" CHEESE DANISH

MAKES 16 SERVINGS

2 packages (8 rolls each) refrigerated
  crescent rolls
2 (8-ounce) packages cream cheese,
  softened
1½ cups sugar, divided
1 large egg
1 teaspoon vanilla extract
8 tablespoons (1 stick) butter, melted
1 teaspoon ground cinnamon
1 cup chopped pecans

Preheat the oven to 350F. Grease a 13 x 9-inch baking dish.

Unroll one can of crescent rolls and press into the bottom of the dish, pressing perforations together to form a flat sheet of dough. Ease the edges of the dough slightly up the sides of the dish.

Combine the cream cheese, 1 cup of the sugar, the egg, and vanilla in a medium bowl. Mix thoroughly. Spread the cheese mixture over the crescent roll dough. Unroll the remaining can of crescent rolls and place over the cream cheese mixture, pinching perforations together. Press the edges together to seal.

Combine the melted butter, remaining ½ cup sugar, the cinnamon, and pecans. Spread evenly over the top layer of crescent roll dough. Bake about 30 minutes or until golden. To serve, cut into rectangles.

Heart & Soul, Memphis, TN

DANISH PUFF PASTRY

4 sticks (1 pound) butter, divided
2 cups all-purpose flour, divided
1 teaspoon almond extract
3 large eggs
2 cups powdered sugar
1 teaspoon vanilla extract
1 tablespoon butter, melted
2-3 tablespoons milk or cream

Preheat the oven to 425F. Cut 2 sticks of the butter into 1 cup of the flour in a large bowl until it resembles coarse meal. Add 2 tablespoons of cold water and toss until well blended. Divide the dough in half. Press each half onto an ungreased baking sheet, shaping into a 12 x 3-inch oblong.

Combine 1 cup of water and the remaining 2 sticks of butter in a saucepan; bring to a boil. Add the almond extract. Remove from the heat and stir in the remaining 1 cup of flour. Add the eggs, one at a time, beating well after each addition. Spread the mixture over the dough. Bake for 50 minutes. Remove from the oven.

Combine the powdered sugar, vanilla, 1 tablespoon melted butter, and milk in a medium bowl; mix well. Spread on the pastry while it is still hot.

Junior League of Philadelphia's Bicentennial Cookbook, Philadelphia, PA

RASPBERRY CREAM CHEESE COFFEECAKE

2¼ cups all-purpose flour
1 cup sugar, divided
12 tablespoons (1½ sticks) butter,
    softened
¾ cup sour cream
2 large eggs, beaten
1 teaspoon almond extract
½ teaspoon baking soda
½ teaspoon baking powder
¼ teaspoon salt
1 (8-ounce) package cream cheese,
    softened
½ cup raspberry preserves
½ cup sliced almonds

Preheat the oven to 350F. Grease and flour the bottom and sides of a 10-inch springform pan.

In a large bowl, combine the flour and ¾ cup of the sugar. Use a pastry blender or fork to cut in the butter until the mixture resembles coarse crumbs. Reserve 1 cup for topping. Combine the remaining crumb mixture with the sour cream, 1 egg, almond extract, baking soda, baking powder, and salt. Mix thoroughly. Spread the dough over the bottom and 2 inches up the sides of the prepared pan.

Beat the cream cheese, the remaining ½ cup sugar, and the remaining egg until blended. Spread over the dough. Spoon the preserves evenly over the cheese filling. Combine the reserved crumb mixture and almonds and sprinkle over the top. Bake for 45 to 55 minutes or until the cheese filling is set and the crust is a deep golden brown. Cool in the pan 15 minutes; remove sides of pan and cut cake into wedges.

Women of Great Taste, Wichita, KS

APPLE BREAKFAST CAKE

12 tablespoons (1½ sticks) butter,
   softened
1½ cups sugar
2 large eggs
2¼ cups all-purpose flour
¾ teaspoon baking powder
1 teaspoon baking soda
¾ cup milk
1½ teaspoons vanilla extract
3 Delicious apples, peeled, cored, and
   sliced or chopped
Streusel (see below)

Preheat the oven to 350F. Have ready an ungreased 13 x 9 x 2-inch baking pan.

Combine the butter, sugar, and eggs in a mixing bowl; beat until smooth. Sift in the flour, baking powder, and baking soda; mix well. Add the milk gradually, mixing until smooth. Stir in the vanilla and apples. Spoon into the baking pan. Sprinkle the streusel over the batter. Bake for 40 to 45 minutes or until a wooden pick inserted near the center of the cake comes out clean. If desired, serve with whipped cream.

STREUSEL:

¾ cup packed brown sugar
3 tablespoons all-purpose flour
3 tablespoons butter, softened
1 teaspoon ground cinnamon
1 cup chopped pecans or walnuts

Mix the brown sugar with the flour in a medium bowl. Cut in the butter with a pastry blender or a fork until well combined. Add the cinnamon and pecans and stir.

The Best of Wheeling, Wheeling, WV

APPLE STREUSEL COFFEECAKE

MAKES 10 TO 12 SERVINGS

4 large eggs, beaten
2½ cups sugar, divided
1 cup vegetable oil
2 teaspoons vanilla extract
3 cups all-purpose flour
1 tablespoon baking powder
1 teaspoon salt
½ cup orange juice
1 tablespoon ground cinnamon
5-6 tart cooking apples, peeled, cored,
    and sliced

Preheat the oven to 325F. Thoroughly grease an 8- to 10-cup Bundt pan.

Mix the eggs, 2 cups of the sugar, oil, and the vanilla in a large bowl. Mix the flour, baking powder, and salt in a medium bowl; add to the egg mixture alternately with the orange juice, beating until smooth after each addition.

Combine the cinnamon with the remaining ½ cup sugar. Layer one-third of the egg mixture, one-third of the apples, and one-third of the cinnamon mixture in the prepared pan. Repeat twice.

Bake for about 1½ hours, or until a wooden pick inserted in the center of the cake comes out clean. Let cool in the pan on a rack for 10 minutes. Tap the pan to loosen the cake on all sides. Invert and cool completely on the rack.

California Sizzles, Pasadena, CA

SOUR CREAM GEMS

MAKES 2 DOZEN MINIATURE
MUFFINS

2 cups unsifted self-rising flour
2 sticks (½ pound) butter, softened
1 cup sour cream

Preheat the oven to 350F. Grease miniature muffin tins. Cut the flour and butter together in a medium bowl with a fork. Add the sour cream, and stir until moistened. Spoon into the prepared tins and bake 20 to 25 minutes.

Uptown Down South, Greenville, SC

ZUCCHINI COFFEECAKE

2 cups all-purpose flour
¾ cup granulated sugar
¾ cup packed dark brown sugar
2 teaspoons baking soda
½ teaspoon baking powder
1 teaspoon salt
¼ teaspoon grated nutmeg
¼ teaspoon ground cinnamon
¾ cup chopped pecans
3 large eggs, slightly beaten
1 cup vegetable oil
1 tablespoon vanilla extract
2 cups shredded zucchini (about 1
    large zucchini)
Topping (see below)

TOPPING:
¼ cup packed dark brown sugar
¼ cup chopped pecans
¼ teaspoon grated nutmeg
¼ teaspoon ground cinnamon

Preheat the oven to 350F. Lightly grease one 13 x 9 x 2-inch pan or two 8-inch square baking pans.

Combine the flour, granulated sugar, brown sugar, baking soda, baking powder, salt, nutmeg, cinnamon, and pecans in a large bowl. Combine the eggs, oil, vanilla, and zucchini in another large bowl; mix well and add to the dry ingredients. Stir just until the dry ingredients are moistened. Pour into the prepared pan or pans. Combine all the topping ingredients in a small bowl. Sprinkle over the batter. Bake 40 minutes.

Winners, Indianapolis, IN

Bananas Foster Pancakes with Butter Rum Syrup

MAKES 4 SERVINGS

1 cup all-purpose flour
1 teaspoon baking powder
¼ teaspoon baking soda
¼ teaspoon ground cinnamon
3 tablespoons light brown sugar
1 banana, mashed
1-1¼ cups milk
1 large egg, beaten
2 tablespoons butter, melted
½ teaspoon vanilla extract
Butter or vegetable oil
Butter Rum Syrup (see below)

Combine the flour, baking powder, baking soda, cinnamon, and brown sugar in a bowl; mix well. Combine the banana, milk, egg, melted butter, and vanilla in a separate bowl; mix well. Pour the banana mixture into the dry ingredients. Stir just until the dry ingredients are moistened; do not overmix.

Heat a griddle or nonstick skillet until a few drops of water dance on the surface. Add a small amount of butter or oil and tilt to coat. Ladle about ⅓ cup of batter for each pancake onto the griddle. Cook the pancakes until the top is speckled with bubbles. Turn and cook the other side until golden brown. Serve immediately with butter rum syrup.

BUTTER RUM SYRUP:

MAKES 1 1/3 CUPS

1 cup maple syrup
2 tablespoons unsalted butter
¼ cup dark rum
¼ teaspoon ground cinnamon

Combine the maple syrup, butter, rum, and cinnamon in a saucepan; mix well. Bring to a simmer and cook for 5 minutes, stirring frequently. Serve warm.

Crescent City Collection: A Taste of New Orleans, New Orleans, LA

GINGERBREAD PANCAKES

MAKES 8 SERVINGS

2¼ cups all-purpose flour
½ teaspoon salt
1 teaspoon ground cinnamon
1 teaspoon grated nutmeg
1 teaspoon ground ginger
½ teaspoon ground cloves
1½ teaspoons baking powder
1½ teaspoons baking soda
1 tablespoon instant coffee granules
4 tablespoons (½ stick) butter, melted
1 large egg, beaten
¾ cup buttermilk
¼ cup packed light brown sugar
¾ cup water

Whisk the flour, salt, spices, baking powder, baking soda, and coffee granules together in a large mixing bowl. Stir in the butter and remaining ingredients. Blend until the dry ingredients are moistened. Pour about ¼ cup batter per pancake onto a hot nonstick skillet. Cook until the tops are speckled with bubbles; turn and cook the other side until brown. Serve right away.

Hearts and Flour, Waco, TX

HOLIDAY BRUNCH TORTE

MAKES 6 TO 8 SERVINGS

1 (15-ounce) package refrigerated pie
  crusts
4 ounces (1 cup) grated Cheddar
  cheese
¾ pound thinly sliced cooked ham
1½ cups thinly sliced unpeeled red
  potatoes
1 medium onion, sliced
1 (9-ounce) package frozen spinach,
  thawed and squeezed between
  paper towels
1 large egg
1 tablespoon water

Allow both crusts to stand at room temperature for 15 to 20 minutes. Preheat the oven to 375F.

Place a cookie sheet in the oven to heat. Prepare the pie crust according to the package directions for a two-crust pie, using a 9-inch springform or a 10-inch deep-dish pie pan. Press 1 crust in the bottom and up the sides of the pan. Sprinkle ⅓ cup of the cheese on the bottom of the crust. Top with half the ham, half the potatoes, and half the onion slices. Distribute the spinach evenly over the onion. Top with ⅓ cup cheese and the remaining ham, potatoes, and onion. Sprinkle the remaining ⅓ cup cheese over the onion. Gently press the mixture into the pan. Cover with the top crust, crimp the edges, and cut a vent in the center for steam to escape. Beat the egg and water together and brush the crust with the egg wash. Place the torte on the hot cookie sheet. Bake for 45 to 60 minutes or until the crust is deep golden brown and the potatoes are tender.

And Roses for the Table, Tyler, TX

STUFFED FRENCH TOAST

MAKES 6 SERVINGS

FILLING:

1 (8-ounce) package cream cheese,
   softened
1 teaspoon vanilla extract
½ cup chopped walnuts

FRENCH TOAST:

1 loaf French bread
4 large eggs
1 cup heavy cream
½ teaspoon vanilla extract
½ teaspoon grated nutmeg

TOPPING:

1 (12-ounce) jar apricot preserves
½ cup orange juice

For the filling, beat the cream cheese and vanilla together until fluffy. Stir in the nuts; set aside.

Cut the bread into 12 (1½-inch) slices; cut a pocket in the top of each. Fill each with 1½ tablespoons of the cheese mixture. Beat the eggs, cream, vanilla, and nutmeg together in a medium bowl. Dip the filled bread slices in the egg mixture, being careful not to squeeze out the filling. Cook on a lightly greased griddle until both sides are golden brown. Keep warm on cookie sheets in a 200F oven until ready to serve. For the topping, heat together the preserves and juice. Drizzle over toast.

Brunch Basket, Rockford, IL

CARAMEL STRATA

MAKES 6 SERVINGS

1 cup packed dark brown sugar
8 tablespoons (1 stick) butter
2 tablespoons light corn syrup
12 slices white sandwich bread, crusts
   removed
1½ cups milk
6 large eggs, beaten
1 teaspoon vanilla extract
¼ teaspoon salt
Assorted fresh fruit, such as sliced
   kiwi, strawberries, and pineapple

Combine the brown sugar, butter, and corn syrup in a small saucepan. Place over medium-low heat until the butter melts and the sugar dissolves, stirring constantly; bring to a boil. Pour into a 13 x 9 x 2-inch glass baking dish, tilting the dish to coat the bottom evenly with the mixture; cool. Arrange 6 slices of the bread over the mixture in the pan, trimming to fit in. Cover with the remaining 6 slices, trimming to fit. Whisk together the milk, eggs, vanilla, and salt in a medium bowl. Pour over the bread. Refrigerate, covered, overnight.

Preheat the oven to 350F. Bake the strata uncovered for 40 minutes or until puffed and lightly browned. Let stand 5 minutes. Cut into 6 portions. Lift with a spatula and invert onto serving plates, caramel side up. Garnish with fresh fruit.

A Capital Affair, Harrisburg, PA

CRISPY SWEET POTATO PANCAKES WITH SOUR CREAM CILANTRO SAUCE

MAKES 4 SERVINGS

3 large eggs, beaten
½ cup plus 1 tablespoon all-purpose
    flour
½ teaspoon salt
1 pound sweet potatoes, peeled and
    grated
1 medium-size onion, minced
Vegetable oil
¼ cup pine nuts
3 cloves garlic, peeled and chopped
1 bunch cilantro, stems removed
½ jalapeño pepper, seeds removed and
    chopped
¼ cup olive oil
3 tablespoons lime juice
⅛ teaspoon salt
¾ cup sour cream

Prepare pancakes by combining the eggs, flour, and salt in a mixing bowl. Stir in the sweet potatoes and onion; mix well. Drop batter by tablespoonfuls into ¼ inch of hot oil in a heavy skillet. Cook, turning once, 6 to 8 minutes or until golden on each side. Drain on paper towels and keep warm.

Combine the pine nuts, garlic, cilantro, jalapeño pepper, olive oil, lime juice, and salt in a food processor; blend to form a smooth paste. Stir in the sour cream. Serve the sauce with the pancakes.

I'll Cook When Pigs Fly, Cincinnati, OH

BREAKFAST PIZZA

MAKES 6 TO 8 SERVINGS

1 (8-count) can crescent rolls
1 pound bulk sausage
2 cups frozen hash brown potatoes,
    thawed
5 large eggs, beaten
¼ cup milk
Salt and freshly ground pepper to
    taste
1½ cups shredded mozzarella cheese
    or Cheddar cheese

Preheat the oven to 350F. Turn the rolls out onto a 14-inch pizza pan, pressing to seal the perforations.

Brown the sausage in a skillet, stirring until crumbly. Drain. Layer the sausage and potatoes over the roll dough. Mix the eggs, milk, salt, and pepper in a bowl. Pour over the potatoes. Sprinkle with the cheese. Bake 35 to 45 minutes or until bubbly and lightly browned.

NOTE: For a change of flavor, spread some spaghetti sauce or pizza sauce over the rolls.

Beyond Burlap: Idaho's Famous Potato Recipes, Boise, ID

BEV'S GREEN CHILE CASSEROLE

MAKES 6 SERVINGS

2 (4-ounce) cans whole green chiles
12 eggs, separated
1 teaspoon salt
16 ounces sour cream
4 cups shredded Monterey Jack cheese
4 cups shredded Cheddar cheese
Seasoned salt to taste

Preheat the oven to 350F.

Rinse the chiles; remove seeds and membranes. Beat the egg whites in a bowl until stiff peaks form. Combine the yolks, salt, and sour cream in a bowl; mix well. Fold in the egg whites gently. Spread 2 tablespoons of the egg mixture over the bottom of a 14 x 10-inch roasting pan. Layer the chiles, cheeses, and egg mixture in the pan, lightly sprinkling each layer with seasoned salt. Make 3 layers, ending with the egg mixture. Bake 50 minutes. Cool for 10 minutes before serving. Serve with sausage and sweet rolls.

Reflections Under the Sun, Phoenix, AZ

FRESH FRUIT PIZZA

MAKES 10 TO 12 SERVINGS

1 (20-ounce) roll refrigerated sugar
  cookie dough
1 (8-ounce) package cream cheese,
  softened
⅔ cup sugar
1 teaspoon vanilla extract
Assorted colorful fresh fruit
  (strawberries, kiwi, peaches,
  blueberries, etc.)
1 (10-ounce) jar peach or apricot jelly

Preheat the oven to 350F. Lightly grease a round pizza pan or jelly roll pan.

Cut the cookie dough into ⅛-inch slices; seal dough edges together to make a crust (dough expands when baked, so leave a little space at edge of the pan, unless the pan has sides). Bake 10 to 12 minutes, or until light brown; cool.

In a bowl, combine the cream cheese, sugar, and vanilla; mix until smooth. Spread over the cooled crust. Arrange the fruit in a decorative pattern on top of the cream cheese mixture. Heat the jelly until slightly runny. Carefully spoon over the fruit to glaze. Refrigerate until ready to serve.

Tampa Treasures, Tampa, FL

WESTSIDE BRUSCHETTA

MAKES 4 TO 6 SERVINGS

1 baguette with sesame seeds
4 to 6 tablespoons extra-virgin olive
   oil
1 tablespoon minced garlic
Freshly grated pecorino Romano
   cheese
¼ teaspoon freshly ground black
   pepper
1 red bell pepper, seeded and cut into
   ¼-inch pieces
1 yellow bell pepper, seeded and cut
   into ¼-inch pieces
2 plum tomatoes, cut into ¼-inch
   slices
3 green onions, cut into ¼-inch slices
½ cup shredded mozzarella, Asiago, or
   crumbled Gorgonzola cheese
4 ounces mushrooms, cut into ⅛-inch
   slices
4 ounces thinly sliced prosciutto or
   smoked ham, cut into ½-inch strips

Preheat the oven to 350F. Slice the baguette lengthwise into halves. Place cut side up on a baking sheet. Combine the olive oil, garlic, 1 tablespoon grated cheese, and ground black pepper in a bowl and mix well. Spread over the cut sides of the bread halves. Arrange the bell peppers, tomatoes, and green onions on each bread half. Sprinkle with the mozzarella cheese. Top with the mushrooms and prosciutto. Bake for 5 to 10 minutes or until the cheese melts. Slide under the broiler for 2 to 3 minutes or just until the cheese begins to brown. Cut into 2-inch slices. Sprinkle with freshly grated pecorino Romano cheese.

Great Lake Effects, Buffalo, NY

DESSERTS

FAMILY AND COMMUNITY CELEBRATIONS

Throughout history and throughout the world, the table has been a place for family, friends, strangers and foes to come together. In ancient Greece, a traveler who showed up at the door was fed first and questioned about his identity later. "Have you eaten?" is a time-honored greeting in Asian countries. Elizabethan kings honored their guests with elaborate feasts featuring such delicacies as swan, eagle and boar.

Today, the tradition of coming together at the table is alive and well. All across America, people sit down to share food in a spirit of community, conviviality and celebration. The occasion can be as spontaneous as an impromptu porch supper or it can be an elaborately planned retirement dinner.

Indeed, the most important milestones in a person's life are accompanied by the sharing of food. Greek-Americans often serve flaky spinach pies and grape leaves stuffed with rice after an infant's vaptisia, or baptism. The Jewish bris and baby-naming ceremonies wouldn't be the same without bagels and lox, whitefish salad and honey cakes. In Korea, on the 100th day of a baby's life, it is customary to celebrate with a "100-day birthday party." On this special day, the baby's family distributes an endless variety of Korean rice cakes—studded with plump dates and nuts, stuffed with sweet bean paste or filled with sesame-infused honey—to 100 friends and family for good luck.

Likewise, a child's passing into adulthood is celebrated with food in many cultures. The Mexican quincenera marks the coming-of-age of fifteen-year-old girls and is celebrated with a lavish feast where the menu might include tamales, empanadas and chile rellenos. At the African rite-of-passage ceremony, adopted by a growing number of African-American families, beloved recipes with their roots in Africa like collard greens, rice and black-eyed peas and spicy stewed pork might be served.

Even in death, food plays an important role. Bereaved family members are comforted by the sharing of food when neighbors arrive at the doorstep bearing noodle casseroles, layer cakes and heaping platters of fried chicken. Food and drinks are essential at an Irish wake, and likewise, according to the Jewish tradition of "sitting shiva," meals are brought to the grieving family.

There are many other types of "feasts"—little and big—that reinforce friendships, kinships and communities. From simple coffee invitations to family reunions, food brings people together. Gatherings can be triggered by a holiday, a season, or the bounty of a prized food: a clambake in Cape Cod; beer and sausage at a Michigan Oktoberfest; a crawfish boil in Louisiana; a glazed ham for Easter. So important is the concept of togetherness to Chinese-Americans that during the Chinese New Year, empty chairs are placed at the banquet table to remember loved ones who couldn't be with them to enjoy Chinese radish cakes and sweets wrapped in red paper for luck and prosperity.

When people sit down together to share a meal of favorite foods prepared with love, cares melt away . . . old grudges are forgotten . . . new alliances are formed . . . and hopes and dreams are spun. Everyone feels nourished and replenished, body and soul, no matter what else is going on in their lives. And in these moments, they are reminded that food has always been—and will continue to be—the tie that binds people to the past, to the future and to each other.

—Nancy Butcher
Saratoga Springs, NY

BIRTHDAY DESSERT BAR

The next time one of your children celebrates a birthday, invite his or her friends for a dessert bar celebration. A table laden with goodies and lots of punch will get things rolling. Then just plan some active play in the backyard or at the skating rink or bowling alley to work off the sugar fix!

PARTY TIME FRUIT PUNCH 49

T. REX PUNCH 49

CHOCOLATE CHIP BUNDT CAKE 315

BUTTER PECAN TURTLE COOKIES 347

CRACKER CANDY 349

PEANUT BUTTER DIAMONDS 370

TEXAS TRASH 40

WEDDING RECEPTION TEA

After a small wedding ceremony, host the bride and groom with a reception in your garden. A selection of hors d'oeuvres and a choice of cake will allow everyone a chance for celebration. And Bubbly Peach Punch will toast the happy couple and send them on their way.

BUBBLY PEACH PUNCH 52

CAVIAR AND EGG HORS D'OEUVRES 35

ERIC'S CHAMPAGNE CHEESE BALL 13

OYSTERS SALISBURY 20

CHOCOLATE-MINT CREAM PUFF 327

SOUR CREAM POUND CAKE 317

RECIPE FOR A BETTER COMMUNITY

JUNIOR LEAGUE OF NEW ORLEANS COMMUNITY PROJECT:

Teen Court of Greater New Orleans

Teen Court of Greater New Orleans is a program for first-time juvenile misde-meanor offenders between the ages of 10 and 18. Offenders admit responsibility and accountability for their offense and are tried by a jury of their peers. Sentenc-ing includes community service, classes, letters of apology, and the imposition of curfews. The project was launched in 1996, and today the Junior League of New Orleans manages and operates Teen Court in partnership with the juvenile courts in two parishes.

The cookbooks that made it happen: Revenue from *Plantation Cookbook, Jam-balaya,* and *Crescent City Collection: A Taste of New Orleans* goes into a general fund that supports all Junior League of New Orleans' community projects.

Did you know? The Junior League of New Orleans launched a media cam-paign to promote its latest cookbook. The League hosted a "launch party," went on TV shows, and took out ads in newspapers and magazines. Sales from the first two cookbooks are over the $1 million mark and sales from the new cookbook, since its November 21, 1999, debut, amount to $190,000!

THE BEST CHOCOLATE CAKE
IN THE WHOLE WIDE WORLD

2 sticks (½ pound) butter, at room temperature
15 ounces Milky Way candy bars
2 cups sugar
4 large eggs
1 teaspoon vanilla extract
1¼ cups buttermilk
½ teaspoon baking soda
3 cups all-purpose flour
1 cup chopped nuts
Chocolate Marshmallow Icing (see below)

Preheat the oven to 325F. Grease and flour a 9-inch tube pan.

Melt 1 stick of the butter in a saucepan; add the candy and place over low heat until the candy melts, stirring constantly. Cool.

Cream the sugar and the remaining stick of butter in a large bowl until light and fluffy. Add the eggs, one at a time, and beat well after each addition. Stir in the vanilla. Combine the buttermilk and baking soda. Add to the creamed mixture alternately with the flour, beating well after each addition. Stir in the candy mixture and nuts. Pour into the prepared pan and bake for 1 hour and 20 minutes. Cool in the pan for 1 hour. Turn out of the pan to complete cooling. Frost cooled cake with chocolate marshmallow icing.

CHOCOLATE MARSHMALLOW ICING:

2½ cups sugar
1 cup evaporated milk
8 tablespoons (1 stick) butter, melted
1 (6-ounce) package semisweet chocolate pieces
1 cup marshmallow creme
Milk, if needed

Combine the sugar, evaporated milk, and butter in a saucepan. Cook on medium heat until a small amount dropped in cold water forms a soft ball (about 30 minutes), or until a candy thermometer registers 138F. Remove from the heat. Add the chocolate and marshmallow creme, stirring until melted. Add milk only if needed for spreading consistency.

Charlotte Cooks Again, Charlotte, NC

MEXICAN CHOCOLATE CAKE
WITH PRALINE FROSTING

1 cup boiling water
3 ounces unsweetened chocolate
8 tablespoons (1 stick) butter, softened
1 teaspoon vanilla extract
1¾ cups packed dark brown sugar
2 large eggs
1¾ cups plus 2 tablespoons all-
   purpose flour
1 teaspoon baking soda
¼ teaspoon salt
½ cup sour cream
Praline Frosting (see below)
½ cup finely chopped pecans

Preheat the oven to 350F. Grease a 9 x 5 x 3-inch loaf pan.

Pour the water over the chocolate in a small bowl. Stir until melted and set aside to cool. With an electric mixer, cream the butter and vanilla; add the brown sugar and blend well. Beat in the eggs, one at a time. Sift the flour, soda, and salt into the creamed mixture; mix well. Blend in the sour cream and chocolate mixture.

Pour the batter into the prepared pan. Bake 1 hour and 15 minutes. Cool in the pan 10 minutes. Turn out of the pan and top with the praline frosting while the cake is still warm. Garnish with pecans.

PRALINE FROSTING:

8 tablespoons (1 stick) butter
1 cup packed dark brown sugar
¼ cup milk
½ teaspoon vanilla extract
1-2 cups powdered sugar, sifted if
   lumpy

Blend the butter and brown sugar in a saucepan. Boil over medium heat for 2 minutes, stirring continuously. Add the milk and bring to a boil. Remove from the heat and cool to lukewarm. Mix in the vanilla. Gradually stir in sugar until the frosting reaches desired consistency.

Plain and Fancy, Richardson, TX

CHOCOLATE CHIP BUNDT CAKE

MAKES 10 TO 12 SERVINGS

Flour for dusting
1 (2-layer) package chocolate cake
  mix
1 (4-ounce) package instant chocolate
  pudding mix
2 cups semisweet chocolate chips
1 cup sour cream
½ cup vegetable oil
½ cup warm water
4 large eggs

Preheat the oven to 350 degrees. Coat a 10-inch Bundt pan with vegetable oil cooking spray. Dust with the flour.

Combine the cake mix and instant pudding mix in a large bowl. Add the chocolate chips, sour cream, oil, water, and eggs, mixing until well blended. Pour into the pan. Bake for 45 to 50 minutes. Cool completely before removing from the pan. Serve warm with vanilla ice cream or chocolate syrup and raspberries.

Dining by Design, Pasadena, CA

CHOCOLATE KAHLÚA DESSERT

MAKES 8 SERVINGS

8 tablespoons (1 stick) butter, melted
1 cup all-purpose flour
¼ cup packed dark brown sugar
½ cup chopped nuts
1 cup powdered sugar
1 (8-ounce) package cream cheese,
  softened
1 (8-ounce) container frozen whipped
  topping, thawed
1 (8-ounce) package chocolate fudge
  instant pudding mix
2½ cups milk
½ cup Kahlúa
Chocolate shavings

Preheat the oven to 350F. Blend the butter, flour, and brown sugar in a large bowl. Mix in the nuts and press into a 13 x 9-inch baking dish. Bake for 15 minutes. Cool.

With an electric mixer, whip the powdered sugar, cream cheese, and half the whipped topping in a large bowl. Spread over the crust and refrigerate for 30 minutes. Combine the pudding mix, milk, and Kahlúa. Spread over the cream cheese layer and refrigerate for 30 minutes. Top with the remaining whipped topping. Refrigerate overnight. Garnish with chocolate shavings.

Plain and Fancy, Richardson, TX

ROULAGE

5 large eggs, separated
1 cup powdered sugar
2 tablespoons all-purpose flour
Unsweetened cocoa powder
1 teaspoon vanilla extract
Pinch of salt
1 cup heavy cream, sweetened and
    whipped
Hot fudge sauce (optional)

Preheat the oven to 325F. Prepare a well-greased and waxed paper-lined jelly roll pan.

Beat the egg whites in a medium bowl until stiff but not dry; set aside. Beat the egg yolks in a large bowl about 2 minutes, until thick and pale yellow. Sift together the flour and 3 tablespoons cocoa in a large bowl; add to the egg yolks and mix well. Add the vanilla and salt; mix well. Fold in the beaten egg whites. Scrape the batter into the prepared pan and spread evenly with a spatula. Bake for 15 minutes.

Let the cake cool completely in the pan on a rack. Run a knife along the edges to release the cake from the pan. Turn the cake out on a damp kitchen towel. Remove the waxed paper. Trim the edges and roll up in the towel, beginning from a short side. Cool in the towel. Remove from the towel and unroll. Sprinkle with cocoa powder. Spread the cake with the whipped cream and roll again; refrigerate. Slice and serve with hot fudge sauce, if desired.

Some Like It South!, Pensacola, FL

CREAM CHEESE POUND CAKE

MAKES 16 SERVINGS

3 sticks (¾ pound) unsalted butter,
    softened
1 (8-ounce) package cream cheese,
    softened
3 cups sugar
¼ teaspoon salt
6 large eggs
1 teaspoon vanilla extract
3 cups all-purpose flour

Preheat the oven to 300F. Grease and flour a 9-inch tube pan.

Cream the butter and cream cheese in a mixing bowl. Add the sugar and salt and beat well. Add 2 of the eggs and the vanilla and beat until fluffy. Add the flour in three parts alternately with the eggs, beginning and ending with flour and beating well after each addition. Scrape the batter into the prepared pan. Spread evenly with a spatula. Bake for 1 hour and 30 minutes to 1 hour and 40 minutes or until a wooden pick inserted in the center comes out clean. Cool completely in the pan on a wire rack. Invert onto a serving plate.

Meet Us in the Kitchen, St. Louis, MO

7UP POUND CAKE

MAKES 16 TO 18 SERVINGS

3 sticks (¾ pound) unsalted butter,
   softened
1½ cups (3 sticks) butter or margarine
3 cups sugar
5 large eggs
3 cups all-purpose flour
¼ teaspoon salt
1 teaspoon lemon extract
¾ cup 7UP

Preheat the oven to 325F. Generously grease and flour a large (10-inch) fluted baking pan.

Cream the sugar and butter together in a large bowl. Beat until light and fluffy. Add the eggs, one at a time. Beat well. Stir in the flour and salt. Add the lemon extract and 7UP; beat well. Scrape the batter into the prepared pan. Bake 1 to 1¼ hours. Cool in pan about 20 minutes before turning out. Frost, if desired.

Charlotte Cooks Again, Charlotte, NC

SOUR CREAM POUND CAKE

MAKES 10 TO 12 SERVINGS

3 cups all-purpose flour
½ teaspoon salt
¼ teaspoon baking soda
3 cups sugar
2 sticks (½ pound) unsalted butter,
   softened
6 large eggs
1 cup sour cream
1 teaspoon vanilla extract
1 teaspoon almond extract
1 teaspoon lemon extract

Preheat the oven to 350F. Grease and flour a medium tube or Bundt pan.

Sift the flour, salt, and baking soda together twice; set aside. Cream the sugar and butter in a large bowl until fluffy. Beat in the eggs, one at a time. Beat in the flour, a little at a time. Add the sour cream and flavorings; mix well. Scrape the batter into the prepared pan and smooth the top. Bake 1½ hours. Cool in the pan on a rack for 5 minutes, then invert on the rack and cool completely.

Cooking Through Rose-Colored Glasses, Tyler, TX

POTATO MOCHA POUND CAKE

MAKES 16 SERVINGS

1 tablespoon instant coffee granules
2 tablespoons hot water
1½ cups low-fat milk
2 cups all-purpose flour
2 cups sugar
1 cup instant potato flakes
4 teaspoons baking powder
½ teaspoon salt
1 (4-ounce) package chocolate instant
  pudding mix
2 sticks (½ pound) butter, softened
4 large eggs

Preheat the oven to 350F. Generously grease and flour a 10-inch Bundt pan.

Combine the coffee granules and the hot water in a small bowl, stirring until the coffee is dissolved. Stir in the milk. Combine the flour, sugar, potato flakes, baking powder, salt, pudding mix, butter, and eggs in a large mixing bowl. Beat at low speed until mixed. Beat in the milk mixture and continue to beat at medium speed for 4 minutes.

Scrape the batter into the prepared pan. Bake 50 to 55 minutes or until a wooden pick inserted near the center comes out clean. Cool in the pan for 30 minutes. Invert onto a serving platter. Top with ice cream, with Kahlúa, or with a chocolate glaze.

Beyond Burlap: Idaho's Famous Potato Recipes, Boise, ID

SANDCAKE WITH RASPBERRY SAUCE

MAKES 12 TO 15 SERVINGS

1 cup sifted all-purpose flour
1 cup sifted cornstarch
2 teaspoons baking powder
¼ teaspoon salt
2½ sticks butter, softened
1¼ cups sugar
3 large eggs
3 tablespoons Cognac or Kirsch
Powdered sugar
Raspberry Sauce (see below)

Preheat the oven to 350F. Generously grease and flour a 10-inch tube pan and set aside.

Sift together the dry ingredients; set aside. Cream the butter and sugar in a large bowl until fluffy. Beat in the eggs one at a time, beating well after each addition. Add the Cognac. Stir in the dry ingredients and mix until the flour just disappears. Pour and scrape into the prepared pan and smooth the top. Bake 40 to 45 minutes. Remove to a wire rack to cool for 5 minutes, then invert and remove the pan. Cool completely. Sift powdered sugar lightly over the top. Serve with raspberry sauce.

RASPBERRY SAUCE:

2½ cups fresh raspberries
2 tablespoons sugar or to taste
Dash of Kirsch (optional)

Combine the berries with sugar in a blender and purée. Press them through a sieve to remove seeds. Add a dash of liqueur, if desired.

Udderly Delicious, Racine, WI

FRUIT COCKTAIL CAKE

MAKES 10 TO 12 SERVINGS

1½ cups sugar
2 large eggs
½ cup vegetable oil
2 cups all-purpose flour
½ teaspoon salt
2 teaspoons baking soda
1 (16-ounce) can fruit cocktail, not
    drained
Coconut Topping (see below)

Preheat the oven to 350F. Grease a 13 x 9 x 2-inch baking pan.

Combine the sugar, eggs, and oil in a large bowl. Whisk together the flour, salt, and soda and add to the sugar mixture. Stir in the fruit cocktail; mix well. Pour into the prepared pan and bake 45 minutes. Pour the topping over the hot cake when you remove it from the oven.

COCONUT TOPPING:

8 tablespoons (1 stick) butter
½ (13-ounce) can evaporated milk
¾ cup sugar
½ cup pecans or walnuts, coarsely
    chopped
½ cup coconut flakes
1 teaspoon vanilla extract

Combine the butter, milk, and sugar in a saucepan; boil for 10 minutes. Add the nuts, coconut, and vanilla; mix well.

The Charlotte Cookbook, Charlotte, NC

FRESH APPLE CAKE WITH VANILLA SAUCE

MAKES 8 TO 10 SERVINGS

4 cups thinly sliced baking apples
3 cups sugar, divided
2 cups all-purpose flour
1½ teaspoons ground cinnamon
1 teaspoon salt
2 large eggs
¾ cup vegetable oil
2 teaspoons vanilla extract, divided
1 cup chopped nuts
8 tablespoons (1 stick) butter
½ cup cream or evaporated milk

Preheat the oven to 350F. Grease a 13 x 9 x 2-inch baking pan.

Combine the apples and 2 cups of the sugar in a large bowl. Add the flour, cinnamon, and salt; stir well. Beat the eggs, oil, and 1 teaspoon of the vanilla in a medium bowl. Combine the egg mixture with the apple mixture; mix well. Stir in the nuts. Spoon into the prepared pan and bake for 50 minutes or until a toothpick inserted in the center of the cake comes out clean.

Combine the remaining 1 cup sugar, the butter, cream, and the remaining 1 teaspoon of vanilla in a saucepan. Bring to a boil over medium-high heat, stirring constantly. Cook for 3 minutes. Serve the warm sauce over the cake.

And Roses for the Table, Tyler, TX

NORWEGIAN GOLD CAKE

MAKES 14 SERVINGS

2 sticks (½ pound) butter, softened
1½ cups sugar
5 large eggs
1 teaspoon vanilla extract
1 teaspoon grated lemon zest
  (optional)
1⅓ cups sifted all-purpose flour
1½ teaspoons baking powder
¼ teaspoon salt
Raspberry Zinfandel Sauce (see
  below)

Preheat the oven to 325F. Generously grease and flour a 10-inch Bundt pan.

Cream the butter in a large bowl; add the sugar and beat until fluffy. Add the eggs one at a time, beating well after each addition. Beat in the vanilla and lemon zest. In a medium bowl, mix the flour with the baking powder and salt. Add to the butter mixture and blend.

Scrape the batter into the prepared pan and bake for 1 hour or until a wooden pick inserted near the center comes out clean. Cool in the pan for 10 minutes. Invert, remove the pan, and finish cooling on a rack. Serve with raspberry zinfandel sauce. Garnish the cake if desired with mint leaves or fresh raspberries.

RASPBERRY-ZINFANDEL SAUCE:

3 cups red zinfandel wine
1½ cups frozen unsweetened
  raspberries
¾ cup sugar
1 (6-inch) and 1 (3-inch) piece
  vanilla bean, split lengthwise

In a medium saucepan, combine the zinfandel, frozen berries, sugar, and vanilla bean. Bring to a boil, reduce the heat, and simmer 5 minutes. Increase the heat and boil until reduced to 1½ cups, stirring occasionally. This will take approximately 15 minutes. Strain the berry mixture through a sieve, pressing berries to extract as much pulp as possible. Cool to room temperature.

Sound Seasonings, Westchester on the Sound, NY

ALLEY SPRING APPLE CAKE

MAKES 12 TO 15 SERVINGS

1 cup vegetable oil
2 cups sugar
3 large eggs, well beaten
1 tablespoon vanilla extract
2½ cups all-purpose flour
2 teaspoons baking powder
1 teaspoon ground cinnamon
1 teaspoon grated nutmeg
1 teaspoon baking soda
1 teaspoon salt
3 cups peeled, chopped apples
1 cup chopped pecans
Brown Sugar Icing (see below)

Preheat the oven to 350F. Generously grease and flour a 10-inch Bundt pan.

In a large bowl, mix the oil, sugar, and eggs. Add the vanilla. Whisk together the flour, baking powder, cinnamon, nutmeg, soda, and salt in a medium bowl. Blend into the oil mixture. Fold in the apples and pecans. Pour and scrape the batter into the prepared pan and bake for 55 to 60 minutes. Cool the cake in the pan for 5 minutes. Invert and finish cooling on a rack. Drizzle brown sugar icing over the cake.

BROWN SUGAR ICING:

1 cup firmly packed light brown sugar
8 tablespoons (½ stick) butter
¼ cup evaporated milk
1 teaspoon vanilla extract

Combine the brown sugar, butter, and milk in a small saucepan; bring to a boil, stirring constantly. Remove from the heat and stir in the vanilla. Beat with a wooden spoon until the icing is cool.

Sassafras! Springfield, MO

BLUEBERRY CITRUS LAYER CAKE

MAKES 12 SERVINGS

1 (2-layer) package lemon cake mix
½ cup orange juice
½ cup water
⅓ cup vegetable oil
3 large eggs
1½ cups fresh blueberries
1½ tablespoons finely shredded orange zest
1½ tablespoons finely shredded lemon zest
Citrus Frosting (see below)
Orange zest curls

Preheat the oven to 350F. Grease and flour two 8- or 9-inch round cake pans.

Combine the cake mix, orange juice, water, oil, and eggs in a large mixer bowl. Beat at low speed for 30 seconds. Beat at medium speed for 2 minutes. Fold in the blueberries, orange zest, and lemon zest. Spoon the batter into the prepared pans. Bake 35 to 40 minutes or until a wooden. pick inserted near the center comes out clean. Cool in the pans on the racks for 10 minutes. Invert the layers onto wire racks to cool completely. Spread citrus frosting between the layers and over the top and side of the cake. Sprinkle with orange zest curls. Store, covered, in the refrigerator.

CITRUS FROSTING:

1 (3-ounce) package cream cheese, softened
4 tablespoons (½ stick) butter, softened
3 cups powdered sugar, sifted if lumpy
2 tablespoons orange juice
1 cup heavy cream, whipped
2 tablespoons finely shredded orange zest
1 tablespoon finely shredded lemon zest

Beat the cream cheese and butter in a medium mixer bowl until light and fluffy. Add the powdered sugar and orange juice and beat until smooth. Add the whipped cream, orange zest, and lemon zest. Beat at low speed until blended.

Sunsational Encore, Greater Orlando, FL

ORANGE BLOSSOMS SPECIAL

MAKES 70 MINIATURE CUPCAKES

1 (2-layer) package yellow cake mix
3½ cups sugar
1 cup orange juice
Juice of 1 lemon
Grated zest of 1 lemon and 3 oranges

Preheat the oven to 350F. Prepare the cake mix according to the directions on the package and pour into greased miniature muffin tins. Bake for 15 minutes.

Combine the sugar and juices in a small bowl; mix until the sugar is dissolved. Add the grated zests and mix well. While the cakes are still hot, turn them out of the muffin tins and dip in the glaze. Place on a cake rack over a sheet of waxed paper to cool. The cakes will keep two days in an airtight tin or they may be frozen.

Dinner on the Diner, Chattanooga, TN

DEB'S BLUEBERRY BUCKLE

MAKES 6 TO 8 SERVINGS

2 cups all-purpose flour
¼ cup sugar
2 teaspoons baking powder
½ teaspoon salt
2 cups small fresh blueberries, rinsed
    and dried
1 large egg
½ cup milk
¼ cup solid vegetable shortening,
    melted

TOPPING:
½ cup sugar
½ teaspoon ground cinnamon
¼ teaspoon freshly grated nutmeg
½ cup all-purpose flour
4 tablespoons (½ cup) butter, melted

Preheat the oven to 375F. Grease an 8-inch-square baking pan.

In a large bowl, whisk together the flour, sugar, baking powder, and salt. Add the blueberries and toss to mix. Beat the egg and milk in a small bowl with the shortening. Add to the flour mixture and stir just until moistened.

Combine the topping ingredients in a medium bowl and mix well. Sprinkle over the top of the cake. Bake for 45 to 60 minutes or until a wooden pick inserted near the center of the cake comes out clean.

RSVP, Portland, ME

LEMONADE CAKE

1 (6-ounce) can frozen lemonade
   concentrate, thawed
½–¾ cup sugar
1 (2-layer) package lemon cake mix
4 large eggs, beaten lightly
1 (3-ounce) package lemon instant
   pudding
¾ cup water
¾ cup vegetable oil

Preheat the oven to 350F. Generously grease and flour a 10-inch tube pan.

Mix the lemonade concentrate with sugar to taste and set aside. Combine the cake mix, eggs, lemon pudding, water, and oil in a large bowl; mix well. Pour into the prepared pan. Bake for 1 hour. Remove the cake from the oven and spoon the lemonade and sugar mixture over the top. Let stand for 1 hour before removing the cake from the pan.

Gracious Gator Cooks, Gainesville, FL

CHOCOLATE-MINT CREAM PUFFS

MAKES 1 DOZEN

8 tablespoons (1 stick) butter
1 cup water
1 cup all-purpose flour
¼ teaspoon salt
4 large eggs
Peppermint Whipped Cream (see below)
Hot Fudge Sauce (see below)

Preheat the oven to 450F. Have ready an ungreased baking sheet.

Melt the butter in the water in a large saucepan and bring the mixture to a full boil. Add the flour and salt all at once and stir vigorously with a wooden spoon until the mixture pulls away from the side of the pan. Cook, stirring constantly, 1 minute longer, until the mixture forms a ball that doesn't separate. Remove from heat and cool for 5 minutes, stirring occasionally. Add the eggs, one at a time, beating vigorously after each addition.

When the dough is smooth and shiny, drop from tablespoons 2 inches apart onto the baking sheet. Bake 25 minutes or until golden brown and very firm to the touch. Turn off the oven, poke a hole in the underside of each puff, and return to the oven to dry out for 10 or more minutes. Remove with a spatula to cool on a wire rack. When thoroughly cool, slice the top off each puff, remove any soft dough inside, and fill the puffs with the peppermint whipped cream. Spoon a generous portion of hot fudge sauce over each puff before serving.

PEPPERMINT WHIPPED CREAM:

1 pint heavy cream
½ pound red soft peppermint candy

Whip the cream to serving thickness. Crush the candy with a rolling pin and gently fold into the whipped cream just before filling the cream puffs.

HOT FUDGE SAUCE:

3 squares unsweetened chocolate
1 cup evaporated milk
1 cup sugar
⅛ teaspoon salt
2 tablespoons butter
1 teaspoon vanilla extract

Mix the chocolate, milk, sugar, and salt in the top of a double boiler set over simmering water. Cook over low heat, stirring constantly, until the chocolate melts. Add the butter and vanilla. Continue to cook, stirring constantly, until the sauce is smooth. Remove from the heat. Serve over the cream puffs.

Smoky Mountain Magic, Johnson City, TN

PUMPKIN CHEESECAKE
WITH BOURBON SOUR CREAM TOPPING

CRUMB CRUST:

¾ cup graham cracker crumbs

½ cup finely chopped pecans

¼ cup packed light brown sugar

¼ cup granulated sugar

4 tablespoons (½ stick) butter, melted
  and cooled

PUMPKIN FILLING:

1 (15-ounce) can pumpkin purée

3 large eggs

2 teaspoons ground cinnamon

¾ teaspoon grated nutmeg

½ teaspoon ground ginger

½ teaspoon salt

½ cup packed light brown sugar

3 (8-ounce) packages cream cheese,
  softened

½ cup granulated sugar

2 tablespoons heavy cream

1 tablespoon cornstarch

1 teaspoon vanilla extract

1 tablespoon bourbon

BOURBON SOUR CREAM
TOPPING:

2 cups sour cream

2 tablespoons sugar

1 tablespoon bourbon

16 pecan halves

For the crust, butter a 9-inch springform pan. Combine the crumbs, pecans, brown sugar, and granulated sugar in a bowl. Stir in the melted butter. Press the mixture over the bottom and ½ inch up the side of the pan. Chill, covered, in the refrigerator for 1 hour.

For the filling, preheat the oven to 350F. Whisk the pumpkin, eggs, cinnamon, nutmeg, ginger, salt, and brown sugar in a large bowl until thoroughly combined. Cut the cream cheese into chunks and cream together with the granulated sugar in the large bowl of an electric mixer. Beat in the heavy cream, cornstarch, vanilla, and bourbon. Add the pumpkin mixture and beat until smooth. Pour the filling into the crust. Bake on the middle rack of the oven for 50 to 55 minutes or until the center is set. Remove from the oven but keep oven heat on. Let the cake stand on a wire rack for 5 minutes while assembling the topping.

For the topping, whisk the sour cream, sugar, and bourbon in a bowl. Spread over the hot cheesecake. Bake for 5 minutes. Let cool in the pan on a wire rack. Chill, covered, for 12 hours. Remove the springform, decorate with the pecans, and serve.

Dining by Design, Pasadena, CA

WALNUT-CRUST CHEESECAKE

Preheat the oven to 350F.

CRUST:
2 cups graham cracker crumbs
¼ cup packed dark brown sugar
½ teaspoon ground cinnamon
8 tablespoons (1 stick) butter, melted
¼ cup finely chopped walnuts

Make the crust: In a bowl, combine the graham cracker crumbs, brown sugar, cinnamon, and butter; mix well. Press into the bottom and partly up the side of a 10-inch springform pan. Sprinkle the walnuts over the bottom crust.

FILLING:
5 (8-ounce) packages cream cheese, softened
1 cup granulated sugar
4 large eggs
1 teaspoon vanilla extract

For the filling: Whip the cream cheese and sugar in a large bowl until smooth. Add the eggs and vanilla; whip until smooth. Pour over the crust. Place on the second rack from the bottom of the oven. Bake 45 minutes or until set.

TOPPING:
1 teaspoon vanilla extract
1 cup sour cream
5 tablespoons granulated sugar

For the topping: Combine the vanilla, sour cream, and sugar in a small bowl; mix well. Spread over the hot cake, return to the oven, and bake 5 minutes. Cool to room temperature on a wire rack. Refrigerate several hours before serving.

Very Virginia, Hampton Roads, VA

CARAMEL CASHEW CHEESECAKE

MAKES 8 SERVINGS

CRUST:

2 cups finely crushed vanilla wafers
½ cup finely chopped cashews
¼ cup granulated sugar
6 tablespoons (¾ stick) butter, melted

CHEESECAKE:

3 (8-ounce) packages cream cheese,
  softened
1 (14-ounce) can sweetened condensed
  milk (not evaporated milk)
3 large eggs
1 tablespoon vanilla extract
1½ tablespoons rum
½ tablespoon butter flavoring

CARAMEL TOPPING:

⅓ cup finely chopped cashews
2 teaspoons granulated sugar
½ cup packed dark brown sugar
3 tablespoons heavy cream
1½ tablespoons butter
¾ teaspoon vanilla extract

Preheat the oven to 325F. Combine the vanilla wafers, cashews, sugar, and butter for the crust. Press firmly onto the bottom and partly up the side of a 9-inch springform pan. In a large mixer bowl, beat the cream cheese until fluffy. Gradually beat in the sweetened condensed milk until smooth. Add the eggs, vanilla, rum, and butter flavoring; mix well. Pour the mixture into the prepared springform pan. Bake 55 to 60 minutes or until the center is set. Allow the cheesecake to cool.

Prior to making the topping, sprinkle the cheesecake with ⅓ cup of finely chopped cashews. For the topping, combine the sugars, cream, and butter in a small saucepan. Heat to boiling, stirring until the sugars dissolve. Cook over low to medium heat until the mixture reaches 225F on a candy thermometer. Remove from the heat and add the vanilla extract. Stir until the topping is creamy. Drizzle the caramel sauce over the top of the cheesecake. Refrigerate overnight before serving. Cut into slices and serve.

First Impressions: Dining with Distinction, Waterloo-Cedar Falls, IA

NEW ENGLAND APPLE PIE

PIE PASTRY:

2 cups all-purpose flour

1 teaspoon salt

⅔ cup plus 2 tablespoons solid
  vegetable shortening

4-5 tablespoons cold water

APPLE FILLING:

¾ cup sugar

¼ cup all-purpose flour

½ teaspoon grated nutmeg

½ teaspoon ground cinnamon

Dash of salt

4 McIntosh apples, peeled, cut into
  slices

2 Granny Smith apples, peeled, cut
  into slices

2 tablespoons butter

For the pie pastry, combine the flour and salt in a bowl. Cut in the shortening with a pastry blender or two knives until crumbly. Add the water 1 tablespoon at a time, mixing with a fork until the mixture forms a ball. Chill, wrapped in plastic wrap, 30 minutes or longer. Divide into two portions. Roll one portion into an 11-inch circle on a lightly floured surface. Fit into a 9-inch pie plate. Roll the remaining portion into a 10-inch circle on a lightly floured surface.

Preheat the oven to 325F. For the pie filling, combine the sugar, flour, nutmeg, cinnamon, and salt in a bowl and mix well. Add the apple slices and toss to coat. Spoon into the pastry-lined pie plate. Dot with the butter. Top with the remaining pastry, sealing the edge and cutting 6 steam vents. Cover the edge with a 3-inch strip of foil. Bake 25 minutes. Remove the foil strip. Bake 15 to 25 minutes longer or until the crust is brown and the juice is bubbly.

Wild Thymes and Other Temptations, Tucson, AZ

GEORGIA PECAN PIE

MAKES 6 TO 8 SERVINGS

1¼ cups sugar
½ cup light corn syrup
4 tablespoons (½ stick) butter
3 large eggs, slightly beaten
1 cup pecans, coarsely chopped
1 teaspoon vanilla extract
1 (9-inch) pie crust

Preheat the oven to 350F. Combine the sugar, corn syrup, and butter in a 2-quart saucepan. Bring to a boil over high heat, stirring constantly, until the butter is melted. Remove from the stove and gradually add the hot syrup to the eggs, stirring constantly. Add the pecans and vanilla to the mixture and cool to lukewarm. Pour into the pie crust and bake 40 to 45 minutes, until the edges are firm and the center is set but quivery, with a gelatin-like consistency. Cool on a rack for at least 1½ hours before serving.

Georgia on My Menu, Cobb-Marietta, GA

PRALINE PUMPKIN PIE

MAKES 6 TO 8 SERVINGS

3 tablespoons butter, softened
½ cup plus ⅓ cup firmly packed light
   brown sugar
⅓ cup chopped pecans
1 (9-inch) pastry crust, unbaked
3 large eggs, lightly beaten
1½ cups canned pumpkin purée
½ cup granulated sugar
1½ teaspoons pumpkin pie spice
1 teaspoon salt
1 cup evaporated milk
½ cup water
½ cup heavy cream, whipped

Preheat the oven to 450F. In a small mixing bowl, cream the butter with the ⅓ cup brown sugar until smooth. Stir in the pecans. Press the mixture into the bottom of the crust. Bake 10 minutes. Let stand 10 minutes to cool. Reduce the oven temperature to 350F.

Combine the eggs, pumpkin, granulated sugar, ½ cup brown sugar, pumpkin pie spice, and salt in a medium mixing bowl. Combine the evaporated milk and water in a small bowl; add to the pumpkin mixture, beating well. Spread the filling into the baked crust. Bake 50 minutes or until a knife tip inserted near the center comes out clean. Let cool. Serve the cooled pie with whipped cream.

I'll Cook When Pigs Fly, Cincinnati, OH

AMELIA ISLAND MUD PIE

SHELL:
12 chocolate cookies (without the
   cream filling), finely crushed
2 tablespoons butter, melted
1 tablespoon perked decaffeinated
   coffee grounds

FILLING:
2-3 cups chocolate ice cream, softened
1 tablespoon perked decaffeinated
   coffee grounds
2 tablespoons brandy
2 tablespoons Kahlúa
2 tablespoons brewed coffee, chilled
4 tablespoons whipped cream (or more
   to taste)

TOPPING:
Fudge topping
¼ cup chopped pecans
Whipped cream, sweetened to taste

To make the shell, mix the chocolate cookie crumbs with the butter and the coffee grounds in a small bowl. Press into a 9-inch pie plate and freeze.

For the filling, whip the ice cream with the coffee grounds, liqueurs, and coffee in a medium bowl. Fold in the whipped cream. Pour into the shell. Freeze until hard.

Cover with a thin layer of fudge topping and the nuts. Garnish with whipped cream.

Tea-Time at the Masters, Augusta, GA

MARGARITA PIE

1½ cups crushed pretzels
¼ cup sugar
8 tablespoons (1 stick) butter, melted
1 (14-ounce) can sweetened condensed
    milk (not evaporated milk)
⅓ cup fresh lime juice
2 tablespoons tequila
2 tablespoons Triple Sec
1-2 drops green food coloring
1 cup heavy cream, whipped
Lime slices

Mix the pretzels and sugar in a bowl. Add the butter, stirring until crumbly. Press the crumb mixture over the bottom and up the sides of a buttered 9-inch pie plate. Chill in the refrigerator.

Combine the condensed milk, lime juice, tequila, and Triple Sec in a bowl and mix well. Stir in the food coloring. Fold in the whipped cream. Spoon into the prepared pie plate. Freeze, covered, 3 to 4 hours or until firm. Top with a lime slice.

NOTE: The pie may be stored in the freezer for several days.

Sunny Side Up, Greater Fort Lauderdale, FL

PEPPERMINT PIE WITH RICE KRISPIES CRUST

MAKES 8 SERVINGS

CRUST:
1 (4-ounce) bar German's Sweet
    Chocolate
4 tablespoons (¼ cup) butter
3 cups Rice Krispies

FILLING:
¾ cup crushed peppermint candy
½ gallon vanilla ice cream, softened

Make the crust: Break the chocolate into pieces and place in the top of a double boiler over simmering water. Add the butter and stir over medium heat until melted. Remove from the heat and add the Rice Krispies; mix well. Press the mixture into the bottom and up the sides of a 10-inch pie pan. Refrigerate.

For the filling, break the candy into very small pieces; stir into the softened ice cream. Spoon into the chocolate crust and freeze for 3 to 4 hours or until firm.

Southern Accent, Pine Bluff, AR

WHIPPED KAHLÚA PIE

MAKES 8 SERVINGS

½ package chocolate wafers, crushed
6 tablespoons butter, melted
½ cup finely chopped pecans
1 tablespoon sugar
1 quart coffee ice cream
2 cups heavy cream
1 teaspoon vanilla extract
⅔ cup Kahlúa
4 Heath candy bars, crushed

Preheat the oven to 350F. Combine the wafer crumbs, melted butter, pecans, and sugar in a medium bowl. Pat the mixture into a greased 10-inch pie pan. Bake 10 minutes; cool.

Soften the ice cream slightly. Whip the cream in a medium bowl until it forms soft peaks. Add the vanilla and Kahlúa. Gently fold in the crushed candy bars, then the ice cream. Pour into the crust and freeze.

Brunch Basket, Rockford, IL

FRESH BLUEBERRY PIE

MAKES 6 TO 8 SERVINGS

2 tablespoons cornstarch
⅛ teaspoon salt
¾ cup sugar
¼ cup water
4½ cups (1 quart) blueberries, rinsed
    and divided
1 tablespoon butter
1 tablespoon lemon juice
1 (9-inch) pie crust, baked and cooled
Whipped cream (optional)
Finely grated lemon zest (optional)

In a medium-size saucepan, mix together the cornstarch, salt, and sugar. Stir in the water. Add 2¼ cups of the blueberries and cook over medium heat, stirring constantly, until the mixture becomes thick. Stir in the butter and lemon juice. Remove from the heat and cool.

Put the remaining blueberries in the bottom of the baked pie crust. Spoon the thickened blueberry mixture on top; chill. Before serving, garnish with fresh whipped cream dusted with finely grated lemon zest, if desired.

A Matter of Taste, Morristown, NJ

MOONLIT BLUEBERRY PIE
WITH ALMOND CRÈME CHANTILLY

MAKES 8 SERVINGS

4 cups fresh blueberries, washed,
    divided
¾ cup sugar
½ cup water
2 tablespoons cornstarch, dissolved in
    2 tablespoons water
1 tablespoon butter
4 tablespoons Cointreau liqueur
¼ cup slivered almonds, toasted
1 (9-inch) deep-dish pie crust, baked
Crème Chantilly (see below)

Combine 1 cup of the blueberries, the sugar, and the water in a blender and purée until smooth. Pour the mixture into a medium saucepan and add the dissolved cornstarch. Heat until thickened, stirring frequently. Stir in the butter and Cointreau. Add the almonds and the remaining 3 cups of blueberries, stirring gently to combine. Pour into the baked pie crust and chill. Top with crème chantilly just before serving.

CRÈME CHANTILLY:

1 cup heavy cream
2 tablespoons sugar
¼ teaspoon almond extract

Combine the cream, sugar, and almond extract in a chilled bowl. Whip until stiff peaks form.

Dining by Fireflies, Charlotte, NC

BLUEBERRY–SOUR CREAM PIE

MAKES 8 SERVINGS

1¼ cups plus 6 tablespoons all-purpose flour
8 tablespoons (1 stick) plus 4 tablespoons (½ stick) chilled unsalted butter, cut up
Pinch of salt
¼ cup sugar, divided
4 tablespoons ice water
Blueberry Filling (see below)
⅓ cup chopped pecans

Process the 1¼ cups flour, 8 tablespoons butter, salt, and 2 tablespoons of the sugar in a food processor until a coarse meal forms. With the machine running, add the ice water, 1 tablespoon at a time, through the food chute until clumps form. Using your hands, gather the dough into a ball and flatten to a disc. Wrap in plastic wrap, and chill 30 minutes or until firm. Roll out the dough on a lightly floured surface to a 13-inch round. Fit into a 9-inch pie plate; trim the edges to ½-inch overhang. Fold the dough under, and crimp. Place in the freezer for 10 minutes.

Preheat the oven to 400F. Line the chilled pie crust with aluminum foil, and fill with dried beans or pie weights. Bake 12 minutes. Remove the foil and beans. Let cool. Spoon blueberry filling into the prepared pie crust. Bake at 400F for 25 minutes or until set.

Meanwhile, mix the 6 tablespoons flour and 4 tablespoons butter, using your fingertips, until small clumps form. Stir in the pecans and the remaining 2 tablespoons sugar. Remove the pie from the oven and top with pecan mixture. Bake an additional 12 minutes or until the topping is lightly browned. Let cool on a wire rack.

BLUEBERRY FILLING:

1 cup sour cream
¾ cup sugar
2½ tablespoons all-purpose flour
1 large egg
¾ teaspoon almond extract
¼ teaspoon salt
2½ cups blueberries

Beat all the ingredients, except blueberries, in a medium bowl at medium speed with an electric mixer until smooth. Stir in the blueberries.

Victorian Thymes & Pleasures, Williamsport, PA

QUAKER BONNET LEMON ANGEL PIES

MAKES 6 TO 8 SERVINGS

6 large egg whites, at room
   temperature
1½ cups superfine sugar
1 cup large egg yolks
½ cup granulated sugar
½ cup lemon juice
1 teaspoon finely chopped lemon zest
1 cup whipped cream

Preheat the oven to 150F to 175F (or as low as possible). Beat the egg whites in a mixing bowl until soft peaks form. Gradually add the 1½ cups of superfine sugar, beating constantly until stiff and glossy. Do not overbeat the meringue or it will break down.

Pipe the meringue into individual nests on a parchment-paper-lined baking sheet sprayed with vegetable oil cooking spray. Bake for 3 hours.

Note: Leave the oven door open if your oven is set higher than 150F or 175F. The shells may be baked at 150F for as long as 12 hours to ensure that they are completely dry.

Combine the egg yolks, ½ cup granulated sugar, lemon juice, and lemon zest in the top of a double boiler set over simmering water. Cook, whisking constantly, until the mixture holds a ribbon for 3 seconds when the whisk is lifted from the mixture. Let stand until cool. Spoon the lemon mixture into the meringue nests. Spread with the whipped cream.

Great Lake Effects, Buffalo, NY

INDIANA RASPBERRY TART

PASTRY:
1 cup all-purpose flour
2 tablespoons sugar
¼ teaspoon salt
8 tablespoons (1 stick) butter, chilled
2-3 tablespoons cold water

FILLING:
¼ teaspoon ground cinnamon
⅔ cup sugar
¼ cup all-purpose flour
6 cups fresh raspberries, divided
Heavy cream

Preheat the oven to 400F.

To prepare the pastry, combine the flour, sugar, and salt in a medium bowl. Cut in the butter with a pastry blender or two knives unil the mixture is crumbly. Sprinkle with the cold water, 1 tablespoon at a time, until the dough is just moist enough to hold together. Press the pastry into the bottom and 1 inch up the side of a 9-inch springform pan. Set aside.

To make the filling, combine the cinnamon, sugar, and flour in a small bowl. Sprinkle half the flour mixture over the bottom of the pastry. Top with 4 cups of the raspberries. Sprinkle the remaining flour mixture over the raspberries. Place in the oven on the lowest rack and bake for 50 to 60 minutes, or until the tart is golden and bubbly. Remove from oven; cool on a wire rack. Remove the springform carefully after the tart has completely cooled. Top with the remaining 2 cups of raspberries. Cut into wedges. To serve, pool 2 tablespoons of cream on each serving plate; arrange a tart wedge on the cream.

Back Home Again, Indianapolis, IN

GANACHE TORTE

*2 cups pecans, diced, plus ½ cup
pecans, coarsely chopped and
toasted*

2⅓ cups sugar, divided

*½ pound (2 sticks) plus 4 tablespoons
(½ stick) butter, melted*

1 large egg yolk

*2 cups heavy cream, heated and
divided*

*10 ounces semisweet chocolate morsels,
melted*

Preheat the oven to 325F. Combine the 2 cups of diced pecans, ⅓ cup of the sugar, and 4 tablespoons of melted butter in a small bowl; press onto the bottom and partly up the side of a 10-inch tart pan with a removable bottom. Bake 15 minutes. Remove from the oven.

Beat the egg yolk and 1 cup of cream at medium speed in an electric mixer until smooth; stir in the melted chocolate. Pour the chocolate mixture into the prepared crust. Top with the ½ cup of toasted pecans; chill.

Cook the remaining 2 cups of sugar and 2 sticks of butter in a small saucepan over medium heat, stirring often, until caramel colored. Remove from the heat and, standing back to avoid possible spatters, stir in the remaining cup of heavy cream. Cut the torte into wedges, and serve with the caramel sauce.

Victorian Thymes & Pleasures, Williamsport, PA

LEMON CURD BARS

MAKES 24 BARS

12 tablespoons (1½ sticks) butter,
  softened
1½ cups plus 3 tablespoons all-
  purpose flour
½ cup powdered sugar, plus additional
  for garnish
3 cups granulated sugar
1 cup plus 2 tablespoons fresh lemon
  juice (about 5 lemons)
6 large eggs, slightly beaten

Preheat the oven to 350F. Mix the butter, 1½ cups of the flour, and the ½ cup of powdered sugar in a bowl until thoroughly combined. Press into the bottom and ¾ inch up the sides of a greased 13 x 9-inch baking pan. Bake 20 minutes.

Meanwhile, whisk the remaining 3 tablespoons of flour, the granulated sugar, lemon juice, and eggs in a small bowl until well blended. Pour over the hot crust and return to the oven. Lower the temperature to 300F and bake until set, about 35 minutes longer. Sprinkle the top with powdered sugar. Cool on a rack completely and cut into squares.

Rare Collections, Galveston County, TX

CHOCONUT CARAMEL BARS

MAKES 12 SERVINGS

1 (12-ounce) package chocolate chips
  (2 cups)
2 tablespoons solid vegetable
  shortening
14 ounces caramels
5 tablespoons butter
2 tablespoons water
1 cup coarsely chopped peanuts

Melt the chocolate chips and shortening in the top of a double boiler over hot, not boiling, water. Stir until the mixture is smooth. Remove from the heat. Pour half the chocolate mixture into a foil-lined 8-inch square pan and spread evenly. Refrigerate until firm (about 15 minutes). Return the remaining chocolate mixture to low heat. Combine the caramels, butter, and water in a small microwave mixing bowl. Microwave, stirring every 1 to 2 minutes, until melted and smooth. Stir in the peanuts and pour over the chocolate-lined pan. Spread evenly. Refrigerate until tacky (15 minutes). Top with the remaining chocolate mixture and spread evenly. Refrigerate for 1 hour. Cut into squares. Refrigerate until ready to serve.

St. Louis Days . . . St. Louis Nights, St. Louis, MO

CHOCOLATE MINT BARS

BROWNIES:

2 squares unsweetened baking
   chocolate
8 tablespoons (1 stick) butter
1 cup sugar
¼ teaspoon salt
¼ teaspoon peppermint extract
1 teaspoon vanilla extract
2 large eggs, beaten
½ cup all-purpose flour
½ cup chopped nuts (optional)

FROSTING:

2 tablespoons butter
2 tablespoons heavy cream
1½ cups powdered sugar
½ teaspoon peppermint extract

GLAZE:

2 squares semisweet baking chocolate
2 tablespoons butter

Preheat the oven to 350F. Line a 9-inch square pan with foil and grease the foil.

Prepare the brownies by melting the unsweetened chocolate and butter together over low heat in a saucepan. Let cool for 10 minutes. Stir in the sugar, salt, peppermint, and vanilla extract. Beat in the eggs one at a time. Mix in the flour, then the nuts. Scrape the batter into the prepared pan, spreading to the edges. Bake for 20 to 25 minutes, or until a toothpick inserted near the center comes out with a few fudgy crumbs. Remove from the oven and place on a rack to cool completely. Turn out of the pan and carefully remove the foil.

Prepare the frosting by combining all the ingredients in a medium bowl and stirring until smooth. Spread on the cooled brownies, then refrigerate for 5 minutes.

Prepare the glaze by melting the chocolate and butter together in a saucepan over very low heat. Spread over the set frosting. Cut into squares.

California Sizzles, Pasadena, CA

CHOCOLATE DELIGHTS

MAKES 16 TO 24 SERVINGS

8 tablespoons (1 stick) plus 4½
    tablespoons butter
¼ cup plus 1 tablespoon unsweetened
    cocoa powder
¼ cup granulated sugar
1 large egg, beaten
1 teaspoon vanilla extract
2 cups graham cracker crumbs
½ cup chopped nuts
2 tablespoons instant vanilla pudding
    mix
2 cups powdered sugar
3 tablespoons milk
4 (1-ounce) squares unsweetened
    chocolate

In a large saucepan, melt 1 stick of butter. Add the cocoa, granulated sugar, egg, and vanilla. Cook and stir over medium heat until thickened. Remove from the heat. Stir in the cracker crumbs and nuts, mixing until blended. Press the mixture into the bottom of an 8-inch or 9-inch square baking pan. Chill.

Cream 3 tablespoons of the butter with the pudding mix. Blend in the powdered sugar and milk. Spread on the chilled crust. Melt the remaining 1½ tablespoons of butter with the chocolate. Spread on the pudding layer. Cut into bars and chill.

I'll Cook When Pigs Fly, Cincinnati, OH

LOCH NESS BARS

MAKES 60 BARS

8 tablespoons (1 stick) butter
2 (6-ounce) packages chocolate chips,
    divided
1 cup peanut butter
1 (10-ounce) package miniature
    marshmallows
4¼ cups crispy rice cereal
1 cup peanuts (optional)
1 (6-ounce) package butterscotch chips

Combine the butter, 1 package of chocolate chips, and the peanut butter in a large saucepan. Cook over low heat until melted, stirring until smooth. Add the marshmallows and stir until melted. Blend in the cereal and peanuts. Spread in a 13 x 9-inch baking pan. Chill until firm. Melt the remaining package of chocolate chips and the butterscotch chips together, blending until smooth. Spread on the chilled cereal mixture. Cut into 1 x 2-inch bars.

Children's Party Book, Hampton Roads, VA

CARAMEL FUDGE BROWNIES

MAKES 16 LARGE OR 40 SMALL BROWNIES

1 (14-ounce) package caramels
⅔ cup evaporated milk, divided
1 (2-layer) package devil's food cake mix
1½ sticks butter, melted
1½ cups semisweet chocolate chips

Preheat the oven to 350F. Grease a 13 x 9-inch baking pan.

In a heavy saucepan, melt the caramels with ⅓ cup of the milk over low heat; keep warm. Combine the cake mix, butter, and the remaining ⅓ cup milk in a large bowl. Stir until the dough begins to stick together. Press two-thirds of the mixture into the prepared baking pan. Bake 6 minutes. Remove the pan from the oven and cover the brownie layer with chocolate chips. Spoon the melted caramels over the chocolate. Press the remaining dough mixture over the caramel layer. Bake 20 to 25 minutes or until done. Cool completely and cut into squares.

Very Virginia, Hampton Roads, VA

EDIE'S BROWNIES

MAKES 30 SMALL BROWNIES

5 ounces unsweetened baking chocolate
3 sticks (¾ pound) butter
2½ cups sugar
5 large eggs, beaten
2½ teaspoons vanilla extract
1¼ cups all-purpose flour
1 teaspoon baking powder
1 cup pecans, chopped
Powdered sugar

Preheat the oven to 350F. Line a 13 x 9-inch metal baking pan with foil; grease the foil.

Melt the chocolate and the butter in a large saucepan over very low heat. Remove from the heat and let cool for 10 minutes. Stir in the sugar and mix well. Beat in the eggs, one at a time, and add the vanilla. Whisk the flour and baking powder together and stir in; fold in the pecans.

Scrape into the prepared pan and bake 30 minutes or until the brownies slightly pull away from the edges of the pan and a toothpick inserted near the center comes out with a few fudgy crumbs. Dust with powdered sugar and cut in small squares when thoroughly cool.

¡Viva! Tradiciones, Corpus Christi, TX

KAHLÚA BROWNIES WITH BUTTERCREAM FROSTING AND CHOCOLATE GLAZE

MAKES 1 DOZEN BROWNIES

CRUST:
⅓ cup packed light brown sugar
5⅓ tablespoons unsalted butter, at
   room temperature
⅔ cup all-purpose flour
½ cup finely chopped pecans

FILLING:
2 ounces unsweetened baking
   chocolate
¼ cup solid vegetable shortening
4 tablespoons (½ stick) unsalted butter
½ cup granulated sugar
½ cup packed light brown sugar
2 large eggs
1 teaspoon vanilla extract
¼ cup Kahlúa
½ cup all-purpose flour
¼ teaspoon salt
½ cup chopped pecans

BUTTERCREAM FROSTING:
6 tablespoons unsalted butter, at room
   temperature
2 cups powdered sugar, sifted if lumpy
1 tablespoon Kahlúa
1 tablespoon heavy cream

GLAZE:
2 ounces semisweet baking chocolate
1 ounce unsweetened baking chocolate
2 teaspoons solid vegetable shortening

Preheat the oven to 350F. Grease and flour a 9-inch square baking pan. To make the crust, cream the sugar and butter until light and fluffy. Slowly add the flour and continue to mix until blended. Add the pecans. When completely combined, press the dough into the bottom of the prepared pan; set aside.

Make the filling: Combine the chocolate, shortening, and butter in a large saucepan over low heat. Stir until the chocolate is melted and the mixture is smooth. Cool for 8 to 10 minutes. Stir in the sugars and add the eggs one at a time, blending well. Add the vanilla and Kahlúa. Slowly add the flour and salt, mixing until the batter is smooth. Stir in the pecans. Pour and scrape the filling into the prepared crust. Bake 25 minutes, or until a tester inserted near the center comes out with a few fudgy crumbs. Be careful not to overbake; cool.

For the frosting, cream the butter, sugar, Kahlúa, and cream in a bowl until smooth and creamy. Spread over the cooled cake and refrigerate 30 minutes. More Kahlúa may be added to make spreading easier.

For the glaze, melt the chocolates and shortening over low heat, stirring constantly. Cool and spread over the frosting.

Stop and Smell the Rosemary, Houston, TX

PREVIEW PARTY BROWNIES

MAKES 1 ½ DOZEN

1 (2-layer) package German chocolate
    cake mix
1½ sticks butter, softened
1 cup evaporated milk, divided
1 (14-ounce) package caramels
1 cup chopped pecans
1 cup chocolate chips

Preheat the oven to 350F. Line a 13 x 9-inch baking pan with foil and grease the foil.

Combine the cake mix, butter, and ⅔ cup of the milk in a large bowl. Beat at low speed until well combined. Press half the mixture into the prepared pan. Bake 10 minutes.

Meanwhile, combine the caramels and the remaining ⅓ cup of evaporated milk in a double boiler. Cook over simmering water until the caramels are melted, stirring frequently. Pour over the hot baked mixture. Spread with the remaining cake batter. Sprinkle with the pecans and chocolate chips.

Bake 20 minutes. Remove to a rack. When completely cool, invert and carefully remove the foil. Cut into squares and serve.

Beyond Cotton Country, Decatur, AL

DEATH-TO-THE-DIET BROWNIES

MAKES 48 BROWNIES

4 squares (4 ounces) unsweetened
    baking chocolate
2 sticks (½ pound) butter
2 cups sugar
4 large eggs, beaten
2 teaspoons coffee liqueur, brandy, or
    vanilla extract
1 cup all-purpose flour
1 cup semisweet chocolate chips
1 cup chopped nuts

Preheat the oven to 325F. Line a 13 x 9-inch baking pan with foil and grease the foil.

In a heavy 1-quart saucepan, melt the unsweetened chocolate and butter over low heat, stirring constantly. Remove from the heat and let cool for 8–10 minutes. Stir in the sugar. Beat in the eggs one at a time, add the coffee liqueur, and stir in the flour. Mix well. Stir in the chocolate chips and nuts.

Scrape the batter into the prepared pan. Bake 35 minutes or until the edges are firm (the center will be soft). Cool for 30 to 60 minutes on a wire rack before cutting. Chill at least 2 hours before serving.

Heart & Soul, Memphis, TN

BUTTER PECAN TURTLE COOKIES

MAKES 35 TO 40 COOKIES

CRUST:
8 tablespoons (1 stick) butter, softened
1 cup packed dark brown sugar
2 cups all-purpose flour
1½ cups pecan halves

CARAMEL LAYER:
10⅔ tablespoons butter
½ cup packed dark brown sugar

TOPPING:
1 cup milk chocolate chips

Preheat the oven to 350F. Have ready a lightly greased 13 x 9-inch baking pan.

In a large bowl, cream the butter and brown sugar together until fluffy. Stir in the flour and mix at medium speed until blended. Put into the prepared pan and sprinkle pecan halves on top.

Prepare the caramel layer by combining the butter and brown sugar in a medium saucepan. Cook over medium heat, stirring constantly, until the entire surface begins to boil. Boil 30 to 60 seconds, while stirring. Pour over the crust. Bake near the center of the oven for 18 to 20 minutes or until the caramel layer is bubbly and the crust is light golden brown. Remove from the oven and sprinkle with chocolate chips. Allow to melt for several minutes, then swirl with a knife. Cool completely before cutting.

Mountain Elegance, Asheville, NC

POUND CAKE COOKIES

MAKES 2 TO 3 DOZEN

1 cup sugar
2 sticks (½ pound) butter
2 cups sifted cake flour
1 large egg yolk
1 teaspoon rum
½ teaspoon salt
½ teaspoon vanilla extract
Pecan halves

Beat the sugar and butter in a mixing bowl until creamy. Add the cake flour and egg yolk and beat well. Stir in the rum, salt, and vanilla. Chill, covered, until firm.

Preheat the oven to 350F. Shape the dough into ½-inch balls. Place on a nonstick cookie sheet. Press 1 pecan half into each cookie. Bake 10 minutes. Cool on the cookie sheet for 2 minutes. Remove to a wire rack to cool completely.

Down by the Water, Columbia, SC

MEXICAN HOLIDAY COOKIES (BIZCOCHOS)

MAKES 8 TO 10 DOZEN

2 cups (1 pound) lard (no substitute)
1 cup sweet wine or any fruit juice
2 cups sugar, divided
1 tablespoon plus 4 teaspoons
    cinnamon, divided
1 tablespoon anise seed
2 large egg yolks
3 cups all-purpose flour

Preheat the oven to 350F. Grease two or more cookie sheets.

Whip the lard until creamy in a large bowl. Mix the wine, 1 cup of the sugar, 1 tablespoon of the cinnamon, and the anise in a medium bowl; add to the lard and mix with a wooden spoon. Add the egg yolks; mix well. Add sufficient flour to make a soft dough; roll out ½ inch thick. Cut in desired shapes and arrange on cookie sheets. Bake for 15 minutes; check often to prevent burning. Mix the remaining 1 cup sugar and the remaining 4 teaspoons cinnamon in a small bowl. Dredge cookies in this mixture while still warm. Cool on a rack.

Seasoned with Sun, El Paso, TX

LEMON CRISPIES

MAKES 25 TO 30 COOKIES

1 package lemon cake mix
8 tablespoons (1 stick) butter, melted
1 egg, beaten
1 cup crisp rice cereal

Preheat the oven to 350F. Combine the cake mix, butter, and egg in a mixing bowl. Gently stir in the rice cereal. Roll the dough into 1½-inch balls. Place 2 inches apart on an ungreased cookie sheet. Bake for 9 minutes or until the edges are golden. Cool on the cookie sheet for 1 minute. Remove and cool on a wire rack.

Capital Celebrations, Washington, D.C.

CRACKER CANDY

MAKES 24 CANDIES

40 saltines (see Note)
2 sticks (½ pound) butter
1 cup packed light or dark brown
   sugar
2 cups chocolate chips (12 ounces)
1 cup chopped pecans (optional)

Preheat the oven to 400F. Place the crackers side by side in a foil-lined jelly-roll pan. Combine the butter and brown sugar in a saucepan. Bring to a boil, stirring constantly. Cook for 3 minutes. Pour the mixture over the crackers. Bake 5 minutes. Sprinkle the chocolate chips over the baked crackers. Let stand 5 minutes; spread the melted chocolate over the top. Sprinkle with nuts if desired. Chill in the refrigerator until firm. Invert onto a flat surface; remove the foil. Break into pieces. Store, covered, in an airtight container in the refrigerator.

NOTE: Matzos can be substituted for the saltines. Break the sheets to fit in one layer.

Dining in the Smoky Mountain Mist, Knoxville, TN

PAN DE POLVO

MAKES SEVERAL HUNDRED
SMALL COOKIES

3 pounds solid vegetable shortening
5 pounds plus 2 cups all-purpose
   flour
5 cups sugar, divided
1 teaspoon salt
1 cup boiling water
1 tablespoon anise seed
6 sticks Mexican cinnamon

Preheat the oven to 300F. Grease two or more cookie sheets.

Cut the shortening into a mixture of the flour, 2 cups of the sugar, and the salt in a large bowl; mix well. Pour the boiling water over the anise seed to make a strong tea. Add about ¾ cup to the flour mixture to make a dough. Roll the dough out between sheets of waxed paper. Cut into desired shapes, arrange on the cookie sheets, and bake 20 minutes. Pulverize the cinnamon in an electric blender and mix with the remaining 3 cups sugar. Roll the hot cookies in the mixture.

Fiesta, Corpus Christi, TX

SAND TARTS (MEXICAN WEDDING CAKES)

MAKES ABOUT 4 DOZEN COOKIES

2 sticks (½ pound) butter, softened
¾ cup powdered sugar, sifted if lumpy,
  plus additional as needed
2 teaspoons vanilla extract
1 cup very finely chopped pecans
2 cups all-purpose flour

Preheat the oven to 325F. Grease two cookie sheets.

Cream the butter, the ¾ cup sugar, and the vanilla in a medium bowl until fluffy. Add the nuts gradually and mix well. Stir in the flour. Roll the dough between your palms into balls or crescents. Arrange on the cookie sheets and bake one sheet at a time about 15 minutes or until cookies are faintly colored. Cool on a rack. Roll in additional powdered sugar until coated all over.

Fiesta, Corpus Christi, TX

PECAN DIAMONDS

MAKES 50 SERVINGS

3 sticks (¾ pound) chilled butter,
  divided
1½ cups all-purpose flour
¼ cup ice water
1½ cups packed light brown sugar
½ cup honey
⅓ cup granulated sugar
1 pound pecan pieces or halves
¼ cup heavy cream

In a bowl, cut 1 stick of the butter into the flour with a pastry blender or two knives until crumbly. Add the ice water, tossing lightly with a fork. Shape into a ball; wrap in plastic wrap. Chill for 1 hour.

Roll the dough into a 14 x 10-inch rectangle on a lightly floured surface. Fit into a greased and floured 13 x 9-inch baking pan; dough will come halfway up sides. Pierce all over with a fork. Chill.

Preheat the oven to 375F. Bring the brown sugar, the remaining 2 sticks of butter, the honey, and granulated sugar to a boil in a saucepan, stirring constantly. Boil for 4 minutes or until thickened, continuing to stir. Remove from the heat. Stir in the pecans and cream. Pour over the chilled layer. Bake for 25 minutes or until the edges are brown. Cool in the pan. Cut lengthwise into 1-inch strips; then cut diagonally into 1-inch strips to create diamond shapes.

The Best of Wheeling, Wheeling, WV

CHOCOLATE ALMOND TERRINE WITH RASPBERRY PURÉE

MAKES 12 SERVINGS

3 large egg yolks, slightly beaten
2 cups heavy cream, divided
16 squares (1 pound) semisweet
    baking chocolate, coarsely chopped
¾ cup light corn syrup, divided
8 tablespoons (1 stick) butter
¼ cup powdered sugar
1 teaspoon vanilla extract
¼ teaspoon almond extract
1 (10-ounce) package frozen red
    raspberries, thawed
1-2 tablespoons raspberry liqueur or
    almond liqueur
Fresh red raspberries
Mint leaves

Line an 8 x 4-inch loaf pan with plastic wrap. In a small bowl, combine the egg yolks and ½ cup of the cream. In a large heat-proof bowl, combine the chocolate, ½ cup of the corn syrup, and the butter. Place the bowl in a large skillet of simmering water. Cook and stir over low heat until the chocolate and butter are melted and smooth. Add the egg yolk mixture, raise the heat to medium, and cook for 3 minutes, stirring constantly. Cool to room temperature.

In a medium bowl, beat the remaining 1½ cups cream, the powdered sugar, and the vanilla and almond extracts with an electric mixer until soft peaks form. Fold into the chocolate mixture until no streaks remain. Pour into the prepared loaf pan. Cover and chill overnight.

Purée the raspberries in a blender container or food processor workbowl; press through a sieve to remove the seeds. Stir in the remaining ¼ cup of corn syrup and the liqueur. To serve, invert the terrine and cut into ⅜-inch slices. Pool some of the purée onto each dessert plate. Place a slice of the terrine over the purée. Garnish with fresh raspberries and mint leaves.

Heart & Soul, Memphis, TN

CHOCOLATE RASPBERRY TRUFFLE TORTE

2 (10-ounce) packages frozen
   raspberries
1 pound plus 2 tablespoons unsalted
   butter, cut into tablespoons
1 cup sugar
12 ounces semisweet chocolate,
   coarsely chopped
4 ounces bittersweet chocolate, coarsely
   chopped, plus 8 ounces, finely
   chopped
½ cup Chambord or raspberry brandy
½ teaspoon raspberry extract
8 large eggs, at room temperature
⅔ cup heavy cream
16 fresh raspberries

Preheat the oven to 325F. Grease the bottom and side of a 10 x 3-inch cake pan; line the bottom with waxed paper and set aside.

Drain the raspberries, reserving ½ cup of juice, and force the berries through a sieve. Combine the 1 pound of butter, the sugar, semisweet chocolate, and 4 ounces of the bittersweet chocolate in the top of a double boiler. Cook over hot water until the sugar dissolves, stirring until the mixture is smooth; remove from the heat. Stir in the liqueur, reserved raspberry juice, and raspberry extract. Whisk in the eggs, one at a time. Stir in the strained raspberries. Spoon into the prepared baking pan. Place in a larger pan and set it in the oven. Pour enough boiling water into the larger pan to come halfway up the cake pan.

Bake for 60 to 70 minutes or until a wooden pick inserted near the center of the torte comes out clean. Cool on a wire rack for 2 to 3 hours or until the torte reaches room temperature. Chill, covered with plastic wrap, for 3 hours or overnight.

Combine the cream, the 8 ounces of finely chopped bittersweet chocolate, and the remaining 2 tablespoons of butter in the top of a double boiler. Cook over hot water until the chocolate and butter melt, stirring to mix well. Cover the chocolate mixture with plastic wrap. Chill for 30 to 45 minutes or until thickened to pudding consistency, stirring occasionally.

Loosen the side of the cake from the pan with a knife; invert the cake onto a serving plate, and remove the waxed paper. Reserve ¾ cup of the chilled chocolate mixture. Spread the remaining chilled chocolate mixture over the top and around the side of the torte. Pipe the reserved chilled chocolate mixture into 16 rosettes on the torte, using a pastry bag fitted with a star tip. Arrange the fresh raspberries on top of the torte. Chill until serving time.

The Best of Wheeling, Wheeling, WV

HEAVENLY APPLE DUMPLINGS

2½ cups sugar, divided
2 cups water
½ teaspoon ground cinnamon, divided
6 tablespoons butter, divided
6 apples
2 cups all-purpose flour
1 teaspoon salt
2 teaspoons baking powder
¾ cup solid vegetable shortening
½ cup milk

Preheat the oven to 375F. Combine the sugar, water, and ¼ teaspoon of the cinnamon in a medium saucepan. Cook 5 minutes. Remove from heat. Stir in the butter; set the sauce aside.

Pare and core the apples. Whisk the flour, salt, and baking powder together in a large bowl. Cut in the shortening with a pastry blender or two knives. Add the milk all at once and stir just until the flour is moistened.

Roll the dough ¼ inch thick; cut into 6-inch squares. Place one apple on each square. Combine the remaining ¼ teaspoon of cinnamon and ½ cup sugar in a small bowl. Sprinkle over the apples generously. Cut the remaining 2 tablespoons of butter into small pieces and dot them on top of the apples. Fold four corners of a pastry square together over the top of an apple to seal. Pinch the edges together. Repeat with the other apples. Place 1 inch apart in a greased baking pan. Pour the sauce over the dumplings. Bake about 35 minutes or until the dumplings are golden. Serve hot with cream or cool and refrigerate, which allows the sauce to thicken.

Almost Heaven, Huntington, WV

FLAN

MAKES 6 SERVINGS

½ cup sugar
6 large eggs
1 (13-ounce) can evaporated milk
1 (14-ounce) can sweetened condensed
   milk
14 ounces water
1 teaspoon vanilla extract
Pinch of salt

Preheat the oven to 350F. Melt the sugar in a dry skillet over low heat until it turns a deep amber. Coat a 2½-quart mold with the caramelized sugar.

Beat the eggs in a medium bowl until well mixed (try not to make air bubbles). Add the evaporated milk, condensed milk, and water. Add the vanilla and salt. Strain the mixture and pour into the mold.

Place the mold in a roasting pan and set on the middle oven rack. Pour enough scalding water into the roasting pan to come halfway up the side of the flan mold. Bake approximately 1 hour or until a knife inserted in the middle comes out clean. After cooling slightly, refrigerate until serving time. When ready to serve, unmold onto a broad or deep platter and ladle the caramel over the custard.

Delicioso, Corpus Christi, TX

FLAN DE LECHE NUEVO

MAKES 8 SERVINGS

*1 cup plus 2 tablespoons sugar,
    divided*
*1 (14-ounce) can sweetened condensed
    milk (not evaporated milk)*
5 large eggs
Dash of salt
1 cup fresh whole milk
1 cup evaporated milk
¼ cup sherry
1 tablespoon vanilla extract

Preheat the oven to 350F. Caramelize 1 cup of the sugar by placing it in a 10-inch flan pan or 1½-quart casserole dish. Sprinkle with water and place in the oven until the sugar starts to turn dark brown; quickly rotate the casserole to coat the bottom and about halfway up the sides with caramel. Let cool to harden before adding the custard.

Combine the condensed milk, eggs, 2 tablespoons of sugar, and the salt in a blender or food processor; blend. Add the fresh and evaporated milks, sherry, and vanilla. Pour through a strainer over the caramelized sugar. Place the casserole in a roasting pan and set on the middle rack of the oven. Pour scalding water into the larger pan to come halfway up the side of the casserole. Bake 1 to 1½ hours, removing when a toothpick inserted in the center comes out clean. Cool slightly, cover, and refrigerate until serving time. To serve, unmold onto a large platter.

Tampa Treasures, Tampa, FL

GRASSHOPPER CRÊPES

MAKES 12 SERVINGS

CHOCOLATE CRÊPES:
6 tablespoons all-purpose flour
2 tablespoons unsweetened cocoa powder
¼ teaspoon salt
2 large eggs
2 large egg yolks
1 tablespoon sugar
¼ cup vegetable oil
⅓ cup milk

FILLING:
2 cups miniature marshmallows
⅓ cup milk
2 tablespoons white crème de cacao
3 tablespoons green crème de menthe
Green food coloring
2 cups heavy cream, divided
*½ ounce square semisweet baking
    chocolate*

Combine all the ingredients for the crêpes in a blender or food processor. Blend until smooth. Pour the batter into a pitcher; cover and let stand for 30 minutes or longer.

Place a lightly oiled 5-inch crêpe pan over medium heat. Stir the batter and pour about ⅛ cup into the pan, lifting the pan and tilting it so that the surface is evenly coated. Cook until the underside is set. Turn and cook until the other side is lightly speckled. Remove to a sheet of waxed paper. Continue until all the batter is used, layering the crêpes between waxed paper.

For the filling: Heat the marshmallows and milk in a saucepan over low heat, stirring constantly, until the mixture mounds slightly when dropped from a spoon (about 30 minutes). Stir in the crème de cacao, crème de menthe, and several drops of food coloring; set aside. Beat 1 cup heavy cream until stiff. Fold the cooled green mixture into the whipped cream.

Fill the cooked crêpes and fold over. Chill until firm. Top with extra whipped cream, if desired. Shave the semisweet chocolate or make chocolate curls and sprinkle over the crêpes.

Rare Collections, Galveston County, TX

STRAWBERRY-RHUBARB SLUMP

1 cup all-purpose flour

1 cup plus 2 tablespoons sugar, divided

1 teaspoon baking powder

¼ teaspoon baking soda

¼ teaspoon salt

4 tablespoons (½ stick) butter, cut into small pieces

6 tablespoons low-fat buttermilk

½ teaspoon almond extract

4 cups whole strawberries, hulled

4 cups cut-up rhubarb

½ cup water

1 tablespoon cornstarch

2 tablespoons apple juice or cider

In a large bowl, whisk together the flour, ¼ cup of the sugar, the baking powder, baking soda, and salt. Cut in the butter with a pastry blender or two knives until the mixture resembles coarse meal. Add the buttermilk and almond extract, and toss with a fork until the dry ingredients are moistened. Set the dough aside.

In a 10-inch ovenproof skillet, combine the strawberries, rhubarb, ¾ cup of the sugar, and the ½ cup of water. Cook, covered, over medium heat for 10 minutes, stirring occasionally. In a small bowl, combine the cornstarch and juice. Add to the fruit mixture. Bring to a boil and cook for 1 minute or until thickened.

Drop the dough by heaping teaspoonfuls onto the fruit mixture. Cook, covered, over low heat for 10 minutes. Remove from the heat and sprinkle the remaining 2 tablespoons sugar over the dumplings and fruit. Broil for 3 minutes or until golden.

Women Who Can Dish It Out, Springfield, MO

ALMOND EMPANADITAS

MAKES 3 DOZEN

Oil or shortening for deep frying
2 cups all-purpose flour
2 teaspoons baking powder
1 teaspoon salt
½ cup solid vegetable shortening
½ to ⅔ cup ice water
¾ cup chopped almonds
½ cup granulated sugar
1 teaspoon ground cinnamon
1 large egg white
¼ teaspoon almond extract
1 cup powdered sugar

You will need a deep-fat fryer fitted with a fryer basket and a deep-fry thermometer for this recipe. Measure out enough cooking fat to fill the fryer no more than halfway. Set aside.

Whisk the flour, baking powder, and salt in a large bowl. Cut in the shortening until the mixture resembles crumbs. Add the ice water, 1 tablespoon at a time, tossing with a fork until all the flour is moistened. Divide the pastry in half and wrap one half in waxed paper. Shape the other half into a ball and roll out on a lightly floured surface to ⅛-inch thickness. Cut into 2½-inch circles. Gather the scraps, reroll, and cut into additional circles.

Mix the almonds, granulated sugar, and cinnamon. Beat the egg white with the almond extract until frothy. Stir in the almond mixture. Place 1 teaspoon of filling on each pastry circle. Fold the pastry over; wet edges and seal with a fork. Repeat with the remaining dough and filling.

Let the turnovers dry at room temperature, uncovered, while you heat the cooking oil over moderate heat to 365F. Fry the turnovers, a few at a time, for 2½ to 3 minutes or until well browned. Drain on paper toweling while you fry the rest. Let the oil temperature come up to the required heat before frying the next batch.

Dredge in powdered sugar while still warm.

Seasoned with Sun, El Paso, TX

SURPRISE PACKAGES

2 cups (about 2) apples, peeled, cored
    and cut into ½-inch chunks
2 cups (about 2) pears, peeled, cored
    and cut into ½-inch chunks
1 tablespoon water
8 prunes, pitted and cut into fourths
¼ teaspoon cinnamon, divided
¼ cup walnuts, chopped (optional)
8 (12 x 16-inch) sheets phyllo
    dough, thawed according to package
    directions
1½ tablespoons butter or margarine,
    melted
4 (12-inch) pieces kitchen string
Vegetable oil cooking spray
2 tablespoons powdered sugar

Place the apples, pears, and water in a saucepan. Cover and cook over low heat for 25 minutes. Uncover, and add the prunes. Cook for about 5 minutes or until all the juice has evaporated. Stir in ¼ teaspoon of the cinnamon and the walnuts, if desired. Remove from the heat and cool.

Preheat the oven to 375F. Brush 1 sheet of phyllo with butter. Stack the second sheet on top and brush with butter. Repeat with the third sheet. Place the fourth sheet on top, but do not brush with butter. Cut the phyllo sheets in half. Spoon one-fourth of the fruit mixture in the center of each phyllo section. Gather the edges of each section together and tie with string. Repeat with the remaining 4 sheets of phyllo.

Place the packages on a cookie sheet coated with vegetable oil cooking spray. Lightly brush with the remaining butter. Bake about 16 minutes or until lightly brown. Sift together the remaining ½ teaspoon cinnamon and the powdered sugar. Sprinkle over the warm packets. Serve warm.

Gold 'n Delicious, Spokane, WA

Fresh Fruit Trifle

2 cups milk

4 large egg yolks

½ cup granulated sugar

3 tablespoons cornstarch

¼ teaspoon salt

2 tablespoons butter

1 teaspoon vanilla extract

2 (12-ounce) packages pound cake,
  cut into ½-inch slices

1½ cups Grand Marnier

1 pound strawberries, cleaned, hulled,
  and sliced

2 bananas, sliced

1 (11-ounce) can mandarin oranges,
  drained

2 kiwifruit, peeled and sliced

1 pint fresh blueberries, rinsed and
  drained

1 cup heavy cream

2 tablespoons powdered sugar

Whole strawberries

Combine the milk, egg yolks, granulated sugar, cornstarch, and salt in a food processor or blender. Process until well blended. Pour into a medium-size glass bowl. Microwave on high for 6 to 7 minutes or until thickened. Stir halfway through cooking. (The custard can also be prepared in a saucepan. Cook over medium heat, stirring constantly, until thickened.) Whisk in the butter and vanilla. Cover and refrigerate until cool and soft-set.

Brush the cake slices with Grand Marnier. Arrange half the slices in a single layer in a trifle dish or a deep glass bowl. Layer half the strawberries, bananas, oranges, kiwis, and blueberries. Spoon half the custard mixture over the fruit. Repeat. Whip the cream until soft peaks form. Add the powdered sugar and continue beating until stiff. Spoon or pipe decoratively over the top of the trifle. Garnish with whole strawberries. Chill until ready to serve.

A Cleveland Collection, Cleveland, OH

TRIFLE

3 large eggs
½ cup sugar
Pinch of salt
2 cups milk
1 teaspoon almond extract
1 sponge cake or 4 packages
    ladyfingers
¾ to 1 cup dry sherry, divided
Fresh (1 quart) or canned (29 ounces)
    fruit (peaches, crushed pineapple,
    mandarin oranges, Bing cherries,
    strawberries, blueberries, or
    raspberries)
1 cup whipped cream
Toasted slivered almonds

Beat the eggs, sugar, and salt in the top of a double boiler. Stir in the milk. Set over boiling water and cook, stirring constantly, until the mixture has thickened. Stir in the almond extract. Chill.

Break the cake into bite-size pieces and arrange half of them in a single layer on the bottom of a glass serving dish. Sprinkle the cake with half the sherry. Arrange half the fruit the same way. Spoon on half the chilled egg custard. Repeat the layers. Top with the whipped cream and the almonds. Chill for several hours before serving.

Junior League of Philadelphia's Bicentennial Cookbook, Philadelphia, PA

COLD LEMON SOUFFLÉ WITH WINE SAUCE

MAKES 8 TO 10 SERVINGS

1 envelope unflavored gelatin
¼ cup cold water
5 large eggs, separated (see Note)
¾ cup fresh lemon juice
2 teaspoons grated lemon zest
1½ cups sugar, divided
1 cup heavy cream
Wine Sauce (see below)

Sprinkle the gelatin over the cold water to soften. Mix the egg yolks with lemon juice, zest, and ¾ cup of the sugar. Place in the top of a double boiler over boiling water and cook, stirring constantly, until the lemon mixture is slightly thickened (about 8 minutes). Remove from the heat and stir in the gelatin until dissolved. Chill for 30 to 40 minutes or until the mixture mounds slightly when dropped from a spoon.

Beat the egg whites until they begin to hold their shape; then gradually add the remaining ¾ cup of sugar until all has been added and the whites are stiff. Beat the cream in a separate bowl until stiff. Fold the whites and cream into the yolk mixture until no white streaks remain. Pour into a 2-quart soufflé dish and chill 4 hours or more. Serve with wine sauce.

WINE SAUCE:

½ cup sugar
1 tablespoon cornstarch
½ cup water
3 tablespoons fresh lemon juice
1 teaspoon grated lemon zest
2 tablespoons butter
½ cup dry white wine

In a small saucepan, mix together the sugar and cornstarch. Stir in the water, lemon juice, and zest until smooth. Add the butter. Bring to a boil, lower the heat, and cook until thickened (about 3 minutes). Remove from the heat and stir in the wine. Chill, stirring occasionally.

Serve this rich soufflé sparingly.

NOTE: This dessert is made with uncooked eggs. Those who are concerned about the possibility of salmonella can substitute pasteurized whites and yolks.

The Silver Collection, Memphis, TN

ROBIN K'S CHOCOLATE MOUSSE

*18 ounces semisweet baking chocolate,
   coarsely chopped*
*2 tablespoons liqueur (crème de cacao
   or Cointreau), optional*
1 tablespoon vanilla extract
2 cups heavy cream
6 large eggs, divided (see Note)
2 tablespoons powdered sugar
Chocolate leaves to garnish
Raspberry Sauce (see below)

Melt the chocolate in the top of a double boiler over simmering water. Add the vanilla and optional liqueur. Cool to room temperature. Whip the cream until medium-stiff.

Separate four of the eggs; set the whites aside. Combine the four egg yolks with the remaining two whole eggs in a large bowl. Beat until thick and lemon colored. Beat the four whites in a medium bowl. Add the powdered sugar. Beat until soft peaks form.

Add the chocolate to the beaten egg yolks. Add the whipped cream to the chocolate mixture. Fold in the egg whites. Garnish with chocolate leaves. Serve with raspberry sauce.

NOTES: This doubles easily and freezes beautifully. Remove from the freezer one day before serving and refrigerate. Pasteurized whites and yolks may be substituted for the raw eggs if you are concerned about the possibility of salmonella.

RASPBERRY SAUCE:

*2 (10-ounce) packages frozen
   raspberries, thawed*
1 tablespoon cornstarch
2 tablespoons fresh lemon juice
2 tablespoons Kirsch

In a blender, purée the raspberries. Press the pulp through a sieve into a saucepan. Combine the cornstarch and lemon juice. Add to the raspberry pulp. Bring to a boil and cook until slightly thickened. Add the Kirsch. Chill before serving.

Second Round: Tea-Time at the Masters, Augusta, GA

WHITE CHOCOLATE MOUSSE

MAKES 12 SERVINGS

9 ounces imported white chocolate,
  broken into pieces
3 large eggs, separated (see Note)
6 tablespoons powdered sugar, divided
2 cups heavy cream
¼ teaspoon cream of tartar

SAUCE:

1 (10-ounce) package frozen
  raspberries, thawed
1 tablespoon Kirsch
2 tablespoons granulated sugar

Heat the white chocolate in the top of a double boiler over boiling water until it melts. Remove immediately. Beat the egg yolks and 2 tablespoons of the sugar until thick and lemon colored. Stir into the chocolate and set aside. Whip the cream with 2 tablespoons of the sugar until soft peaks form. Whip the egg whites, cream of tartar, and the remaining 2 tablespoons of sugar to stiff peaks. Add enough whipped cream to the white chocolate mixture to achieve a thick stirring consistency. Fold the chocolate into the whipped cream, blending just enough to achieve uniform color. Gently fold the egg whites into the chocolate mixture just to achieve uniform color. Chill in cups or shallow parfait glasses. Spoon the sauce over the mousse before serving.

To make the sauce, blend the raspberries in a blender and strain to remove seeds. Add the kirsch and sugar.

NOTE: This dessert is made with uncooked eggs. Substitute pasteurized whites and yolks if you are concerned about salmonella.

Treasures of the Smokies, Johnson City, TN

AMARETTO MOUSSE

5 large eggs, separated (see Note)
½ cup sugar
Pinch of salt
1 teaspoon vanilla extract
1 cup milk
1 envelope gelatin
2 tablespoons cold water
1 pint heavy cream, whipped
Amaretto

Beat the egg yolks with the sugar in a medium bowl until thick and lemon-colored. Add the salt and vanilla to the milk in a saucepan and bring to a boil. Add a little of the hot milk to the beaten yolks, mixing thoroughly. Add the warmed yolk mixture to the milk in the saucepan. Cook over low heat, stirring constantly, until thickened, but don't boil.

Soften the gelatin in the cold water in a small bowl. Add to the milk, and strain the mixture through a cheesecloth into a clean bowl. Cool on a big bowl of ice. Fold in the whipped cream. In a separate bowl, beat the egg whites until stiff and fold into the mixture.

Spoon the mousse into wine glasses and chill in the refrigerator. Before serving, float amaretto on top.

NOTE: This dessert is made with uncooked egg whites. Substitute pasteurized whites if you are concerned about salmonella.

Selections, Huntsville, AL

TEQUILA MOUSSE

MAKES 6 SERVINGS

2 large egg yolks
1 tablespoon lime juice
⅔ cup water, divided
1 whole vanilla bean
½ cup sugar
⅛ teaspoon salt
2-2½ tablespoons golden tequila to
    taste
1 tablespoon orange liqueur
½ teaspoon grated lime zest
1 envelope (1 tablespoon) unflavored
    gelatin
1 cup heavy cream
Lime slices or grated lime zest for
    garnish (optional)

Whisk the egg yolks in a large heatproof bowl for approximately 10 minutes, or until pale and creamy. Add the lime juice and half the water and beat for 1 more minute. Add the vanilla bean.

Prepare a water bath by heating 1 inch of water in a large skillet until bubbles form along the bottom. Set the bowl containing the egg yolk mixture in the water bath and cook, stirring constantly, over low heat for 5 minutes. Remove the mixture from the heat. Take out the vanilla bean, split it open lengthwise, and scrape the vanilla seeds back into the mixture; discard the rest of the bean. Add the sugar, salt, tequila, orange liqueur, and lime zest and mix until well combined.

Sprinkle the gelatin over the remaining water in a small saucepan; let it stand for 5 minutes to soften, then melt the gelatin by gently heating, stirring constantly, until it has dissolved.

Stir the dissolved gelatin into the tequila mixture and put aside to cool until the mixture partly sets. Beat the heavy cream in a chilled bowl, preferably copper, until stiff. Gently fold the whipped cream into the tequila mixture and spoon the mousse into a serving bowl. Refrigerate for 3 hours, or until firm. Serve decorated with lime slices or grated lime zest, if you desire.

Behind the Walls, Mexico City, Mexico

CREAMY PEACH-BLACKBERRY COBBLER

MAKES 8 SERVINGS

TOPPING:
1 cup all-purpose flour
½ cup granulated sugar
6 tablespoons butter
1 teaspoon vanilla extract

FILLING:
⅔ cup all-purpose flour
1¾ cups granulated sugar
¼ teaspoon ground cinnamon
5 large eggs
1 teaspoon vanilla extract
2 cups milk
½ cup heavy cream
4 cups peaches, peeled and cut into
    ¼-inch wedges
2 cups blackberries, rinsed

OPTIONAL GARNISH:
2 cups heavy cream
2 tablespoons powdered sugar

To make the topping, combine the flour and sugar; cut in the butter until the mixture resembles coarse cornmeal. Add the vanilla extract; mix thoroughly and set aside.

Preheat the oven to 400F. Lightly butter a 13 x 9-inch baking pan.

To make the batter, combine the flour, sugar, cinnamon, eggs, vanilla extract, milk, and ½ cup cream in a blender or food processor. Process until smooth.

Line the prepared baking dish with the peaches and berries. Carefully spoon the batter over the fruit and bake 30 minutes. Sprinkle the topping over the cobbler and bake 15 to 20 minutes longer, until the topping is brown and the fruit is tender when pierced with a skewer. Serve warm.

If desired, sweeten the 2 cups of heavy cream with the powdered sugar; whip until stiff. Serve on the side.

Of Tide & Thyme, Annapolis, MD

TOO-EASY PEACH COBBLER

MAKES 6 SERVINGS

6 medium peaches, peeled and sliced
5 slices white bread, crusts removed
1 to 1½ cups sugar
2 tablespoons all-purpose flour
1 large egg, beaten
8 tablespoons (1 stick) butter, melted

Preheat the oven to 350F. Place the peaches in an 8-inch square baking dish coated with vegetable oil cooking spray. Cut each slice of bread into 5 long strips. Place evenly over the fruit. Combine the sugar, flour, egg, and melted butter in a medium bowl; mix well. Pour over the fruit and bread. Bake 35 minutes or until golden brown.

Food for Thought, Birmingham, AL

PEACH COBBLER

MAKES 4 TO 6 SERVINGS

6 tablespoons butter
¾ cup all-purpose flour
2 cups sugar, divided
2 teaspoons baking powder
⅛ teaspoon salt
¾ cup milk
2 cups sliced fresh or frozen peaches
   (see Note)
Cream, whipped cream, or ice cream

Preheat the oven to 350F. Melt the butter in a deep 1½-quart casserole.

Combine the flour, 1 cup of the sugar, baking powder, and salt in a large bowl; mix well and stir in the milk. Pour the batter evenly into the melted butter without additional stirring. Combine the peaches with the remaining cup of sugar; pour into the middle of the batter without stirring. Bake about 30 minutes or until lightly browned. Serve warm with cream, whipped cream, or ice cream.

NOTE: You may substitute apples, blueberries, or blackberries for the peaches.

Atlanta Cooknotes, Atlanta GA

APPLE BLACKBERRY CRISP

MAKES 6 SERVINGS

6 Golden Delicious or Granny Smith
   apples
2 cups blackberries, fresh or frozen
½ cup granulated sugar
½ cup plus 2 tablespoons all-purpose
   flour
½ cup rolled oats
½ cup chopped nuts (optional)
5⅓ tablespoons butter, melted
⅓ cup packed light brown sugar
1 teaspoon ground cinnamon

Preheat the oven to 350F. Grease a 13 x 9-inch baking dish.

Peel and core the apples. Cut into thin slices. Place the apples in the prepared baking dish. Top with blackberries (if using frozen berries, do not thaw first). Sprinkle with the granulated sugar and the 2 tablespoons flour.

Combine the remaining ½ cup of flour with the oats, nuts, melted butter, brown sugar, and cinnamon in a small bowl; mix until crumbly. Sprinkle the crumbly mixture evenly over the filling. Bake for 35 to 40 minutes or until the fruit is soft and bubbly and topping is browned. Serve warm, topped with vanilla ice cream or whipped cream.

Simply Classic Cookbook, Seattle, WA

MINT JULEP SORBET

MAKES 4 SERVINGS

1½ cups water
¾ cup lightly packed fresh mint
½ cup sugar
3 tablespoons bourbon
1 tablespoon crème de menthe
1 teaspoon minced fresh mint
4 fresh mint sprigs for garnish

Place the first three ingredients in a heavy saucepan over medium heat until the sugar is dissolved, stirring constantly. Increase the heat; bring to a boil. Remove from the heat, cover, and chill for two hours. Strain into a bowl. Press the leaves to extract all the liquid. Discard the mint.

Stir the bourbon, crème de menthe, and 1 teaspoon minced mint into the syrup. Freeze in an ice cream maker, following the manufacturer's directions. Spoon into a chilled container. Freeze, covered, for two hours or until firm. Place 4 parfait glasses in the freezer for one hour. Scoop the sorbet into the frosted glasses. Garnish with mint.

Crescent City Collection: A Taste of New Orleans, New Orleans, LA

STRAWBERRIES ROMANOFF

MAKES 8 SERVINGS

1 pint vanilla ice cream, softened
1 cup heavy cream, whipped
9 tablespoons Cointreau, divided
1 quart strawberries, cleaned and
    slightly mashed
½ cup powdered sugar

Whip the ice cream until creamy and fold in the whipped cream and 6 tablespoons of the Cointreau. Mix the strawberries with the powdered sugar and the remaining 3 tablespoons of Cointreau. Blend the ice cream and strawberry mixtures quickly and lightly. Serve in chilled stemmed glasses.

Winning Seasons, Tuscaloosa, AL

DREAMY VANILLA ICE CREAM

MAKES 1 GALLON

4 large eggs
1½ cups sugar
1 tablespoon all-purpose flour
Pinch of salt
1½ quarts milk
1 (14-ounce) can sweetened condensed
    milk (not evaporated milk)
1 teaspoon vanilla extract
2 cups half-and-half

Combine the eggs, sugar, flour, and salt in the container of a blender. Process until blended and smooth. Heat the 1½ quarts milk in a medium saucepan until hot. Stir a small amount of the milk into the egg mixture; stir the warmed egg mixture into the milk. Cook over low heat for 5 minutes or until slightly thickened, stirring constantly. Remove from the heat. Stir in the condensed milk and the vanilla. Pour the custard into a 1-gallon ice cream freezer container. Stir in the half-and-half. Freeze according to the manufacturer's directions.

Beyond Cotton Country, Decatur, AL

PEANUT BUTTER DIAMONDS

MAKES 20 TO 25 BARS

2 cups graham cracker crumbs
4 cups powdered sugar
3 sticks (¾ pound) butter, divided
2 cups creamy peanut butter
2 cups (12 ounces) chocolate chips

Combine the graham cracker crumbs and powdered sugar. Melt 2 sticks of the butter in a small saucepan; mix with the peanut butter. Add to the crumb mixture. Press into the bottom of a 15 x 10-inch jelly roll pan.

Melt the chocolate chips and the remaining stick of the butter in the top of a double boiler over simmering water, stirring until smooth. Pour over the crust. Refrigerate 5 minutes and cut into bars.

Great Beginnings, Grand Finales, South Bend, IN

LOUISIANA PECAN PRALINES

MAKES 2 DOZEN

1 cup light brown sugar, not packed
1 cup granulated sugar
½ cup evaporated milk
2 tablespoons butter
2 tablespoons light corn syrup
Pinch of salt
1 teaspoon vanilla extract
1¾ cups pecan halves

Using a wooden spoon, combine the brown sugar, granulated sugar, milk, butter, corn syrup, and salt in a saucepan. Cook for 10 minutes or to the soft-ball stage (238F on a candy thermometer). Test for doneness by slipping a drop of the mixture into cold water. The drop should be soft when picked up with the fingers.

Remove the saucepan from the heat. Stir in the vanilla and pecans. Beat 1 minute or until the mixture starts to thicken. Drop by teaspoonfuls onto greased waxed paper. Cool.

Jambalaya, New Orleans, LA

CARAMEL PEANUT BARS

MAKES 9 TO 12 BARS

1 (14-ounce) package caramels
2 tablespoons milk
3 tablespoons butter
1 cup powdered sugar
2½ cups peanuts

Heat the caramels and milk together in the top of a double boiler over simmering water until the caramels are melted, stirring constantly. Remove from the heat and stir in the butter. Add the powdered sugar gradually, stirring until smooth. Stir in the peanuts. Spread in a greased 8 x 8-inch pan. Chill, covered; cut into squares for serving.

Beyond Cotton Country, Decatur, AL

WHITE CHOCOLATE CRUNCH

MAKES 8 SERVINGS

1 pound white chocolate
6 cups Rice Chex cereal
3 cups Cheerios cereal
2 cups pretzel sticks
2 cups cashews
12 ounces plain M&M's

Melt the white chocolate in the top of a double boiler over simmering water or in the microwave. Mix together the remaining dry ingredients in a large bowl. Place the dry ingredients in a flat baking pan. Pour the white chocolate over the dry mixture and let harden in a cool place. Break into bite-sized pieces and store in an airtight container. (Can be made 3 days ahead.)

Dining by Fireflies, Charlotte, NC

CHRISTMAS BOURBON BALLS

MAKES 40 CANDIES

1 (6-ounce) package chocolate chips
¼ cup water
2 tablespoons light corn syrup
¼ cup bourbon
1 cup chopped pecans
2½ cups vanilla wafers, crushed fine
½ cup powdered sugar

In a large saucepan over low heat, melt the chocolate chips in ¼ cup water. Stir in the corn syrup and the bourbon. (Add more bourbon if you like stronger flavor.) Add the pecans and wafer crumbs. Mix well and let stand for 20 minutes. Roll into small balls, then roll in powdered sugar.

The Charlotte Cookbook, Charlotte, NC

FUDGE

MAKES 18 TO 20 SERVINGS

3 cups sugar
12 tablespoons (1½ sticks) butter
⅔ cup evaporated milk
1 (12-ounce) package chocolate chips
1 (17-ounce) jar marshmallow cream
1 cup chopped pecans
1 teaspoon vanilla extract

Combine the sugar, butter, and milk in a medium saucepan. Bring to a boil, stirring constantly. Boil for 5 minutes. Remove the saucepan from the heat; stir in the chocolate chips until melted. Add the marshmallow cream, pecans, and vanilla. Beat until blended. Pour into a greased 13 x 9–inch pan. Cool, then cut into squares.

Cooking Through Rose-Colored Glasses, Tyler, TX

JUNIOR LEAGUE COOKBOOKS

Abilene, TX, *Landmark Entertaining;* Albany, GA; *Quail Country;* Albuquerque, NM, *Simply Simpatico;* Ann Arbor, MI, *The Bountiful Arbor;* Annapolis, MD, *Of Tide & Thyme;* Asheville, NC, *Mountain Elegance;* Atlanta, GA, *Atlanta Cooknotes, True Grits: Tall Tales and Recipes from the New South, The Cotton Blossom;* Augusta, GA, *Tea-Time at the Masters, Second Round: Tea-Time at the Masters;* Austin, TX, *Necessities and Temptations;* Baltimore, MD, *Hunt to Harbor;* Baton Rouge, LA, *Savor the Moment, River Roads I, II, III;* Birmingham, AL, *Food for Thought, Magic;* Boise, ID, *Beyond Burlap: Idaho's Famous Potato Recipes, Bound to Please;* Buffalo, NY, *Great Lake Effects: Buffalo Beyond Winter and Wings;* Charleston, SC, *Charleston Party Receipts, Charleston Receipts, Charleston Receipts Repeats;* Charleston, WV, *Mountain Measures I, II;* Charlotte, NC, *Charlotte Cooks Again, The Charlotte Cookbook, Dining by Fireflies;* Chattanooga, TN, *Dinner on the Diner;* Chicago, IL, *Celebrate Chicago: A Taste of Our Town, Soupçon I, II;* Cincinnati, OH, *I'll Cook When Pigs Fly;* Cleveland, OH, *A Cleveland Collection;* Cobb-Marietta, GA, *Georgia on My Menu, Southern on Occasion;* Colorado Springs, CO, *Nuggets;* Columbia, SC, *Down by the Water;* Columbus, GA, *A Southern Collection—Then & Now;* Corpus Christi, TX, *Delicioso, Fiesta, ¡Viva! Tradiciones;*

Decatur, AL; *Beyond Cotton Country;* DeKalb County, GA, *Peachtree Bouquet, Puttin' on the Peachtree;* Denver, CO, *Colorado Cache, Colorado Collage, Crème de Colorado;* El Paso, TX, *Seasoned with Sun;* Eugene, OR, *A Taste of Oregon, Savor the Flavor;* Gainesville, FL, *Gracious Gator Cooks;* Gainesville–Hall County, FL, *Perennials: A Southern Celebration of Food and Flavor;* Galveston County, TX, *Rare Collections;* Gaston County, NC, *Southern Elegance, Southern Elegance: A Second Course;* Grand Rapids, MI, *Cookbook I;* Greater Fort Lauderdale, FL, *Made in the Shade, Sunny Side Up;* Greater Orlando, FL, *Sunsational Encore;* Greensboro, NC, *Out of Our League, Out of Our League Too, Holiday Flavors and Favors;* Greenville, SC, *Uptown Down South, Two Hundred Years of Carolina Cooking;* Hampton Roads, VA, *Very Virginia, Virginia Hospitality, Children's Party Book;* Harlingen, TX, *Rio Riches;* Harrisburg, PA, *A Capital Affair;* Honolulu, HI, *A Taste of Aloha, Another Taste of Aloha;* Houston, TX, *Houston Junior League Cookbook, Stop and Smell the Rosemary, The Star of TX Cookbook;* Huntington, WV, *Almost Heaven;* Huntsville, AL, *Huntsville Heritage Cookbook, Selections, Sweet Home Alabama;* Indian River, FL, *Back Home Again;* Indianapolis, IN, *Winners;* Jackson County, OR, *Rogue River Rendezvous;* Jackson, MS, *Come On In!,*

Southern Sideboards; Jacksonville, FL, *A River Runs Backwards;* Johnson City, TN, *Smoky Mountain Magic, Treasures of the Smokies;* Kansas City, MO, *Above & Beyond Parsley, Beyond Parsley, Company's Coming;* Knoxville, TN, *Dining in the Smoky Mountain Mist;* Lafayette, LA, *Talk About Good, Talk About Good II, Tell Me More;* Lake Charles, LA, *Pirate's Pantry;* Little Rock, AR, *Apron Strings;* Long Island, NY, *It's Our Serve;* Lynchburg, VA, *Good Cookin' From the Heart of Virginia;* McAllen, TX, *La Piñata, Some Like It Hot;* Memphis, TN, *Heart & Soul, Memphis Cook Book, Party Potpourri, The Silver Collection;* Mexico City, Mexico, *Buen Provecho, Behind the Walls;* Mobile, AL, *Bay Tables, One of a Kind, Recipe Jubilee;* Monroe, LA, *Celebrations on the Bayou, The Cotton Country Collection;* Morgan County, AL, *Cotton Country Cooking (25th Anniversary Edition);* Morristown, NJ, *A Matter of Taste;* New Orleans, LA, *Jambalaya, Plantation Cookbook, Crescent City Collection: A Taste of New Orleans;* Norfolk–Virginia Beach, VA, *Tidewater on the Half Shell;* North Little Rock, AR, *Rave Reviews;* Northern Virginia, VA, *What Can I Bring?;* Odessa, TX, *Blue Denim Gourmet, The Wild Wild West;* Ogden, UT, *The UT Dining Car;* Oklahoma City, OK, *Superlatives;* Pasadena, CA, *California Sizzles, Dining by Design, The California Heritage Cookbook;* Pensacola, FL, *Some Like It South!;* Philadelphia, PA, *Settings—From Our Past to Your Presentation, Junior League of Philadelphia's Bicentennial Cookbook;* Phoenix, AZ, *Desert Treasures, Reflections Under the Sun;* Pine Bluff, AR, *Southern Accent;* Portland, ME, *Maine Ingredients, RSVP;* Portland, OR, *From Portland's Palate;* Racine, WI, *Udderly Delicious;* Raleigh, NC, *You're Invited;* Richardson, TX, *Appetites & Victuals, Plain and Fancy, Texas Sampler;* Richmond, VA, *Virginia Fare, Virginia Seasons;* Rochester, NY, *Applehood & Motherpie, For Goodness Taste;* Rockford, IL, *Brunch Basket, Generations, Cotton Country Collection (25th Anniversary Edition);* Salt Lake City, UT, *Always in Season, Heritage Cookbook, Pinch of Salt;* San Angelo, TX, *Pearls of the Concho, The Junior League of San Angelo Cookbook;* San Francisco, CA, *San Francisco à la Carte, San Francisco Flavors;* Santa Barbara, CA, *Slice of Santa Barbara;* Savannah, GA, *Downtown Savannah Style, Savannah Style;* Seattle, WA, *Simply Classic Cookbook;* South Bend, IN, *Great Beginnings, Grand Finales, Nutbread & Nostalgia;* Spokane, WA, *Gold 'n Delicious;* Springfield, IL, *Honest to Goodness;* Springfield, MO, *Sassafras!, Women Who Can Dish It Out;* St. Louis, MO, *St. Louis Days . . . St. Louis Nights, Meet Us in the Kitchen;* Tallahassee, FL, *Thymes Remembered;* Tampa, FL, *Gasparilla Cookbook, Tampa Treasures;* The City of New York, NY, *I'll Taste Manhattan;* The Emerald Beaches, FL, *Sugar Beach;* Tucson, AZ, *Purple Sage and Other Pleasures, Wild Thymes and Other Temptations;* Tuscaloosa, AL, *Winning Seasons;* Tyler, TX, *And Roses for the Table, Cooking Through Rose-Colored Glasses;* Waco, TX, *Hearts and Flour;* Washington, D.C., *Capital Celebrations, Capital Classics;* Waterloo–Cedar Falls, IA, *First Impressions: Dining with Distinction, Buttercups and Brandy, Pig Out;* Westchester on the Sound, NY; *Sound Seasonings;* West Palm Beach, FL, *Heart of the Palms;* Wheeling, WV, *The Best of Wheeling, Treat Yourself to the Best;* Wichita, KS, *Women of Great Taste;* Williamsport, PA, *Victorian Thymes & Pleasures;* Wilmington, DE, *Savor the Brandywine Valley;* Wilmington, NC, *Seaboard to Sideboard;* Worcester, MA, *A Taste of New England;* Wyandotte & Johnson Co., *Treasures of the Great Midwest.*

THE JUNIOR LEAGUE MOVEMENT: A HISTORY OF GROWTH AND COMMUNITY SERVICE

In 1901, Mary Harriman, a nineteen-year-old New York City debutante with a social conscience, founded the first Junior League. Moved by the suffering she saw around her, Harriman mobilized a group of eighty other young women, hence the name "Junior" League, to work to improve the squalid conditions in which immigrants were living on the Lower East Side of Manhattan. Mary Harriman's vision for improving communities by using the energy and commitment of trained volunteers caught on. The second Junior League was started in Boston, Massachusetts, in 1907 and was soon followed by the founding of the Brooklyn, New York, Junior League in 1910. The rest is history.

During the 1910s, Junior Leagues shifted their focus from settlement house work to social, health, and educational issues that affected the community at large. The Junior League of Brooklyn successfully petitioned the Board of Education to provide free lunches in city schools. During World War I, the San Francisco Junior League formed a motor delivery service that served as a model for the nationwide Red Cross Motor Corps. In 1921, the Association was formed to provide professional support to the Leagues. During the 1920s, the Junior League of Chicago pioneered children's theater and the idea was taken up by more than one hundred Leagues across the country.

Junior Leagues responded to the Depression during the 1930s by opening nutrition centers and milk stations. They operated baby clinics, day nurseries for working mothers, birth control clinics, and training schools for nurses. Junior Leagues also established volunteer bureaus to recruit, train, and place much-needed volunteers in the community. During World War II, Junior League members played a major role in the war effort by chairing hundreds of war-related organizations in virtually every city where Junior Leagues operated.

In the 1950s, nearly one hundred and fifty Junior Leagues were involved in remedial reading centers, diagnostic testing programs, and programs for gifted and challenged children. Leagues collaborated in the development of educational television and were among the first to promote quality programming for children. In 1952, the Mexico City League created a comprehensive, internationally recognized center for the blind. By the end of the decade, Junior Leagues were involved in more than three hundred arts projects and multiple partnerships in many cities to establish children's museums.

During the 1960s, many Junior Leagues added environmental issues to their agendas. The Junior League of Toledo produced the educational film *Fate of a River,* a report on the devastating effects of water pollution. Leagues also established programs addressing the education, housing, social services, and employment needs of urban residents.

Throughout the 1970s, the Association expanded its participation in public affairs issues, especially in the areas of child health and juvenile justice. In 1973, almost two hundred Leagues worked with the National Commission on Crime and Delinquency and the U.S. Justice Department on a four-year program that sought to improve the criminal justice system.

During the 1980s, Junior Leagues gained recognition for national advocacy efforts to improve the nation's child welfare system. Leagues helped gain passage of the first federal legislation to address domestic violence. Leagues also developed a campaign that actively and comprehensively tackles the impact of alcohol abuse on women. The campaign, called Woman to Woman, involved more than one hundred League communities. In 1989, the Association was presented with the prestigious U.S. President's Volunteer Action Award.

In the early 1990s, two hundred and thirty Leagues participated in a public awareness campaign to encourage early childhood immunization called Don't Wait To Vaccinate. At the end of the decade, the Leagues prepared to launch a public awareness campaign on domestic violence.

In 2000, with nearly two hundred thousand members in Canada, Great Britain, Mexico, and the U.S., the two hundred and ninety-six Junior Leagues of The Association of Junior Leagues International begin to plan for the Centennial celebration in 2001 of the Junior League movement.

The Junior Leagues will celebrate the 100th anniversary of the movement's founding.

INDEX